# SHUTTERBOX

## Book Two:
## First School Quarter

By

Tavisha
and
Rikki Simons

TOKYOPOP®

HAMBURG • LONDON • LOS ANGELES • TOKYO

Tavisha/Wired Psyche - Story and Illustrations
Rikki Simons - Writer, tones and letters
Tavisha and Rikki Simons - Front cover
Patrick Hook - Graphic Designer
Tim Beedle - Associate Editor
Suzanne Waldman - Copy Editor

Mark Paniccia - Editor
Chris Buford - Digital Imaging Manager
Antonio DePietro - Pre-Press Manager
Jennifer Miller and Mutsumi Miyazaki - Production Managers
Matt Alford - Art Director
Jill Freshney - Managing Editor
Jeremy Ross - Director of Original Manga
Ron Klamert - VP of Production
John Parker - President and C.O.O.
Stuart Levy - Publisher and C.E.O.

Email: info@TOKYOPOP.com

Come visit us online at www.TOKYOPOP.com

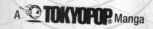

A TOKYOPOP® Manga

TOKYOPOP Inc.
5900 Wilshire Blvd. Suite 2000
Los Angeles, CA 90036

*ShutterBox Vol. 2*



ISBN: 1-59532-201-9

First TOKYOPOP printing: July 2004

10 9 8 7 6 5 4 3 2 1

Printed in the USA

M. U.          S.E.

# An Introduction by the Wired Psyche

As we've discussed with you previously, dear reader, for some time now, we here in this afterlife have been searching for a human capable of describing our tale to you in the mortal world below. We beseeched our usual throng of clients, mad jugglers, hackneyed writers, cloying animators, and so forth...but being that our realm here within the ninth level of imperception is only communicable to you in the shortest bursts of time, the usual clients failed us in a most predictable fashion.

The five senses are inside humans, humans are inside the nine dimensions, the nine dimensions are inside the universe, and the universe is inside the infinite multiverse...and as such, an artist cursed with a nearly schizophrenic sense of their own work was needed to translate our tale in full. A comic book artist, preferably a Gemini, we soon discovered, was the only person truly capable of fully receiving us. Thus we have whispered our tale to Tavisha for many years, and she has been so kind as to force her Virgo husband's hand in writing it all down.

The work does not go easy for Tavisha and Rikki. They toil for us without sleep, for half-lit days and withdrawn nights. Their blood pressures rise and yet they neglect exercise, friends, family, and the grotesque peepshows of the wretched television machine. Now they have lost their only pet of nine years, poor Chibi bunny, to death's careless kiss. They work alone...but at least they work for us.

Being that this is the second part of six, we feel it only fair, dear reader, that we illustrate here, in words and in pictures, what has come before.

*Megan Amano*
 Mortal Age: 18
 Birthday: May 25
 Blood Type: O+
 Soul: possibly new

Megan is a young photography student attending Santa Monica Community College. She began having very real and troubling dreams the night she saw a suicidal young man named AJ Crandall walk fully clothed into the ocean and vanish in the fog. Since then, Megan's curious therapist, Petier Troia, seemed to provide little comfort from Megan's dreams, dreams where she visited with the deceased AJ in a tranquil summer-set meadow.

Events took a turn for the bizarre during one troubled sleep. Megan found herself enlisted as a living ShutterBox exchange student at Merridiah University of Spiritual Education. Now she finds she must return there again on December 25, to begin her education as a living Muse, where she is sure to encounter once again the brothers AJ and Dane, the ghost living in her camera, and the rabbit-like creatures who seemed to have placed themselves in her servitude, the Beebos.

**_Damien "Dane" Crandall_**
  _Mortal Age: varies_
  _Birthday: usually August 8_
  _Blood Type: varies_
  _Soul: maybe old, maybe new_
  _University Position: the_
  _Angel of Death_
  _Unbalanced_

**_Adrien "AJ" Crandall_**
  _Mortal Age: varies (never_
  _more than 18)_
  _Birthday: usually August 8_
  _Blood Type: varies_
  _Soul: maybe old, maybe new_
  _University Position: the_
  _Angel of Childhood's End_

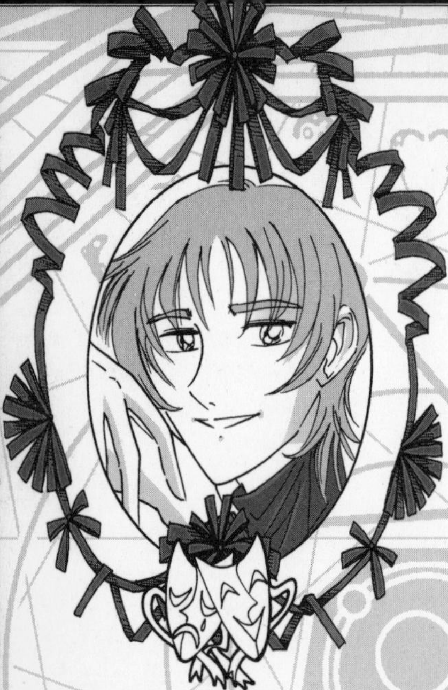

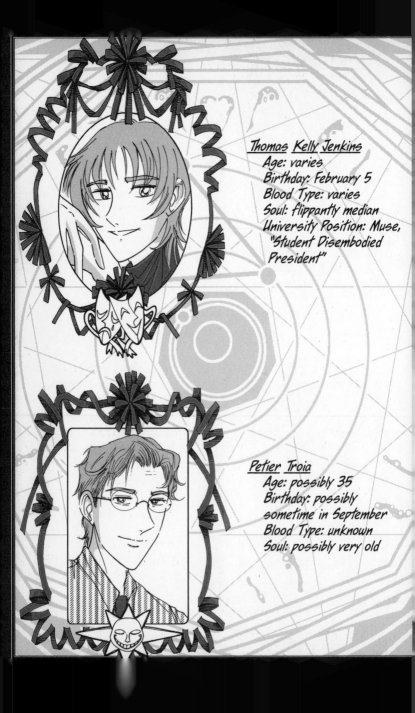

Thomas Kelly Jenkins
Age: varies
Birthday: February 5
Blood Type: varies
Soul: flippantly median
University Position: Muse, "Student Disembodied President"

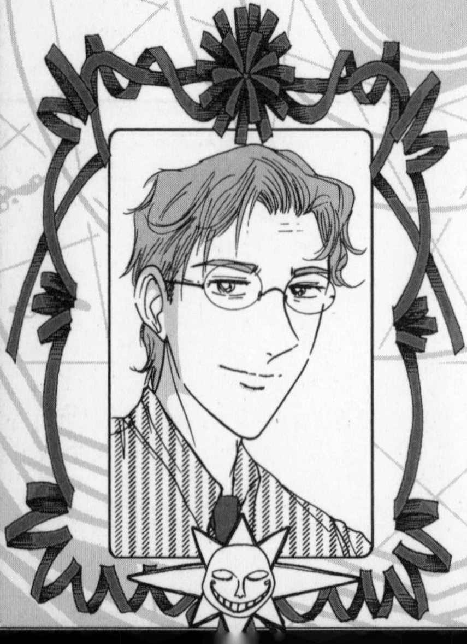

Petier Troia
Age: possibly 35
Birthday: possibly sometime in September
Blood Type: unknown
Soul: possibly very old

_Megan's Mother:_
_Francine "Frankie" Amano;_
_and_
_Megan's Best Friend:_
_Dagny Gilhooley..._
_both a mystery... for now..._

Here now, is the second part of six, of the true story of how our realm was changed forever by the addition of one small mortal girl to our Merridiah University. May the telling of the tale further free you from the corruption of the banshees and the otherwise sad horror of living.

_Eternally Nocturnally Yours,_
_The Inhabitants of Merridiah,_
_speaking through this Wired_
_Psyche_

# CHAPTER ONE:
# THIS IS PHOTOGENIC

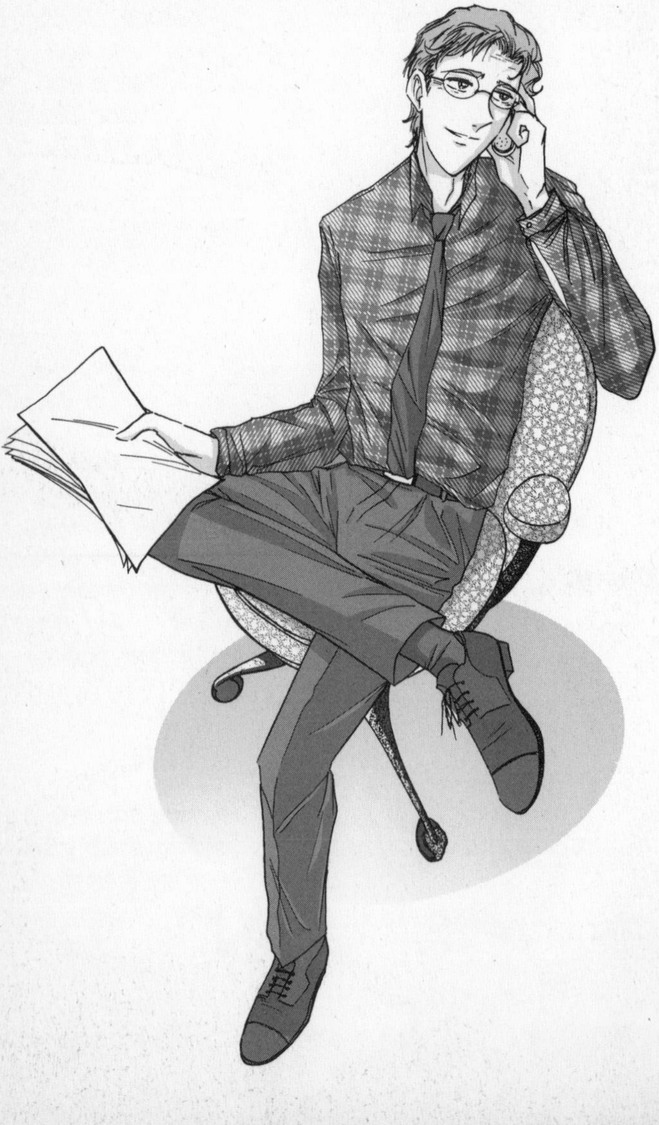

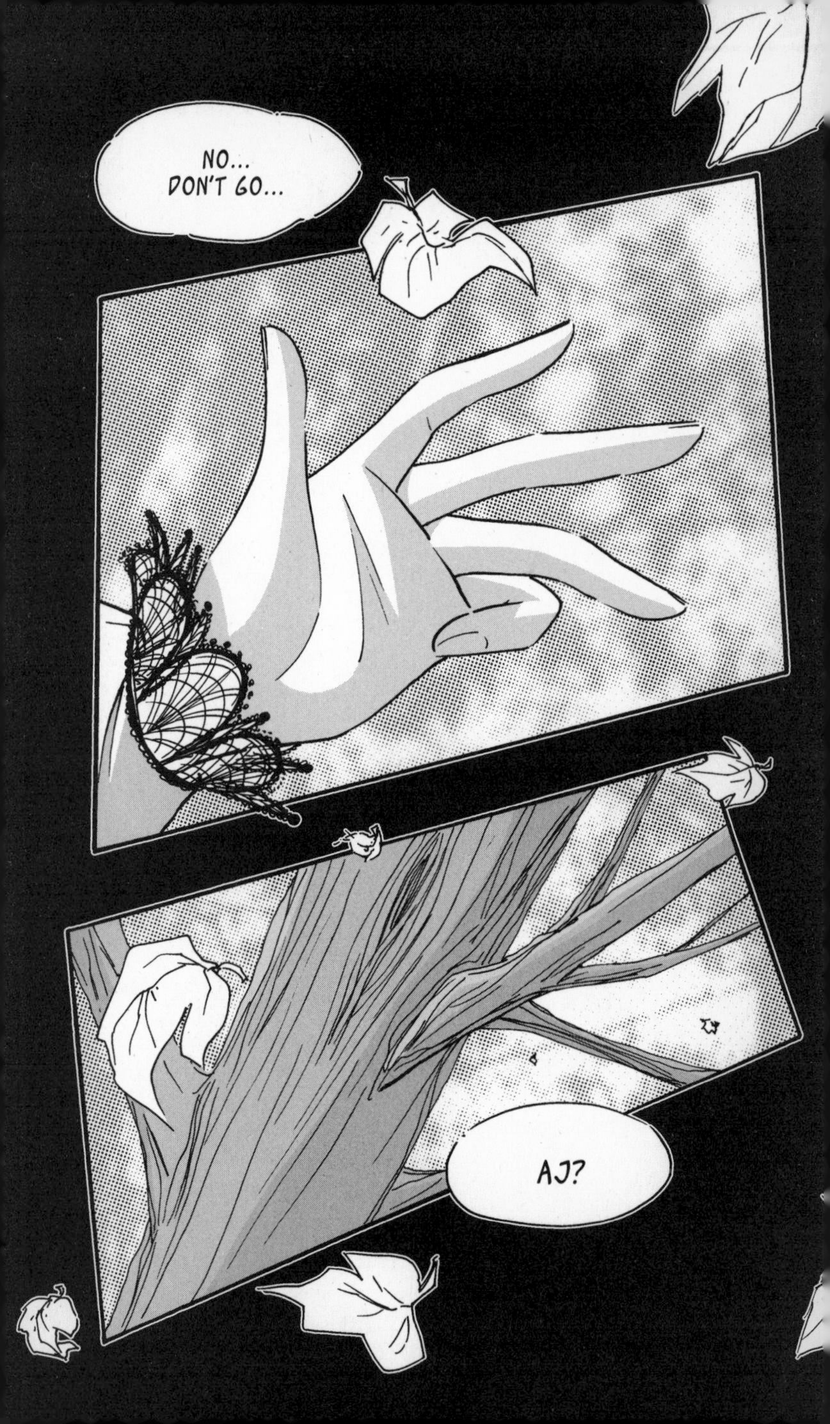
NO...
DON'T GO...
AJ?

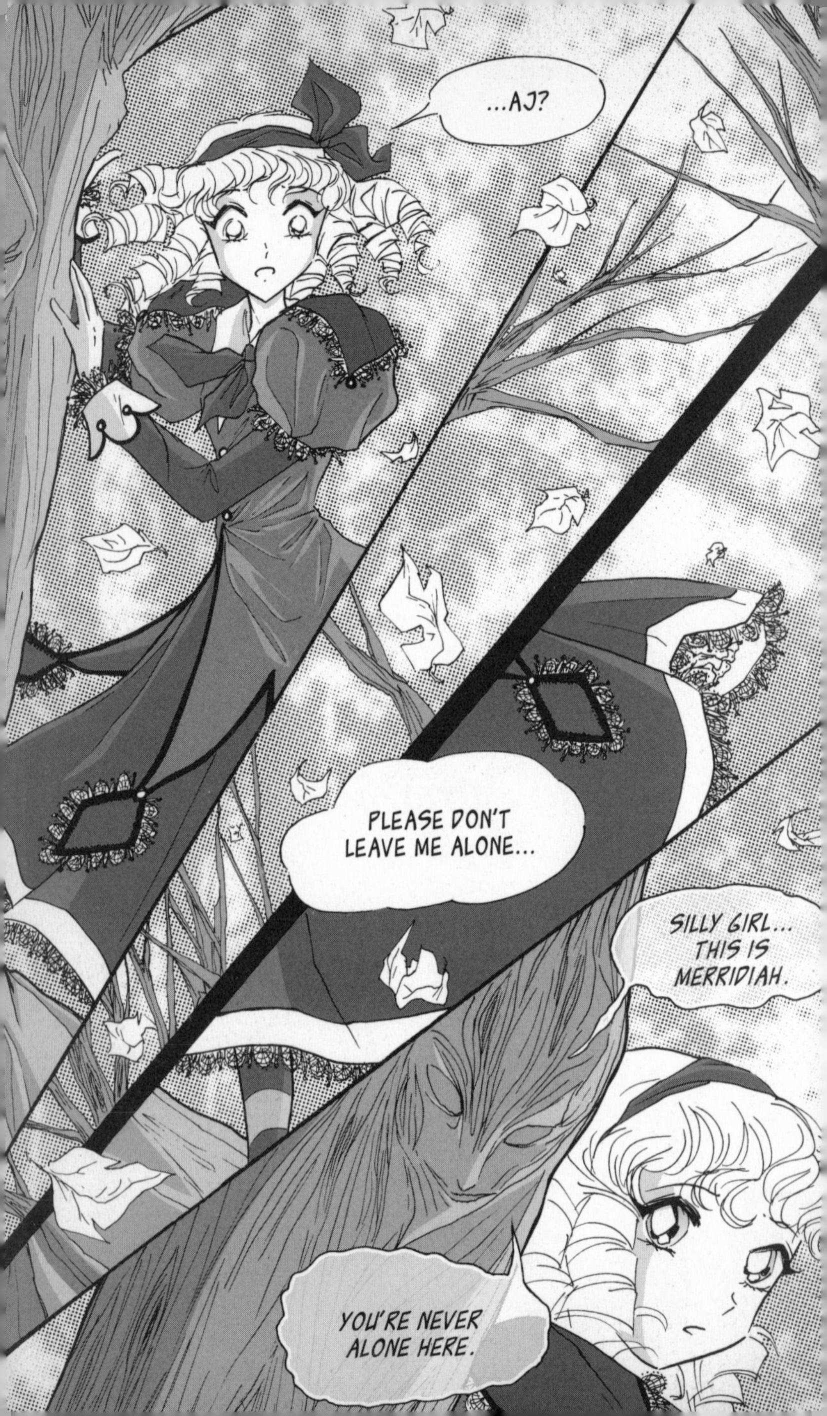
...AJ?
PLEASE DON'T LEAVE ME ALONE...
SILLY GIRL... THIS IS MERRIDIAH.
YOU'RE NEVER ALONE HERE.

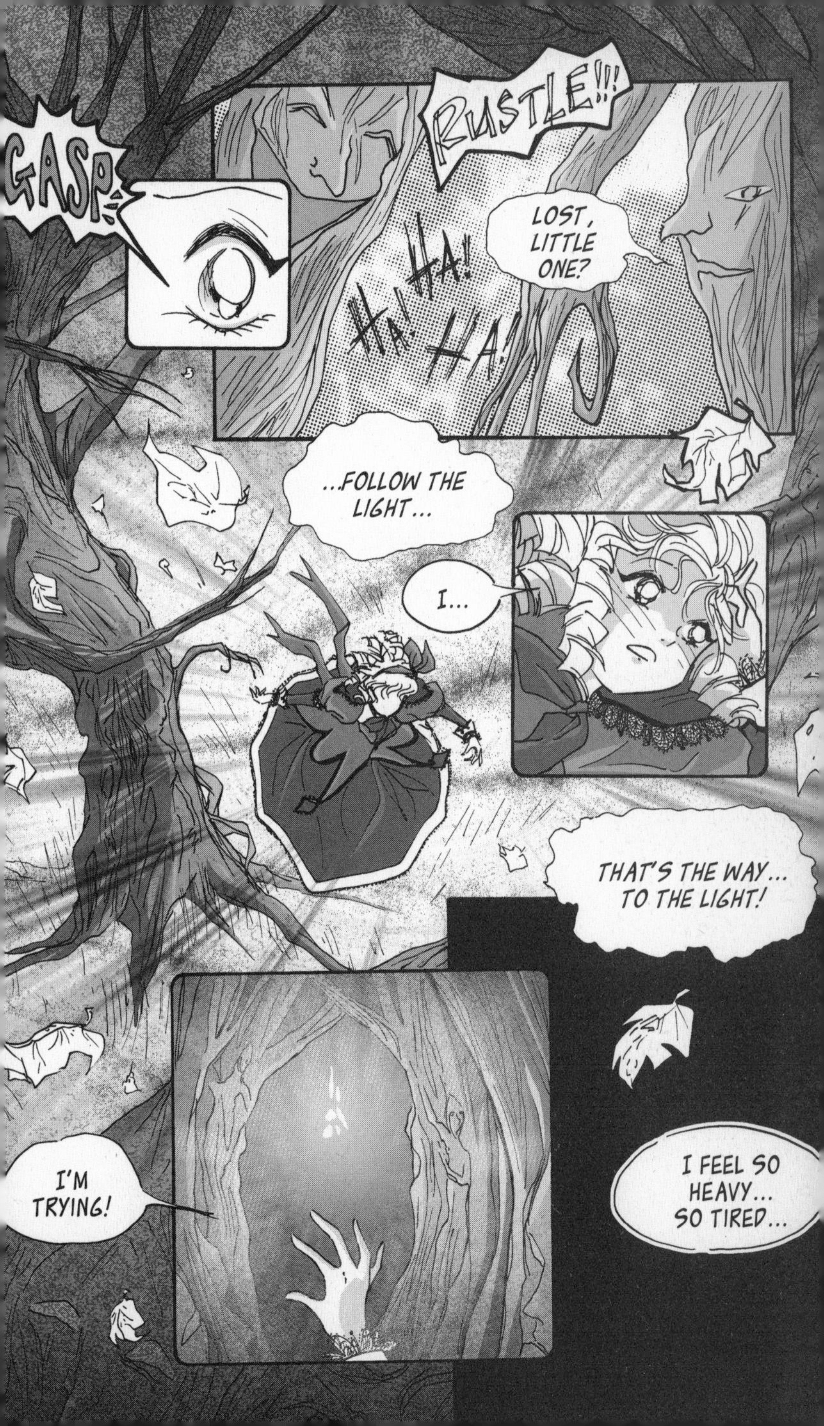
RUSTLE!!!
LOST, LITTLE ONE?
HA! HA! HA!
GASP!
...FOLLOW THE LIGHT...
I...
THAT'S THE WAY... TO THE LIGHT!
I FEEL SO HEAVY... SO TIRED...
I'M TRYING!

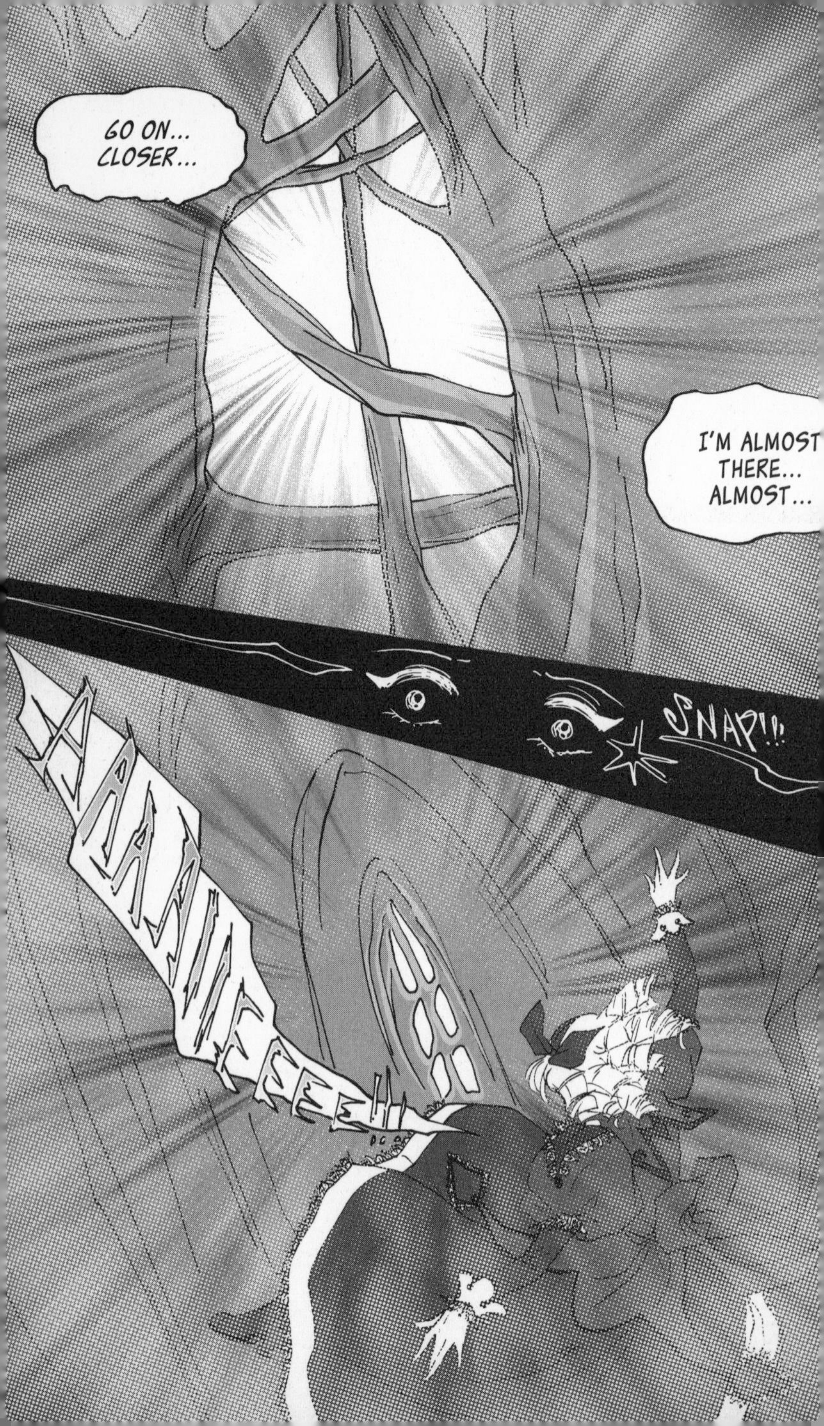
I'M ALMOST THERE... ALMOST...
GO ON... CLOSER...
SNAP!!
AAAAIIIEEEE!!

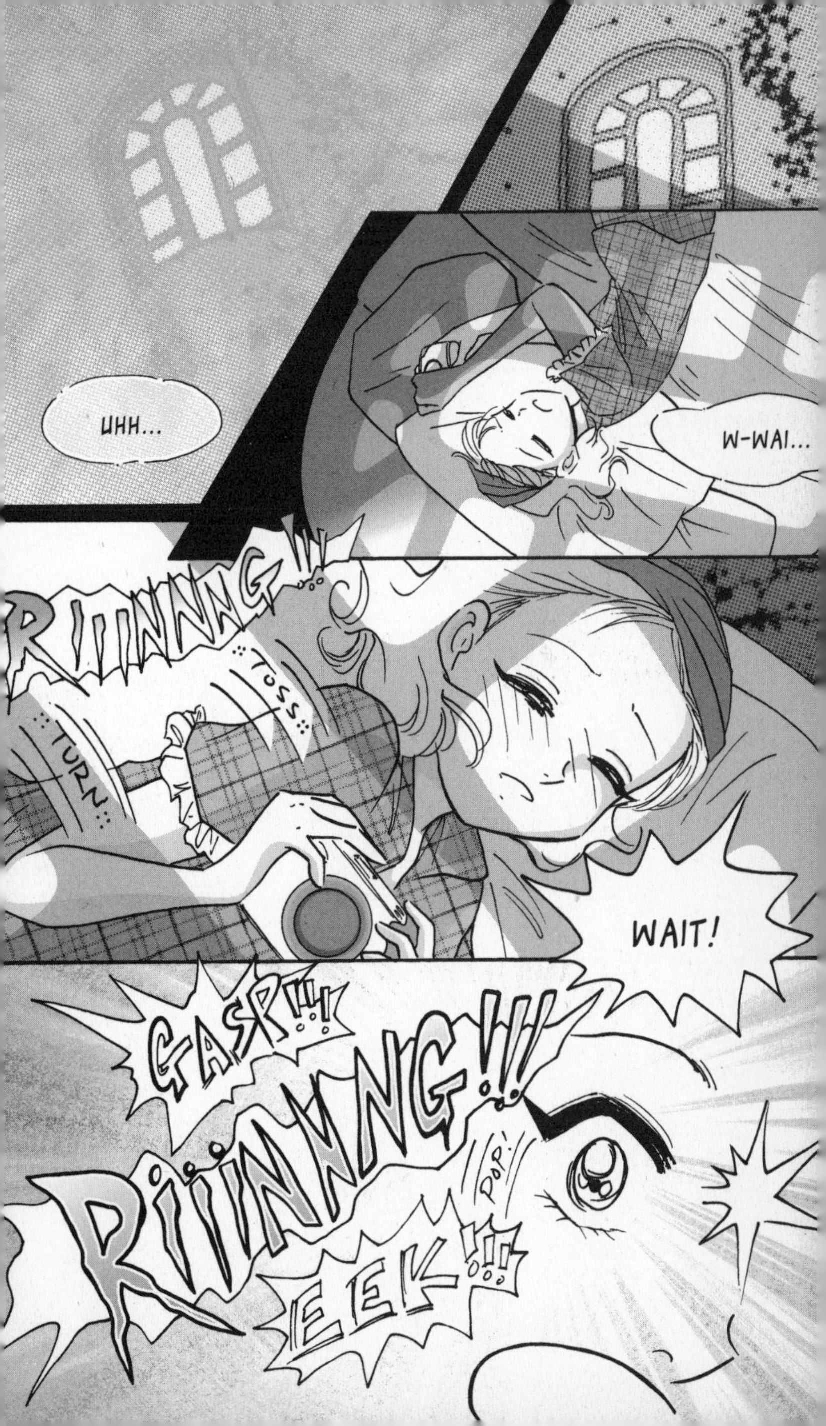
W-WAI...
UHH...
RIINNNG!!!
TOSSS
TURN
WAIT!
GASP!!!
RIIINNNG!!!
POP!
EEK!!!

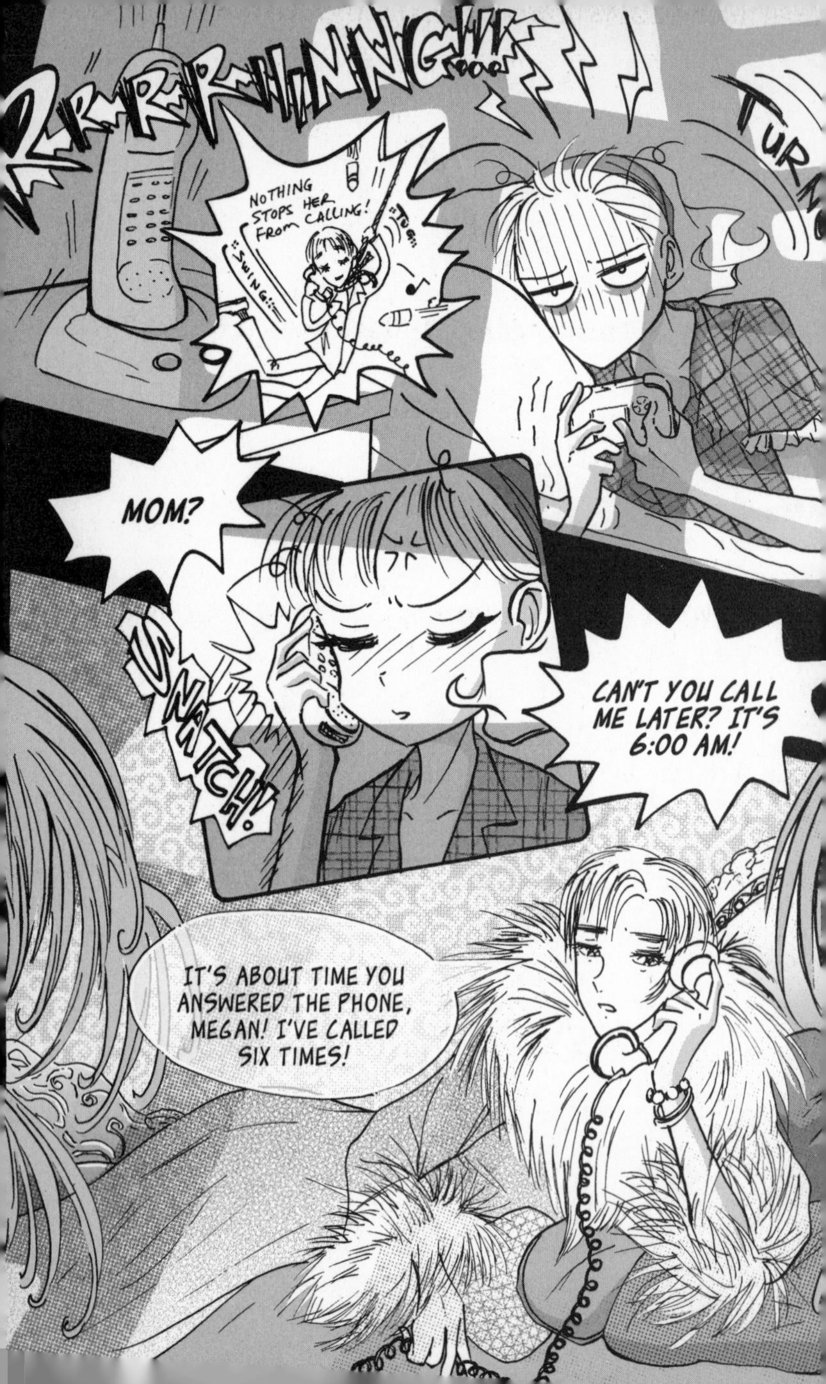
RRRRIIINNNG!!!
TURN
NOTHING STOPS HER FROM CALLING!
SWING
TUG
MOM?
SNATCH!
CAN'T YOU CALL ME LATER? IT'S 6:00 AM!
IT'S ABOUT TIME YOU ANSWERED THE PHONE, MEGAN! I'VE CALLED SIX TIMES!

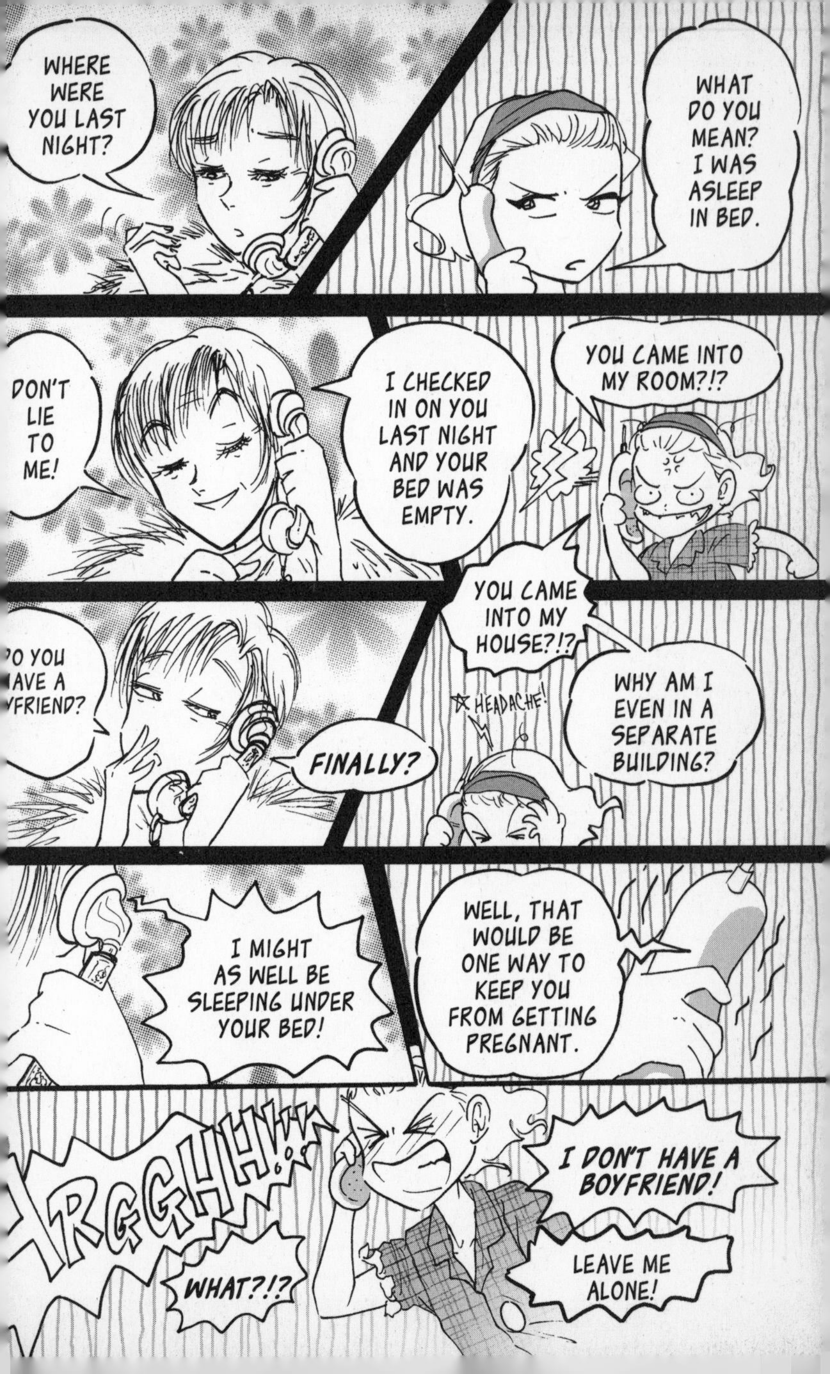
WHERE WERE YOU LAST NIGHT?
WHAT DO YOU MEAN? I WAS ASLEEP IN BED.
DON'T LIE TO ME!
I CHECKED IN ON YOU LAST NIGHT AND YOUR BED WAS EMPTY.
YOU CAME INTO MY ROOM?!?
YOU CAME INTO MY HOUSE?!?
O YOU AVE A YFRIEND?
FINALLY?
HEADACHE!
WHY AM I EVEN IN A SEPARATE BUILDING?
I MIGHT AS WELL BE SLEEPING UNDER YOUR BED!
WELL, THAT WOULD BE ONE WAY TO KEEP YOU FROM GETTING PREGNANT.
RGGHH!!
WHAT?!?
I DON'T HAVE A BOYFRIEND!
LEAVE ME ALONE!

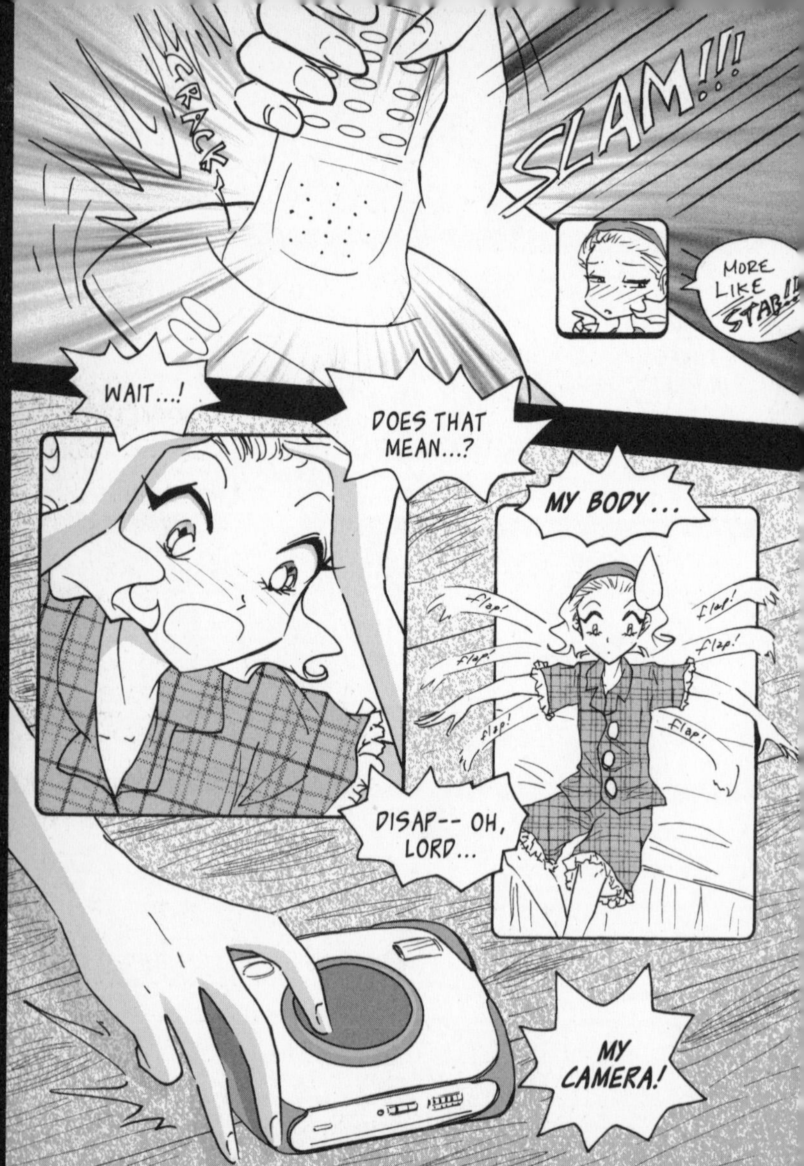
SLAM!!!
CRACK
MORE LIKE STAB!!
WAIT...!
DOES THAT MEAN...?
MY BODY...
flap!
flap!
flap!
flap!
flap!
flap!
DISAP-- OH, LORD...
MY CAMERA!

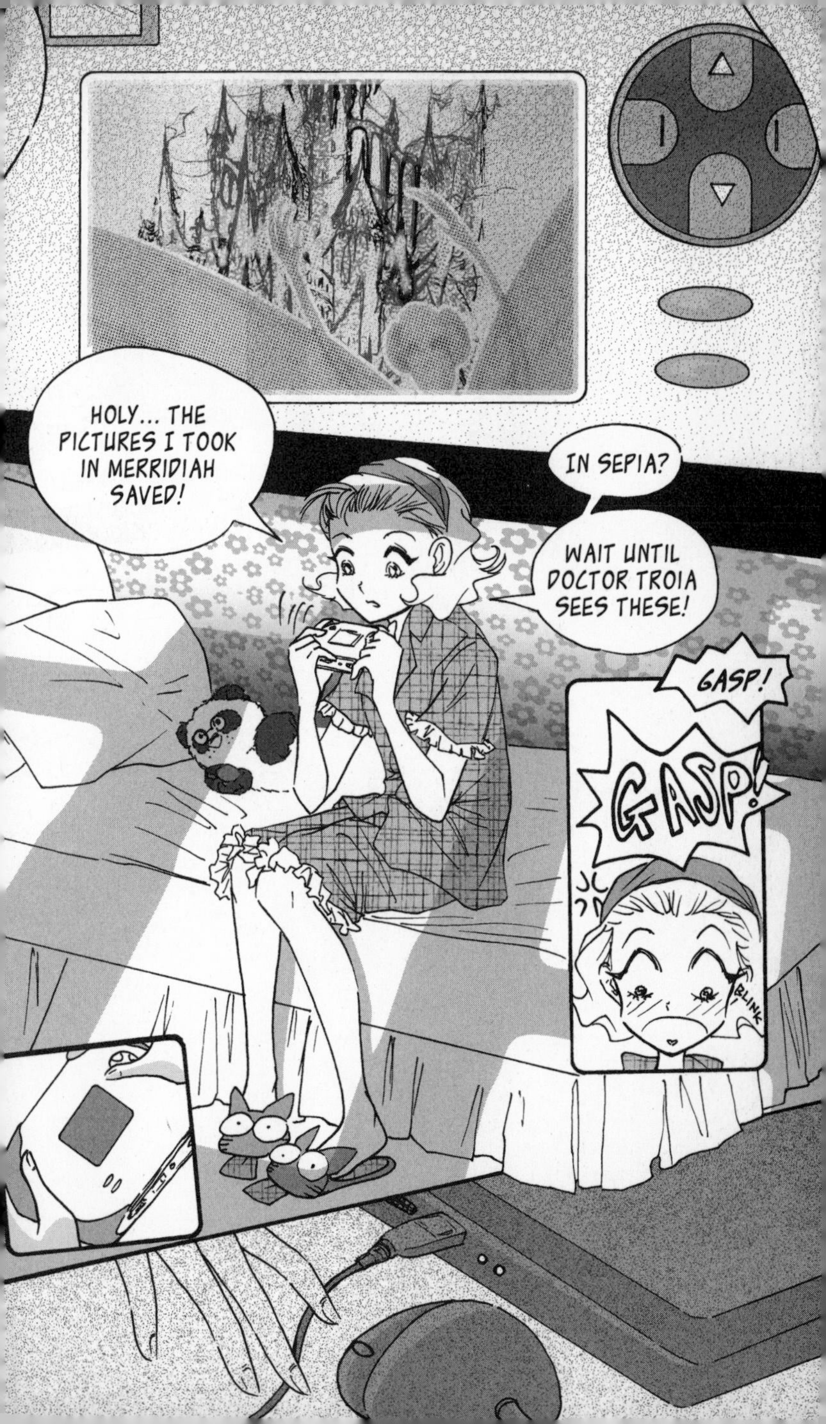
HOLY... THE PICTURES I TOOK IN MERRIDIAH SAVED!
IN SEPIA?
WAIT UNTIL DOCTOR TROIA SEES THESE!
GASP!
GASP!
BLINK

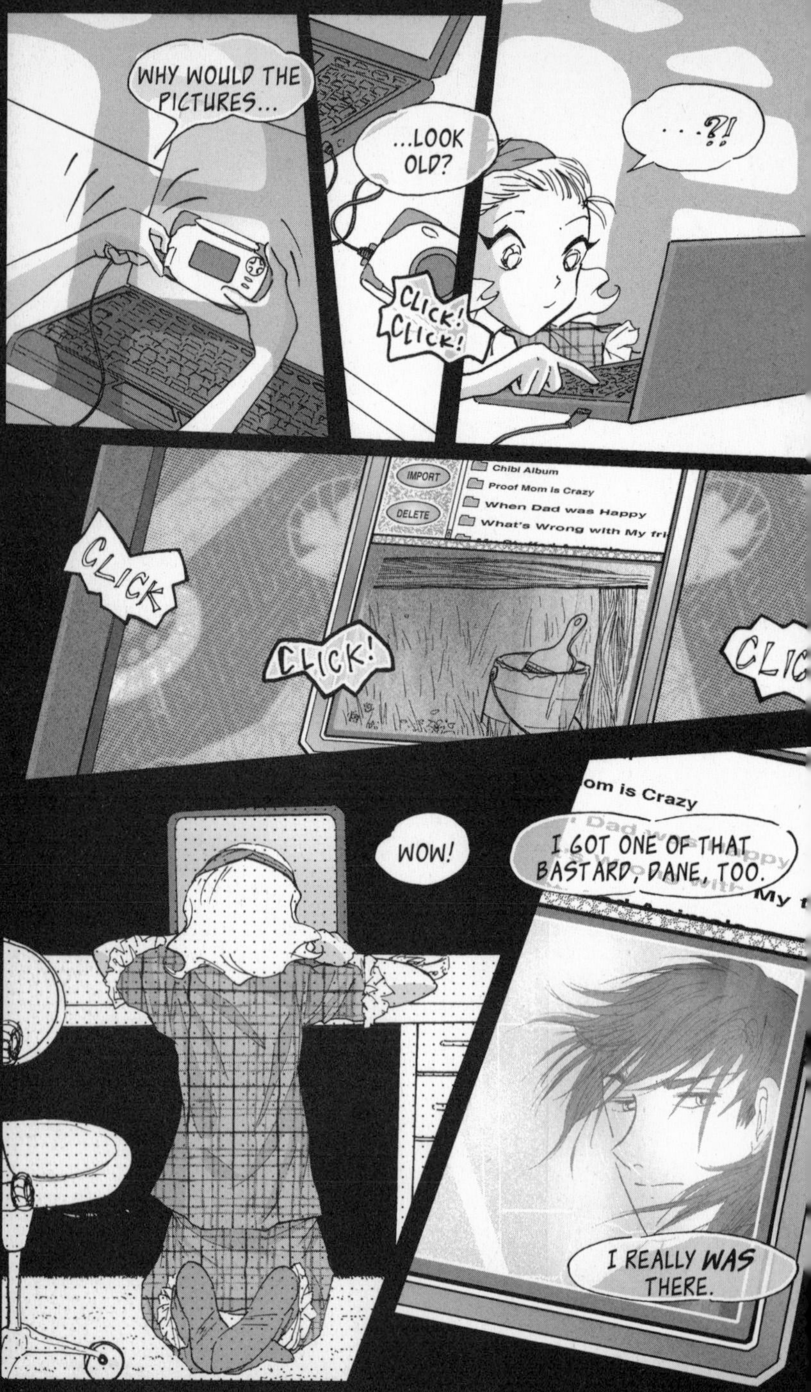
WHY WOULD THE PICTURES...
...LOOK OLD?
CLICK! CLICK!
...?!
CLICK
IMPORT
DELETE
Chibi Album
Proof Mom is Crazy
When Dad was Happy
What's Wrong with My fri
CLICK!
CLIC
WOW!
om is Crazy
I GOT ONE OF THAT BASTARD, DANE, TOO.
I REALLY WAS THERE.

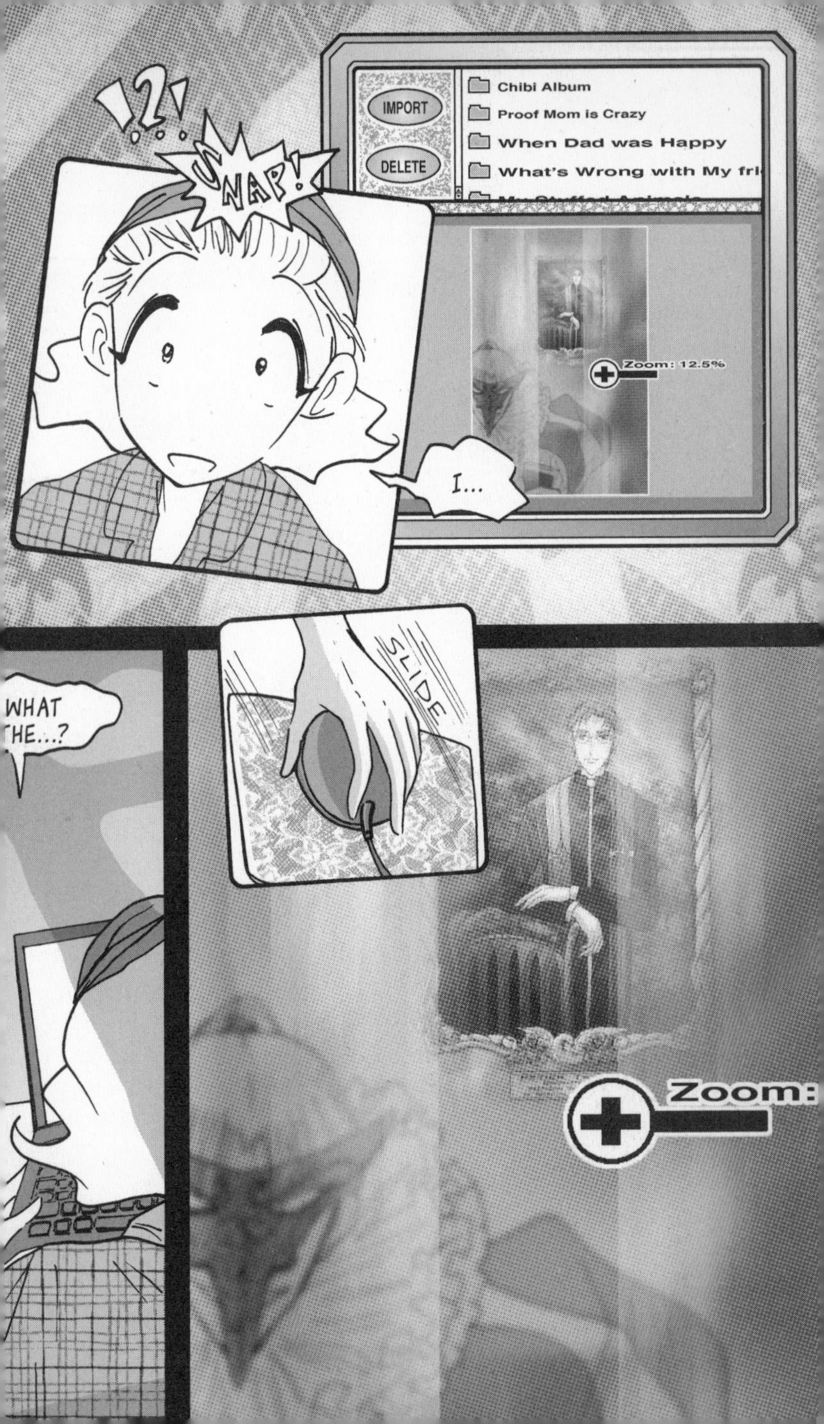
IMPORT
DELETE
Chibi Album
Proof Mom is Crazy
When Dad was Happy
What's Wrong with My fri
Zoom: 12.5%
!?!
SNAP!
I...
SLIDE
Zoom:
WHAT THE...?

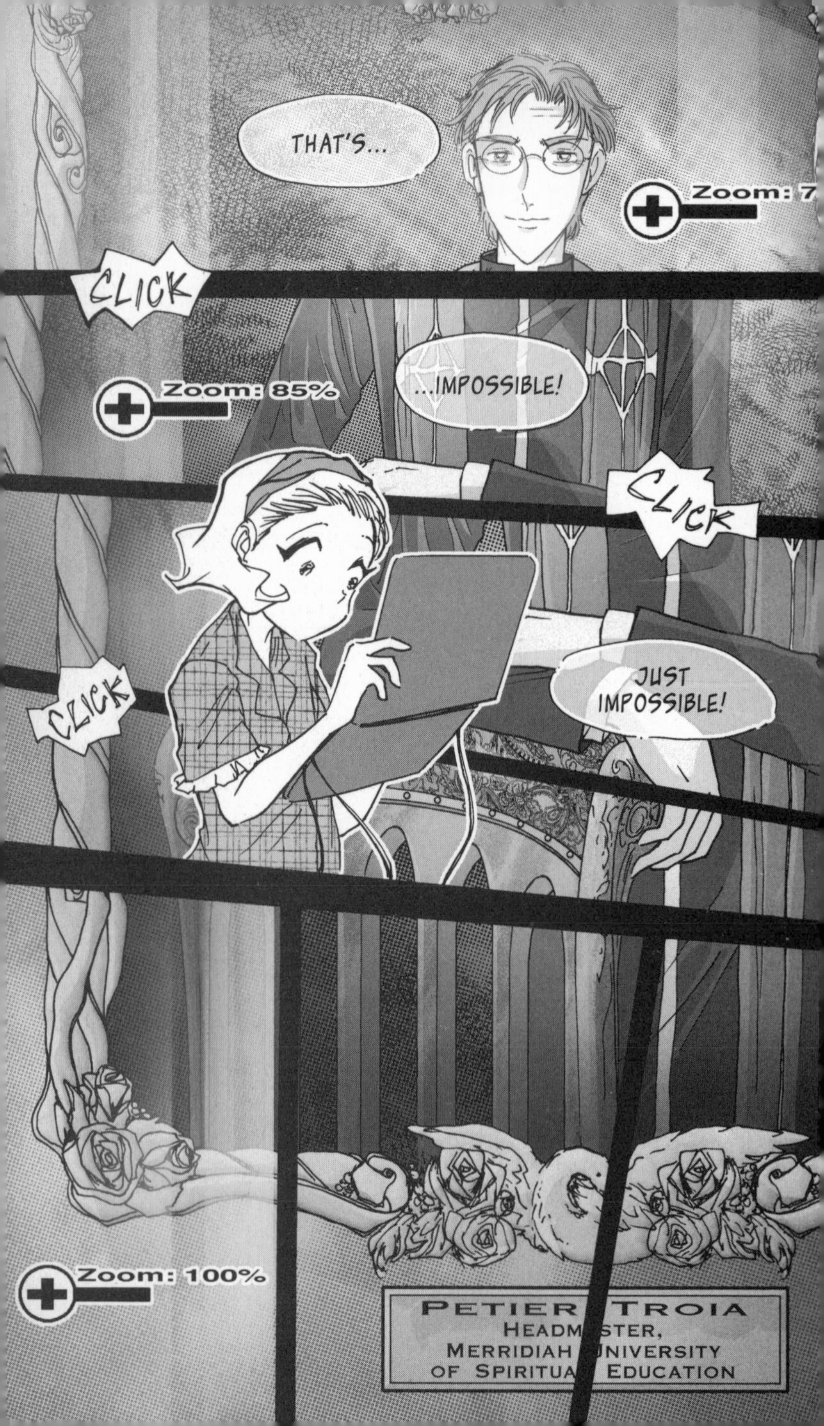

Zoom: 7
THAT'S...
CLICK
...IMPOSSIBLE!
Zoom: 85%
CLICK
JUST IMPOSSIBLE!
CLICK
Zoom: 100%
PETIER TROIA
HEADM STER,
MERRIDIAH NIVERSITY
OF SPIRITUA EDUCATION

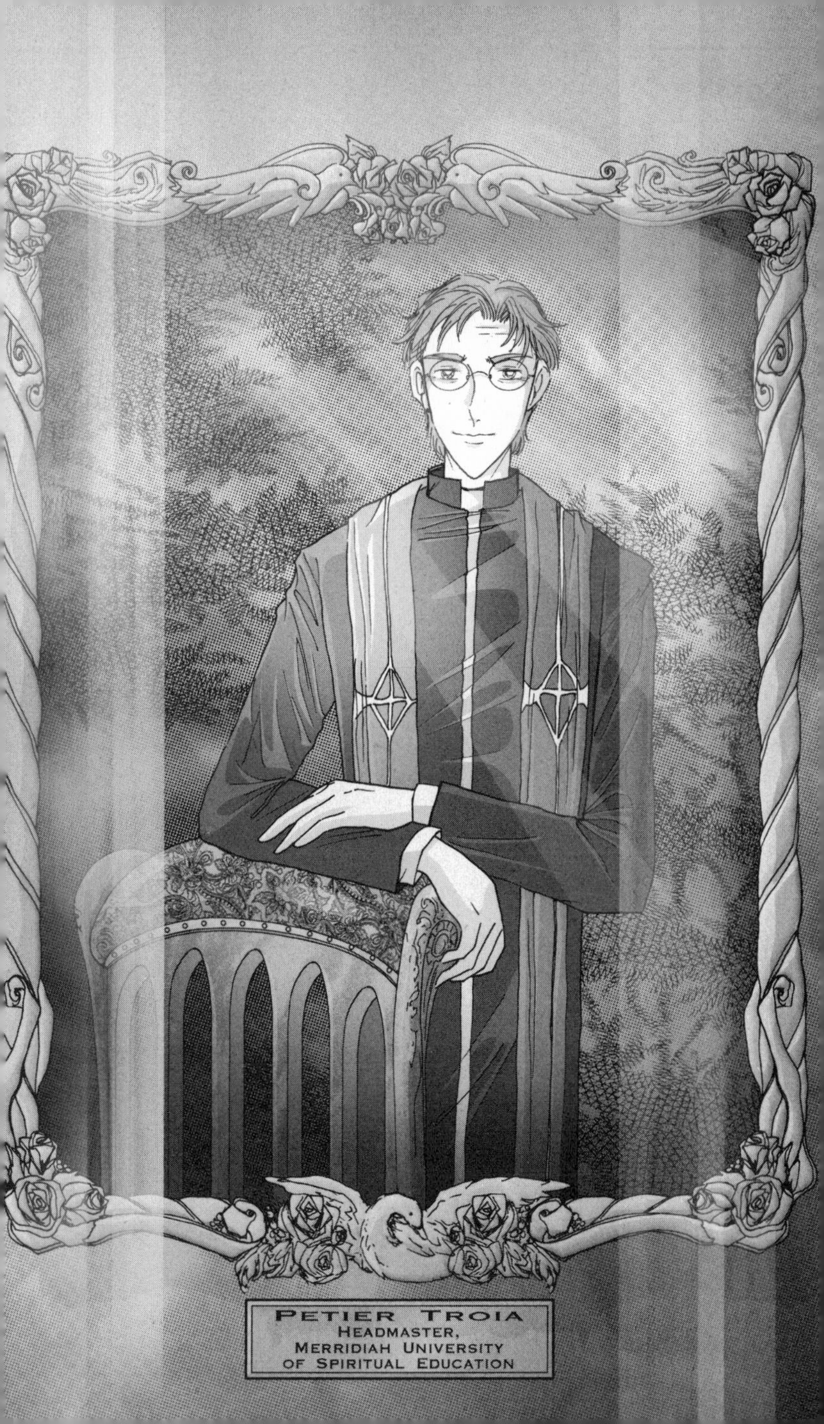
PETIER TROIA
HEADMASTER,
MERRIDIAH UNIVERSITY
OF SPIRITUAL EDUCATION

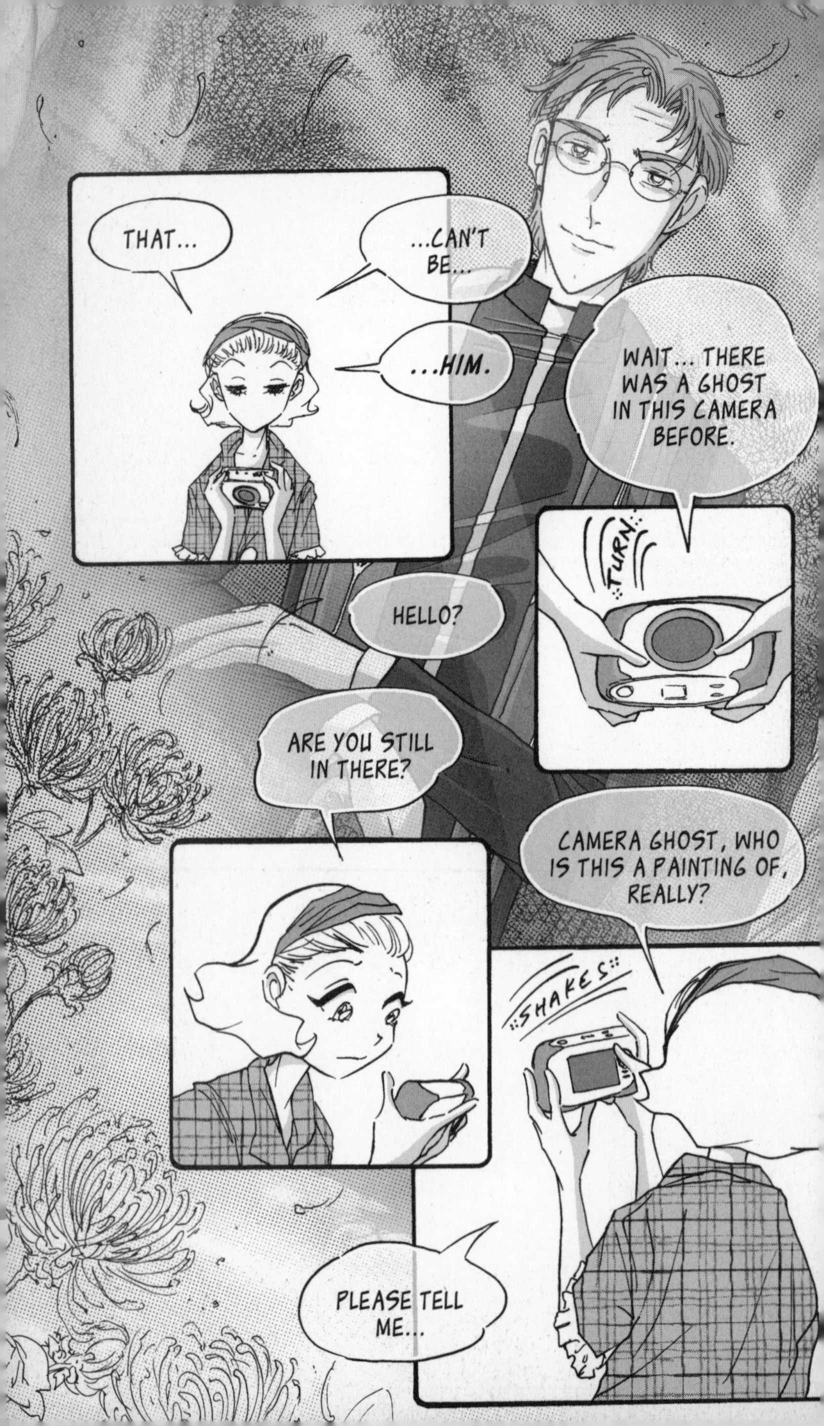
THAT...
...CAN'T BE...
...HIM.
WAIT... THERE WAS A GHOST IN THIS CAMERA BEFORE.
TURN
HELLO?
ARE YOU STILL IN THERE?
CAMERA GHOST, WHO IS THIS A PAINTING OF, REALLY?
SHAKES
PLEASE TELL ME...

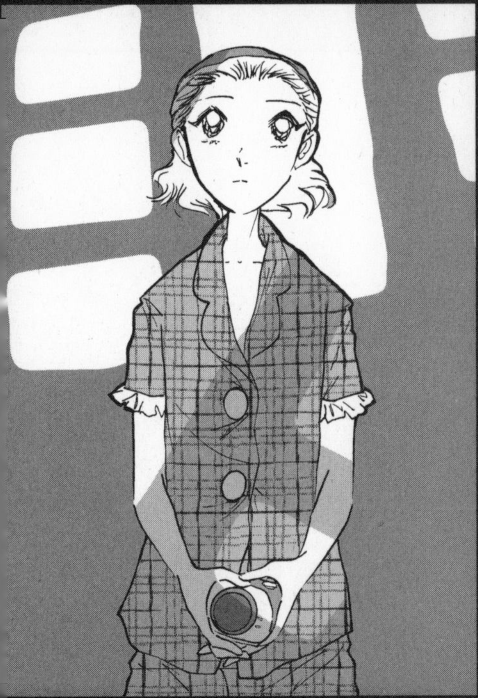

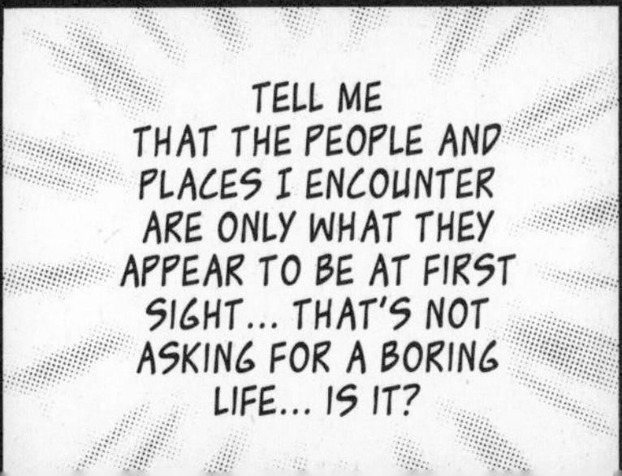
TELL ME THAT THE PEOPLE AND PLACES I ENCOUNTER ARE ONLY WHAT THEY APPEAR TO BE AT FIRST SIGHT... THAT'S NOT ASKING FOR A BORING LIFE... IS IT?

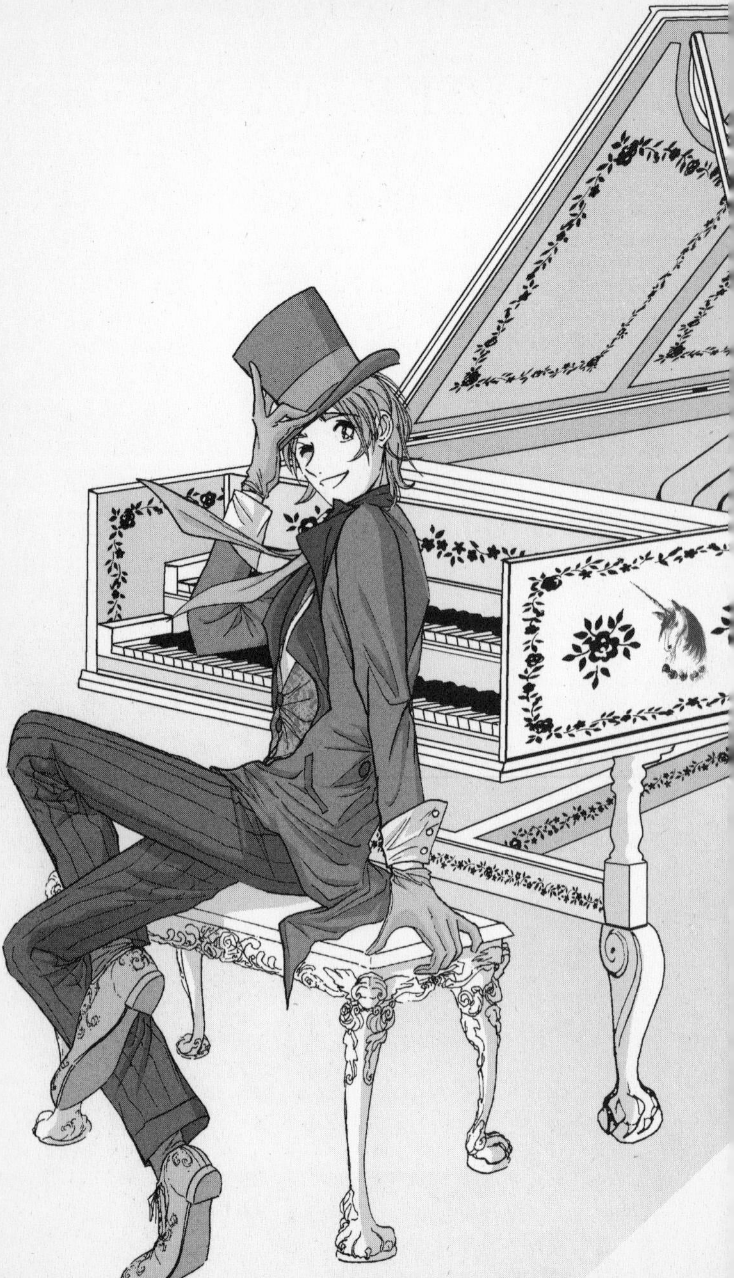

# CHAPTER TWO:

# THIS IS HETEROGENEOUS

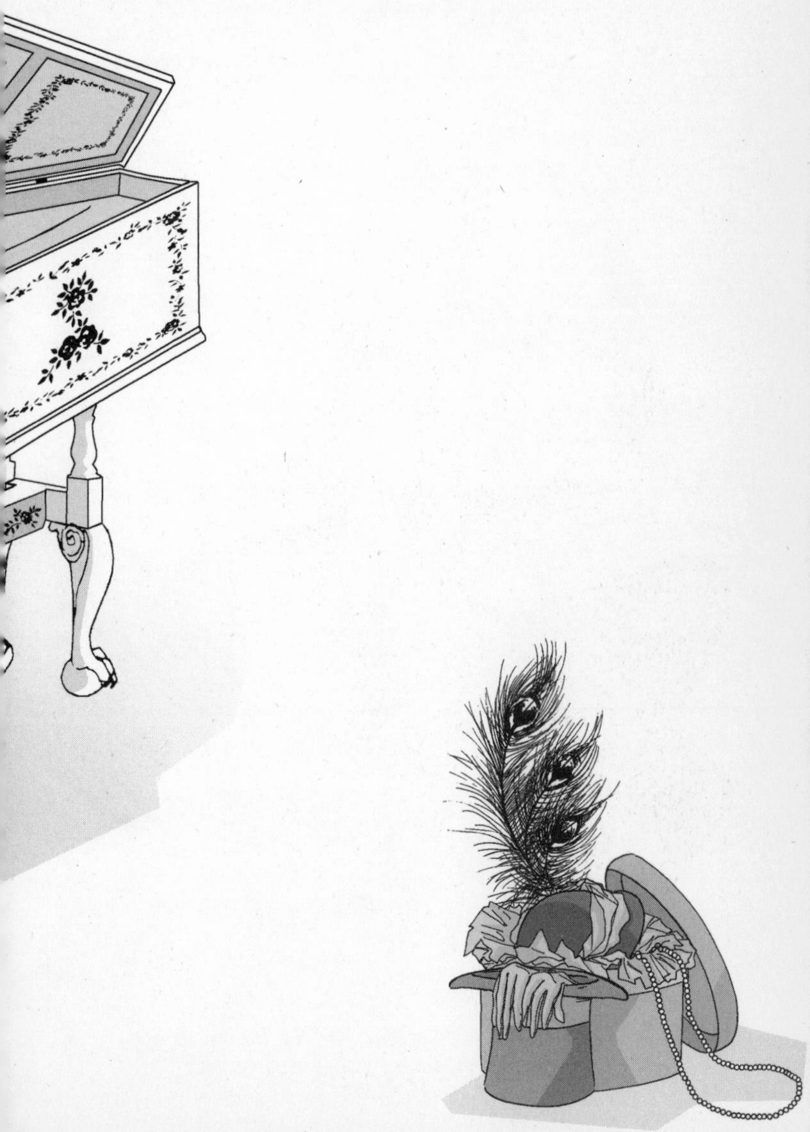

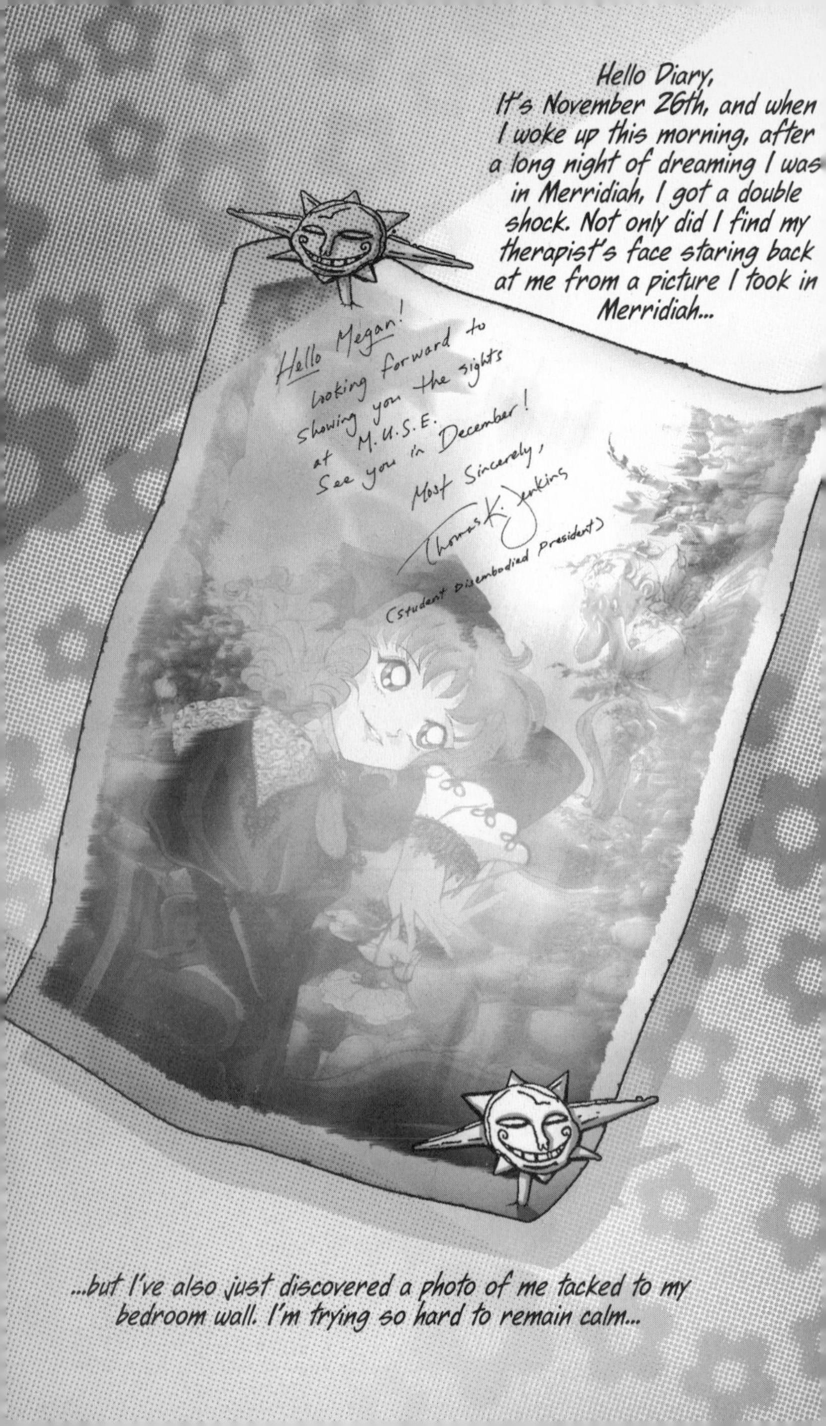
Hello Diary,
It's November 26th, and when I woke up this morning, after a long night of dreaming I was in Merridiah, I got a double shock. Not only did I find my therapist's face staring back at me from a picture I took in Merridiah...
Hello Megan! Looking forward to showing you the sights at M.U.S.E. See you in December! Most Sincerely, Thomas K. Jenkins (Student Disembodied President)
...but I've also just discovered a photo of me tacked to my bedroom wall. I'm trying so hard to remain calm...

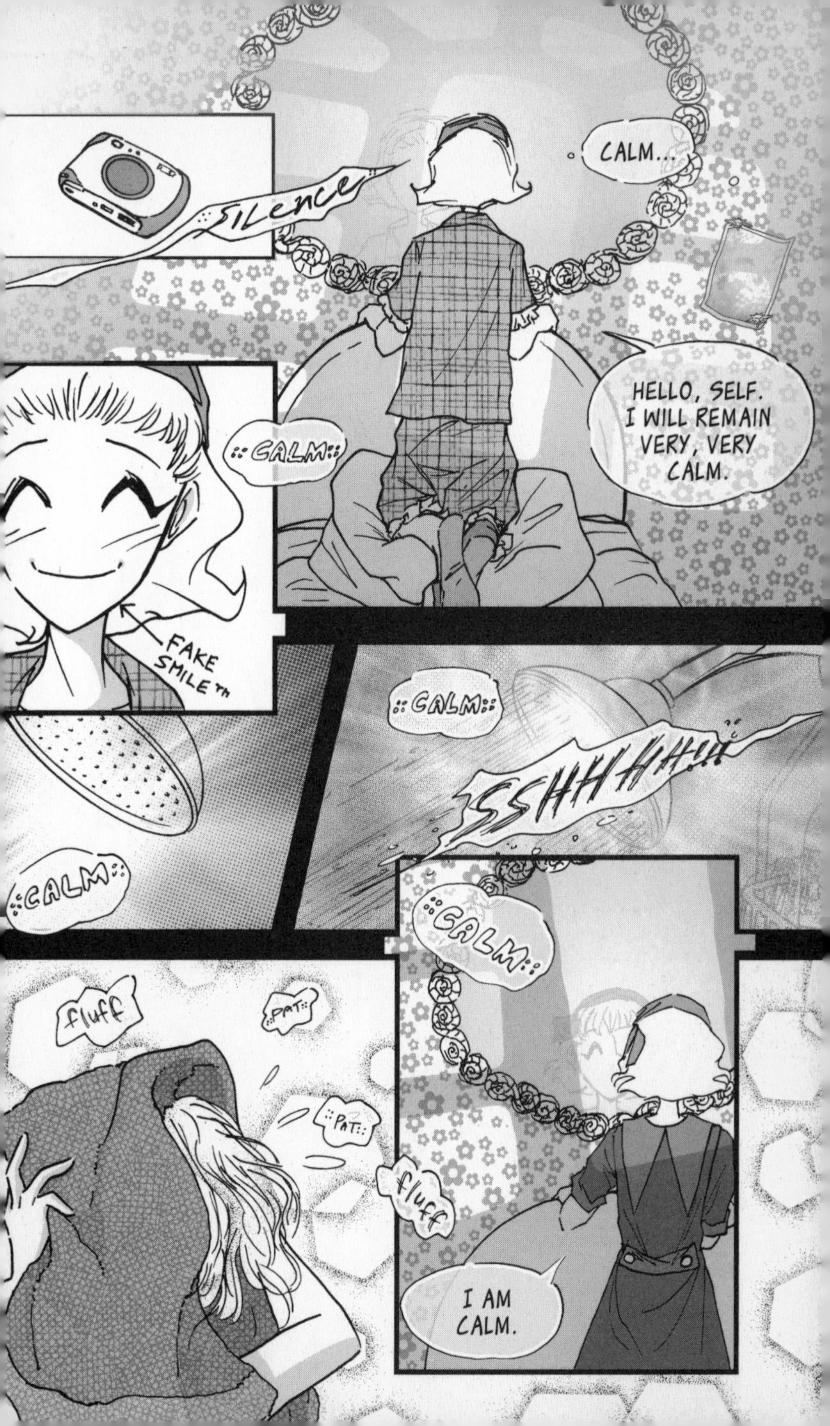

CALM...
HELLO, SELF. I WILL REMAIN VERY, VERY CALM.
SILENCE
::CALM::
SSHHHHH!!!
::CALM::
FAKE SMILE™
::CALM::
::CALM::
I AM CALM.
fluff
::PAT::
::PAT::
fluff

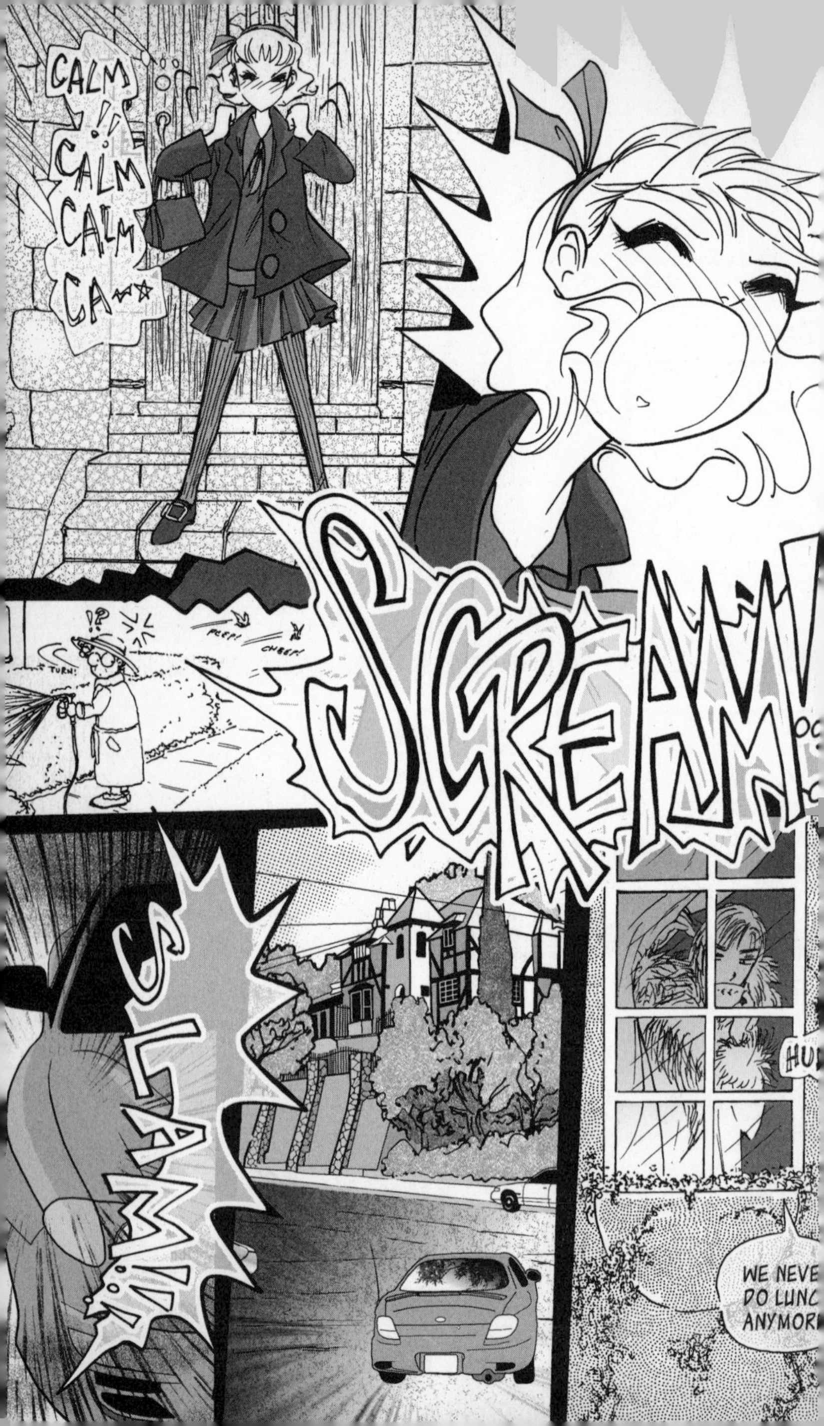
CALM !! CALM CALM CA☆
SCREAM!
!?
TURN!
PEEP!
CHEEP!
SLAM!!
HU
WE NEVE DO LUNC ANYMOR

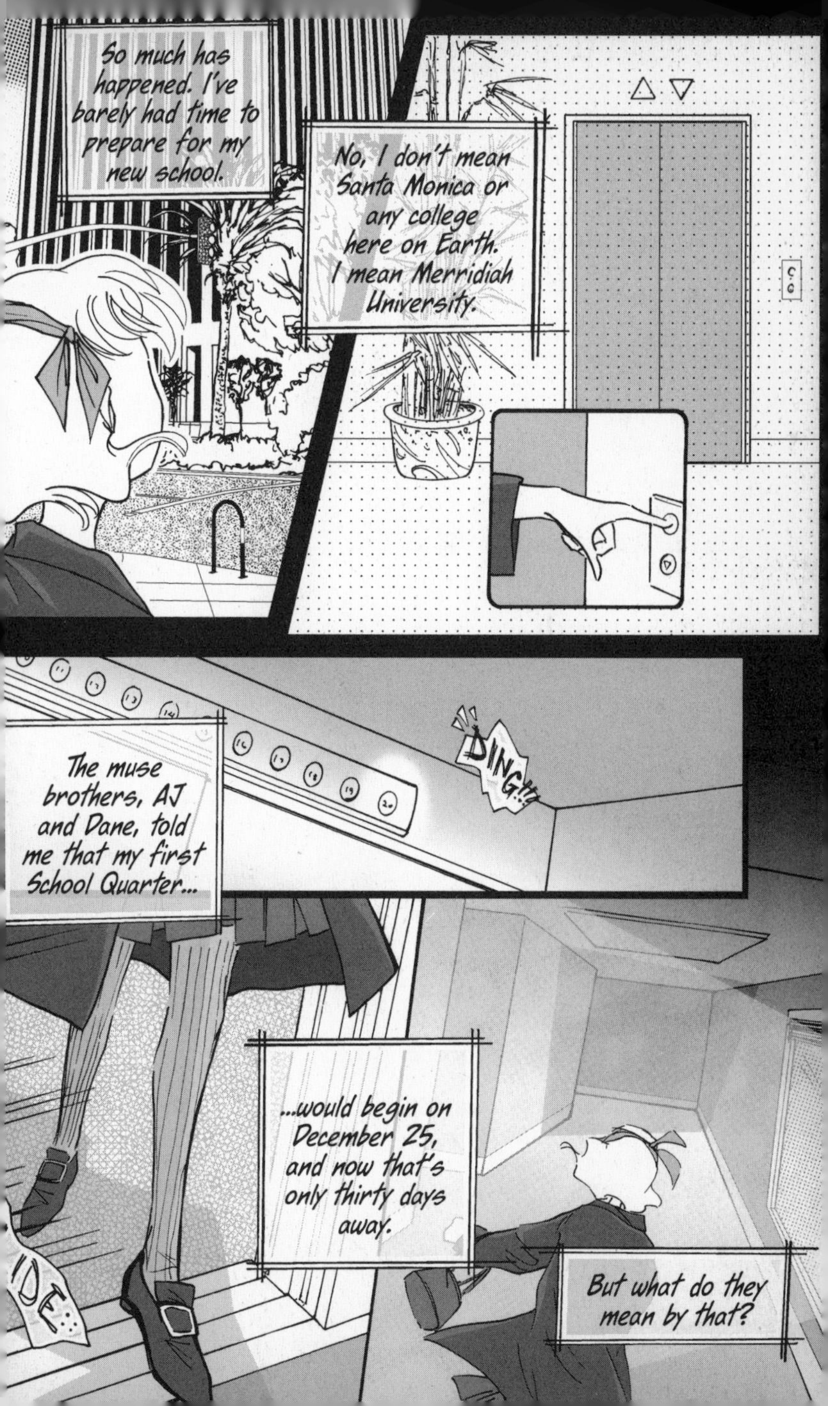

So much has happened. I've barely had time to prepare for my new school.
No, I don't mean Santa Monica or any college here on Earth. I mean Merridiah University.
The muse brothers, AJ and Dane, told me that my first School Quarter...
DING!!!
...would begin on December 25, and now that's only thirty days away.
But what do they mean by that?

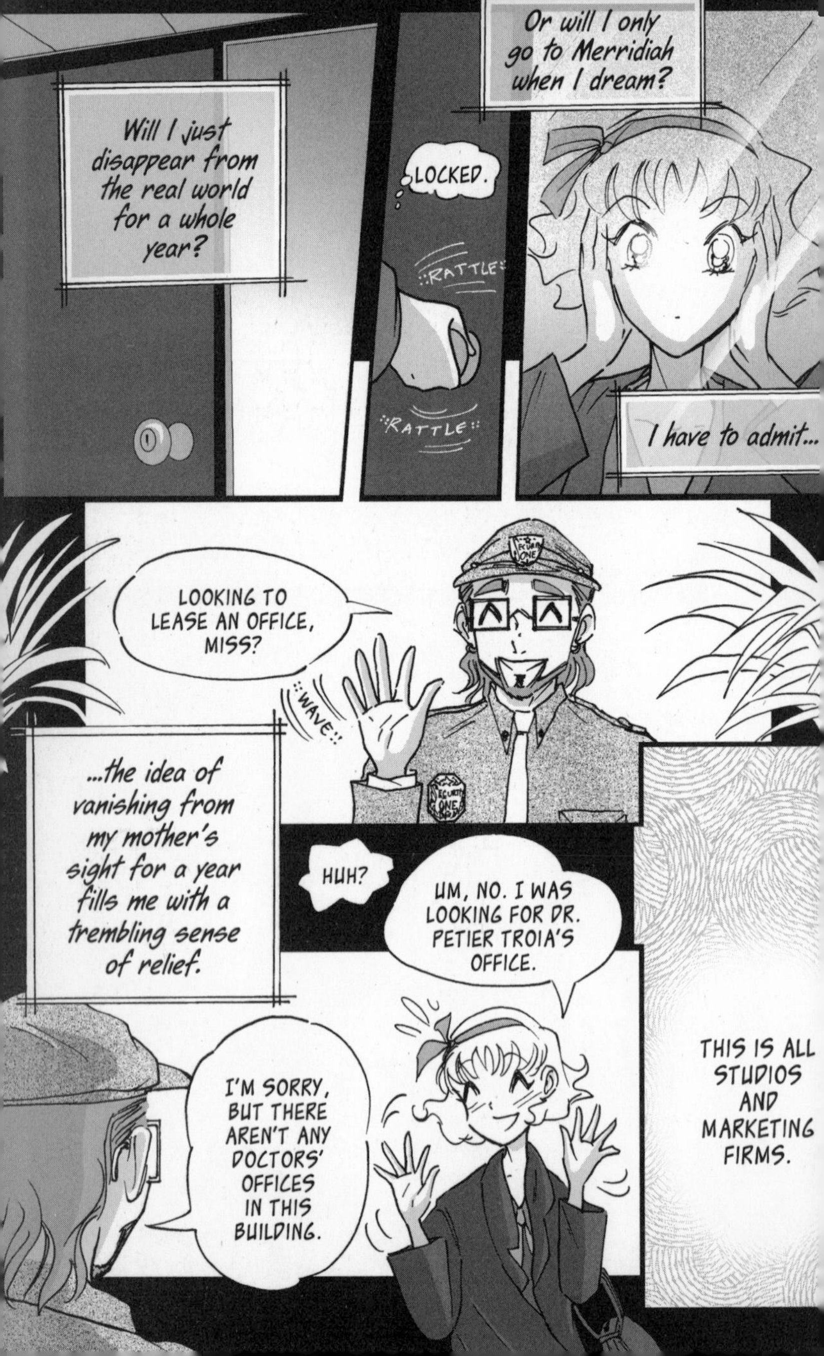
Will I just disappear from the real world for a whole year?
LOCKED.
RATTLE
RATTLE
Or will I only go to Merridiah when I dream?
I have to admit...
LOOKING TO LEASE AN OFFICE, MISS?
WAVE
...the idea of vanishing from my mother's sight for a year fills me with a trembling sense of relief.
HUH?
UM, NO. I WAS LOOKING FOR DR. PETIER TROIA'S OFFICE.
I'M SORRY, BUT THERE AREN'T ANY DOCTORS' OFFICES IN THIS BUILDING.
THIS IS ALL STUDIOS AND MARKETING FIRMS.

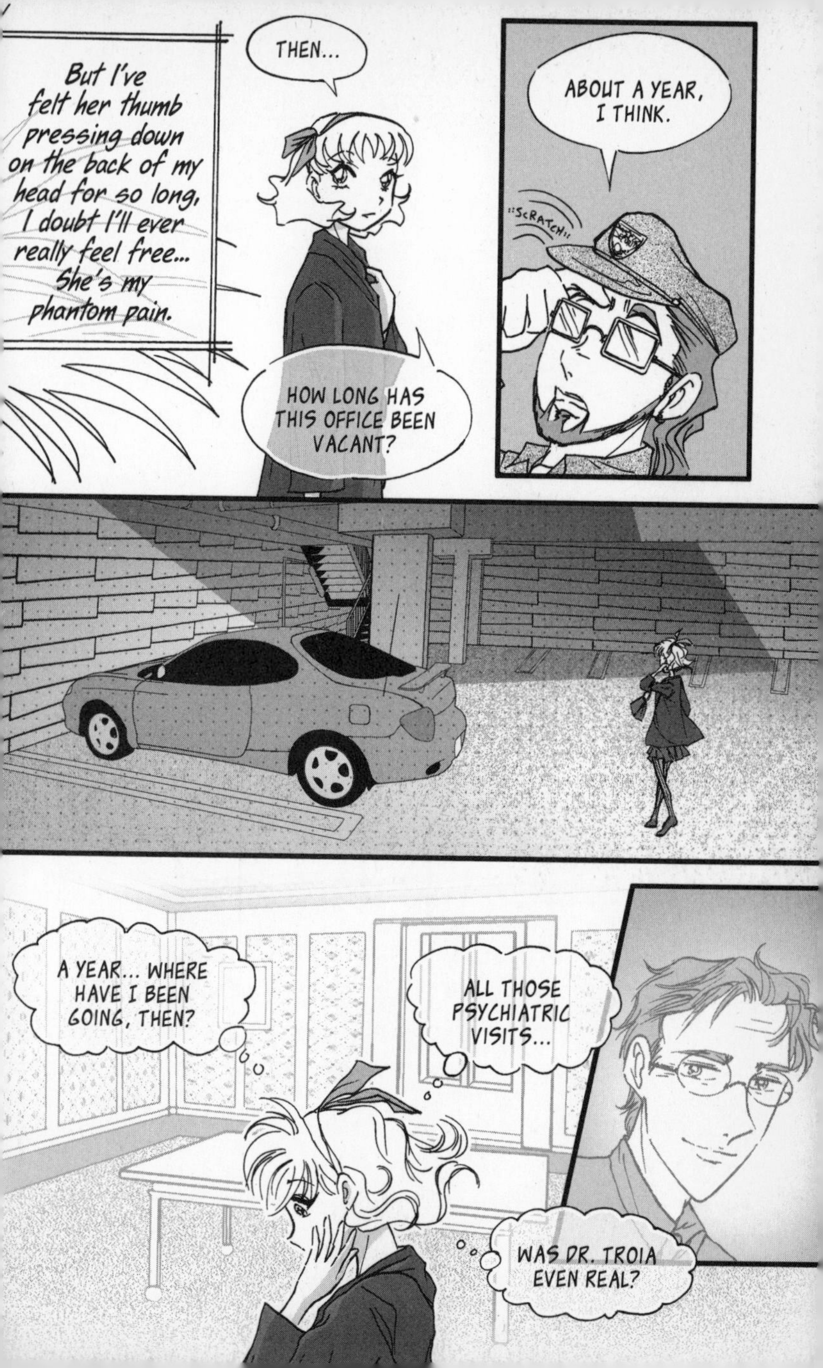
But I've felt her thumb pressing down on the back of my head for so long, I doubt I'll ever really feel free... She's my phantom pain.
THEN...
HOW LONG HAS THIS OFFICE BEEN VACANT?
::SCRATCH::
ABOUT A YEAR, I THINK.
A YEAR... WHERE HAVE I BEEN GOING, THEN?
ALL THOSE PSYCHIATRIC VISITS...
WAS DR. TROIA EVEN REAL?

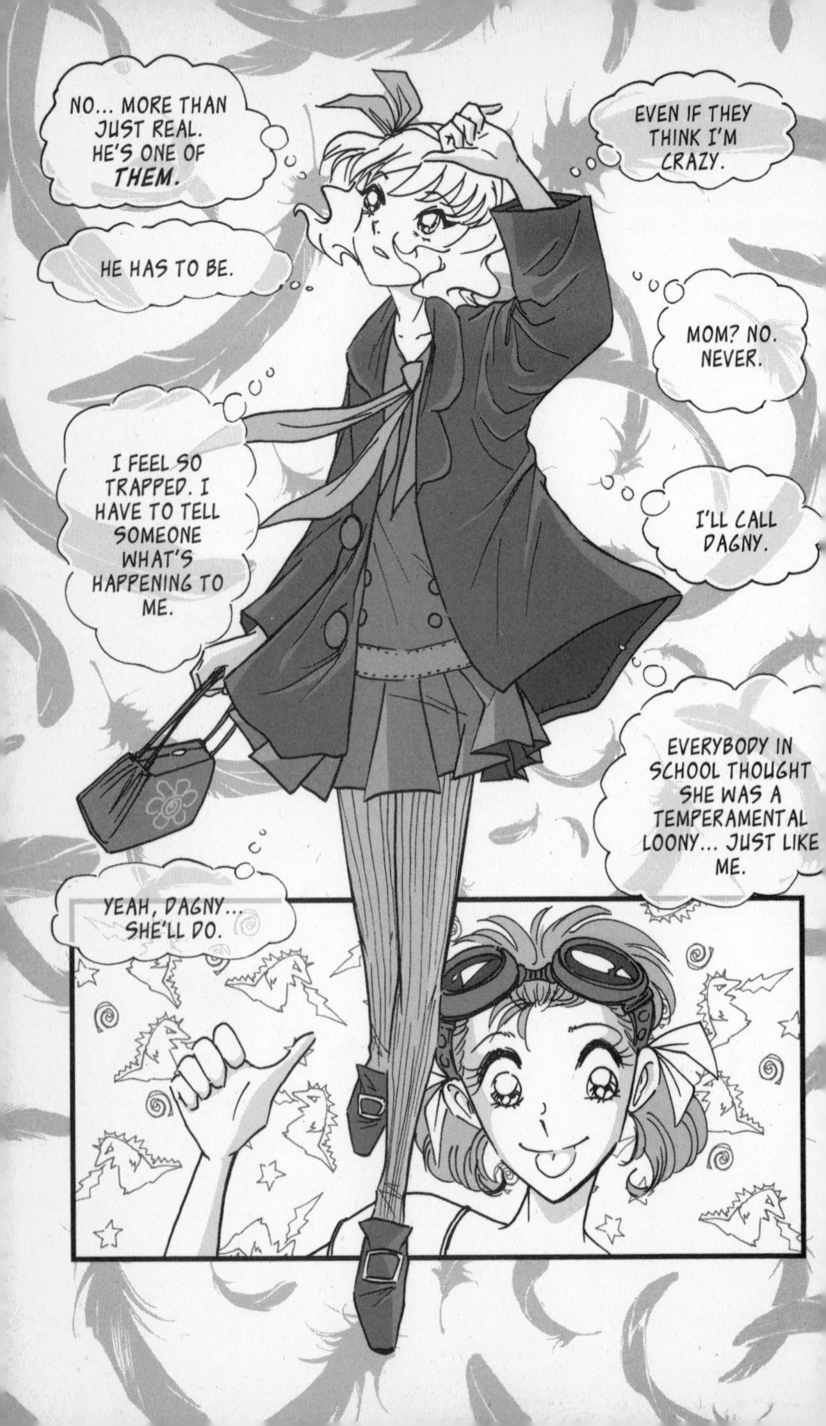
NO... MORE THAN JUST REAL. HE'S ONE OF *THEM*.
HE HAS TO BE.
I FEEL SO TRAPPED. I HAVE TO TELL SOMEONE WHAT'S HAPPENING TO ME.
EVEN IF THEY THINK I'M CRAZY.
MOM? NO. NEVER.
I'LL CALL DAGNY.
EVERYBODY IN SCHOOL THOUGHT SHE WAS A TEMPERAMENTAL LOONY... JUST LIKE ME.
YEAH, DAGNY... SHE'LL DO.

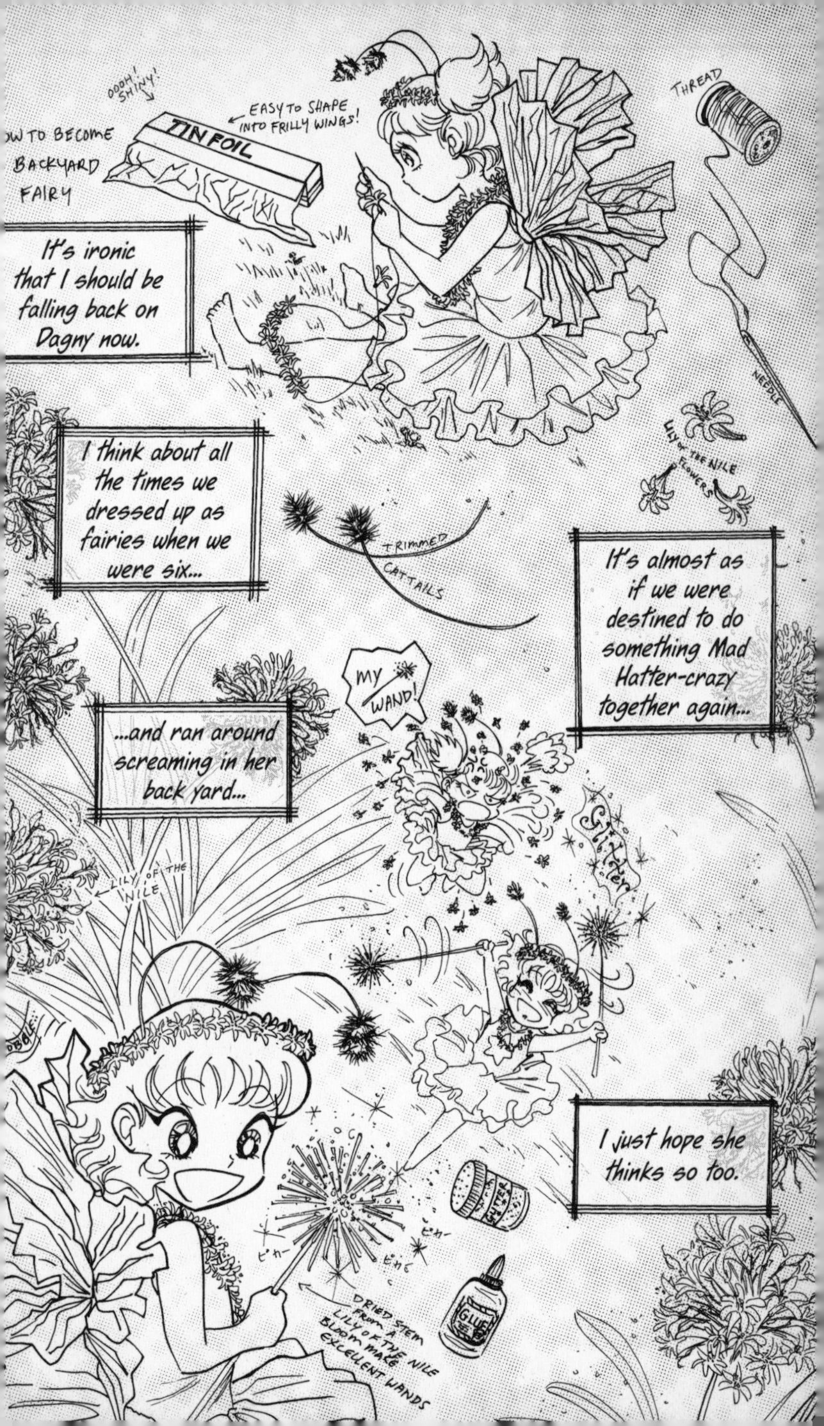
OW TO BECOME BACKYARD FAIRY
OOOH! SHINY!
TIN FOIL
EASY TO SHAPE INTO FRILLY WINGS!
THREAD
NEEDLE
It's ironic that I should be falling back on Dagny now.
LILY OF THE NILE FLOWERS
I think about all the times we dressed up as fairies when we were six...
TRIMMED CATTAILS
It's almost as if we were destined to do something Mad Hatter-crazy together again...
MY WAND!
...and ran around screaming in her back yard...
Glitter
LILY OF THE NILE
I just hope she thinks so too.
GLITTER
GLUE
DRIED STEM FROM A LILY OF THE NILE BLOOM MAKE EXCELLENT WANDS

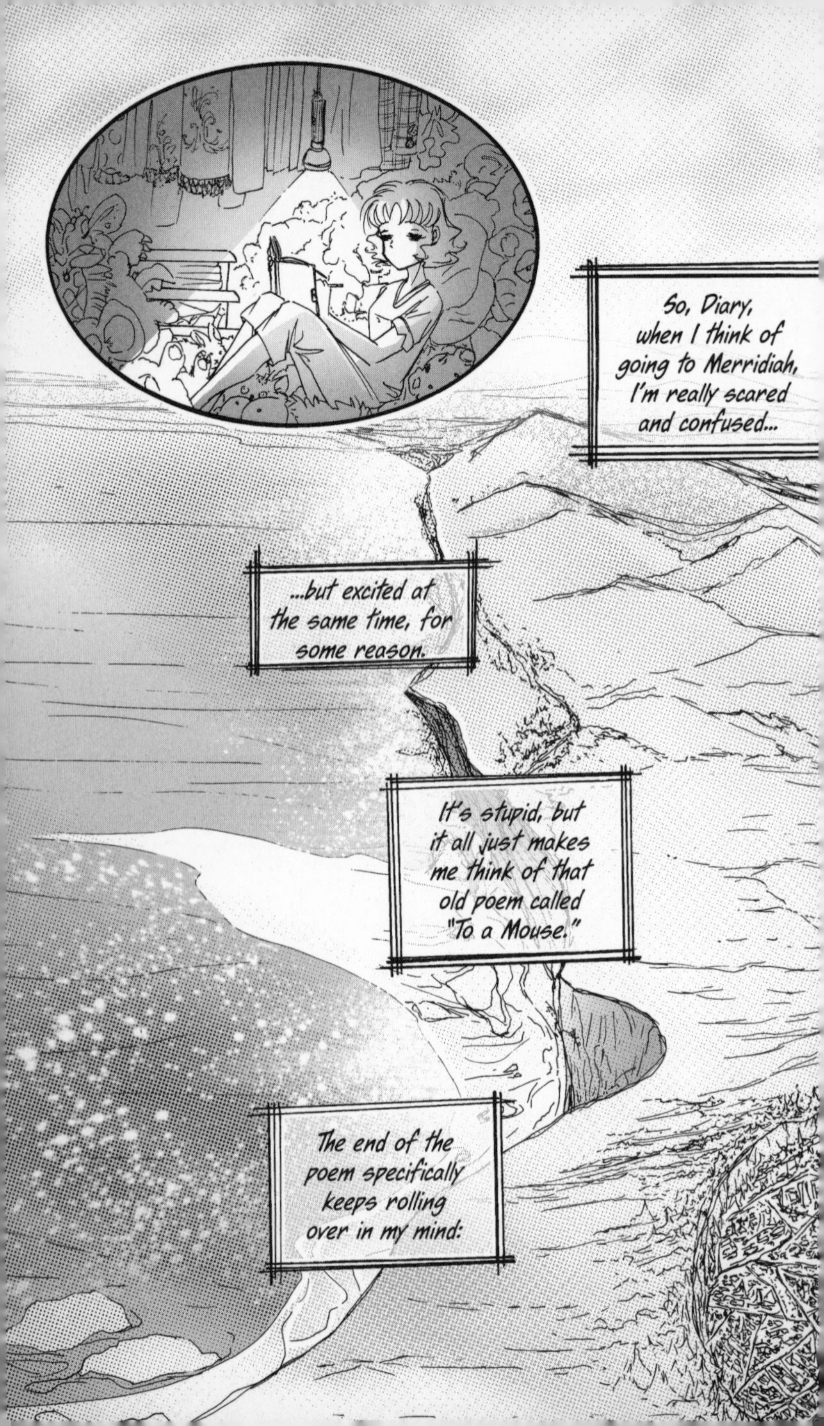
So, Diary, when I think of going to Merridiah, I'm really scared and confused...
...but excited at the same time, for some reason.
It's stupid, but it all just makes me think of that old poem called "To a Mouse."
The end of the poem specifically keeps rolling over in my mind:

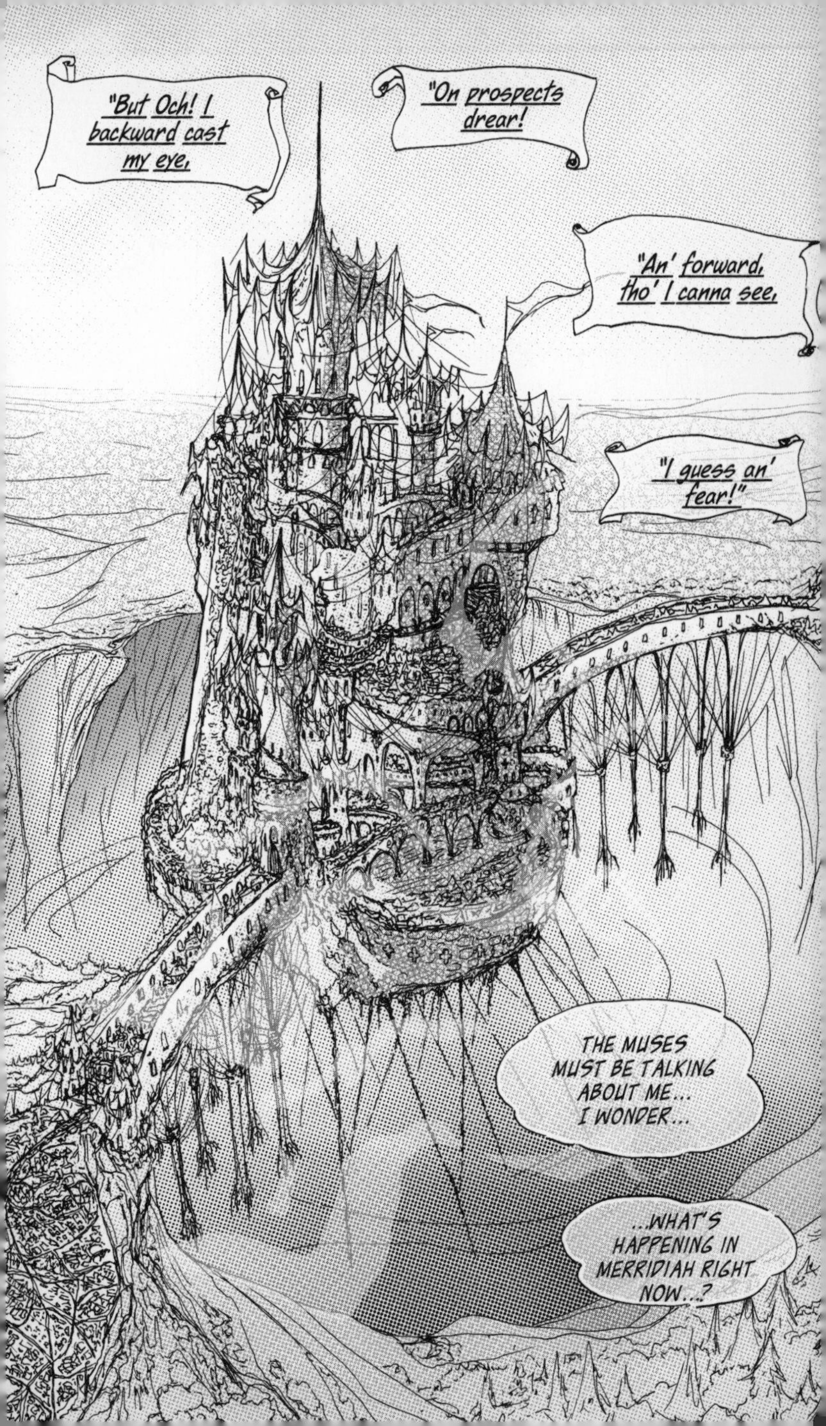
"But Och! I backward cast my eye,
"On prospects drear!
"An' forward, tho' I canna see,
"I guess an' fear!"
THE MUSES MUST BE TALKING ABOUT ME... I WONDER...
...WHAT'S HAPPENING IN MERRIDIAH RIGHT NOW...?

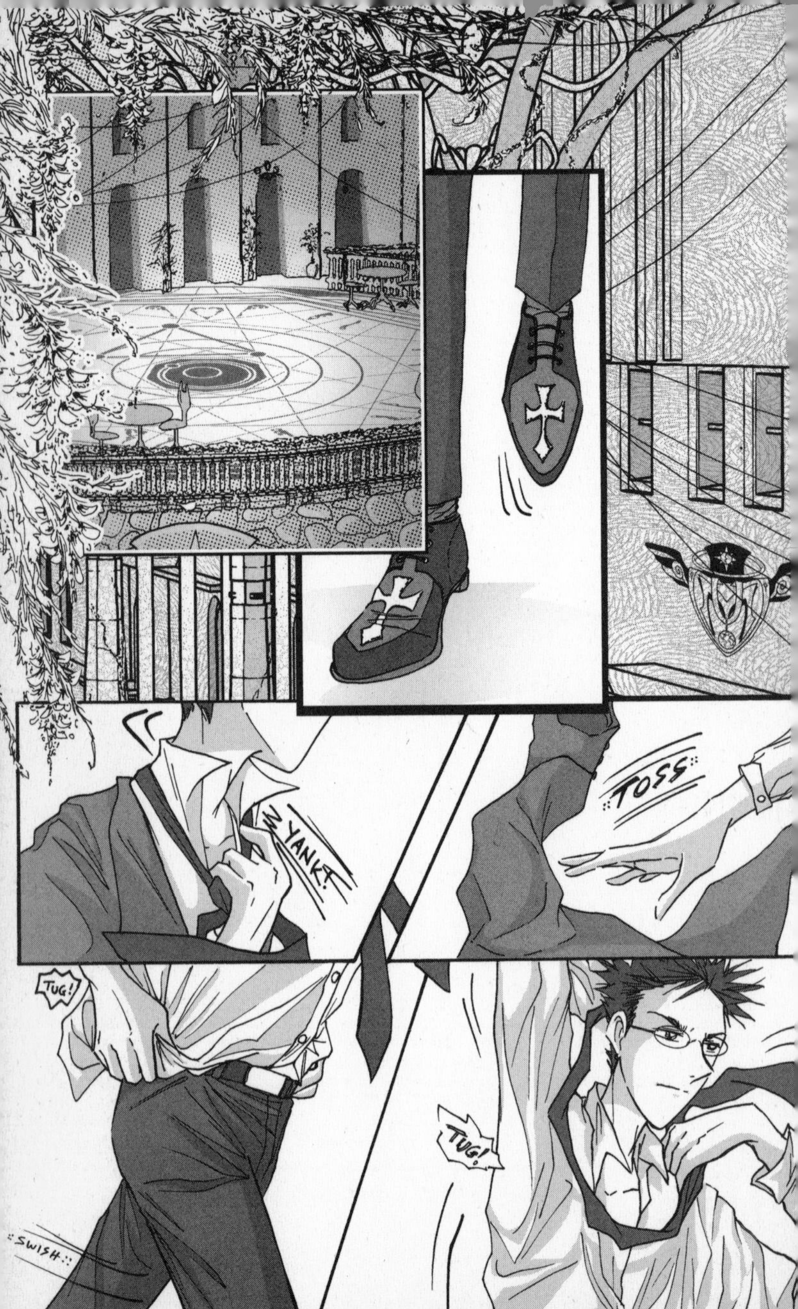

TOSS
YANK!
TUG!
TUG!
SWISH

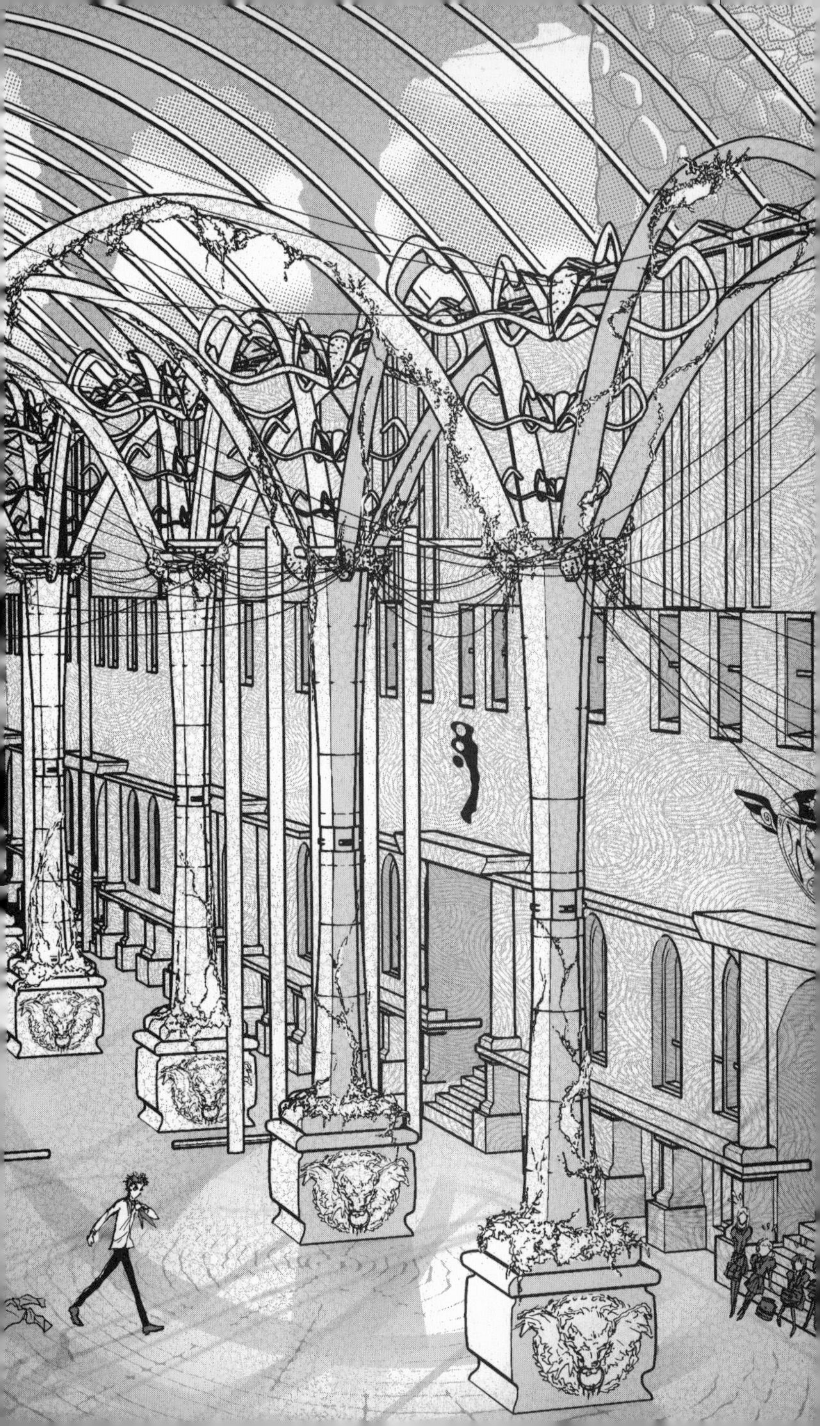

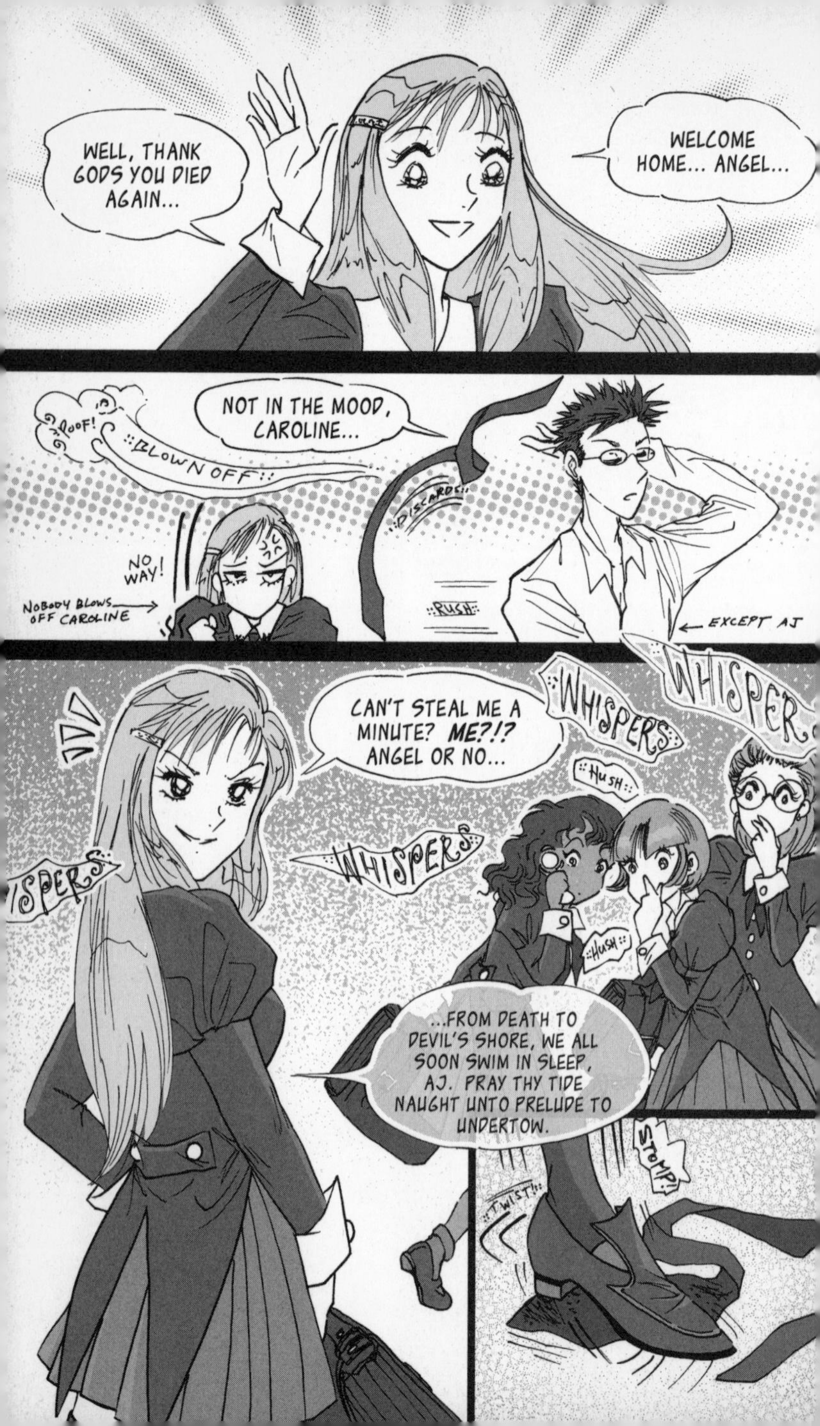
WELL, THANK GODS YOU DIED AGAIN...
WELCOME HOME... ANGEL...
POOF!
BLOWN OFF!
NOT IN THE MOOD, CAROLINE...
DISCARDS
NO WAY!
NOBODY BLOWS OFF CAROLINE
RUSH
EXCEPT AJ
CAN'T STEAL ME A MINUTE? ***ME?!?*** ANGEL OR NO...
WHISPERS
WHISPER
HUSH
WHISPERS
HUSH
...FROM DEATH TO DEVIL'S SHORE, WE ALL SOON SWIM IN SLEEP, AJ. PRAY THY TIDE NAUGHT UNTO PRELUDE TO UNDERTOW.
TWIST!
STOMP!

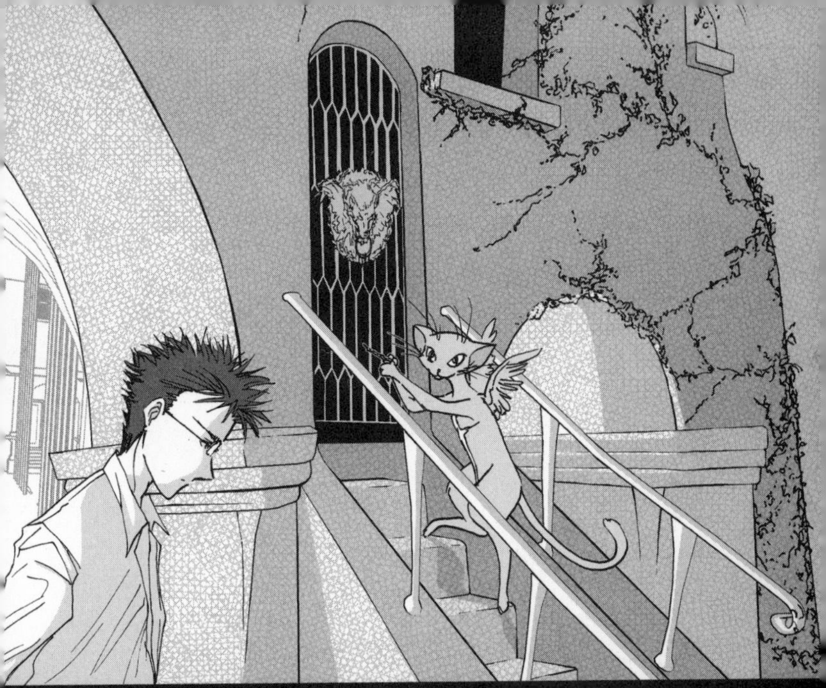
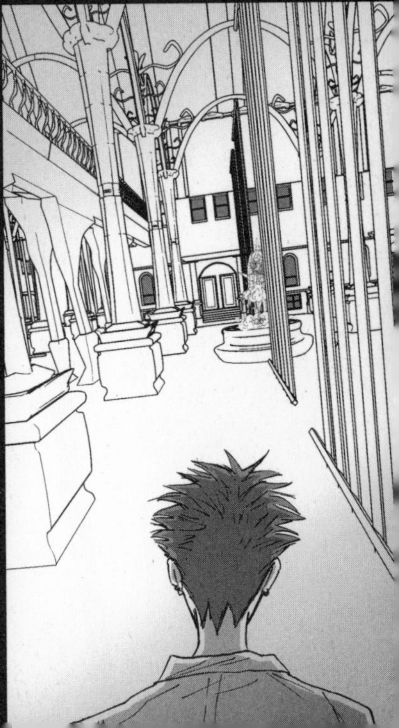
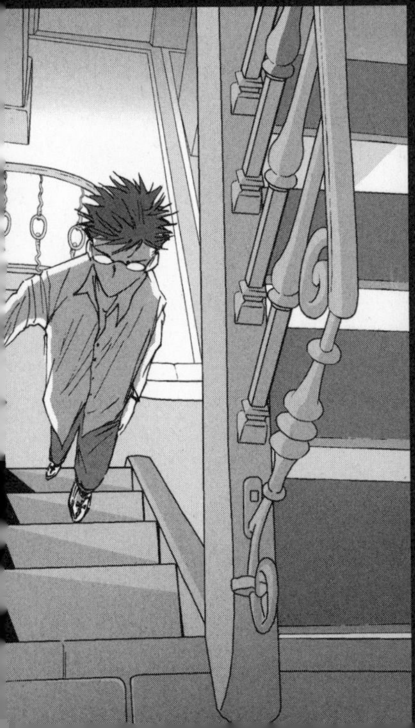

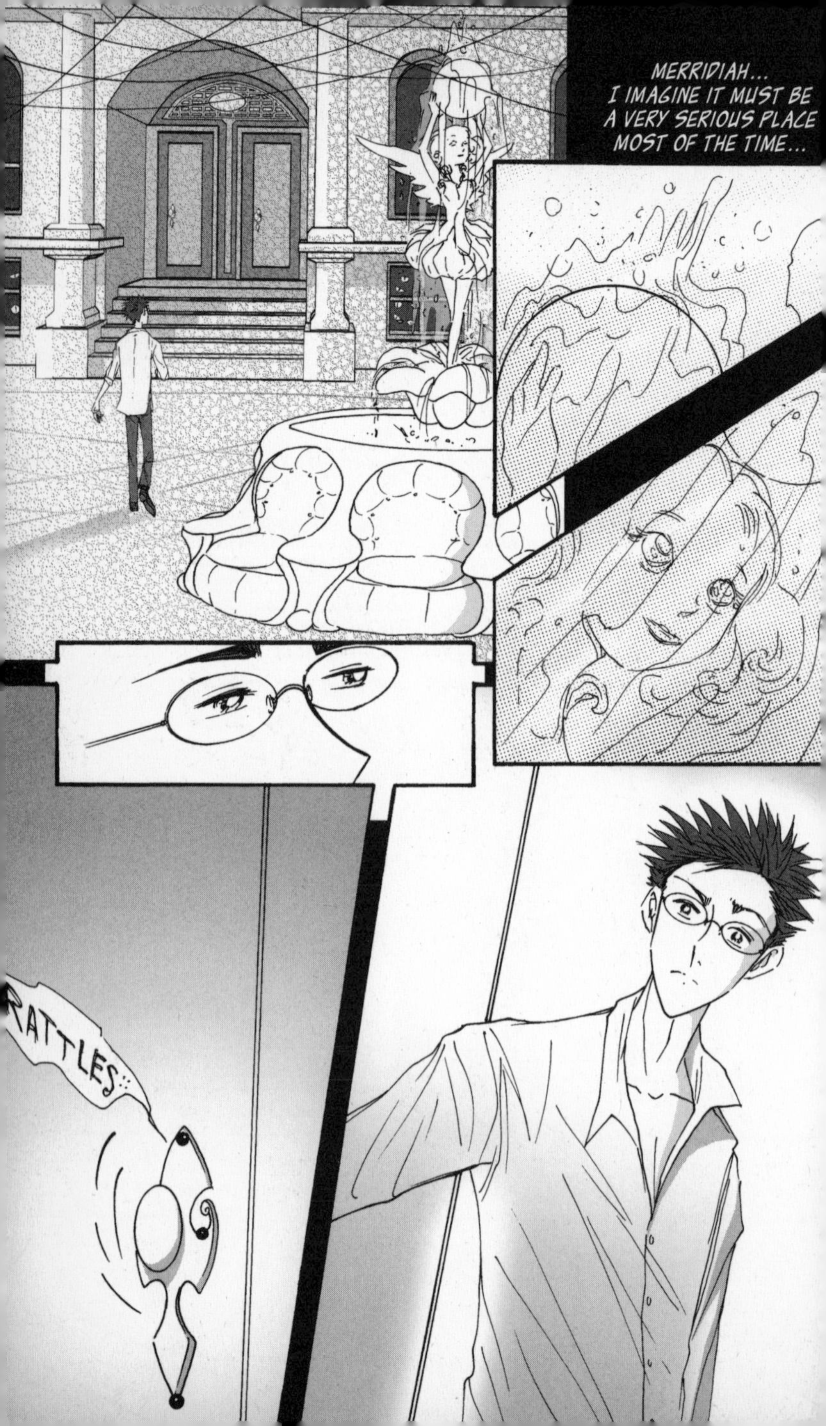
MERRIDIAH...
I IMAGINE IT MUST BE
A VERY SERIOUS PLACE
MOST OF THE TIME...
RATTLES

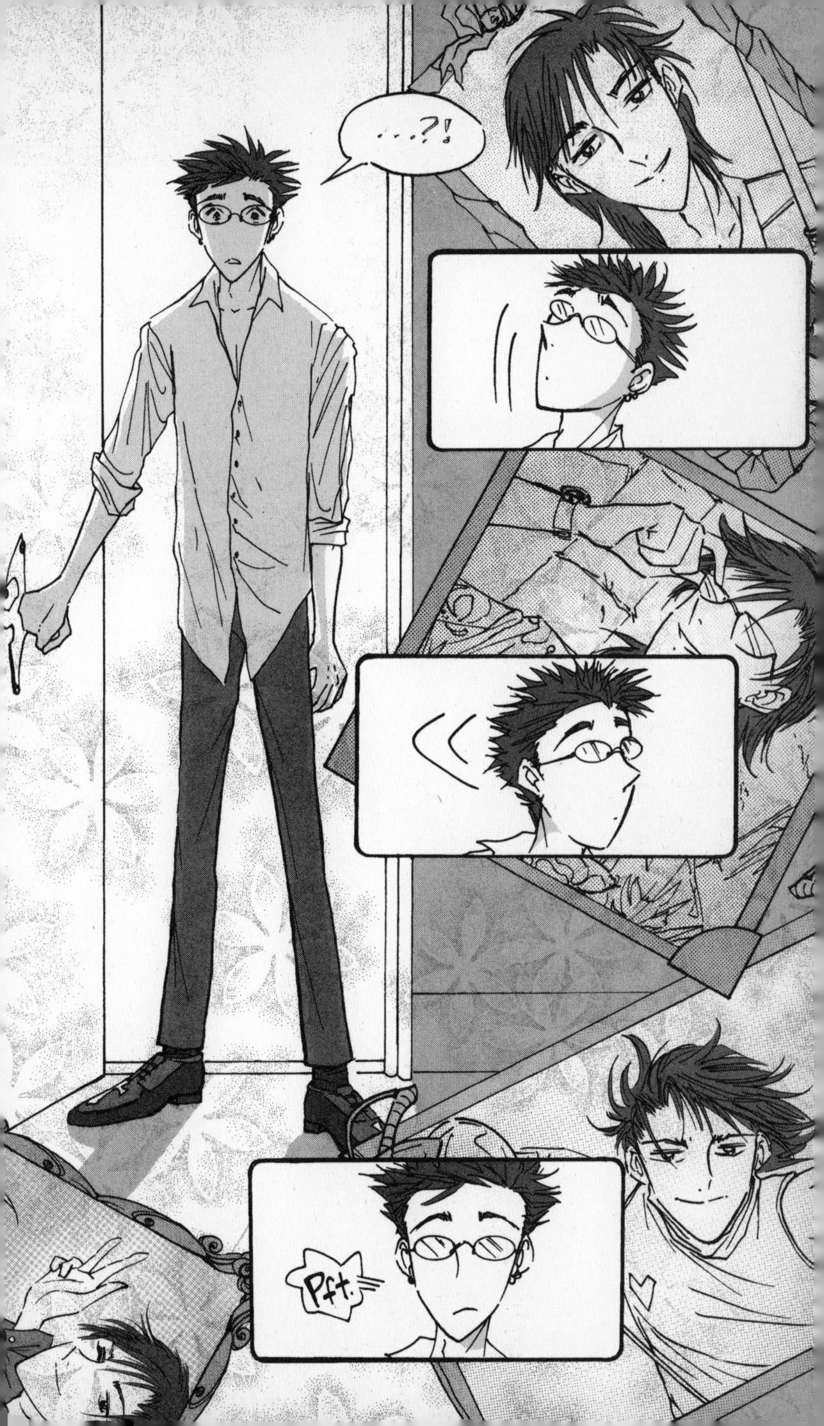
...?!
Pft.

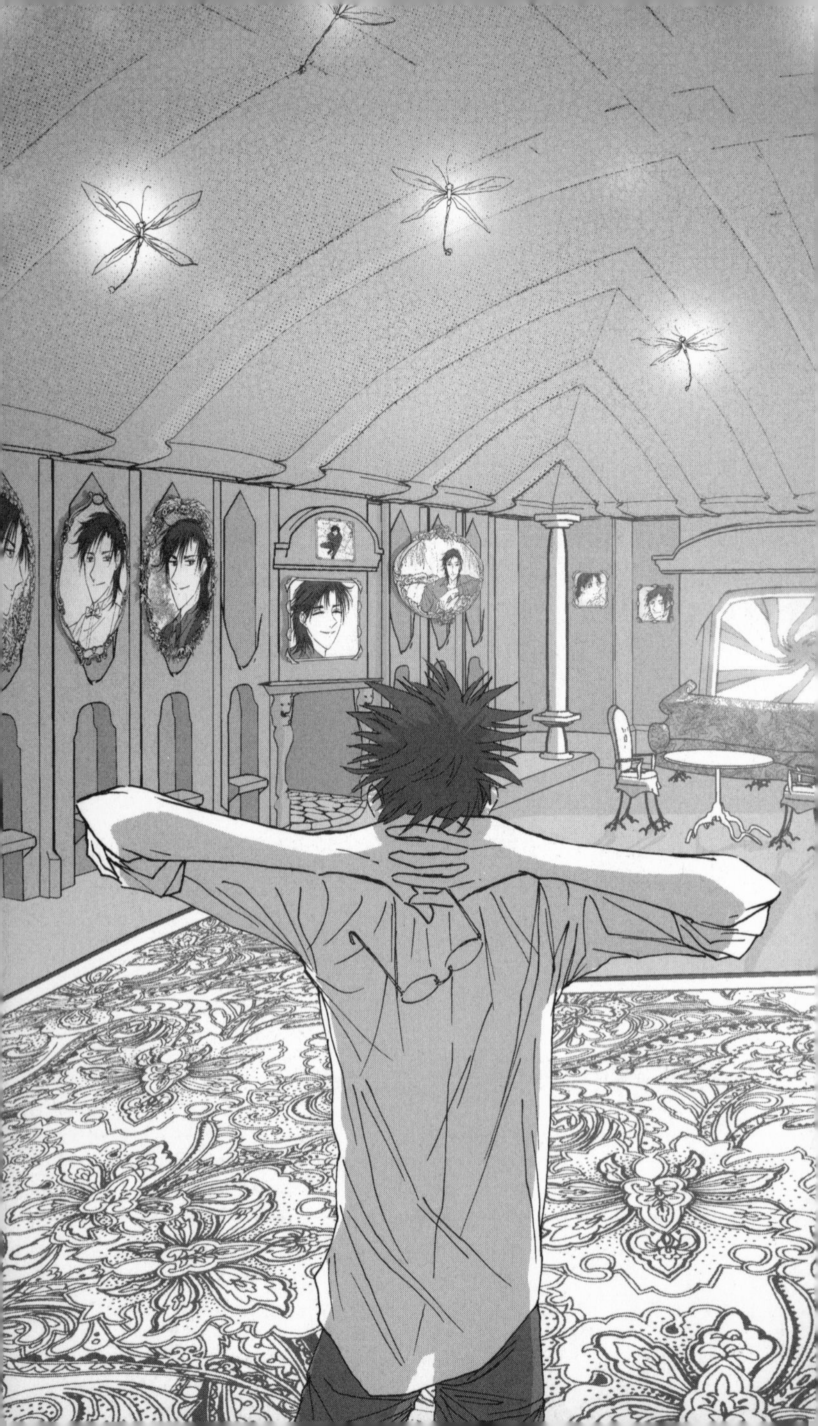

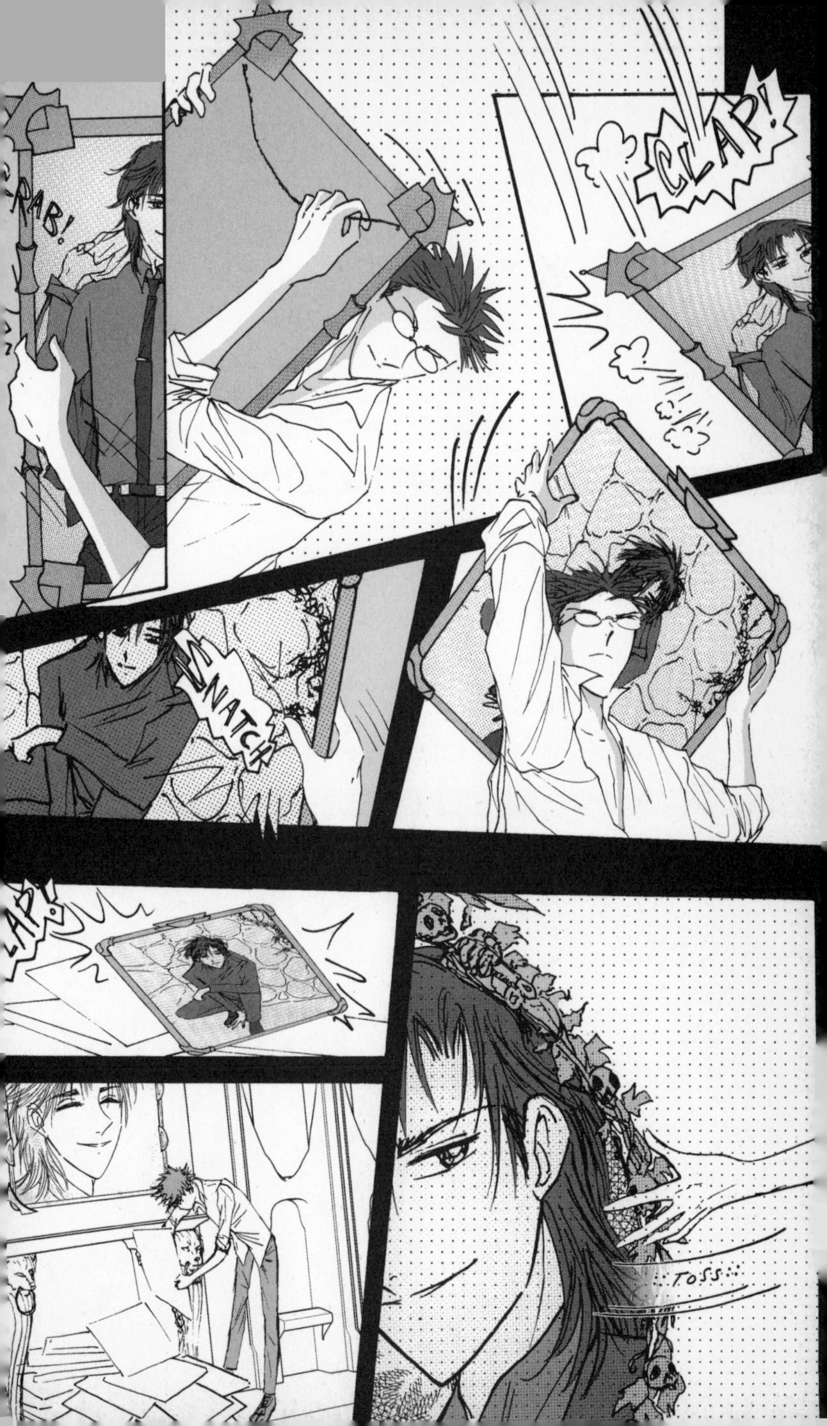
CLAP!
-RAB!
SNATCH
LAP!
TOSS

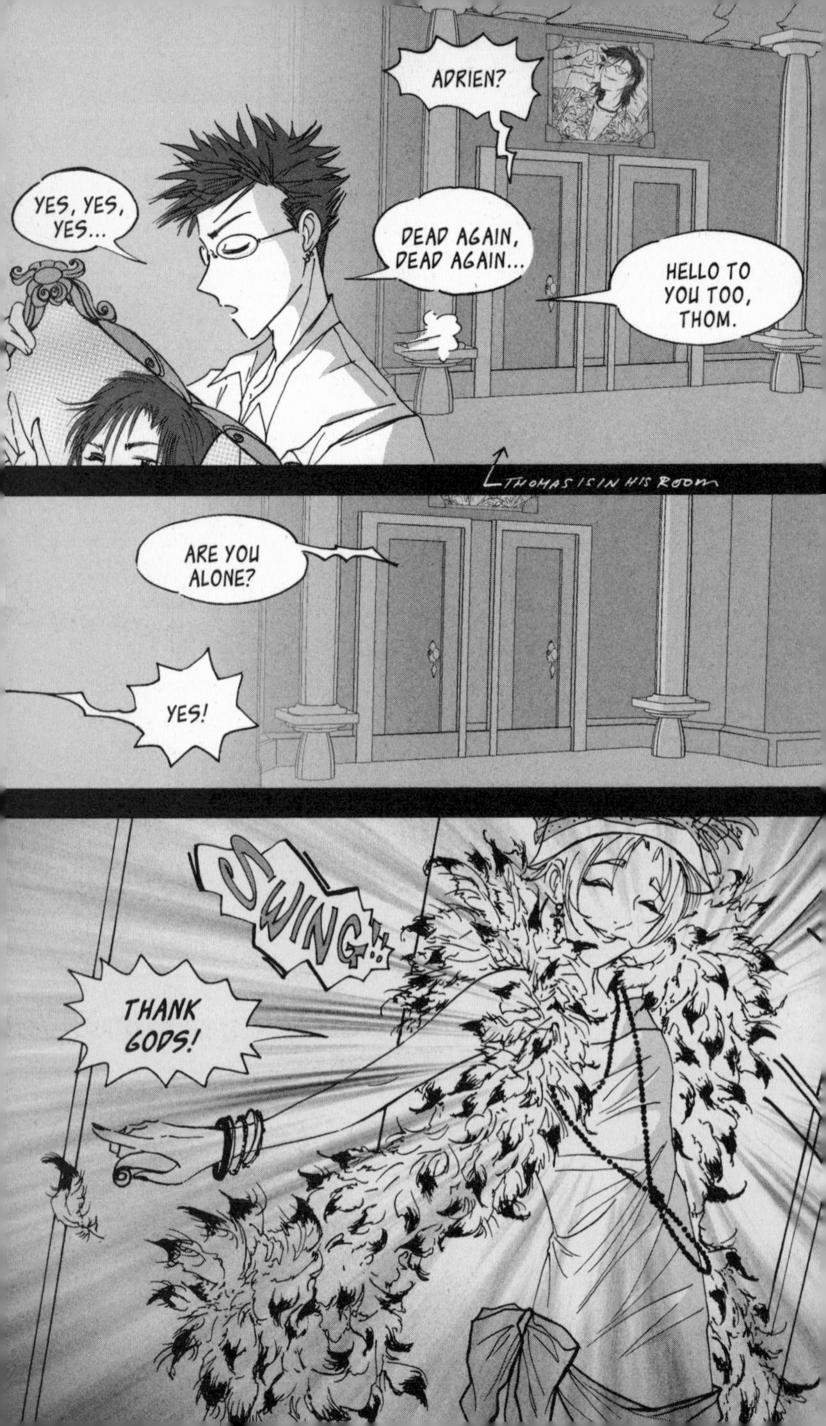
ADRIEN?
HELLO TO YOU TOO, THOM.
DEAD AGAIN, DEAD AGAIN...
YES, YES, YES...
THOMAS IS IN HIS ROOM
ARE YOU ALONE?
YES!
SWING!!
THANK GODS!

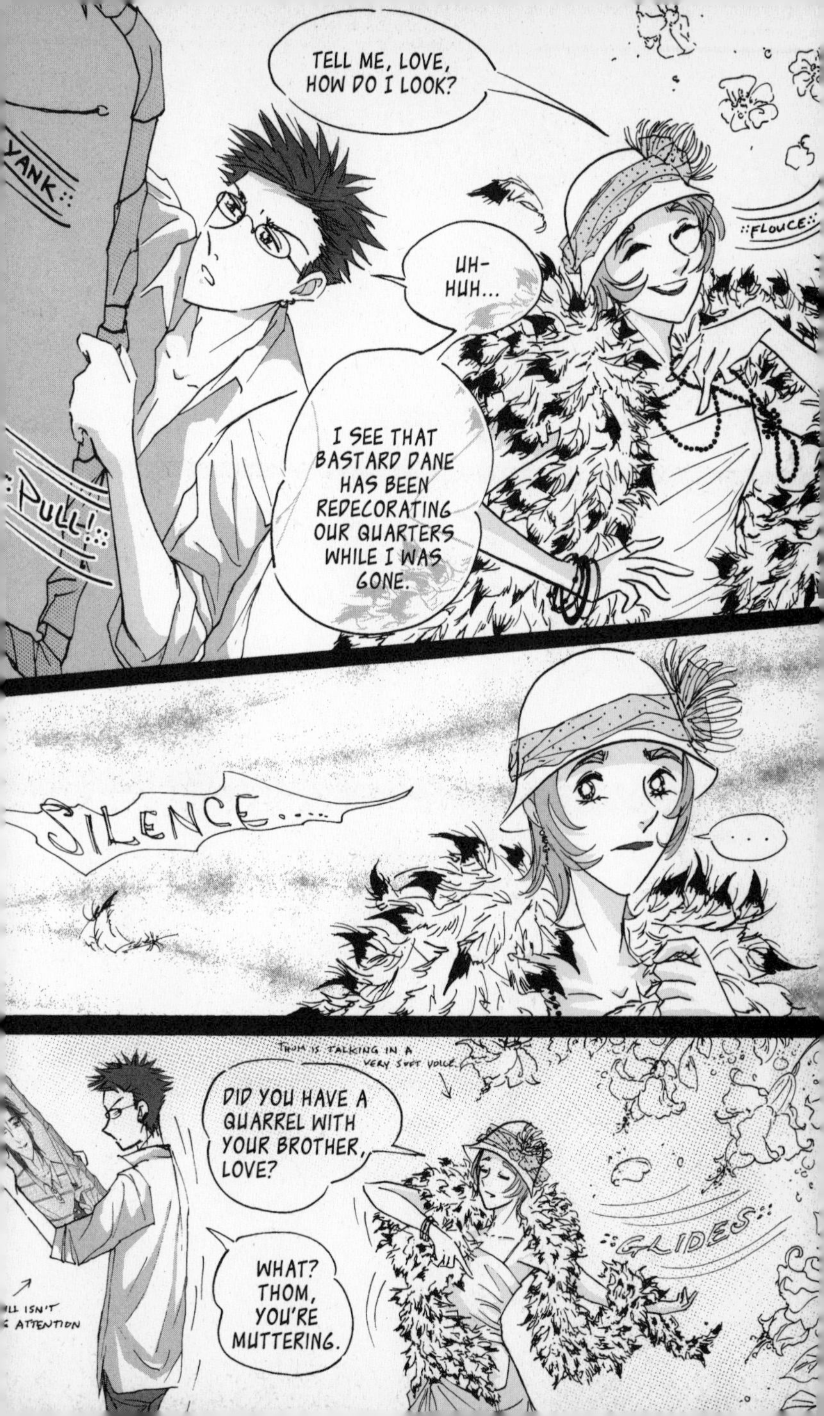
TELL ME, LOVE, HOW DO I LOOK?
::YANK::
::FLOUCE::
UH-HUH...
I SEE THAT BASTARD DANE HAS BEEN REDECORATING OUR QUARTERS WHILE I WAS GONE.
::PULL!::
SILENCE....
...
THOM IS TALKING IN A VERY SOFT VOICE.
DID YOU HAVE A QUARREL WITH YOUR BROTHER, LOVE?
::GLIDES::
WHAT? THOM, YOU'RE MUTTERING.

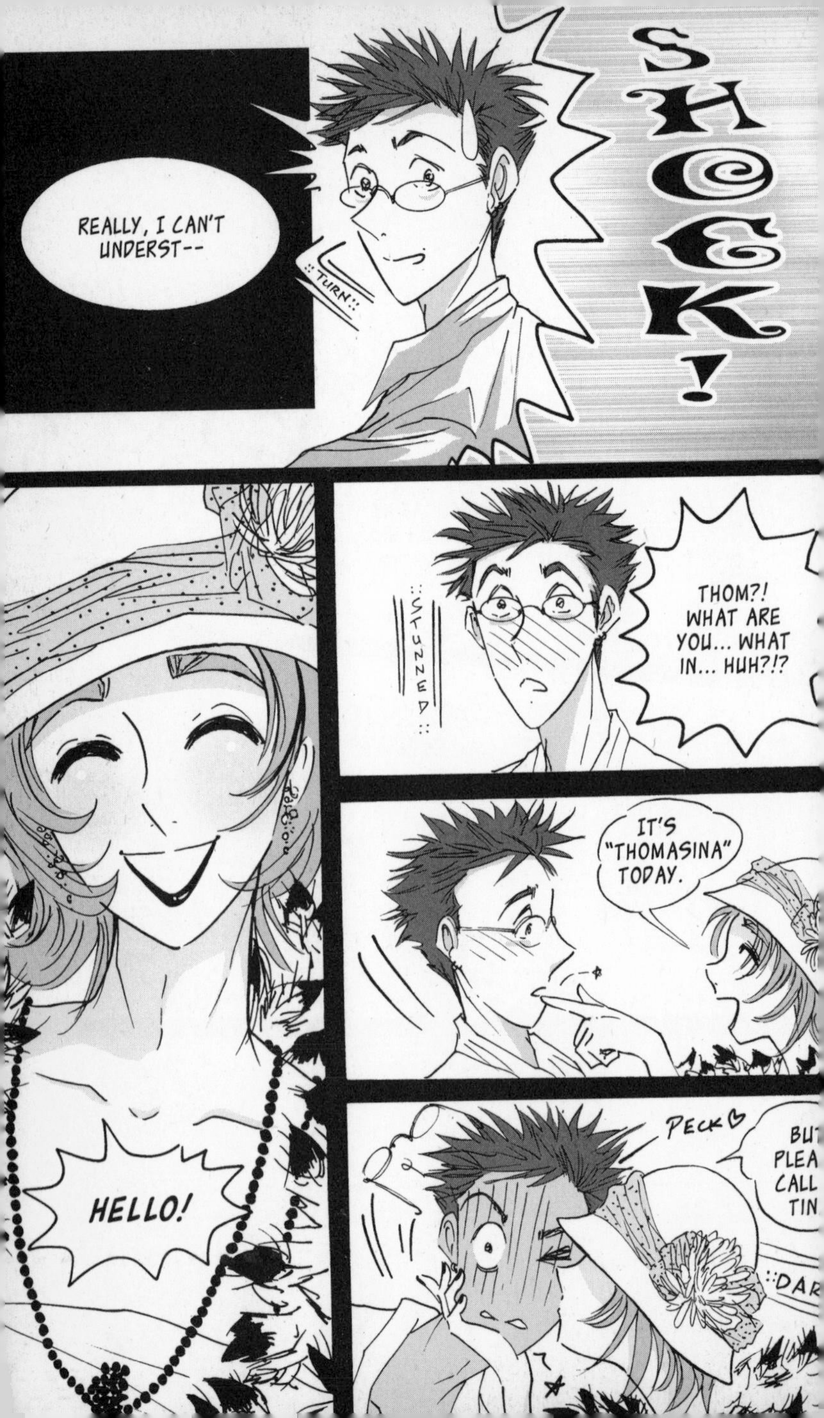
REALLY, I CAN'T UNDERST--
TURN
SHOCK!
THOM?! WHAT ARE YOU... WHAT IN... HUH?!?
STUNNED
IT'S "THOMASINA" TODAY.
PECK♡
BU
PLEA
CALL
TIN
DAR
HELLO!

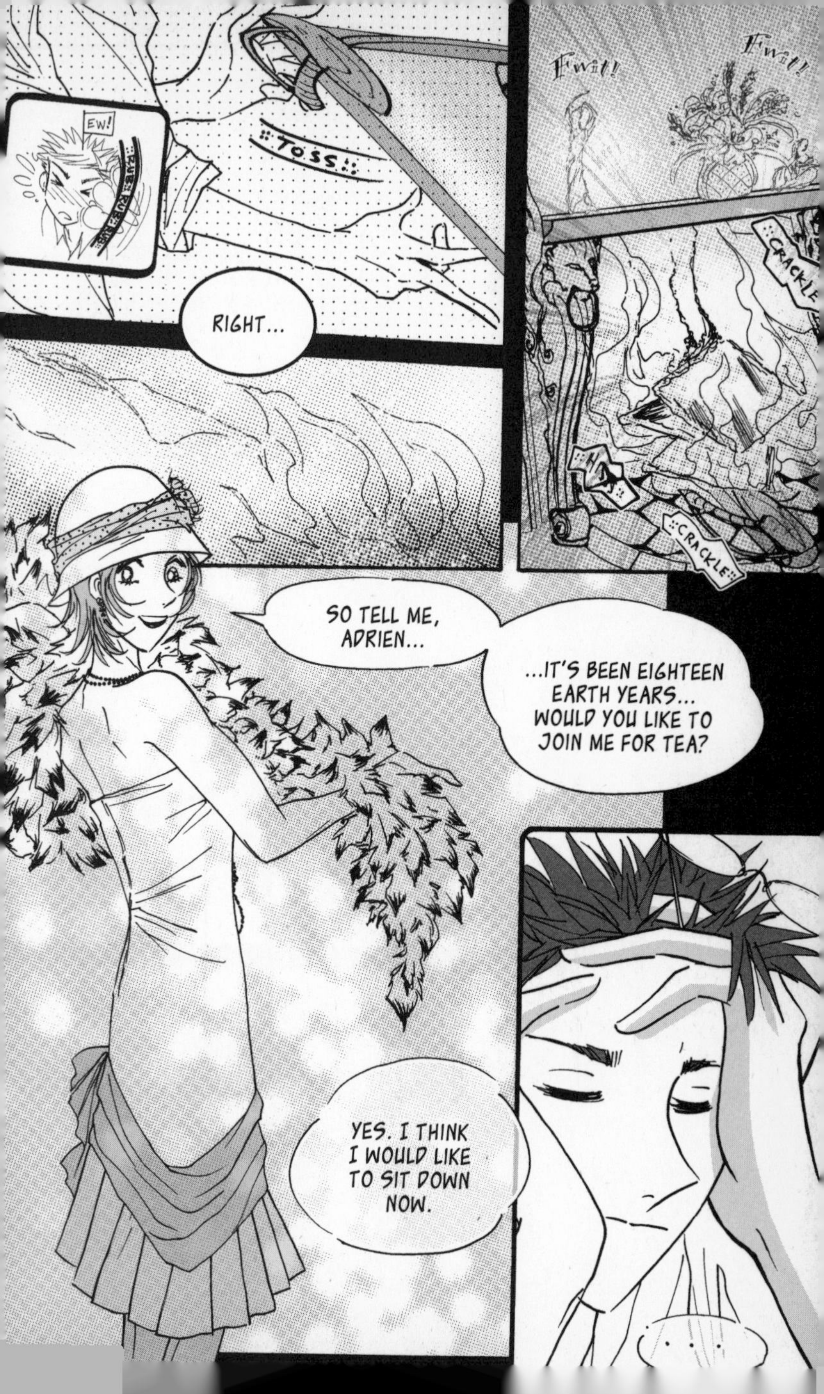
Fwit!
Fwit!
CRACKLE
CRACKLE
TOSS
EW!
RUB RUB RUB
RIGHT...
SO TELL ME, ADRIEN...
...IT'S BEEN EIGHTEEN EARTH YEARS... WOULD YOU LIKE TO JOIN ME FOR TEA?
YES. I THINK I WOULD LIKE TO SIT DOWN NOW.

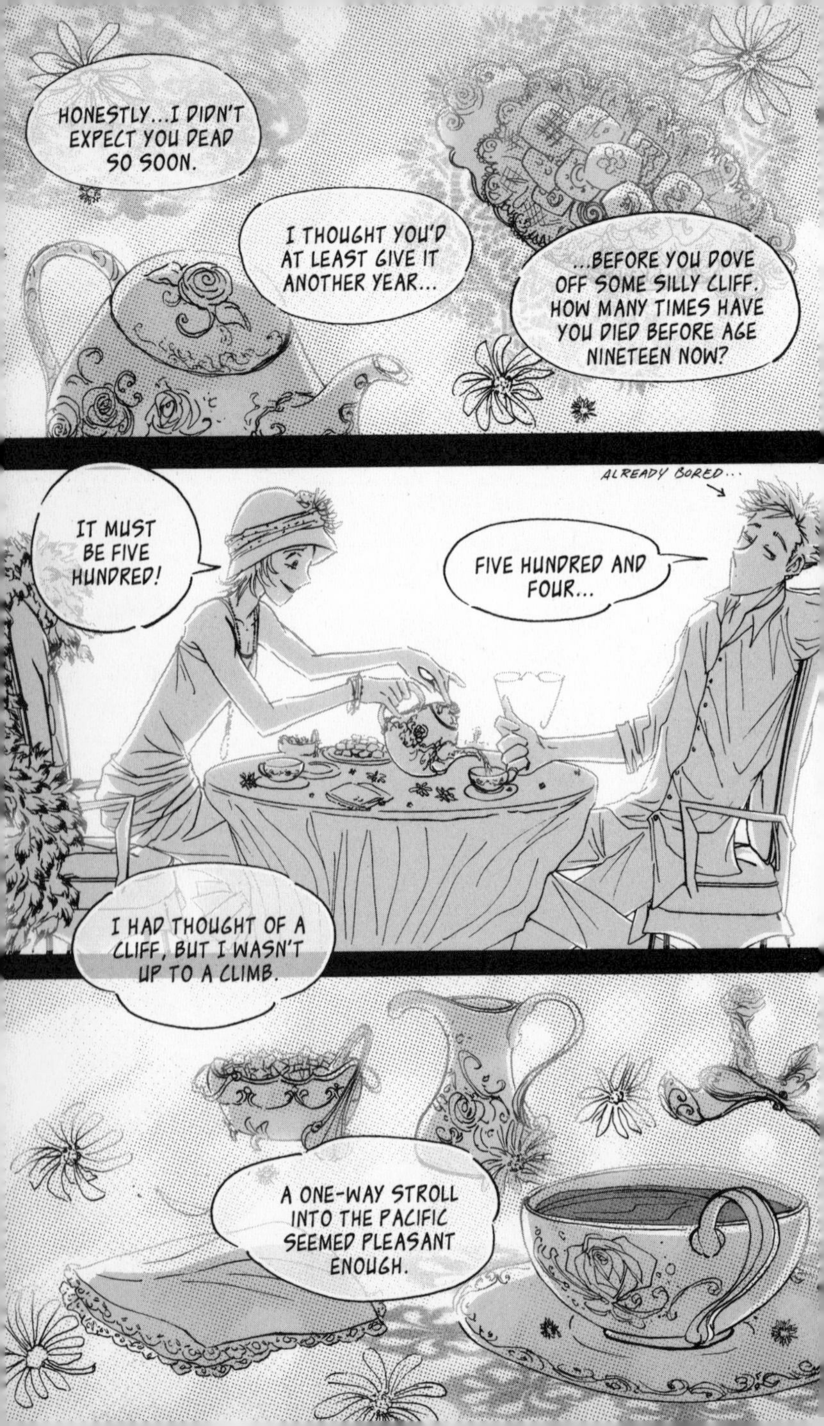
HONESTLY...I DIDN'T EXPECT YOU DEAD SO SOON.
I THOUGHT YOU'D AT LEAST GIVE IT ANOTHER YEAR...
...BEFORE YOU DOVE OFF SOME SILLY CLIFF. HOW MANY TIMES HAVE YOU DIED BEFORE AGE NINETEEN NOW?
IT MUST BE FIVE HUNDRED!
ALREADY BORED...
FIVE HUNDRED AND FOUR...
I HAD THOUGHT OF A CLIFF, BUT I WASN'T UP TO A CLIMB.
A ONE-WAY STROLL INTO THE PACIFIC SEEMED PLEASANT ENOUGH.

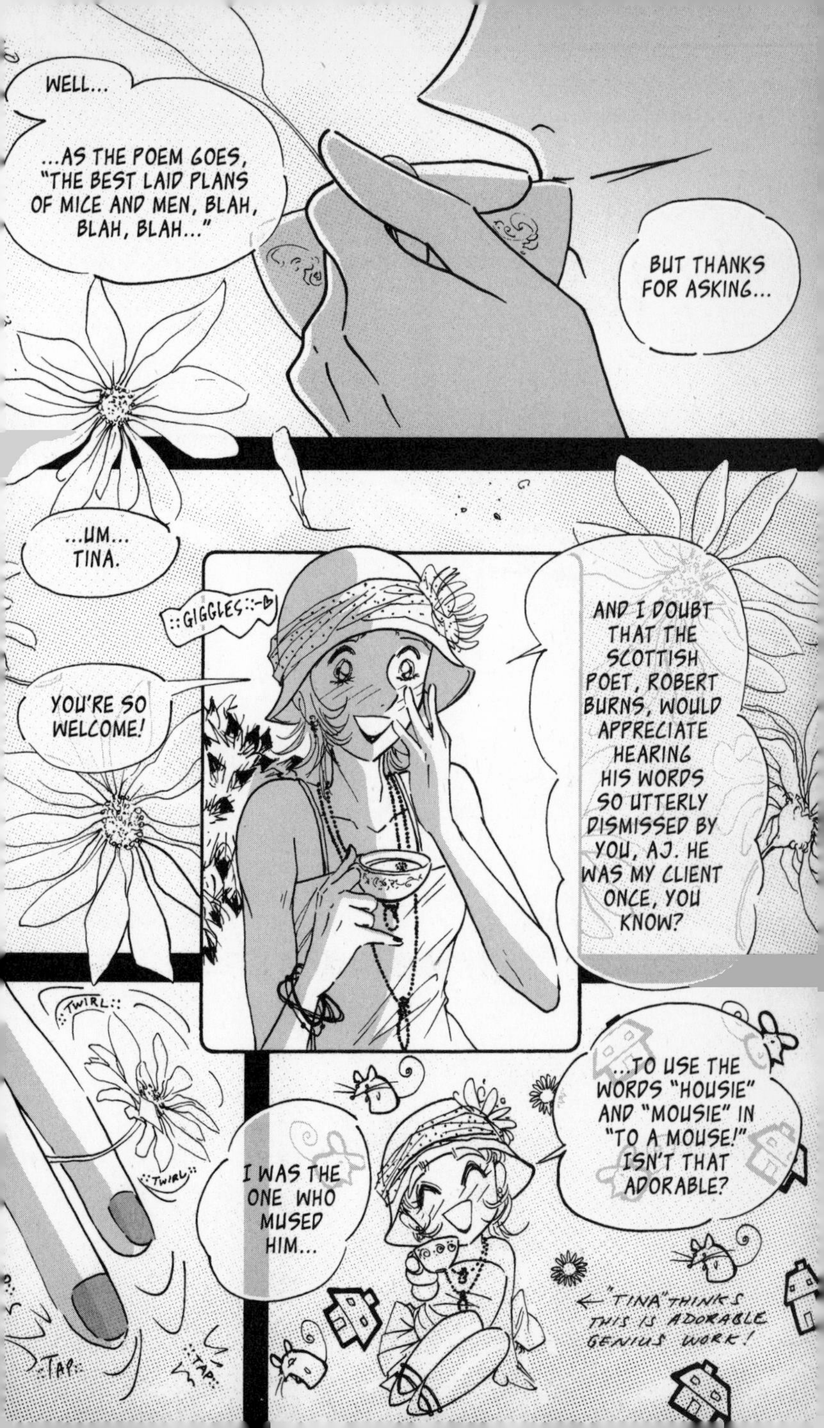
WELL...
...AS THE POEM GOES, "THE BEST LAID PLANS OF MICE AND MEN, BLAH, BLAH, BLAH..."
BUT THANKS FOR ASKING...
...UM... TINA.
::GIGGLES::
YOU'RE SO WELCOME!
AND I DOUBT THAT THE SCOTTISH POET, ROBERT BURNS, WOULD APPRECIATE HEARING HIS WORDS SO UTTERLY DISMISSED BY YOU, AJ. HE WAS MY CLIENT ONCE, YOU KNOW?
::TWIRL::
::TWIRL::
::TAP::
::TAP::
I WAS THE ONE WHO MUSED HIM...
...TO USE THE WORDS "HOUSIE" AND "MOUSIE" IN "TO A MOUSE!" ISN'T THAT ADORABLE?
← "TINA" THINKS THIS IS ADORABLE GENIUS WORK!

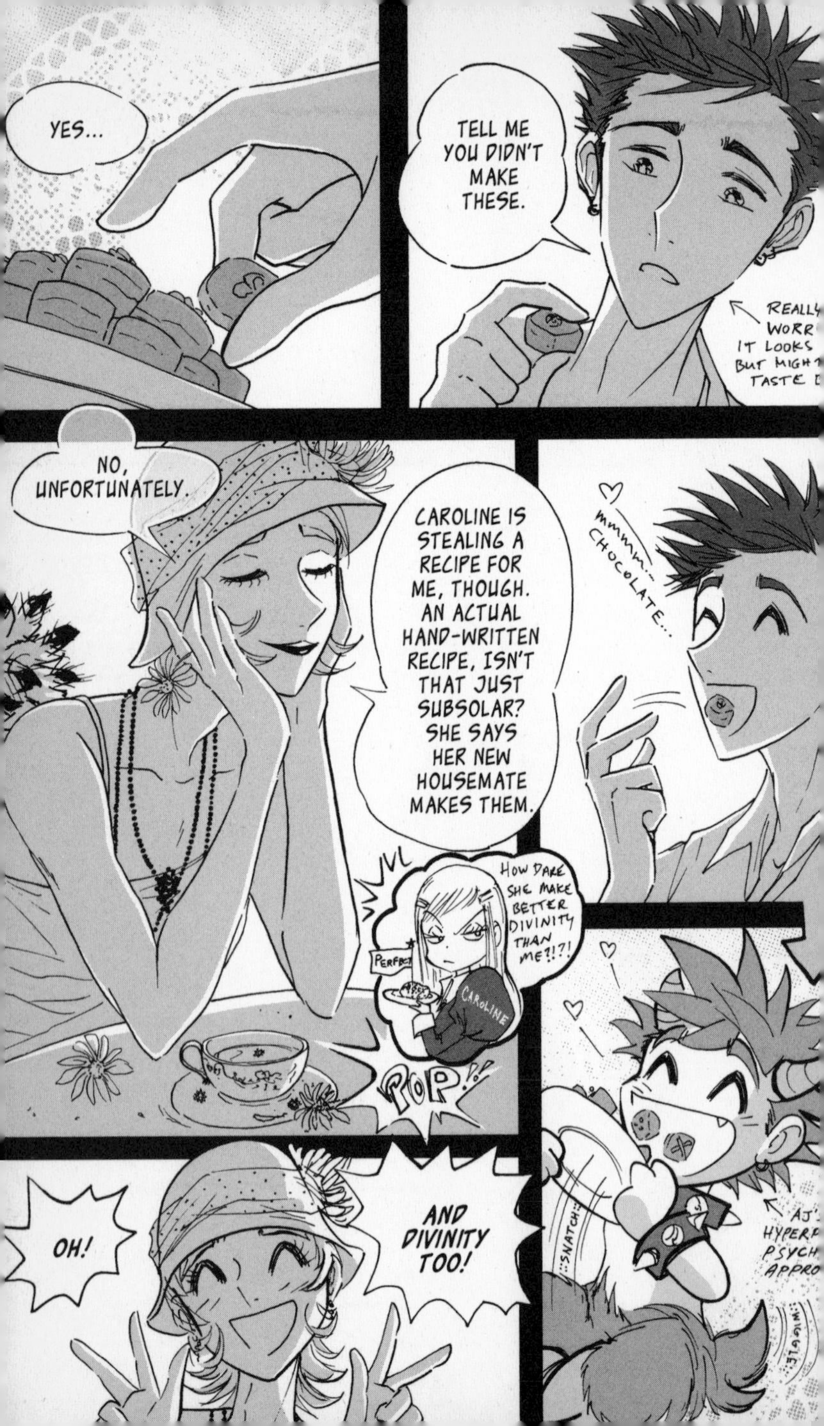
YES...
TELL ME YOU DIDN'T MAKE THESE.
REALLY WORR IT LOOKS BUT MIGH TASTE
NO, UNFORTUNATELY.
CAROLINE IS STEALING A RECIPE FOR ME, THOUGH. AN ACTUAL HAND-WRITTEN RECIPE, ISN'T THAT JUST SUBSOLAR? SHE SAYS HER NEW HOUSEMATE MAKES THEM.
HOW DARE SHE MAKE BETTER DIVINITY THAN ME?!?!
PERFECT
CAROLINE
POP!?!
MMMM... CHOCOLATE...
OH!
AND DIVINITY TOO!
::SNATCH::
AJ'S HYPER PSYCH APPRO
::WIGGLE::

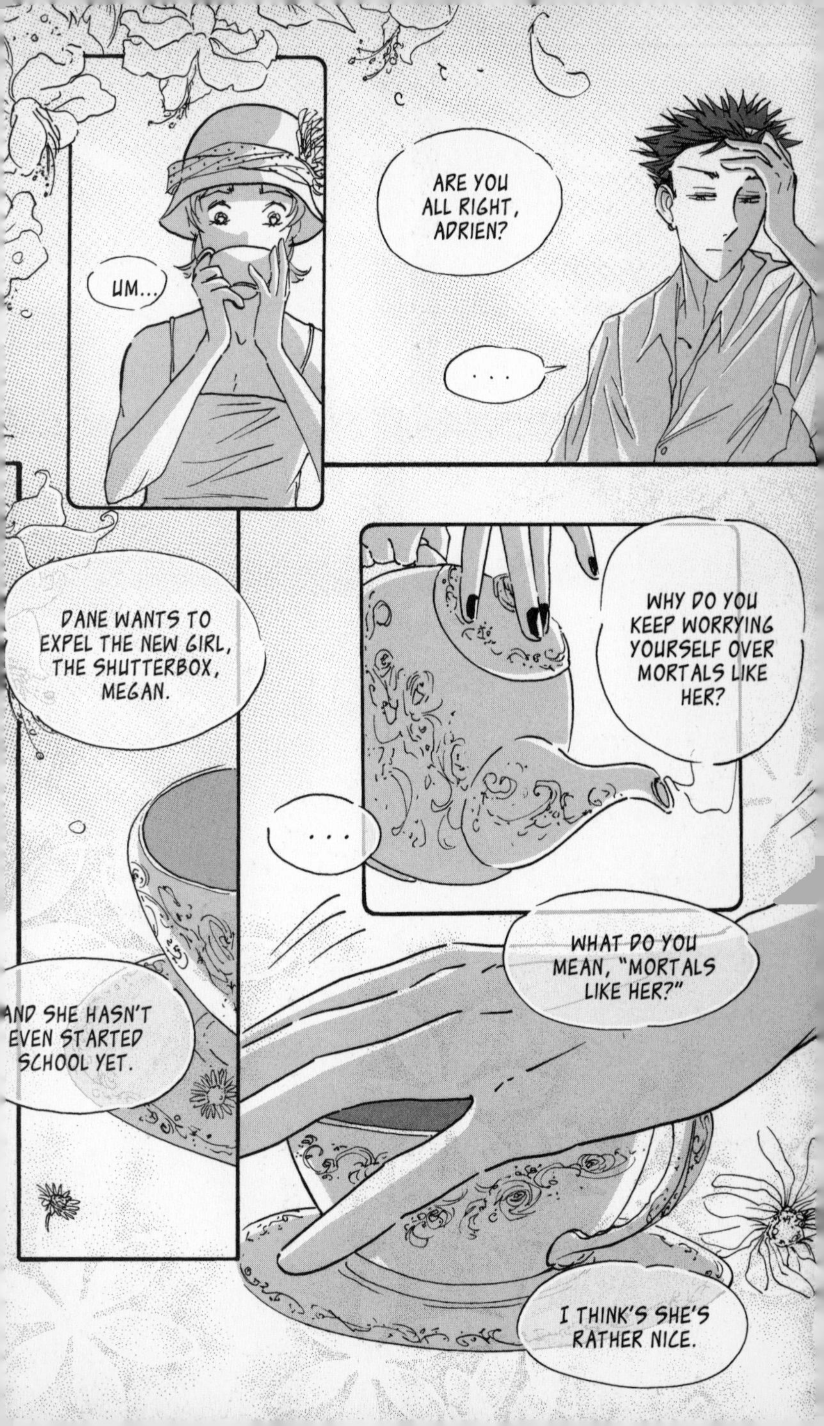
UM...
ARE YOU ALL RIGHT, ADRIEN?
. . .
DANE WANTS TO EXPEL THE NEW GIRL, THE SHUTTERBOX, MEGAN.
AND SHE HASN'T EVEN STARTED SCHOOL YET.
WHY DO YOU KEEP WORRYING YOURSELF OVER MORTALS LIKE HER?
. . .
WHAT DO YOU MEAN, "MORTALS LIKE HER?"
I THINK'S SHE'S RATHER NICE.

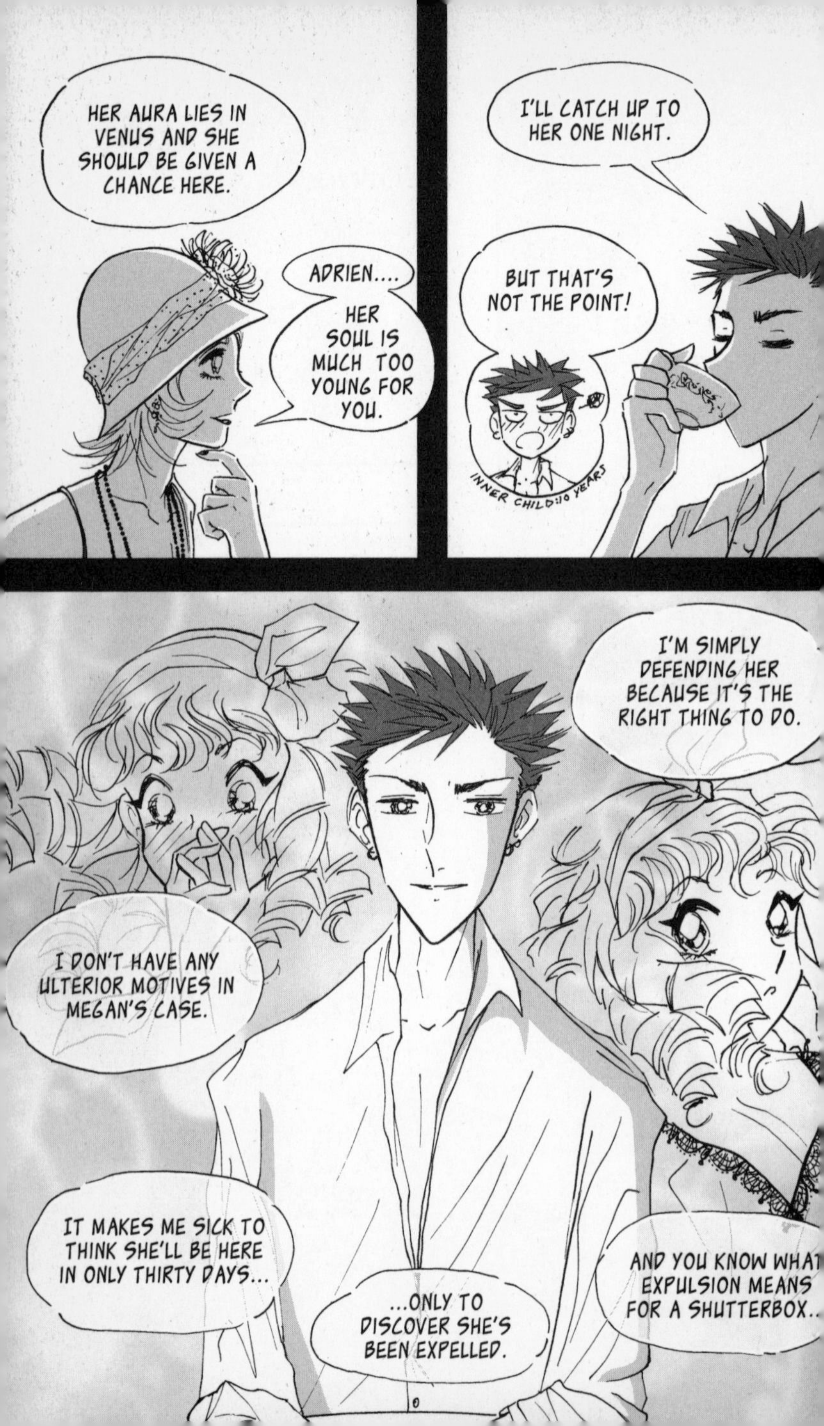
HER AURA LIES IN VENUS AND SHE SHOULD BE GIVEN A CHANCE HERE.
ADRIEN....
HER SOUL IS MUCH TOO YOUNG FOR YOU.
I'LL CATCH UP TO HER ONE NIGHT.
BUT THAT'S NOT THE POINT!
INNER CHILD: 10 YEARS
I DON'T HAVE ANY ULTERIOR MOTIVES IN MEGAN'S CASE.
I'M SIMPLY DEFENDING HER BECAUSE IT'S THE RIGHT THING TO DO.
IT MAKES ME SICK TO THINK SHE'LL BE HERE IN ONLY THIRTY DAYS...
...ONLY TO DISCOVER SHE'S BEEN EXPELLED.
AND YOU KNOW WHAT EXPULSION MEANS FOR A SHUTTERBOX...

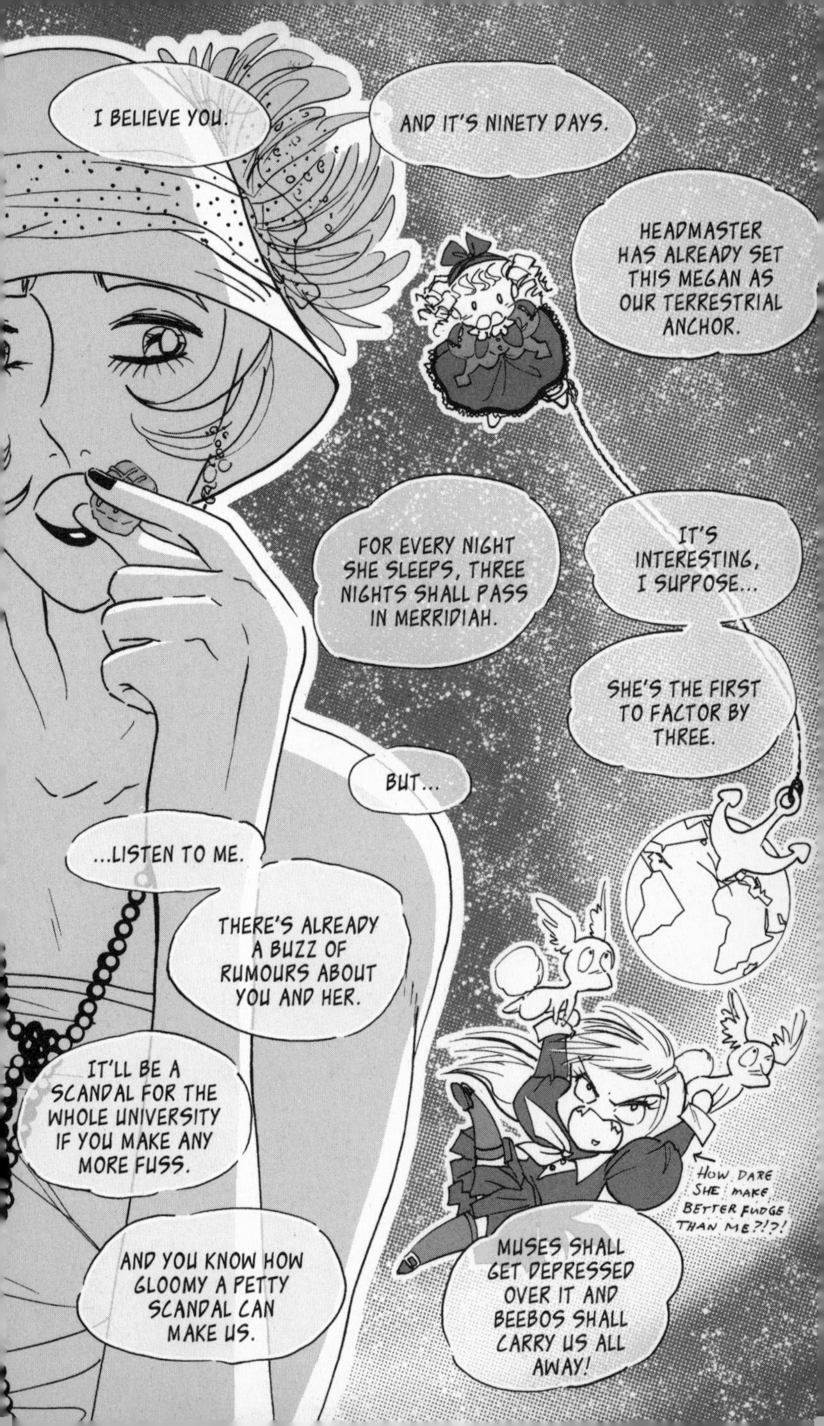

I BELIEVE YOU.
AND IT'S NINETY DAYS.
HEADMASTER HAS ALREADY SET THIS MEGAN AS OUR TERRESTRIAL ANCHOR.
FOR EVERY NIGHT SHE SLEEPS, THREE NIGHTS SHALL PASS IN MERRIDIAH.
IT'S INTERESTING, I SUPPOSE...
SHE'S THE FIRST TO FACTOR BY THREE.
BUT...
...LISTEN TO ME.
THERE'S ALREADY A BUZZ OF RUMOURS ABOUT YOU AND HER.
IT'LL BE A SCANDAL FOR THE WHOLE UNIVERSITY IF YOU MAKE ANY MORE FUSS.
AND YOU KNOW HOW GLOOMY A PETTY SCANDAL CAN MAKE US.
MUSES SHALL GET DEPRESSED OVER IT AND BEEBOS SHALL CARRY US ALL AWAY!
HOW DARE SHE MAKE BETTER FUDGE THAN ME?!?!

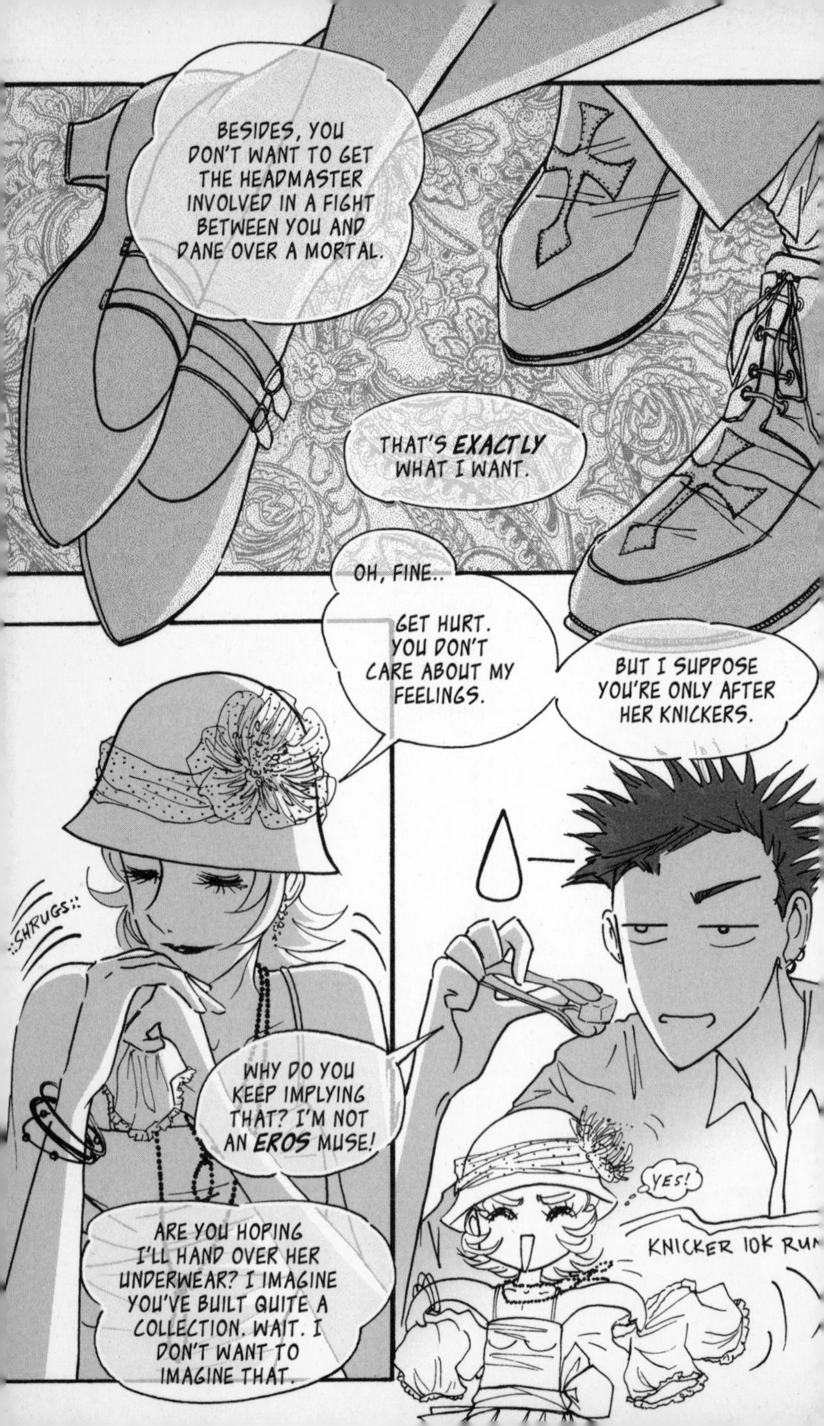
BESIDES, YOU DON'T WANT TO GET THE HEADMASTER INVOLVED IN A FIGHT BETWEEN YOU AND DANE OVER A MORTAL.
THAT'S EXACTLY WHAT I WANT.
OH, FINE..
GET HURT. YOU DON'T CARE ABOUT MY FEELINGS.
::SHRUGS::
BUT I SUPPOSE YOU'RE ONLY AFTER HER KNICKERS.
WHY DO YOU KEEP IMPLYING THAT? I'M NOT AN EROS MUSE!
ARE YOU HOPING I'LL HAND OVER HER UNDERWEAR? I IMAGINE YOU'VE BUILT QUITE A COLLECTION. WAIT. I DON'T WANT TO IMAGINE THAT.
YES!
KNICKER 10K RU

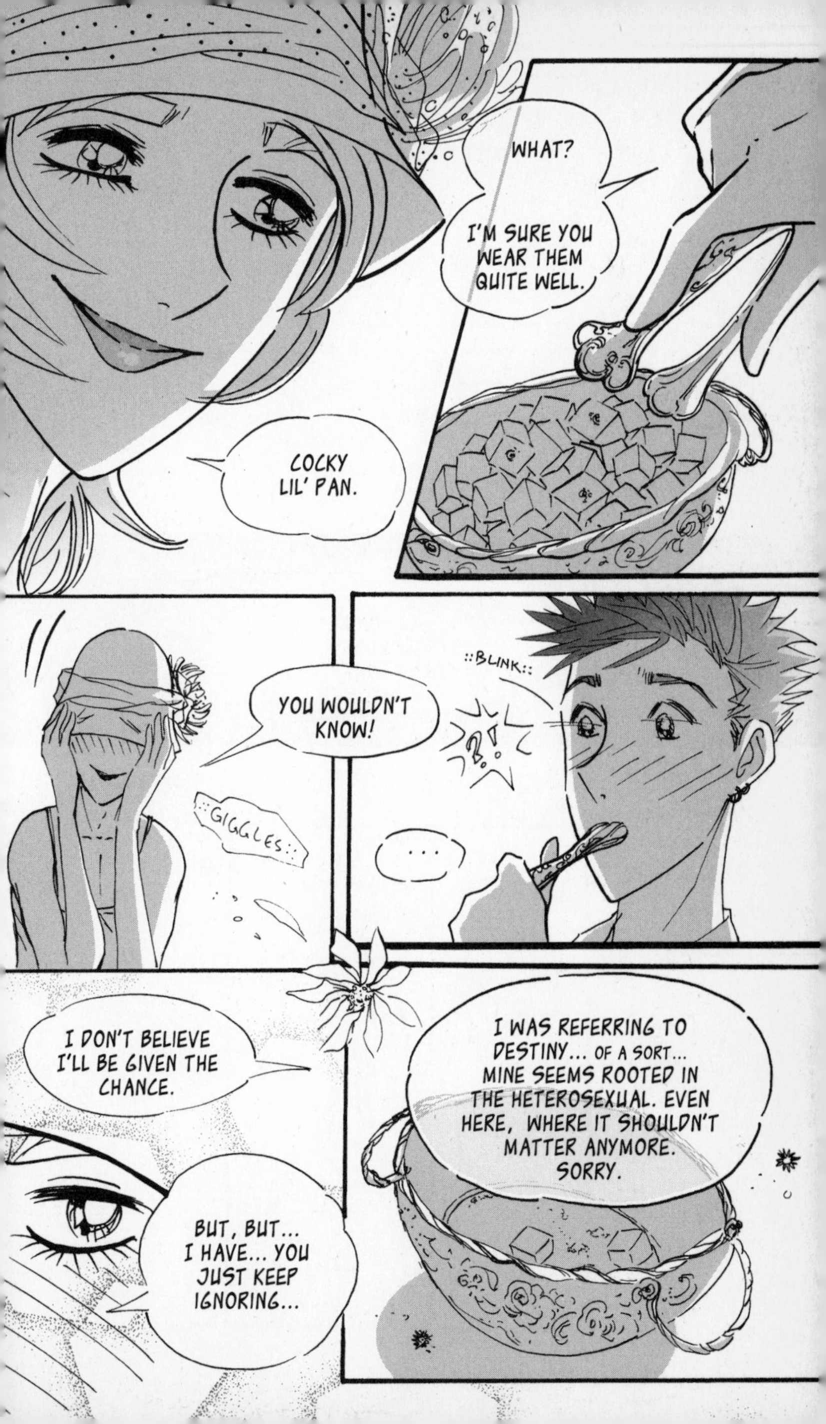
WHAT?
I'M SURE YOU WEAR THEM QUITE WELL.
COCKY LIL' PAN.
::BLINK::
...
YOU WOULDN'T KNOW!
::GIGGLES::
I WAS REFERRING TO DESTINY... OF A SORT... MINE SEEMS ROOTED IN THE HETEROSEXUAL. EVEN HERE, WHERE IT SHOULDN'T MATTER ANYMORE. SORRY.
I DON'T BELIEVE I'LL BE GIVEN THE CHANCE.
BUT, BUT... I HAVE... YOU JUST KEEP IGNORING...

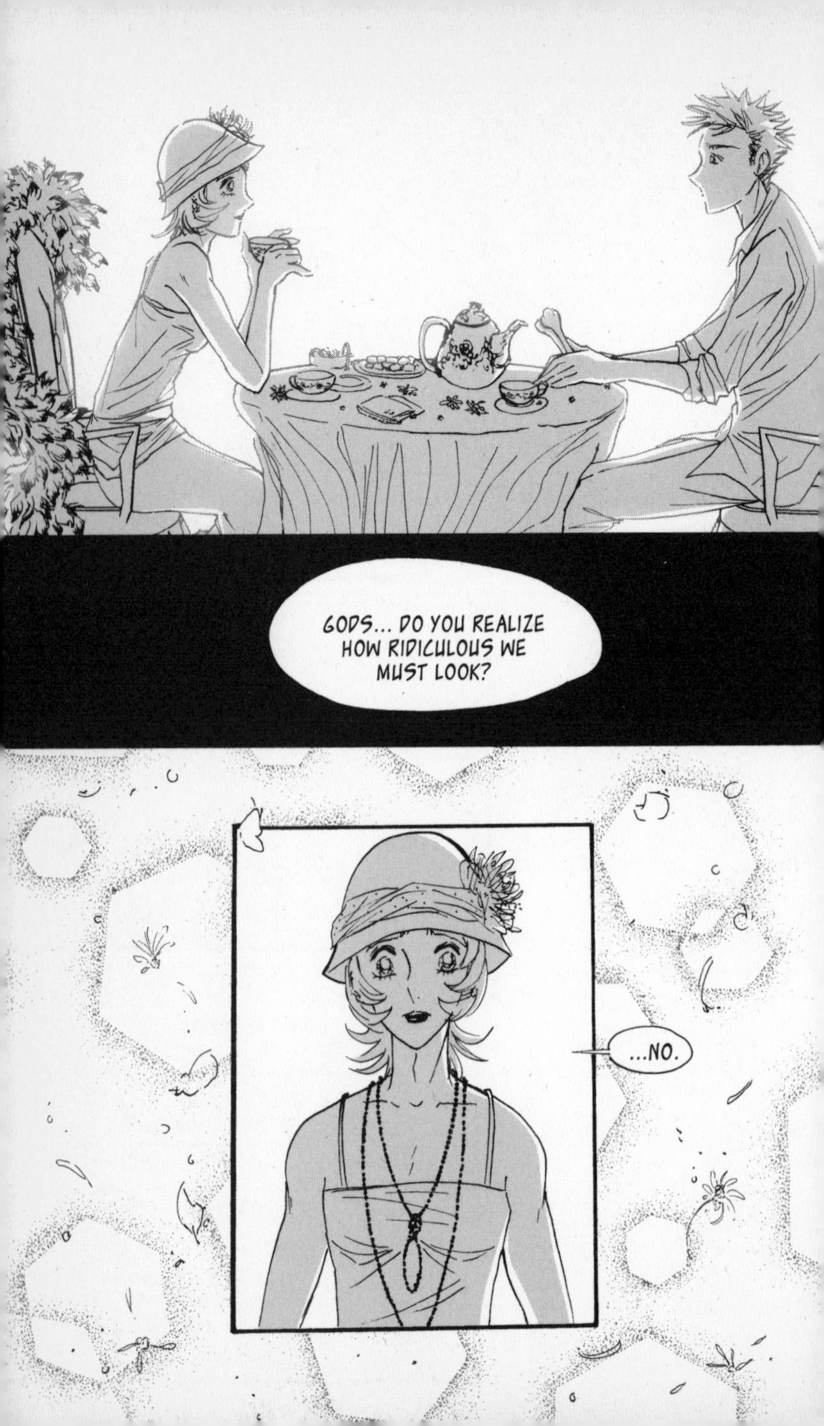
GODS... DO YOU REALIZE HOW RIDICULOUS WE MUST LOOK?
...NO.

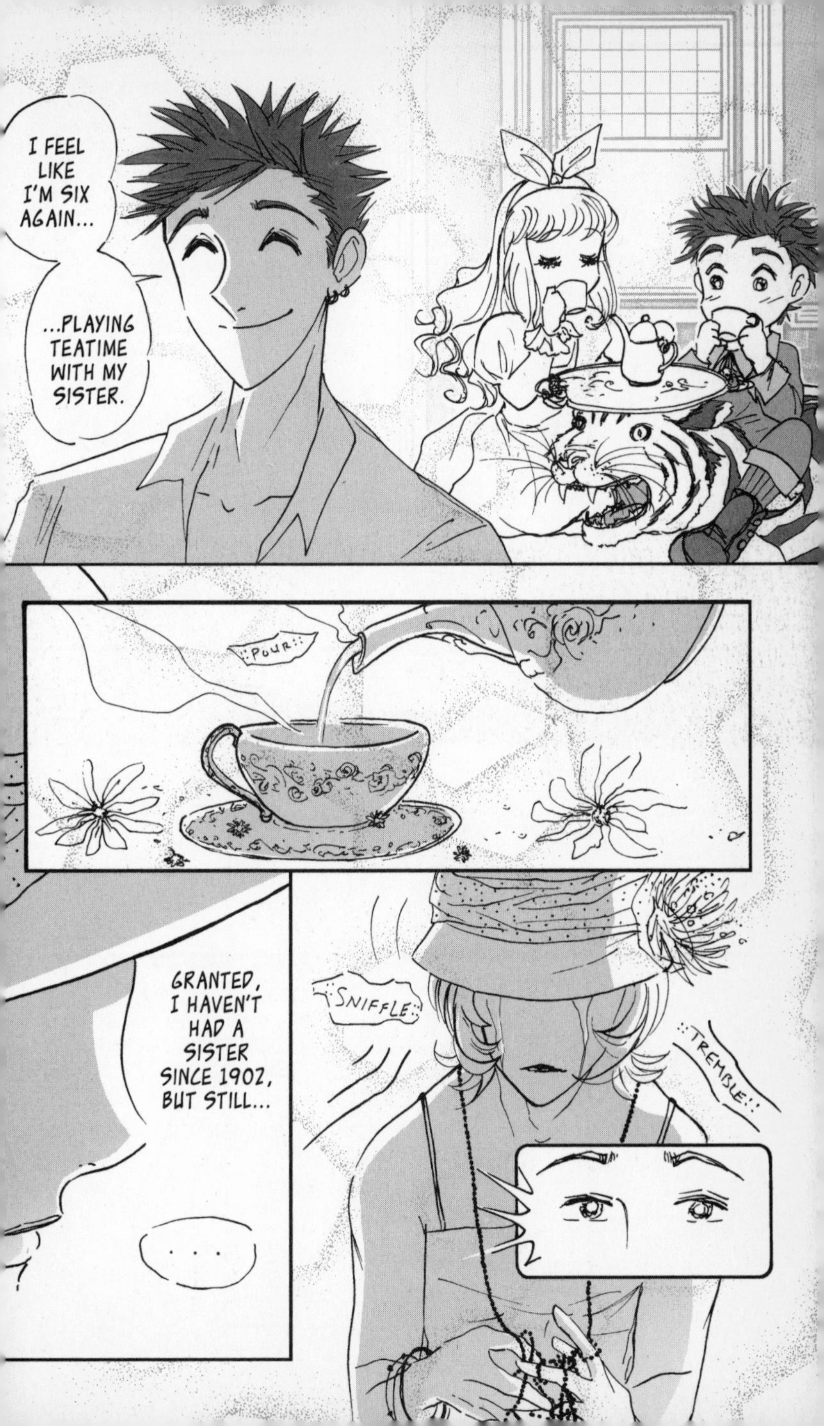
I FEEL LIKE I'M SIX AGAIN...
...PLAYING TEATIME WITH MY SISTER.
POUR
SNIFFLE
TREMBLE
GRANTED, I HAVEN'T HAD A SISTER SINCE 1902, BUT STILL...
...

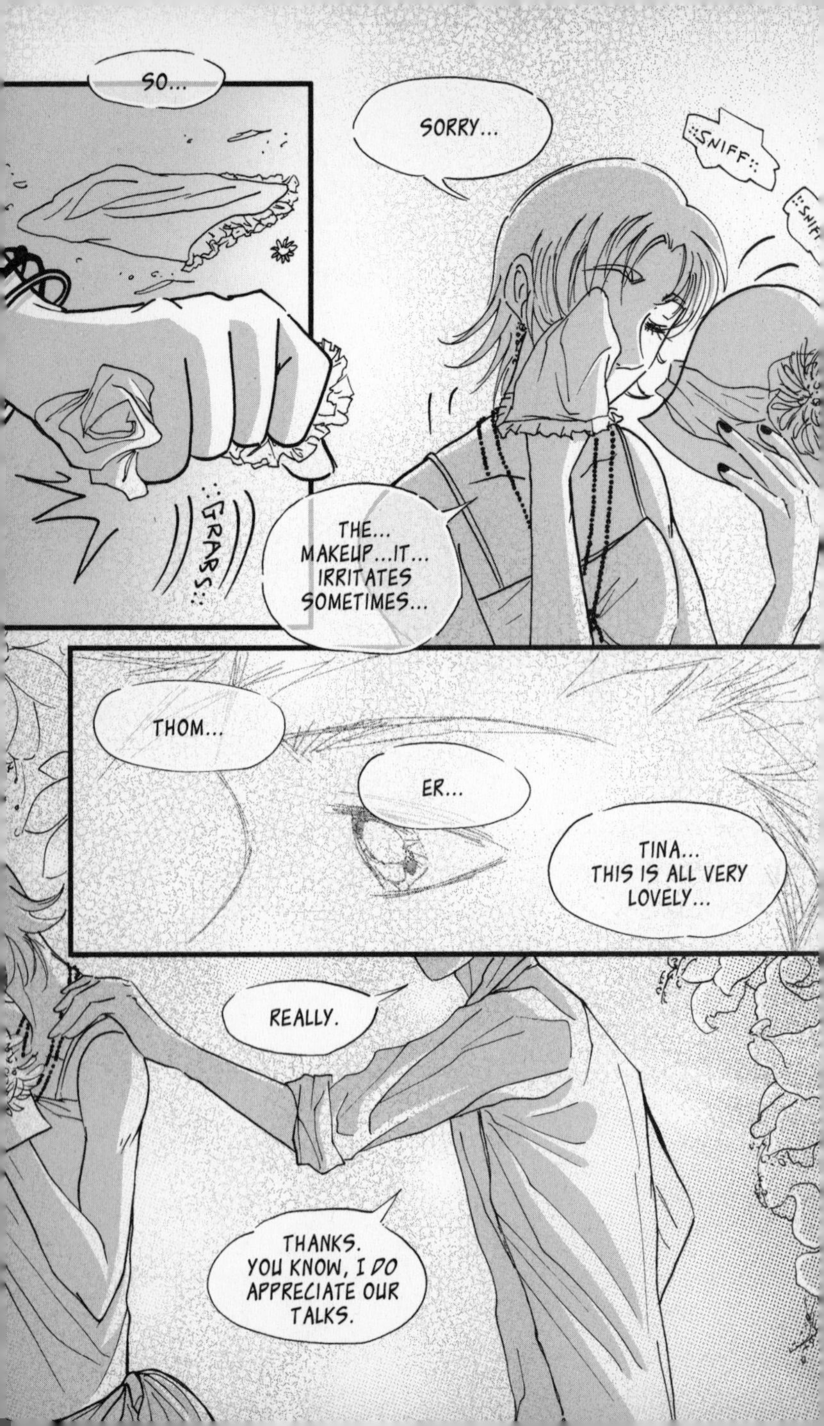
SO...
::GRABS::
SORRY...
::SNIFF::
::SNIFF
THE... MAKEUP...IT... IRRITATES SOMETIMES...
THOM...
ER...
TINA... THIS IS ALL VERY LOVELY...
REALLY.
THANKS. YOU KNOW, I DO APPRECIATE OUR TALKS.

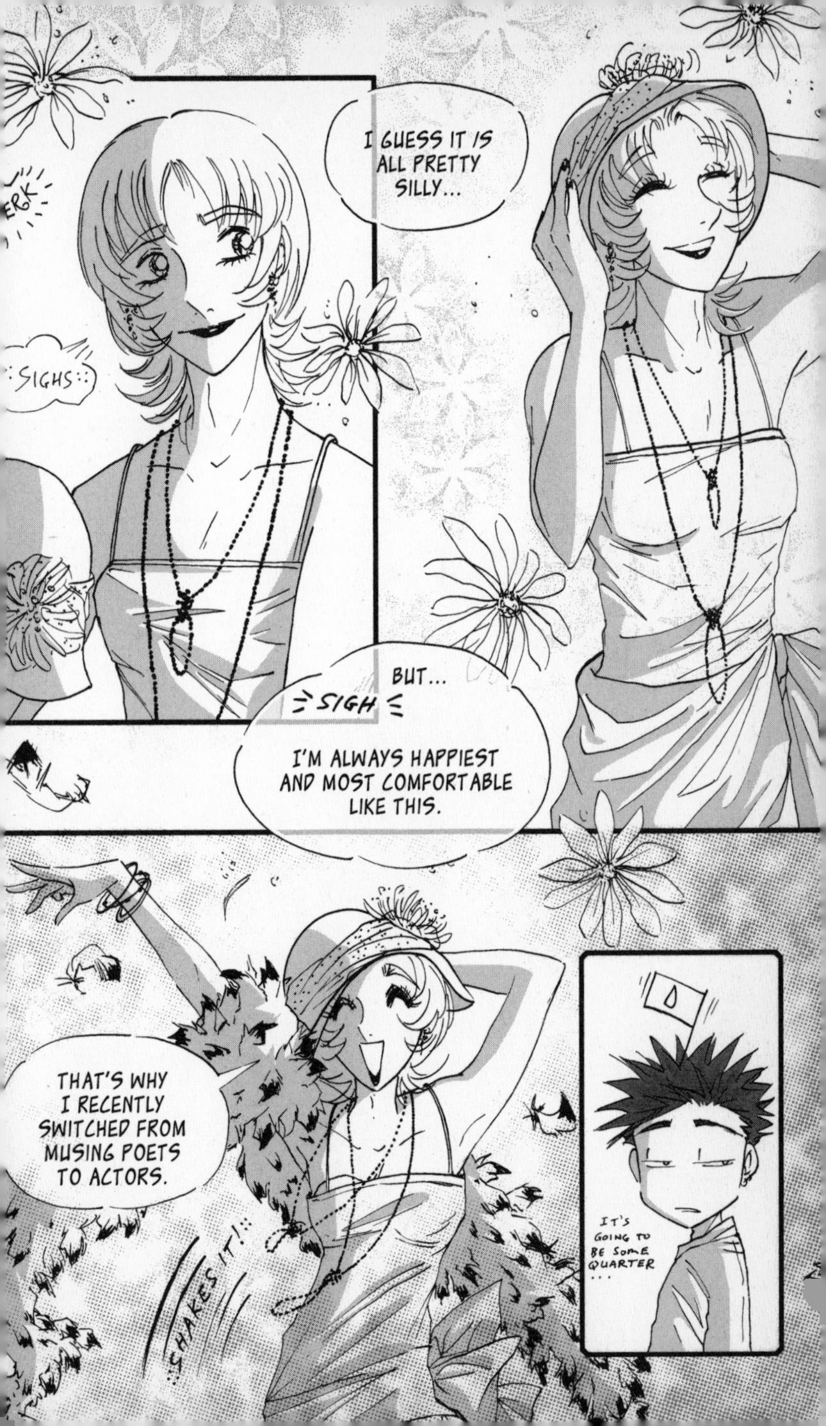
ERK
SIGHS
I GUESS IT IS ALL PRETTY SILLY...
BUT...
SIGH
I'M ALWAYS HAPPIEST AND MOST COMFORTABLE LIKE THIS.
THAT'S WHY I RECENTLY SWITCHED FROM MUSING POETS TO ACTORS.
SHAKES IT!
IT'S GOING TO BE SOME QUARTER...

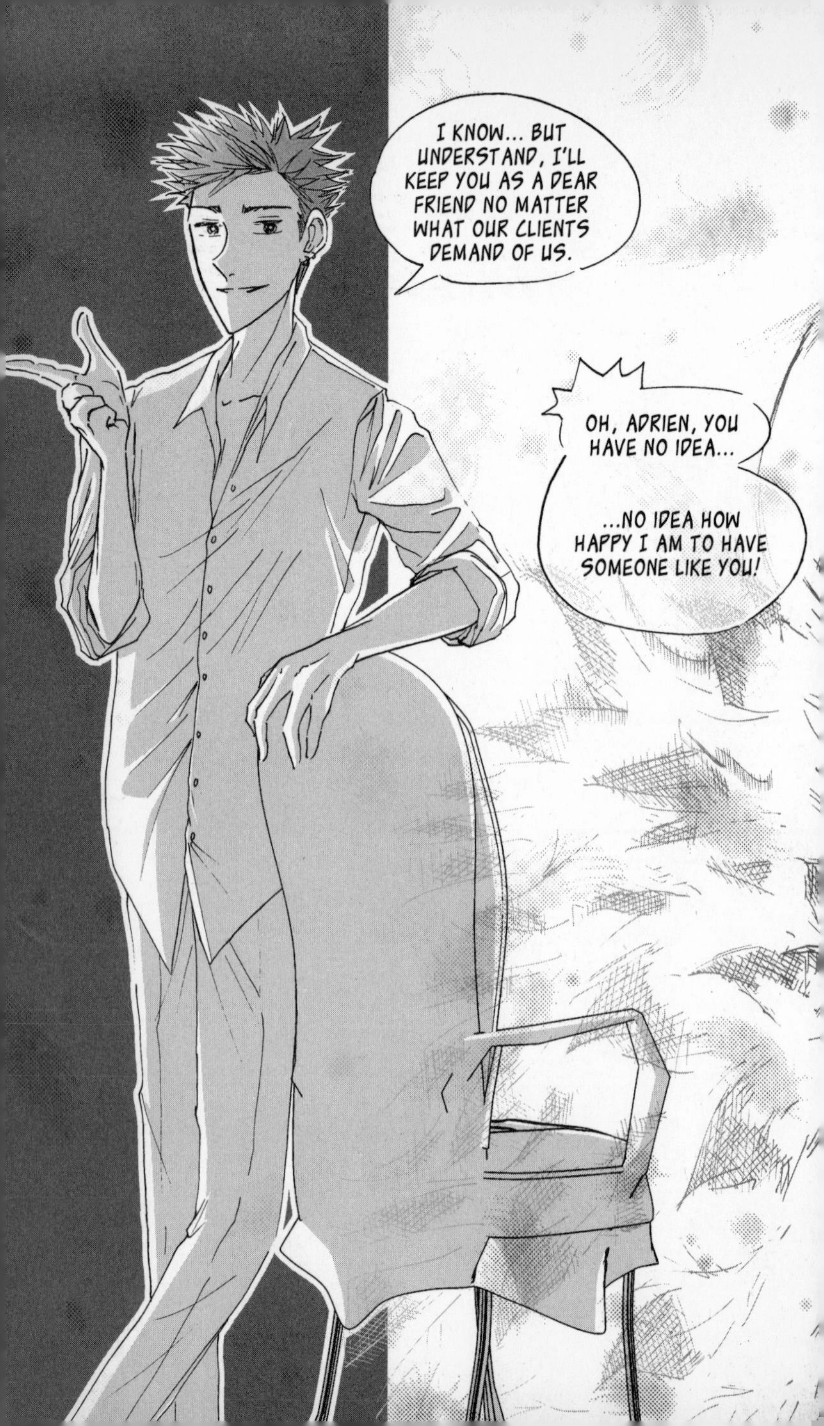
I KNOW... BUT UNDERSTAND, I'LL KEEP YOU AS A DEAR FRIEND NO MATTER WHAT OUR CLIENTS DEMAND OF US.
OH, ADRIEN, YOU HAVE NO IDEA...
...NO IDEA HOW HAPPY I AM TO HAVE SOMEONE LIKE YOU!

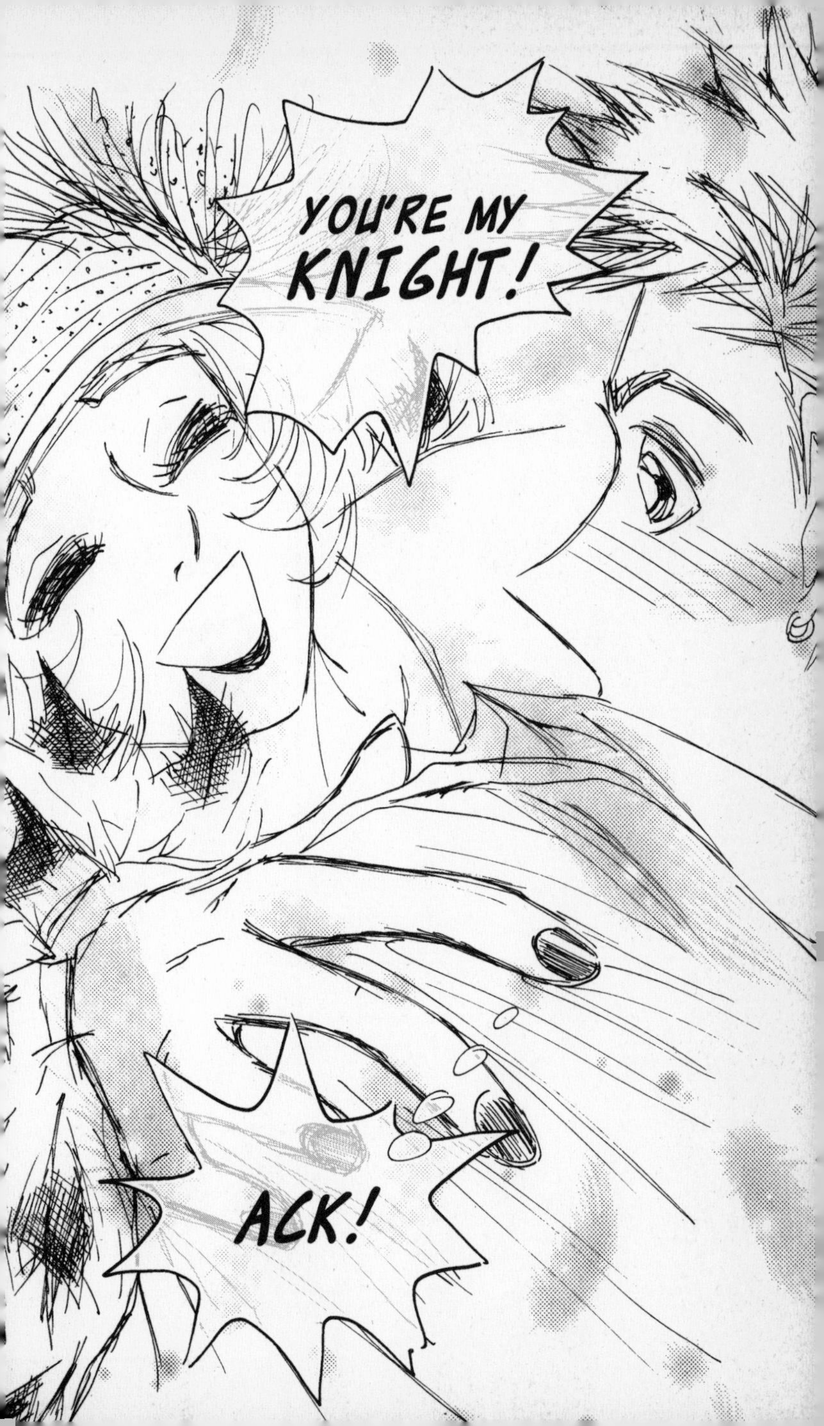
YOU'RE MY KNIGHT!
ACK!

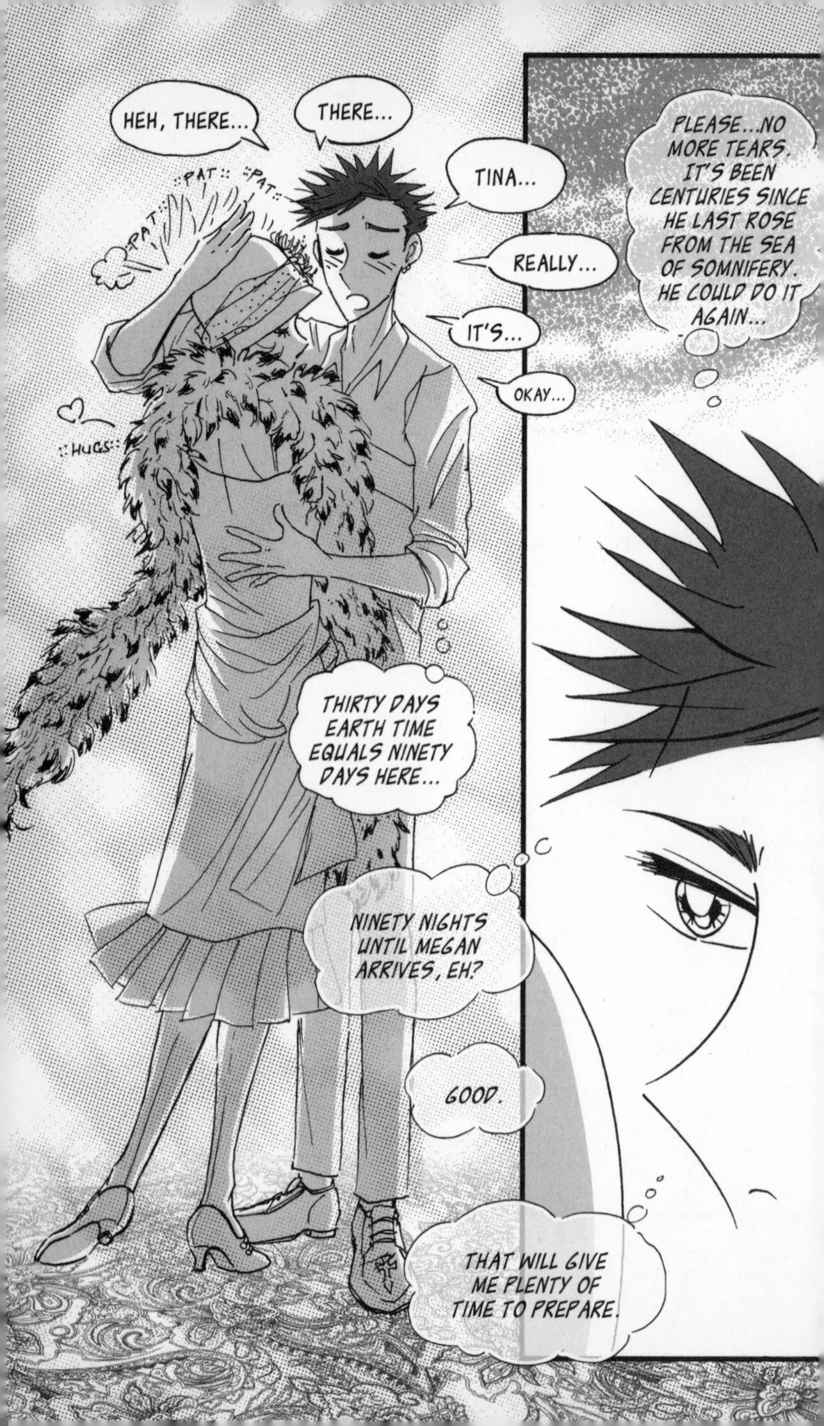
HEH, THERE...
THERE...
PAT PAT PAT
TINA...
REALLY...
IT'S...
OKAY...
HUGS
PLEASE...NO MORE TEARS. IT'S BEEN CENTURIES SINCE HE LAST ROSE FROM THE SEA OF SOMNIFERY. HE COULD DO IT AGAIN...
THIRTY DAYS EARTH TIME EQUALS NINETY DAYS HERE...
NINETY NIGHTS UNTIL MEGAN ARRIVES, EH?
GOOD.
THAT WILL GIVE ME PLENTY OF TIME TO PREPARE.

# Chapter Three: this is Yuletide

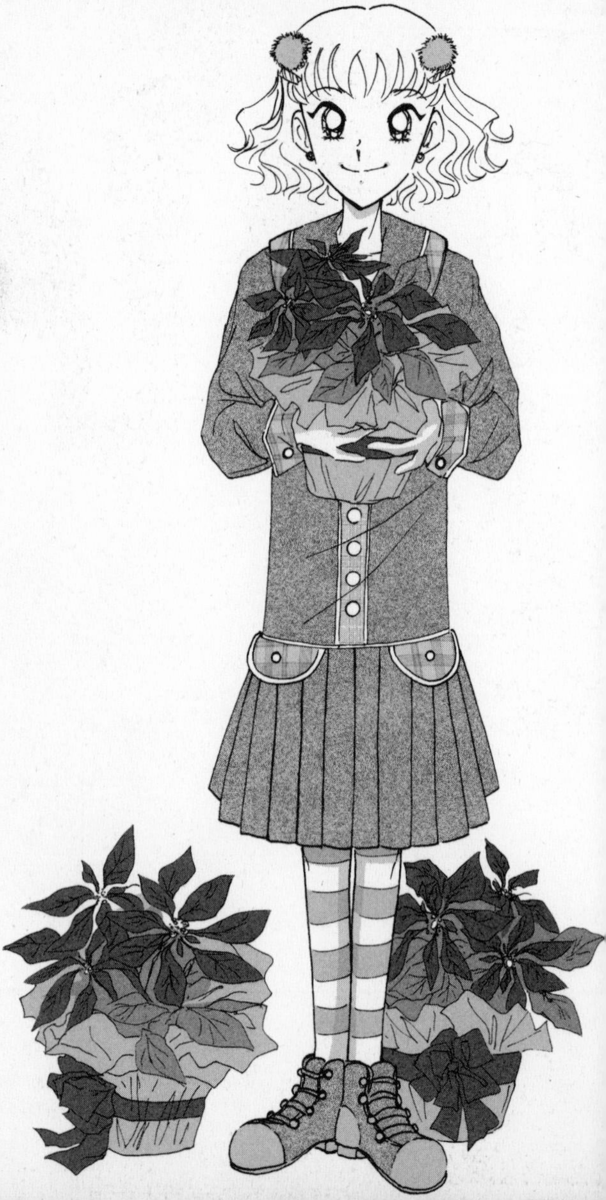

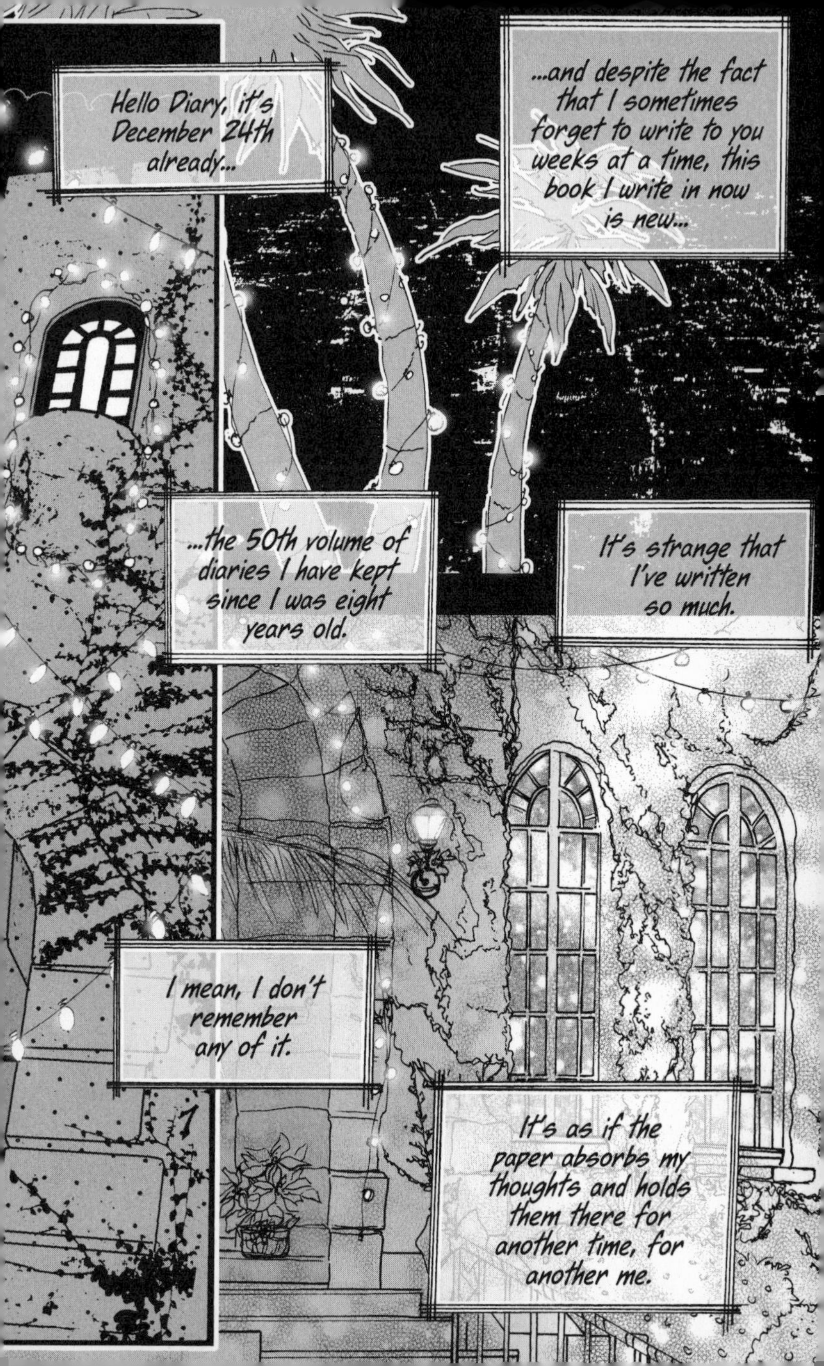
Hello Diary, it's December 24th already...
...and despite the fact that I sometimes forget to write to you weeks at a time, this book I write in now is new...
...the 50th volume of diaries I have kept since I was eight years old.
It's strange that I've written so much.
I mean, I don't remember any of it.
It's as if the paper absorbs my thoughts and holds them there for another time, for another me.

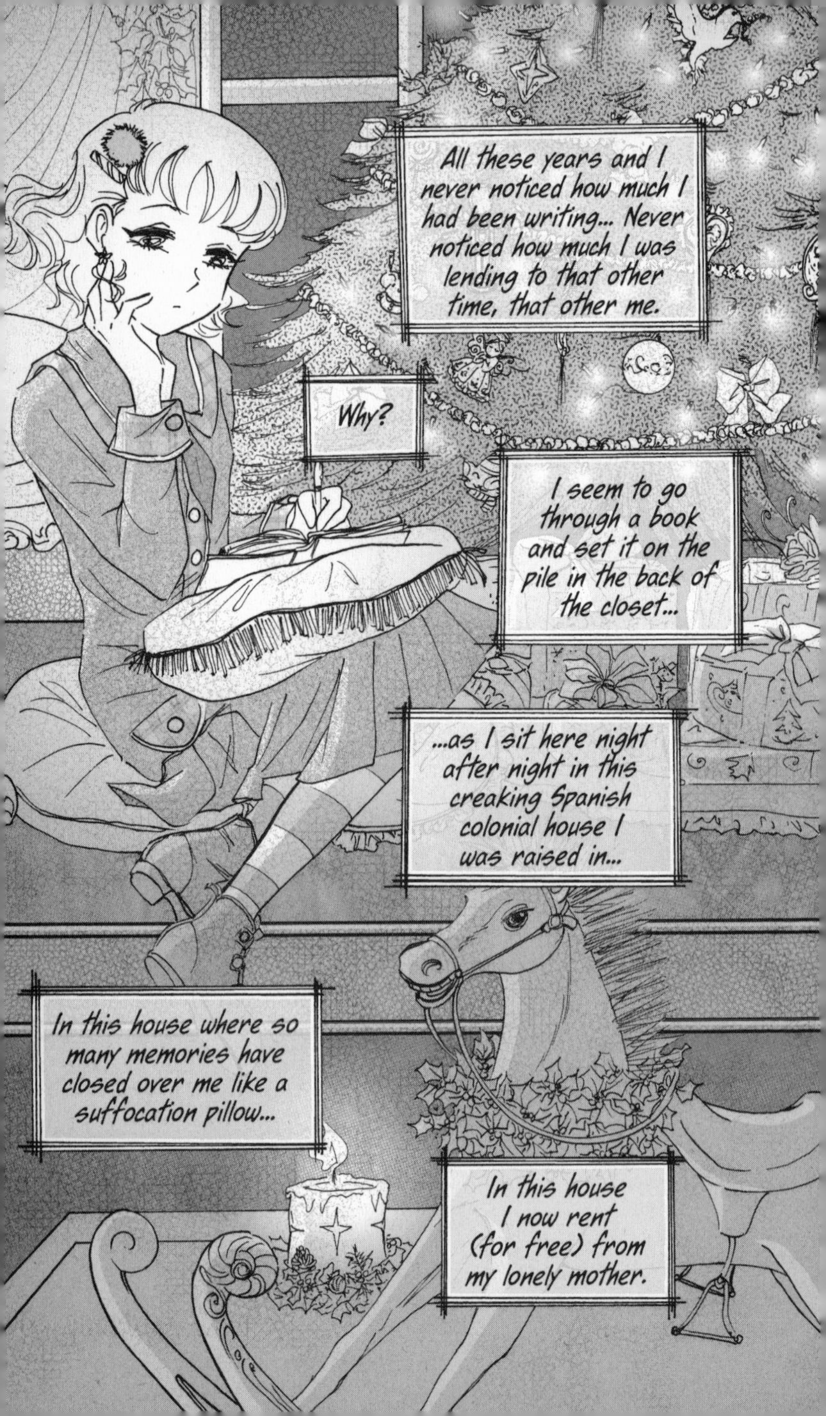
All these years and I never noticed how much I had been writing... Never noticed how much I was lending to that other time, that other me.
Why?
I seem to go through a book and set it on the pile in the back of the closet...
...as I sit here night after night in this creaking Spanish colonial house I was raised in...
In this house where so many memories have closed over me like a suffocation pillow...
In this house I now rent (for free) from my lonely mother.

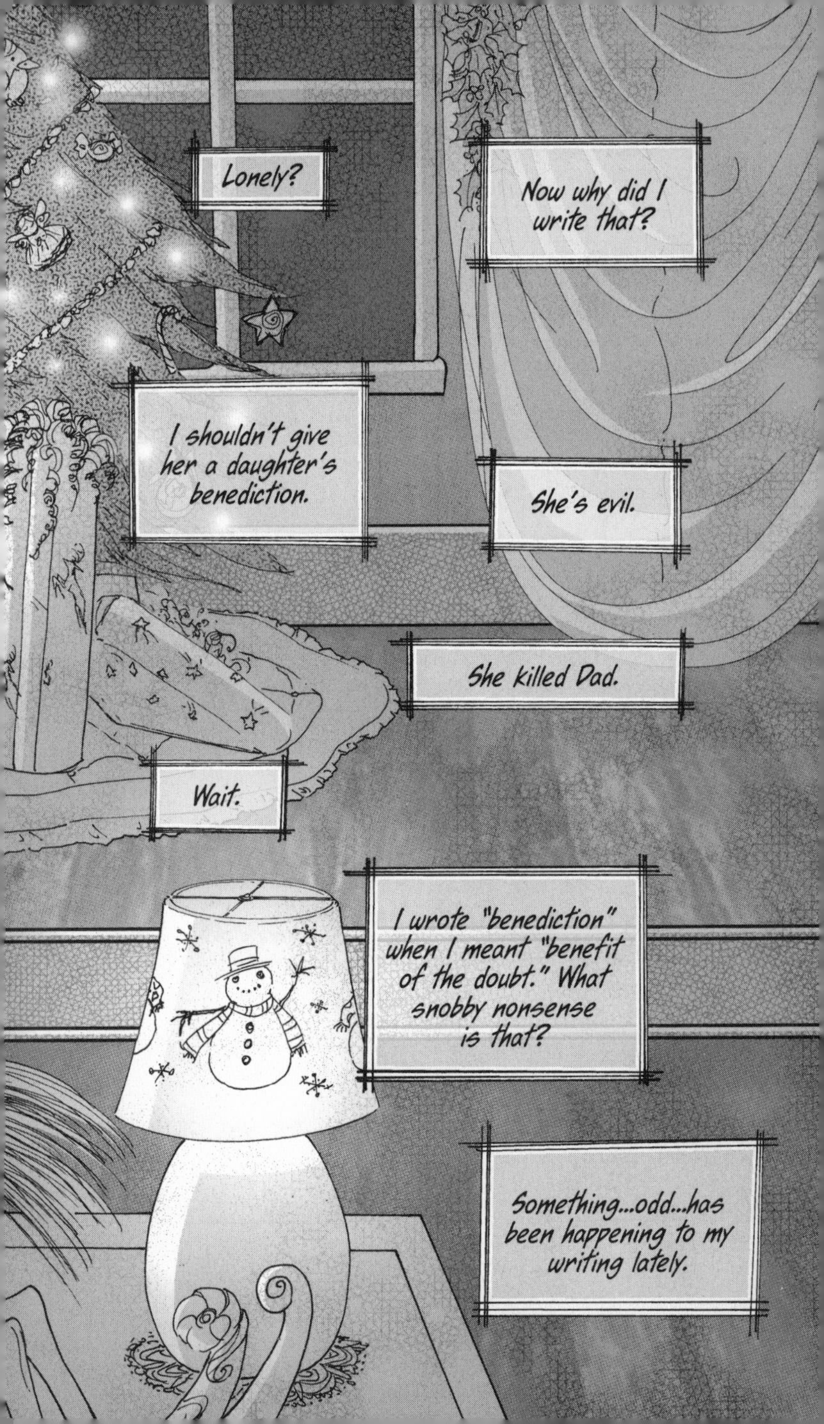
Now why did I write that?
Lonely?
I shouldn't give her a daughter's benediction.
She's evil.
She killed Dad.
Wait.
I wrote "benediction" when I meant "benefit of the doubt." What snobby nonsense is that?
Something...odd...has been happening to my writing lately.

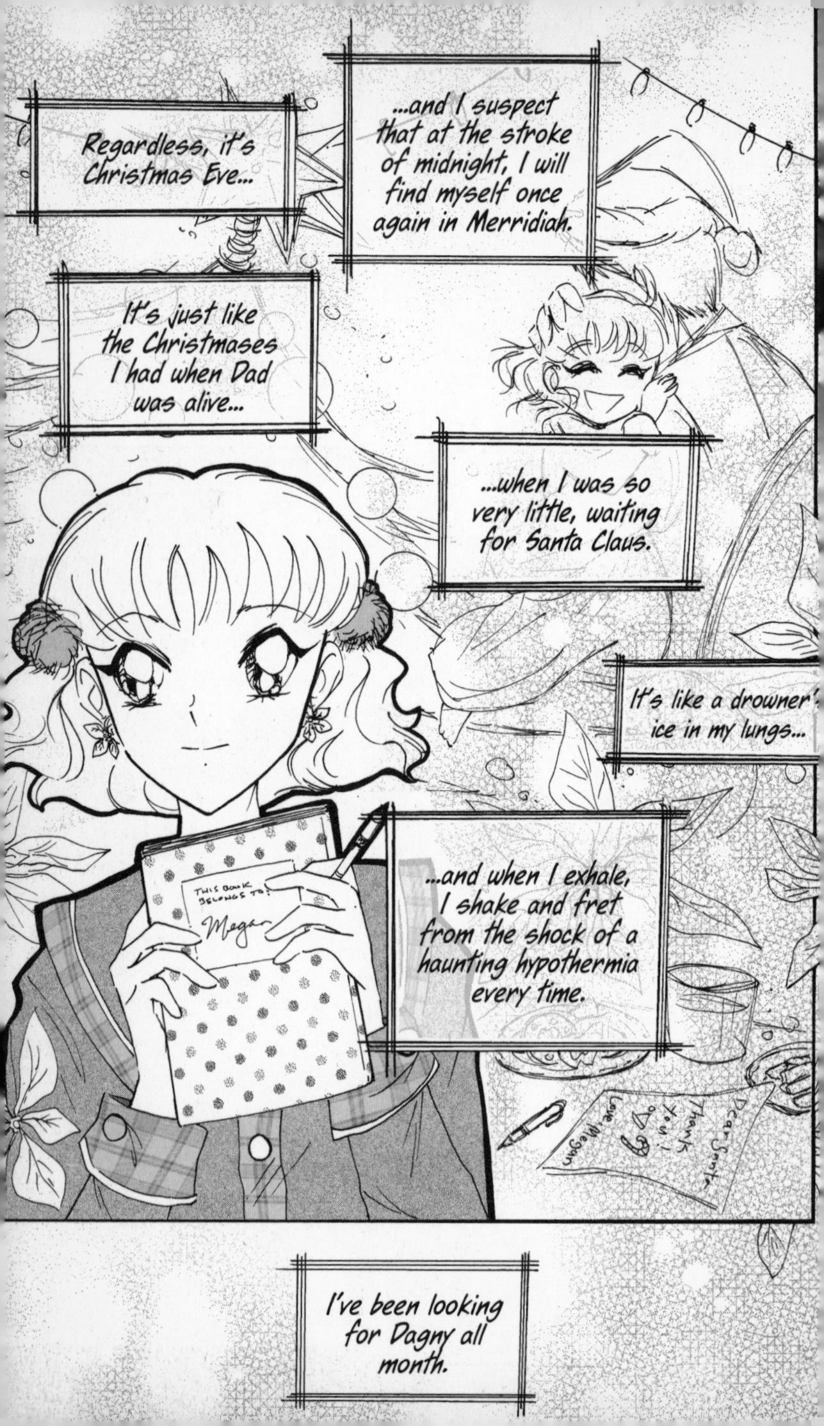
Regardless, it's Christmas Eve...
...and I suspect that at the stroke of midnight, I will find myself once again in Merridiah.
It's just like the Christmases I had when Dad was alive...
...when I was so very little, waiting for Santa Claus.
It's like a drowner' ice in my lungs...
THIS BOOK BELONGS TO: Megan
...and when I exhale, I shake and fret from the shock of a haunting hypothermia every time.
Dear Santa Thank you! Love, Megan
I've been looking for Dagny all month.

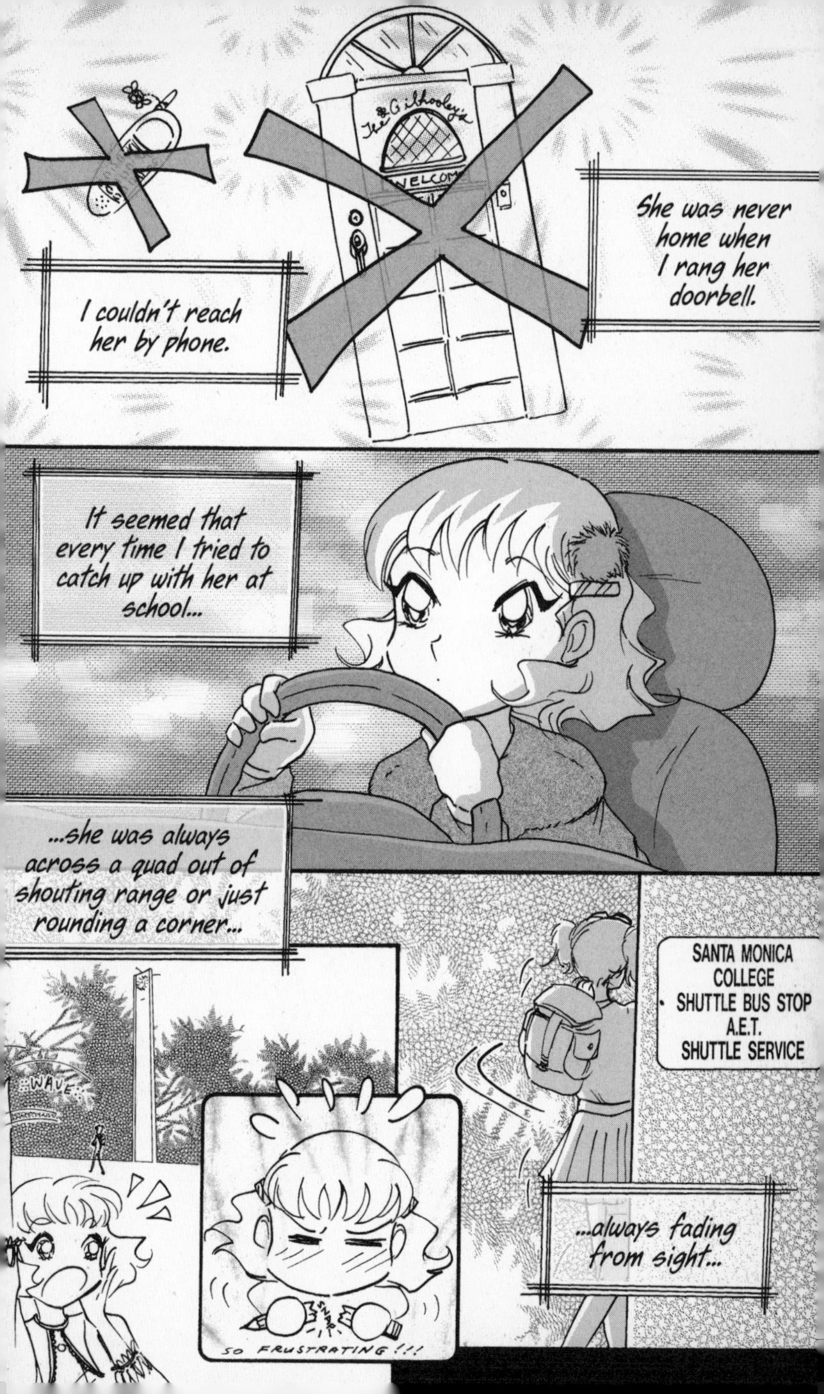

I couldn't reach her by phone.
The Gilhooley's
WELCOME
She was never home when I rang her doorbell.
It seemed that every time I tried to catch up with her at school...
...she was always across a quad out of shouting range or just rounding a corner...
WAVE
SO FRUSTRATING!!!
SANTA MONICA COLLEGE
• SHUTTLE BUS STOP
A.E.T.
SHUTTLE SERVICE
...always fading from sight...

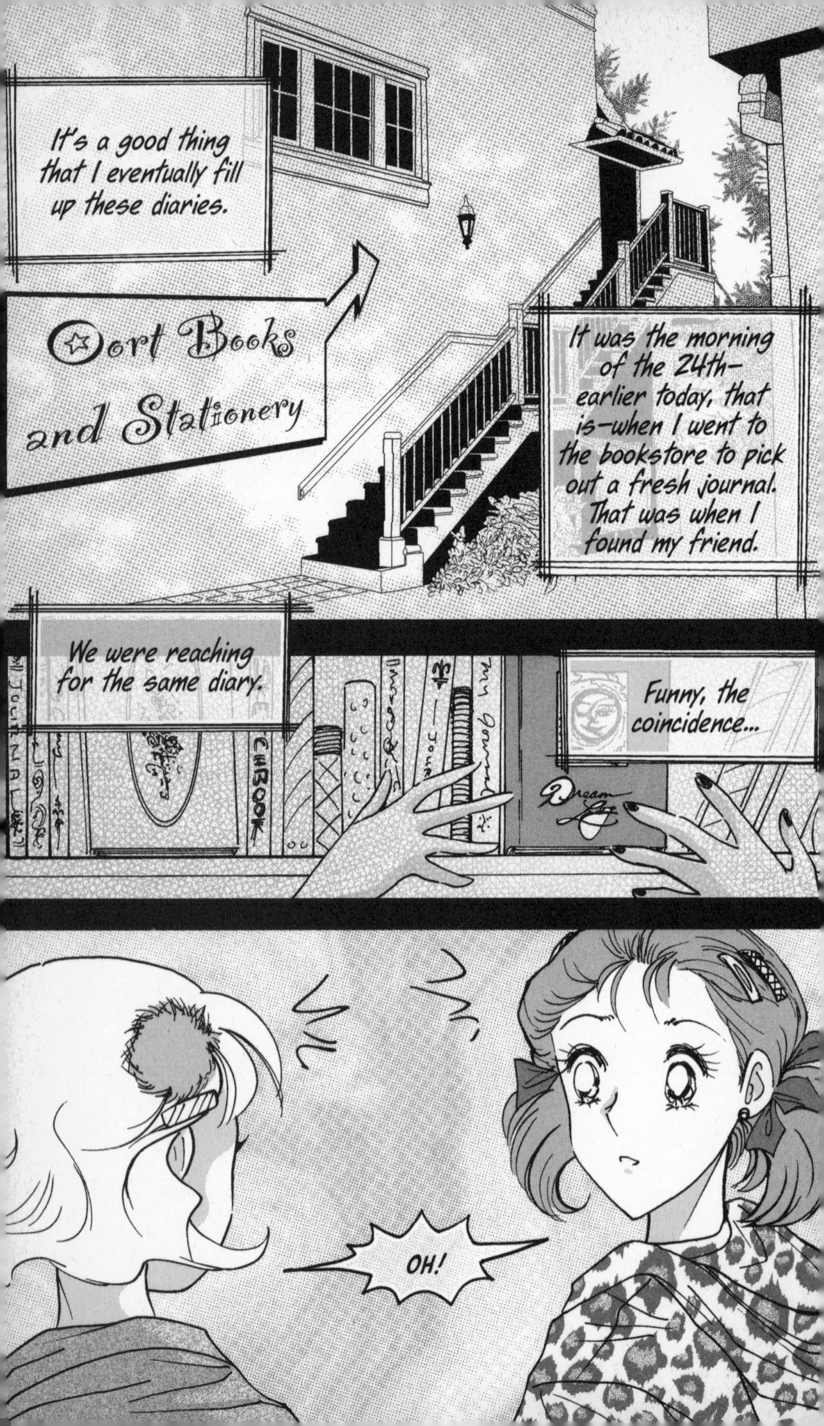
It's a good thing that I eventually fill up these diaries.
Oort Books and Stationery
It was the morning of the 24th— earlier today, that is—when I went to the bookstore to pick out a fresh journal. That was when I found my friend.
We were reaching for the same diary.
Funny, the coincidence...
OH!

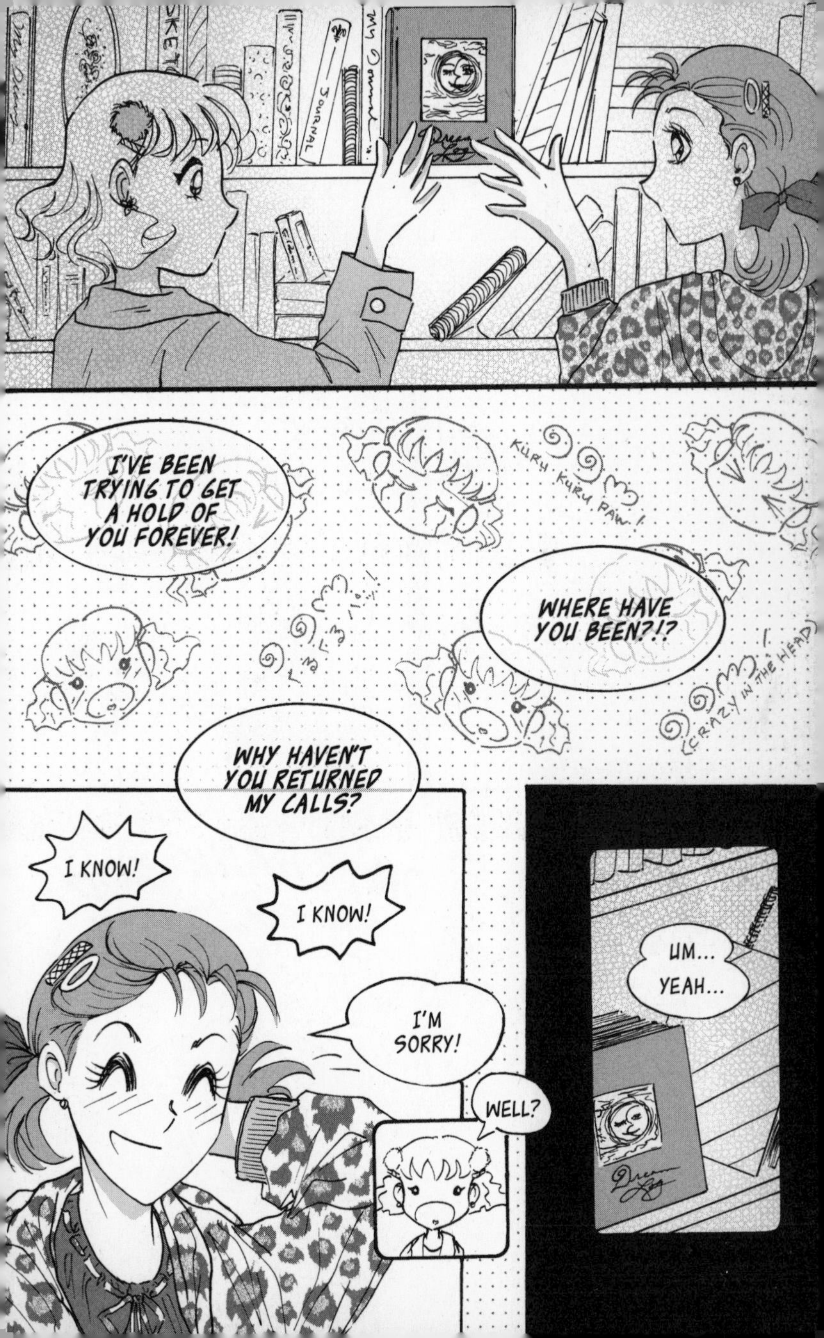
I'VE BEEN TRYING TO GET A HOLD OF YOU FOREVER!
KURU KURU PAW!
WHERE HAVE YOU BEEN?!?
(CRAZY IN THE HEAD)
WHY HAVEN'T YOU RETURNED MY CALLS?
I KNOW!
I KNOW!
I'M SORRY!
WELL?
UM... YEAH...

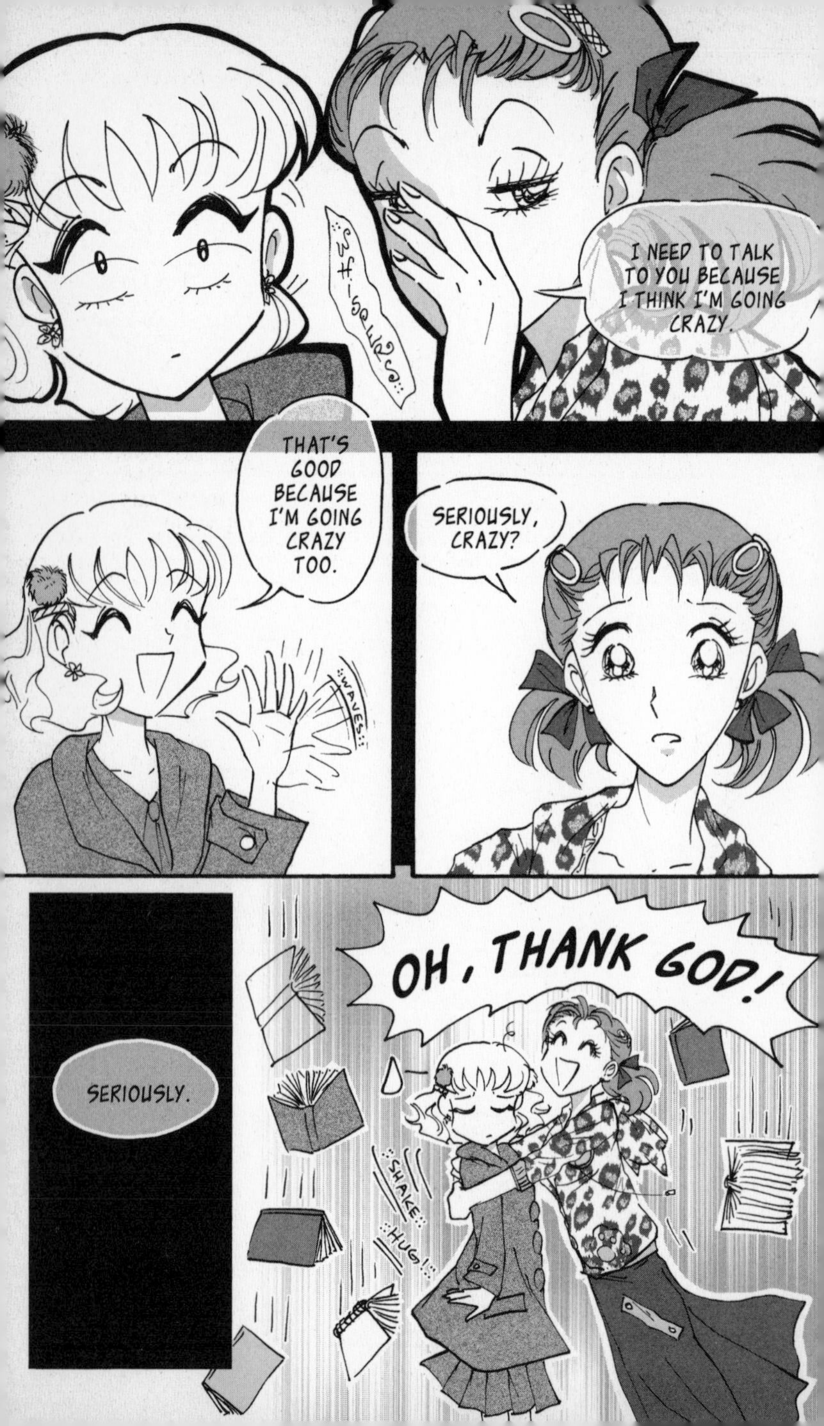
::whispers::
I NEED TO TALK TO YOU BECAUSE I THINK I'M GOING CRAZY.
THAT'S GOOD BECAUSE I'M GOING CRAZY TOO.
::WAVES::
SERIOUSLY, CRAZY?
SERIOUSLY.
OH, THANK GOD!
::SHAKE::
::HUG!::

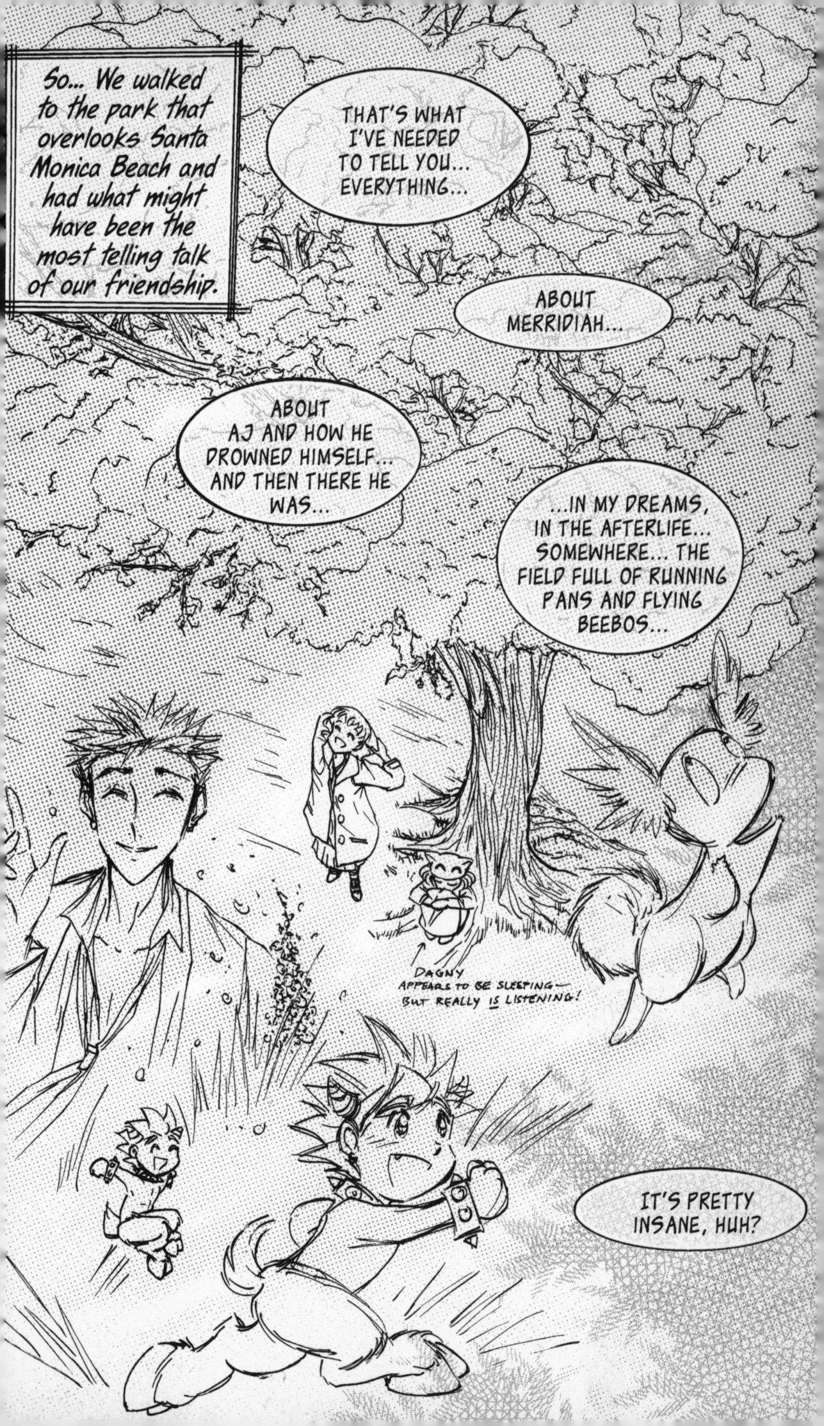
So... We walked to the park that overlooks Santa Monica Beach and had what might have been the most telling talk of our friendship.
THAT'S WHAT I'VE NEEDED TO TELL YOU... EVERYTHING...
ABOUT MERRIDIAH...
ABOUT AJ AND HOW HE DROWNED HIMSELF... AND THEN THERE HE WAS...
...IN MY DREAMS, IN THE AFTERLIFE... SOMEWHERE... THE FIELD FULL OF RUNNING PANS AND FLYING BEEBOS...
DAGNY APPEARS TO BE SLEEPING— BUT REALLY IS LISTENING!
IT'S PRETTY INSANE, HUH?

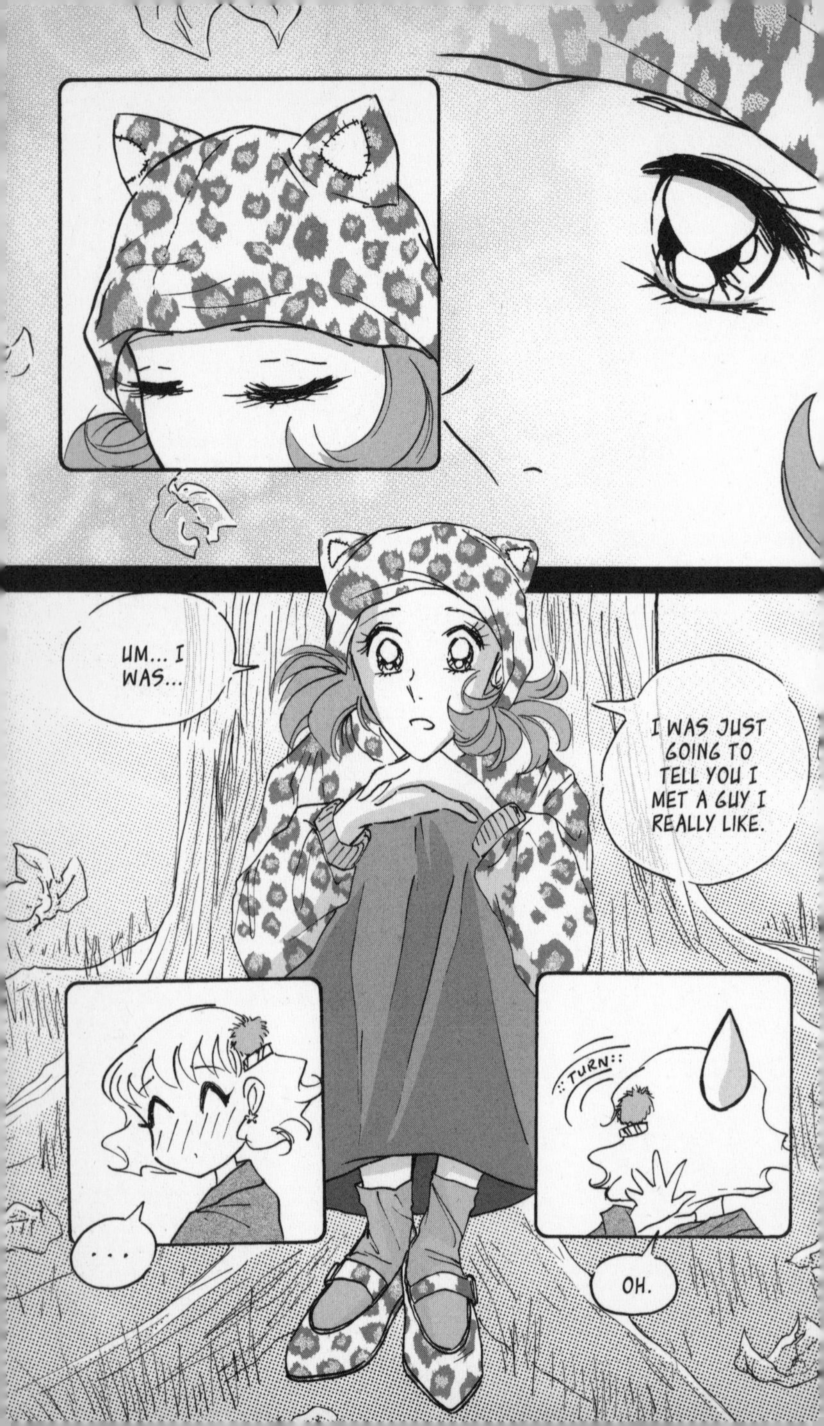
UM... I WAS...
I WAS JUST GOING TO TELL YOU I MET A GUY I REALLY LIKE.
...
::TURN::
OH.

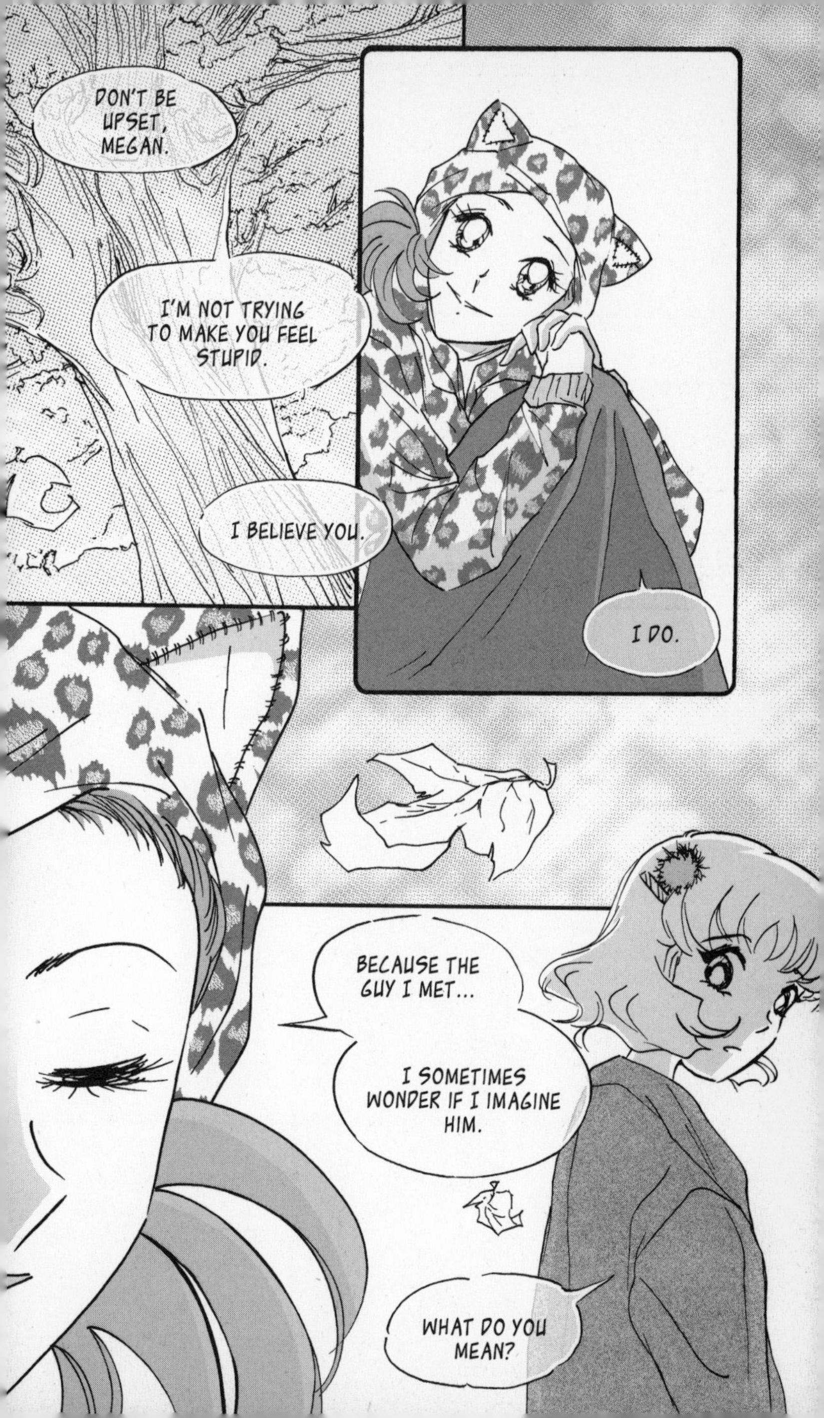
DON'T BE UPSET, MEGAN.
I'M NOT TRYING TO MAKE YOU FEEL STUPID.
I BELIEVE YOU.
I DO.
BECAUSE THE GUY I MET...
I SOMETIMES WONDER IF I IMAGINE HIM.
WHAT DO YOU MEAN?

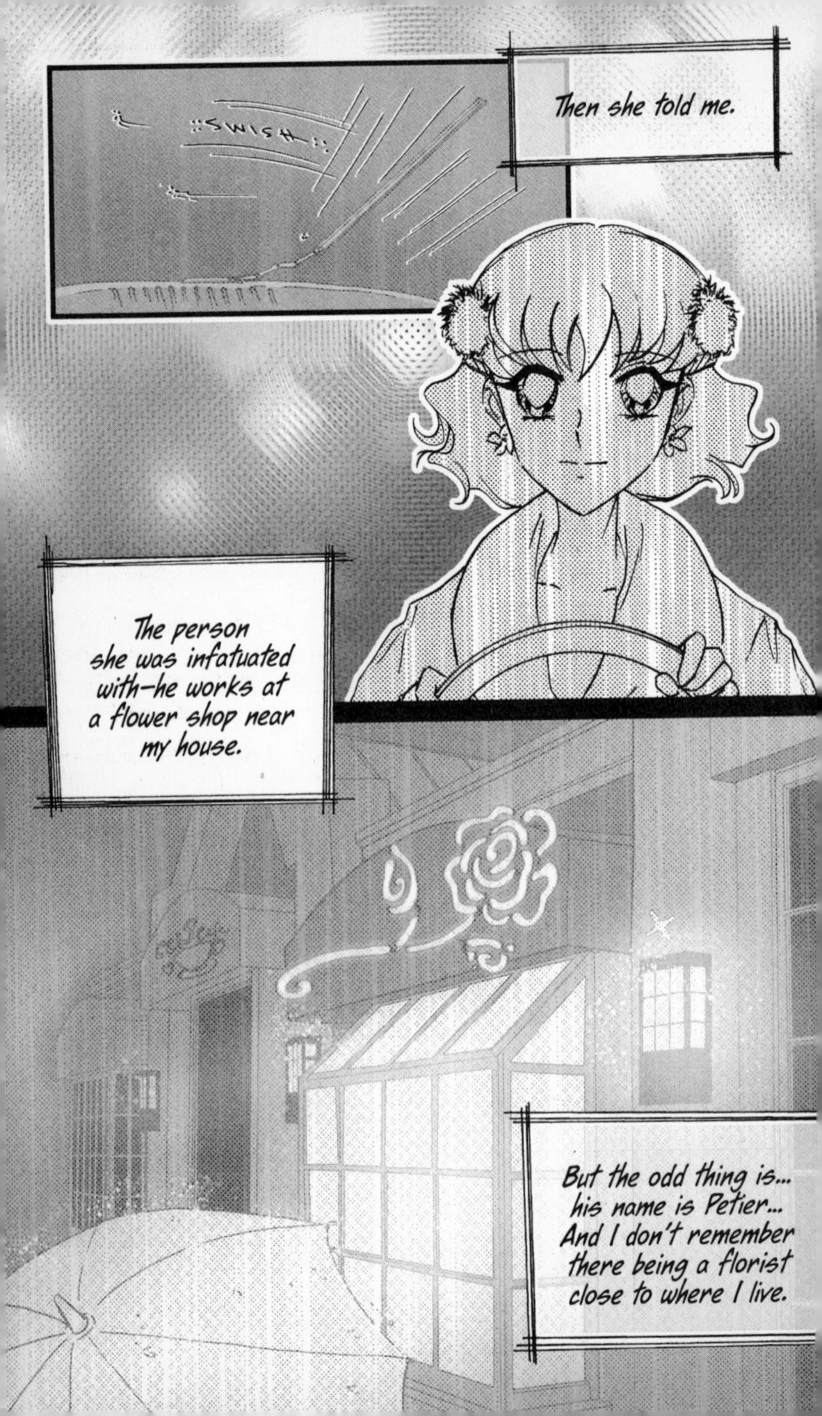
Then she told me.
::SWISH::
The person she was infatuated with–he works at a flower shop near my house.
But the odd thing is... his name is Petier... And I don't remember there being a florist close to where I live.

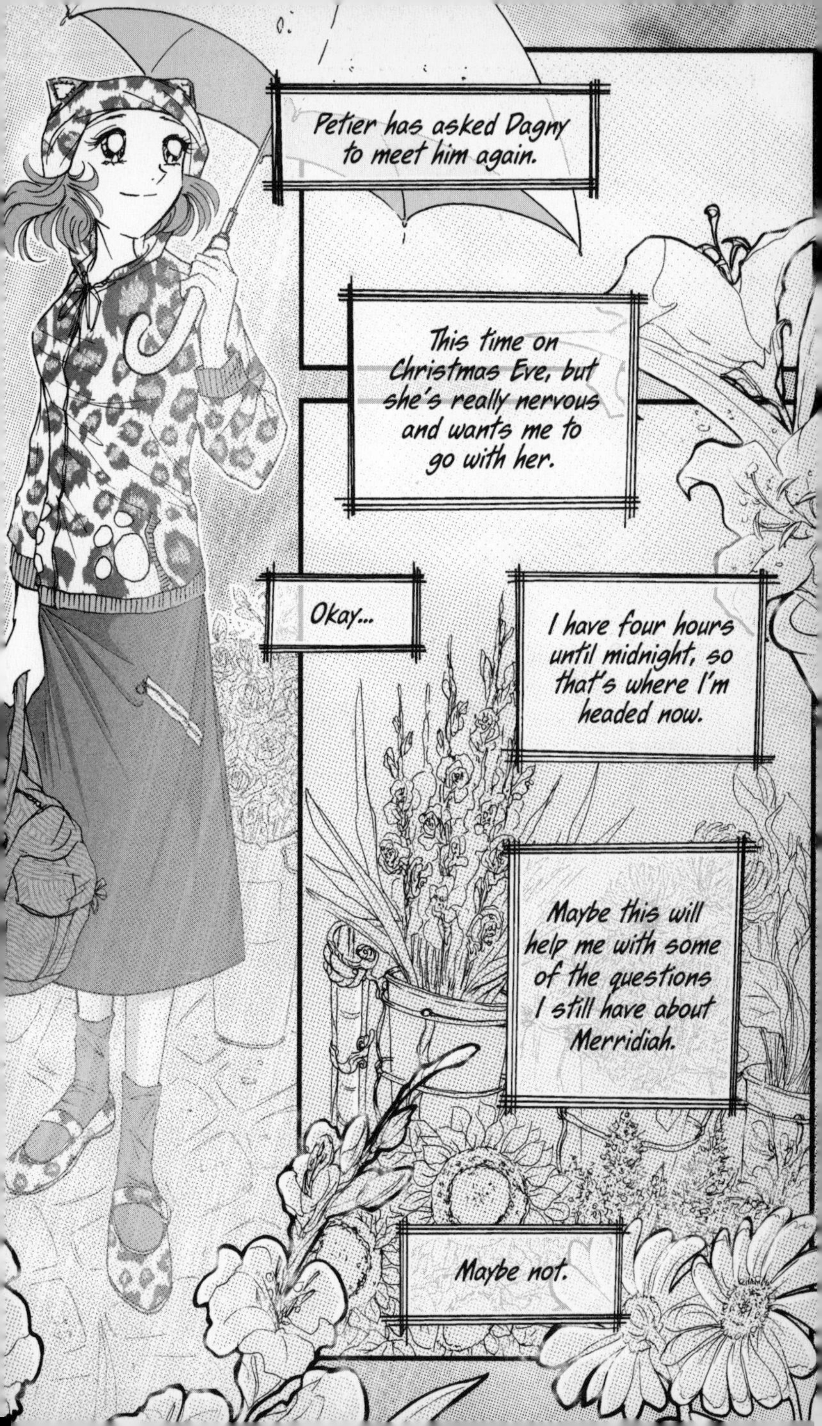
Petier has asked Dagny to meet him again.
This time on Christmas Eve, but she's really nervous and wants me to go with her.
I have four hours until midnight, so that's where I'm headed now.
Okay...
Maybe this will help me with some of the questions I still have about Merridiah.
Maybe not.

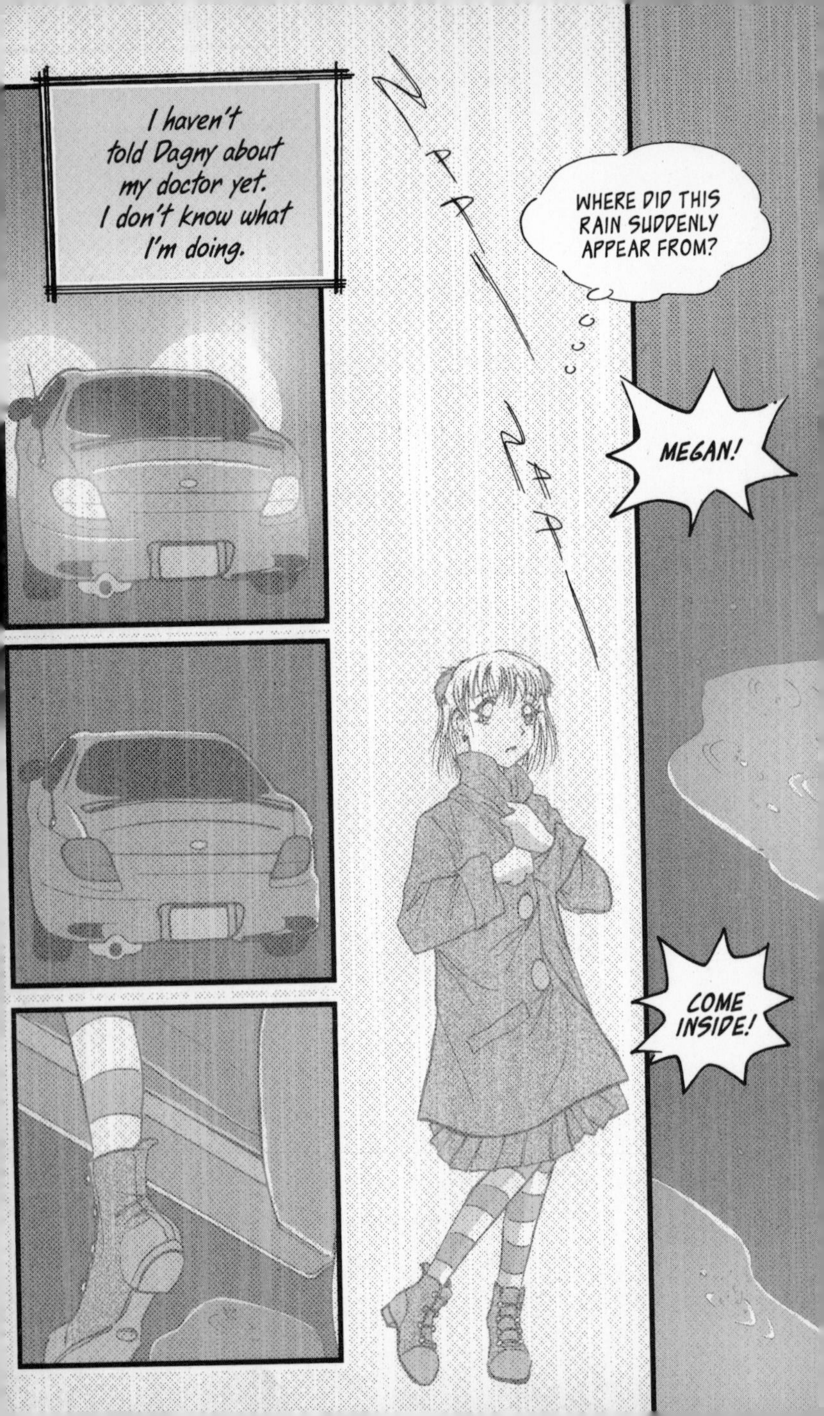
I haven't told Dagny about my doctor yet. I don't know what I'm doing.
WHERE DID THIS RAIN SUDDENLY APPEAR FROM?
MEGAN!
COME INSIDE!

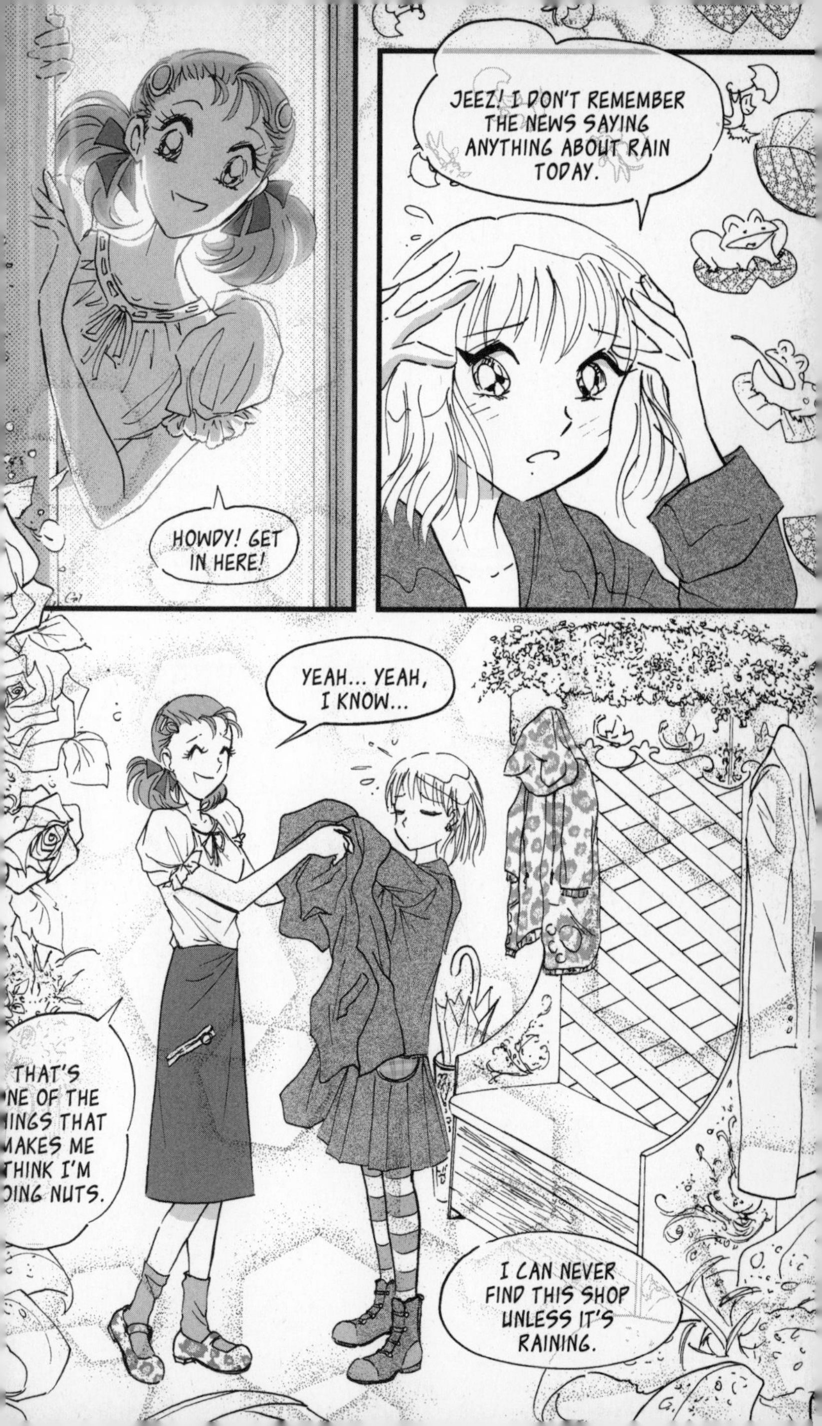
JEEZ! I DON'T REMEMBER THE NEWS SAYING ANYTHING ABOUT RAIN TODAY.
HOWDY! GET IN HERE!
YEAH... YEAH, I KNOW...
I CAN NEVER FIND THIS SHOP UNLESS IT'S RAINING.
THAT'S NE OF THE INGS THAT MAKES ME THINK I'M OING NUTS.

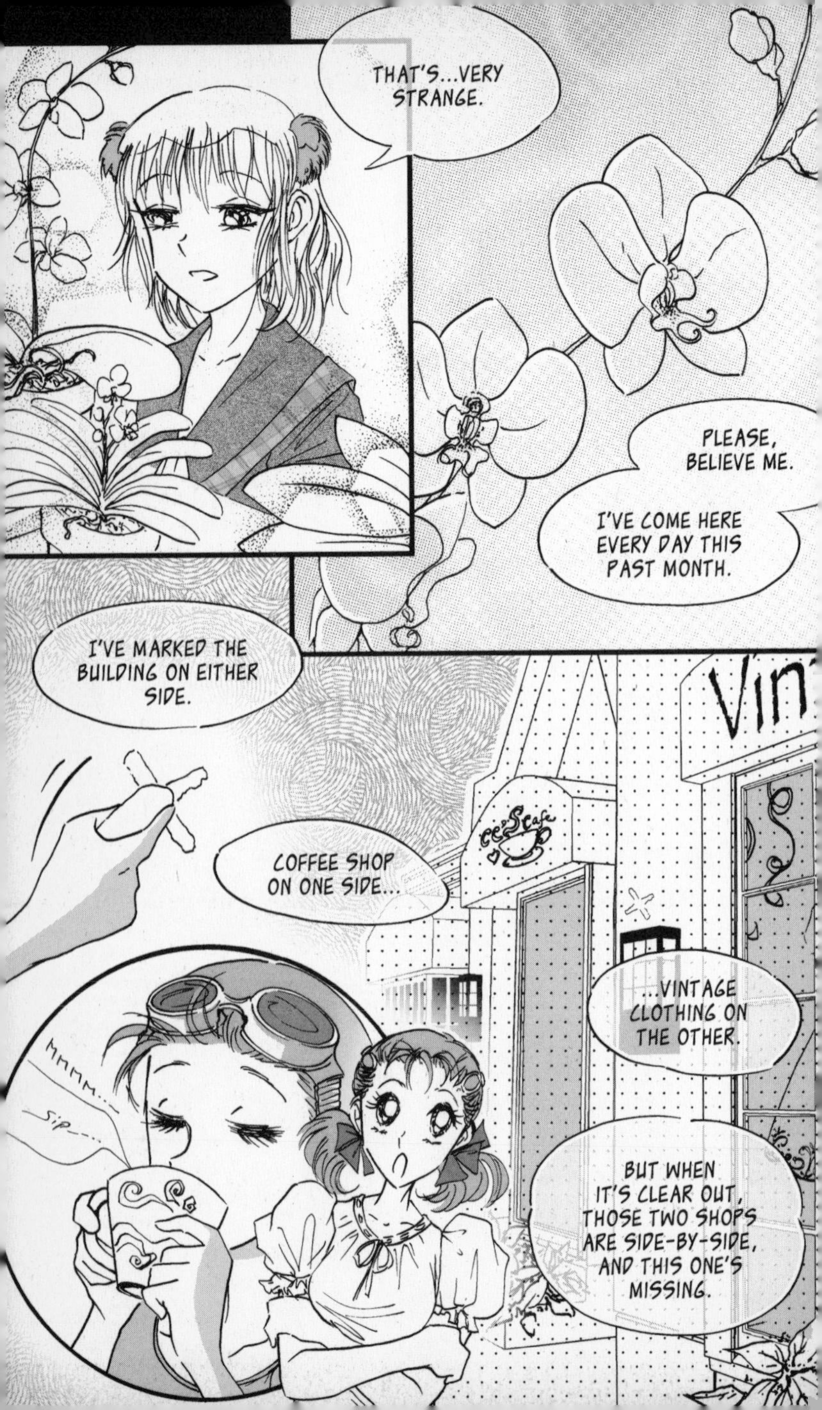
THAT'S...VERY STRANGE.
PLEASE, BELIEVE ME.
I'VE COME HERE EVERY DAY THIS PAST MONTH.
I'VE MARKED THE BUILDING ON EITHER SIDE.
Vin
COFFEE SHOP ON ONE SIDE...
...VINTAGE CLOTHING ON THE OTHER.
MMMM...
Sip---
BUT WHEN IT'S CLEAR OUT, THOSE TWO SHOPS ARE SIDE-BY-SIDE, AND THIS ONE'S MISSING.

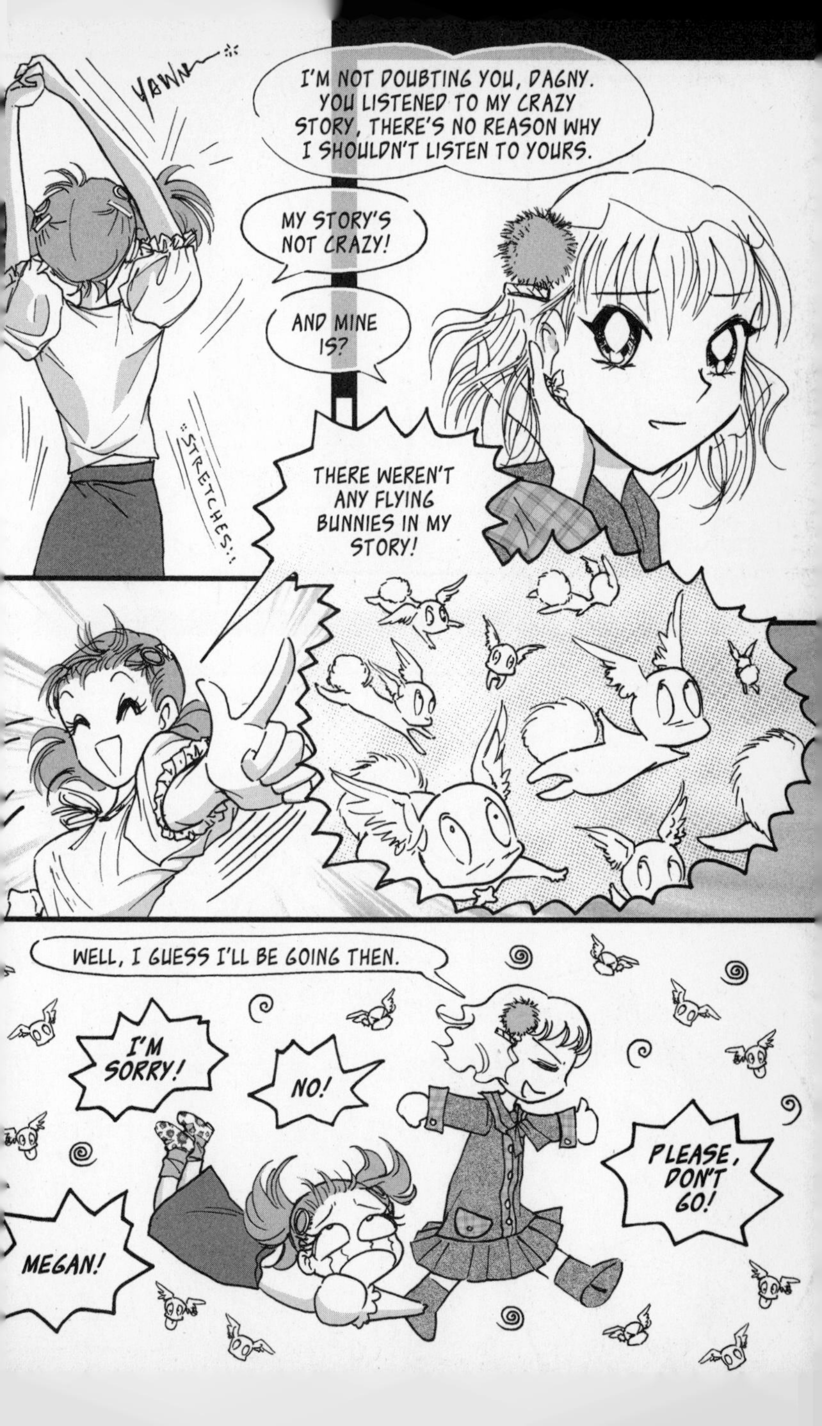
YAWN
STRETCHES
I'M NOT DOUBTING YOU, DAGNY. YOU LISTENED TO MY CRAZY STORY, THERE'S NO REASON WHY I SHOULDN'T LISTEN TO YOURS.
MY STORY'S NOT CRAZY!
AND MINE IS?
THERE WEREN'T ANY FLYING BUNNIES IN MY STORY!
WELL, I GUESS I'LL BE GOING THEN.
I'M SORRY!
NO!
PLEASE, DON'T GO!
MEGAN!

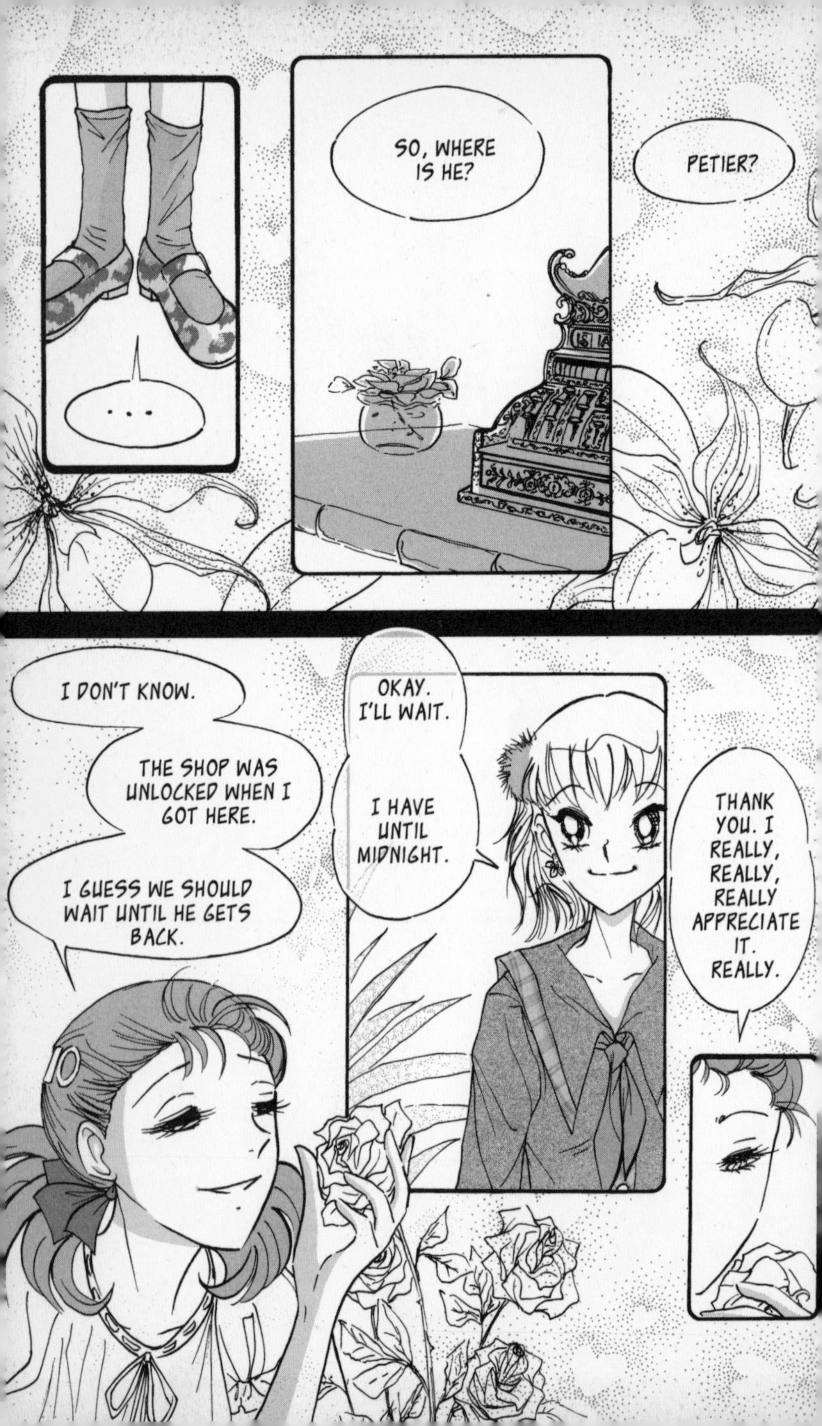
...
SO, WHERE IS HE?
PETIER?
I DON'T KNOW.
THE SHOP WAS UNLOCKED WHEN I GOT HERE.
I GUESS WE SHOULD WAIT UNTIL HE GETS BACK.
OKAY. I'LL WAIT.
I HAVE UNTIL MIDNIGHT.
THANK YOU. I REALLY, REALLY, REALLY APPRECIATE IT. REALLY.

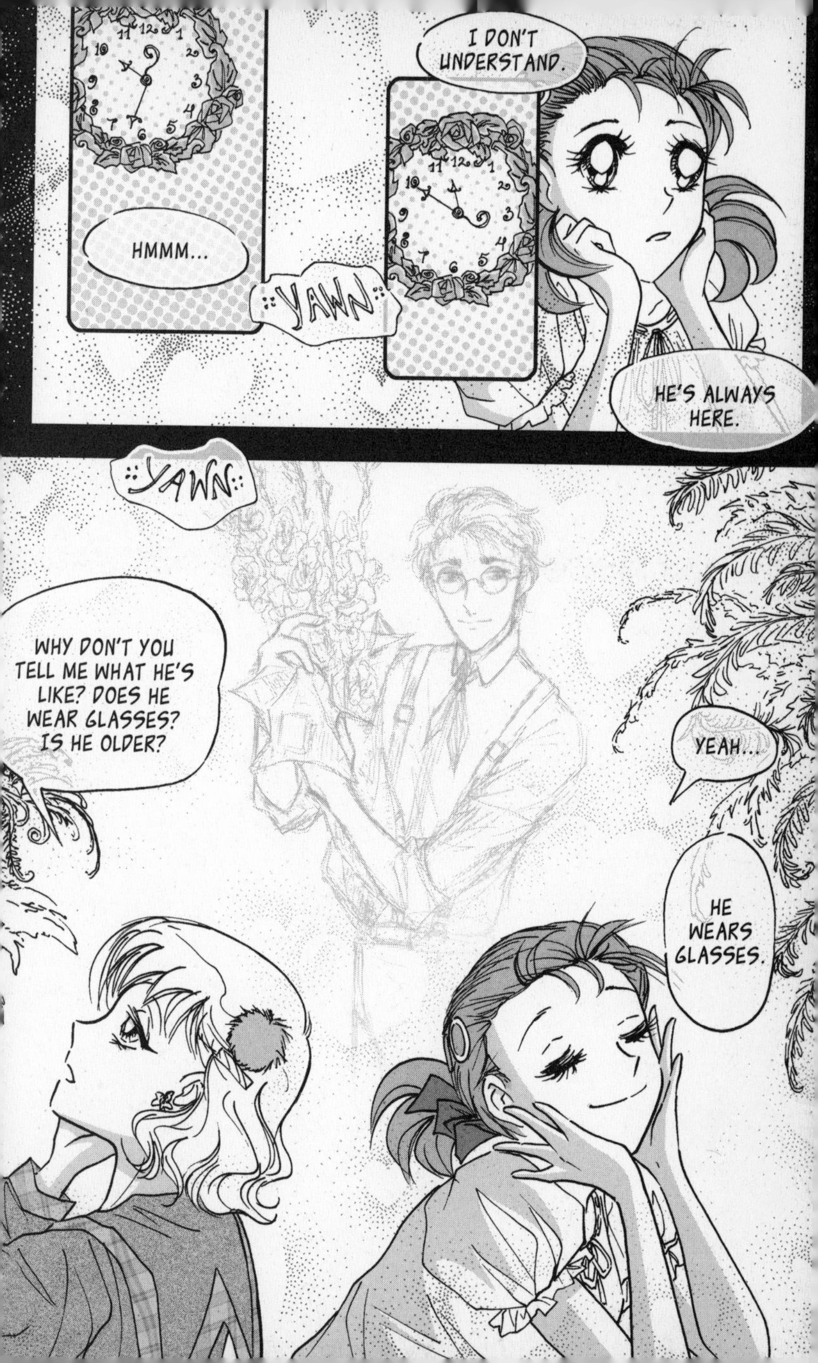
I DON'T UNDERSTAND.
HMMM...
::YAWN::
HE'S ALWAYS HERE.
::YAWN::
WHY DON'T YOU TELL ME WHAT HE'S LIKE? DOES HE WEAR GLASSES? IS HE OLDER?
YEAH...
HE WEARS GLASSES.

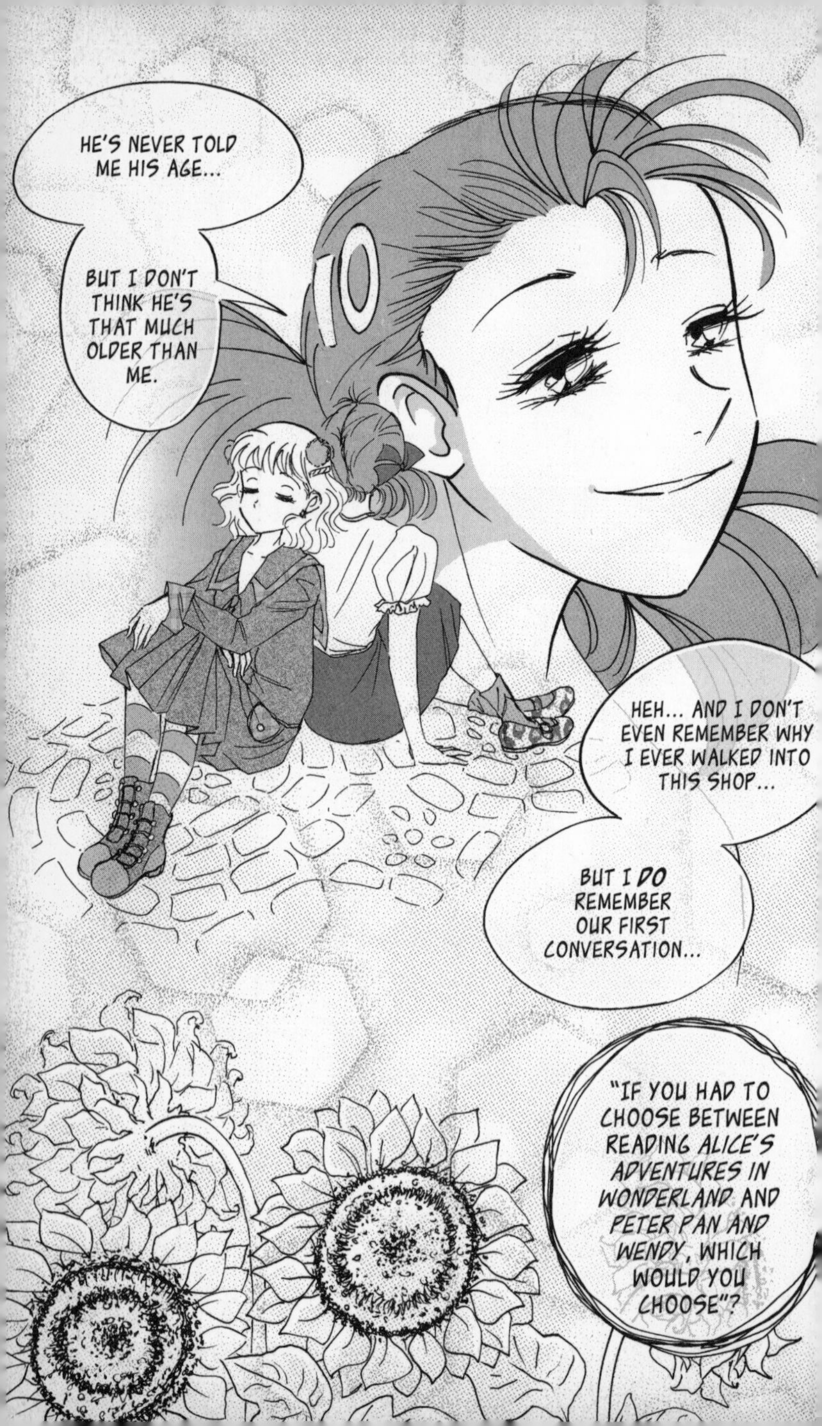
HE'S NEVER TOLD ME HIS AGE...
BUT I DON'T THINK HE'S THAT MUCH OLDER THAN ME.
HEH... AND I DON'T EVEN REMEMBER WHY I EVER WALKED INTO THIS SHOP...
BUT I *DO* REMEMBER OUR FIRST CONVERSATION...
"IF YOU HAD TO CHOOSE BETWEEN READING *ALICE'S ADVENTURES IN WONDERLAND* AND *PETER PAN AND WENDY*, WHICH WOULD YOU CHOOSE"?

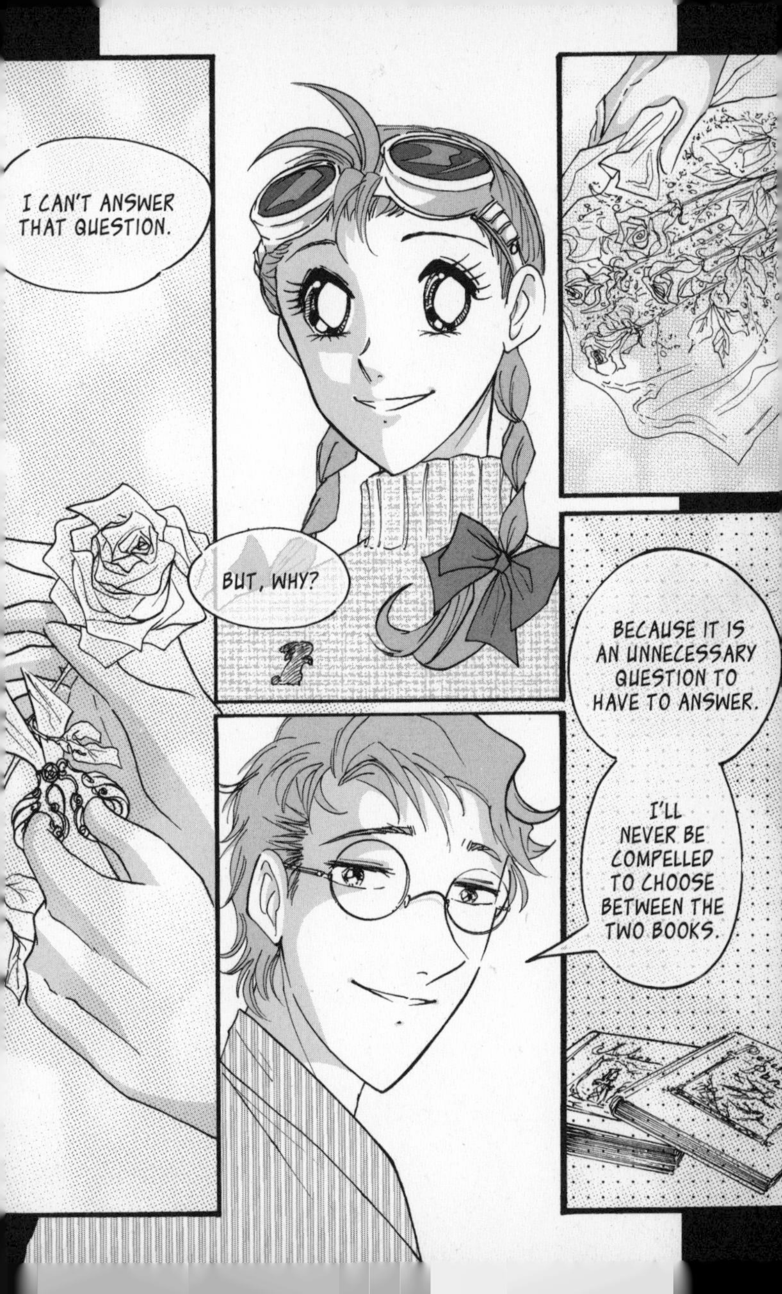
I CAN'T ANSWER THAT QUESTION.
BUT, WHY?
BECAUSE IT IS AN UNNECESSARY QUESTION TO HAVE TO ANSWER.
I'LL NEVER BE COMPELLED TO CHOOSE BETWEEN THE TWO BOOKS.

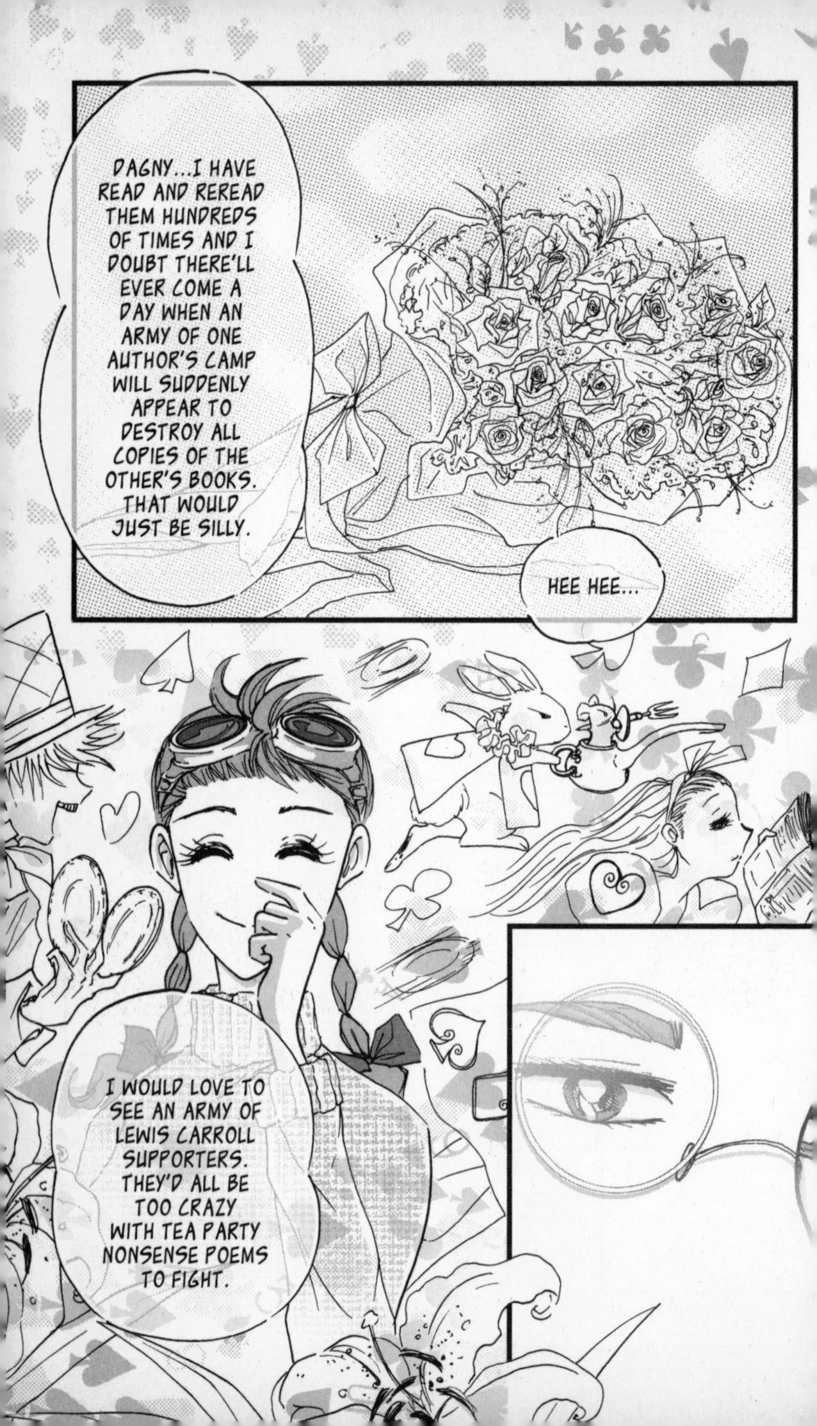
DAGNY...I HAVE READ AND REREAD THEM HUNDREDS OF TIMES AND I DOUBT THERE'LL EVER COME A DAY WHEN AN ARMY OF ONE AUTHOR'S CAMP WILL SUDDENLY APPEAR TO DESTROY ALL COPIES OF THE OTHER'S BOOKS. THAT WOULD JUST BE SILLY.
HEE HEE...
I WOULD LOVE TO SEE AN ARMY OF LEWIS CARROLL SUPPORTERS. THEY'D ALL BE TOO CRAZY WITH TEA PARTY NONSENSE POEMS TO FIGHT.

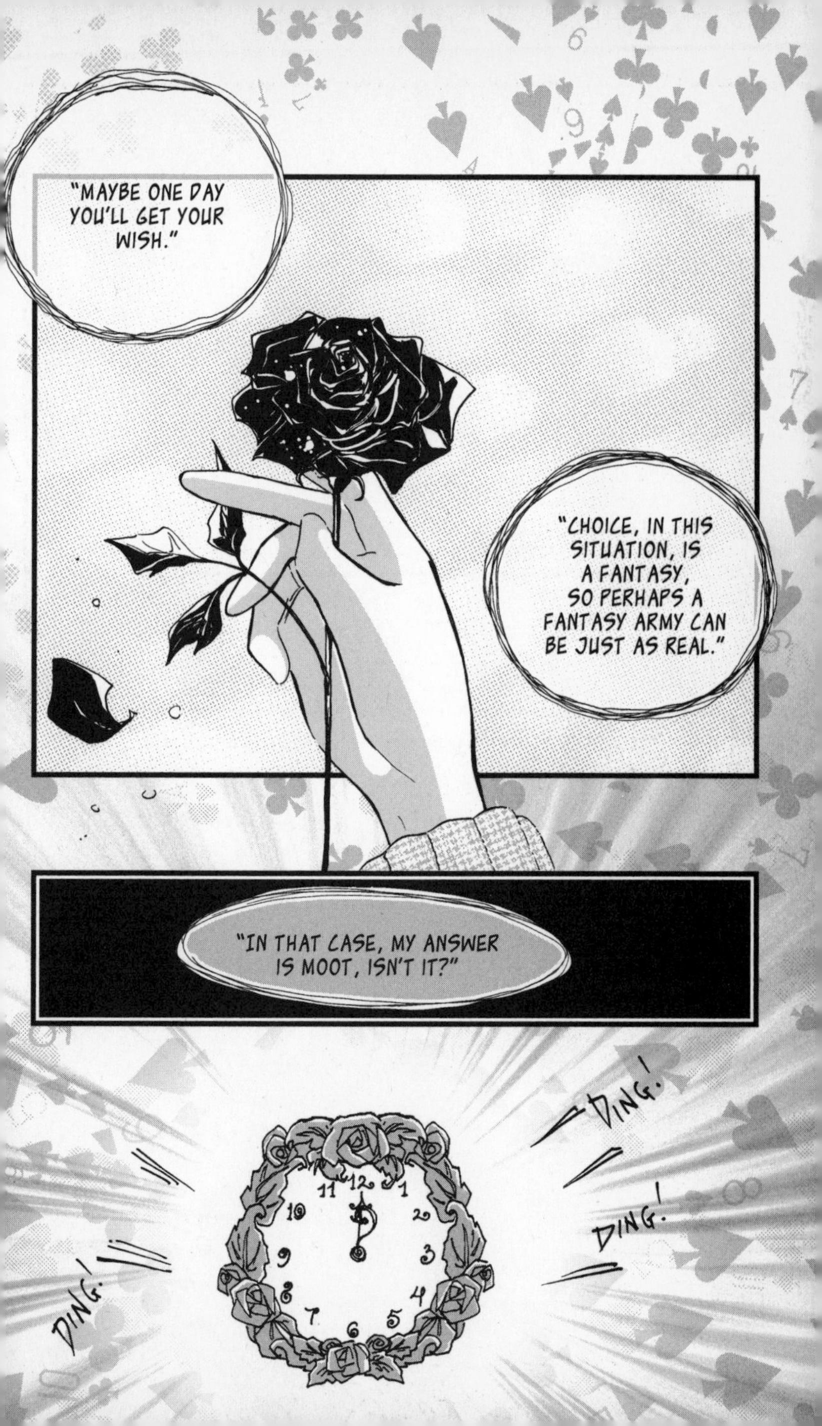
"MAYBE ONE DAY YOU'LL GET YOUR WISH."
"CHOICE, IN THIS SITUATION, IS A FANTASY, SO PERHAPS A FANTASY ARMY CAN BE JUST AS REAL."
"IN THAT CASE, MY ANSWER IS MOOT, ISN'T IT?"
DING!
DING!
DING!

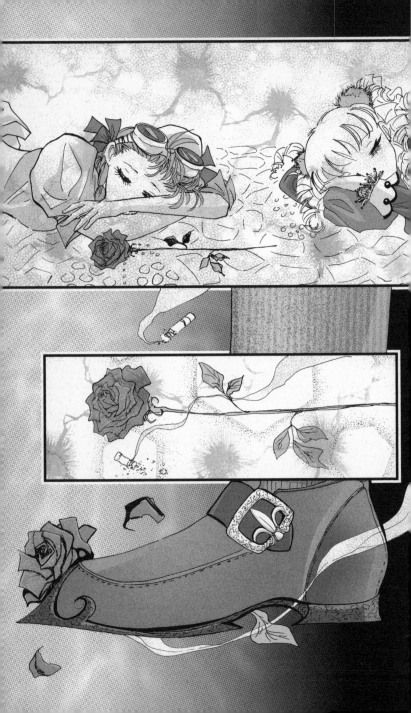

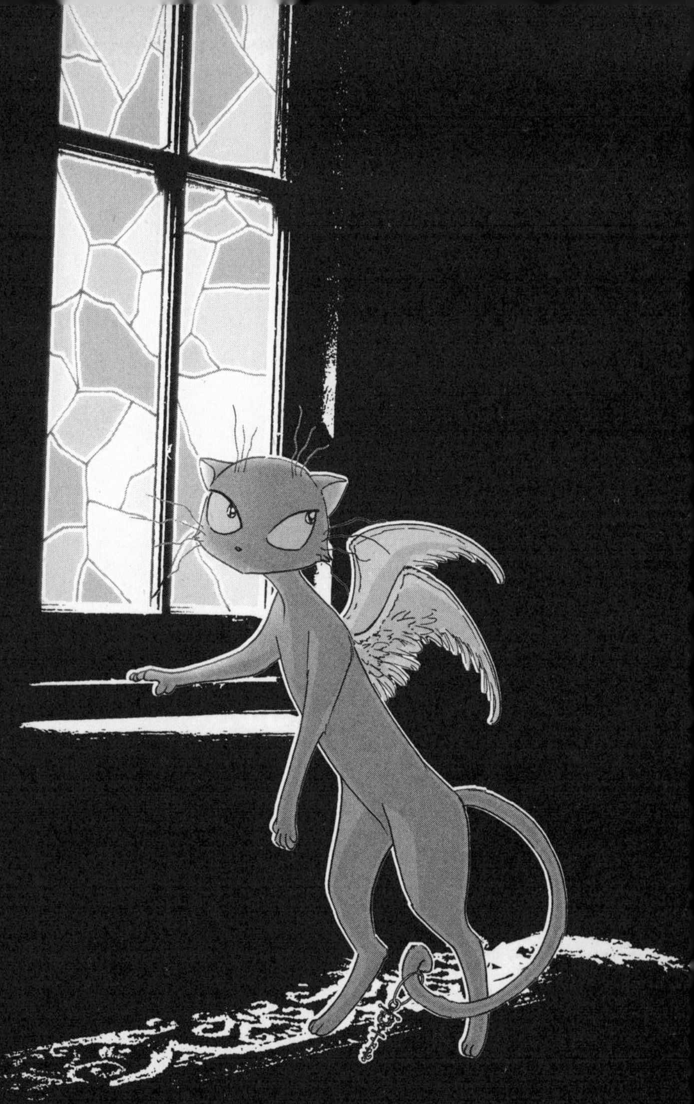

# CHAPTER FOUR:
## THIS IS ENIGMATIC

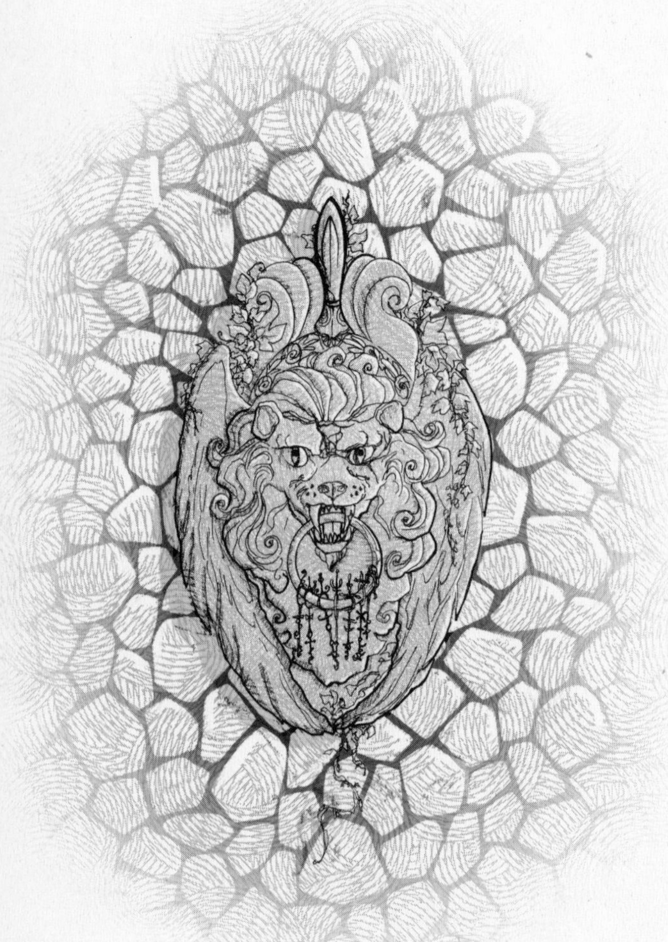

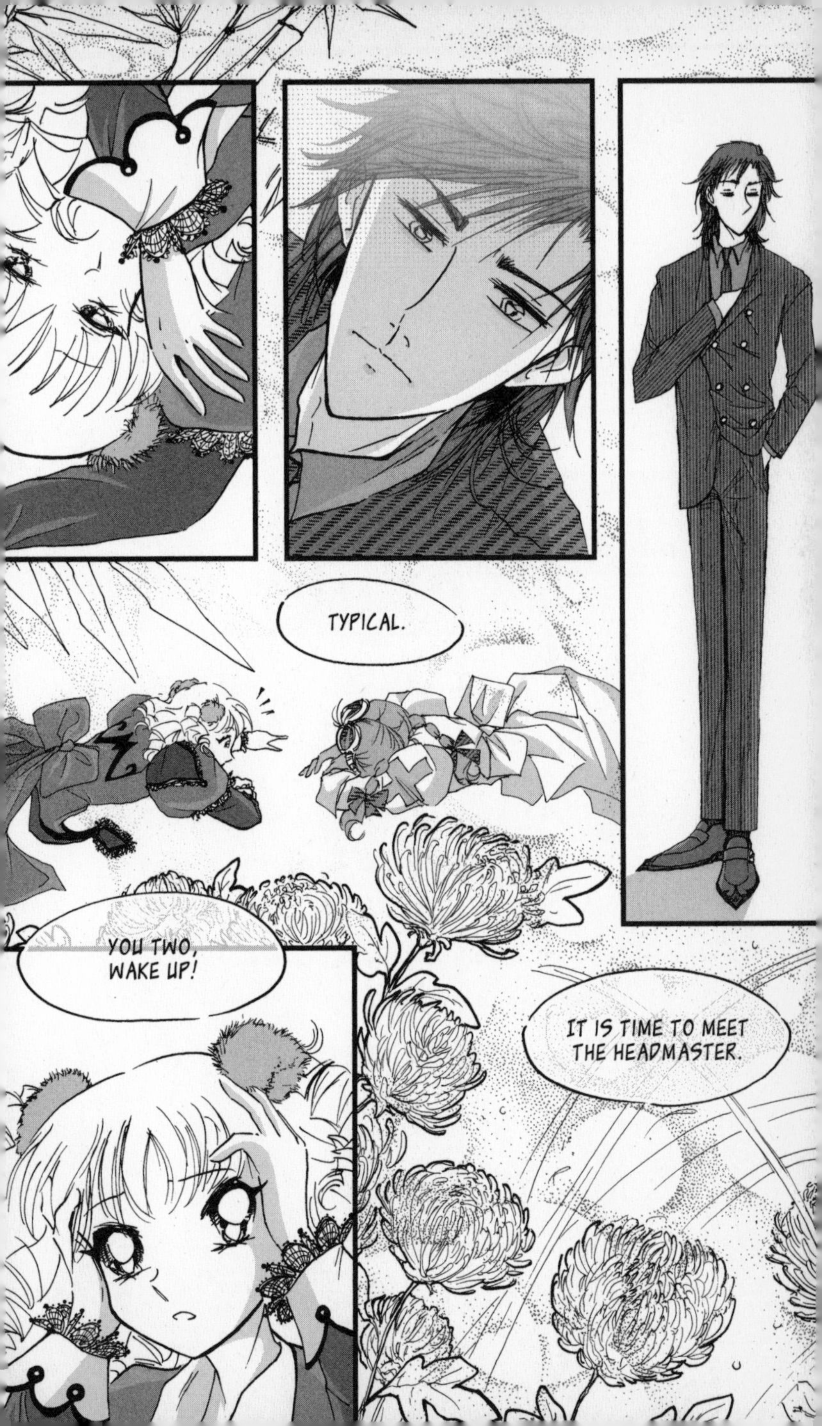
TYPICAL.
YOU TWO, WAKE UP!
IT IS TIME TO MEET THE HEADMASTER.

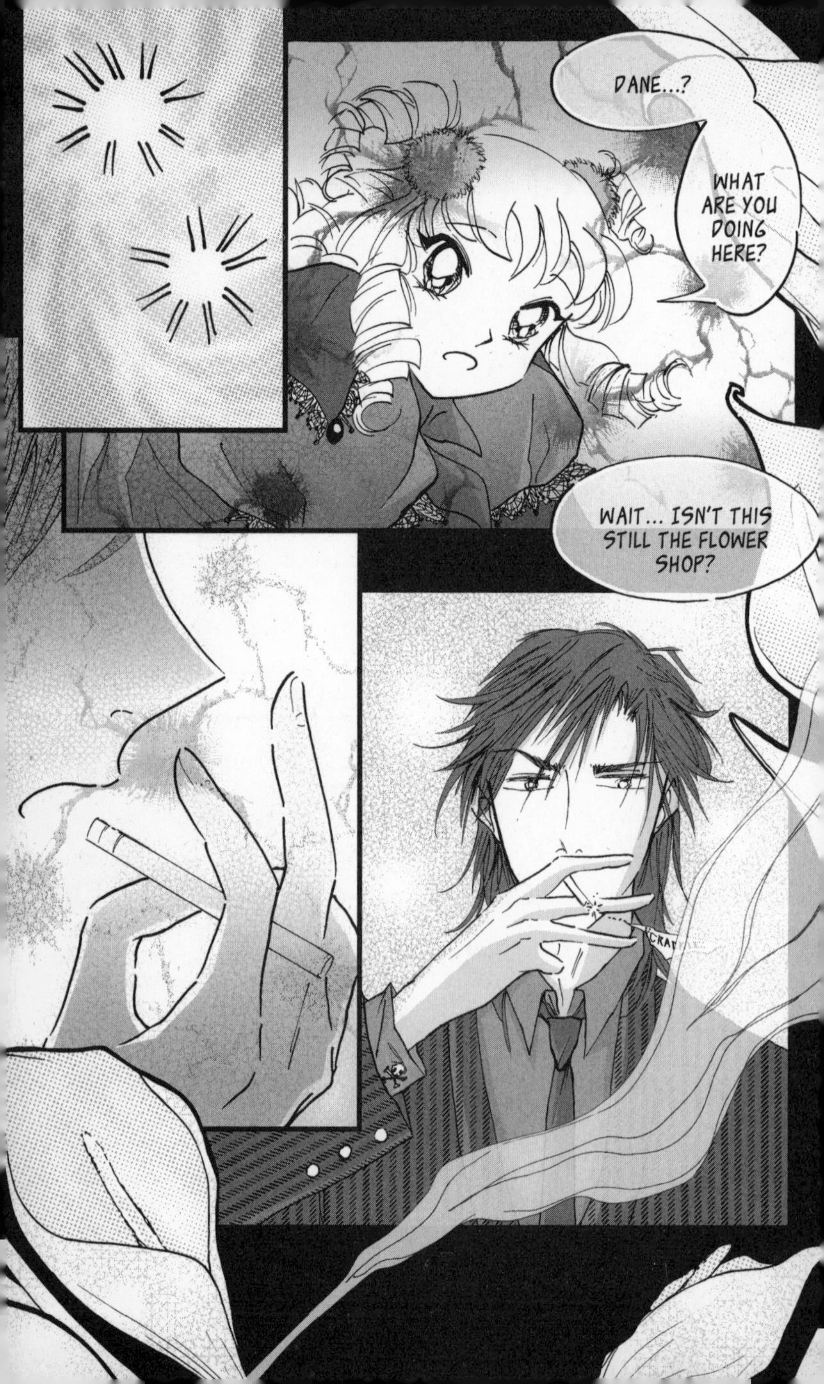
DANE...?
WHAT ARE YOU DOING HERE?
WAIT... ISN'T THIS STILL THE FLOWER SHOP?

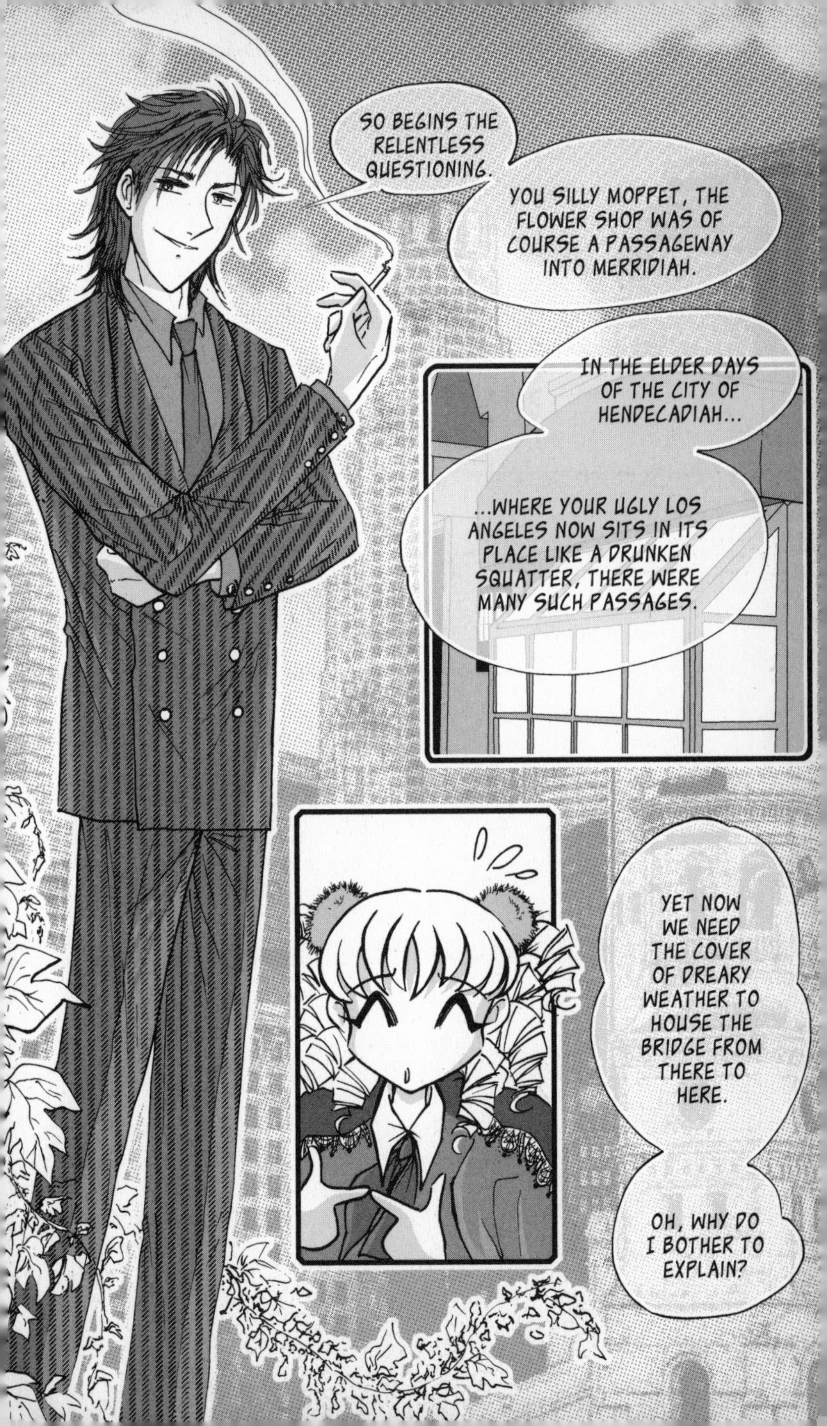
SO BEGINS THE RELENTLESS QUESTIONING.
YOU SILLY MOPPET, THE FLOWER SHOP WAS OF COURSE A PASSAGEWAY INTO MERRIDIAH.
IN THE ELDER DAYS OF THE CITY OF HENDECADIAH...
...WHERE YOUR UGLY LOS ANGELES NOW SITS IN ITS PLACE LIKE A DRUNKEN SQUATTER, THERE WERE MANY SUCH PASSAGES.
YET NOW WE NEED THE COVER OF DREARY WEATHER TO HOUSE THE BRIDGE FROM THERE TO HERE.
OH, WHY DO I BOTHER TO EXPLAIN?

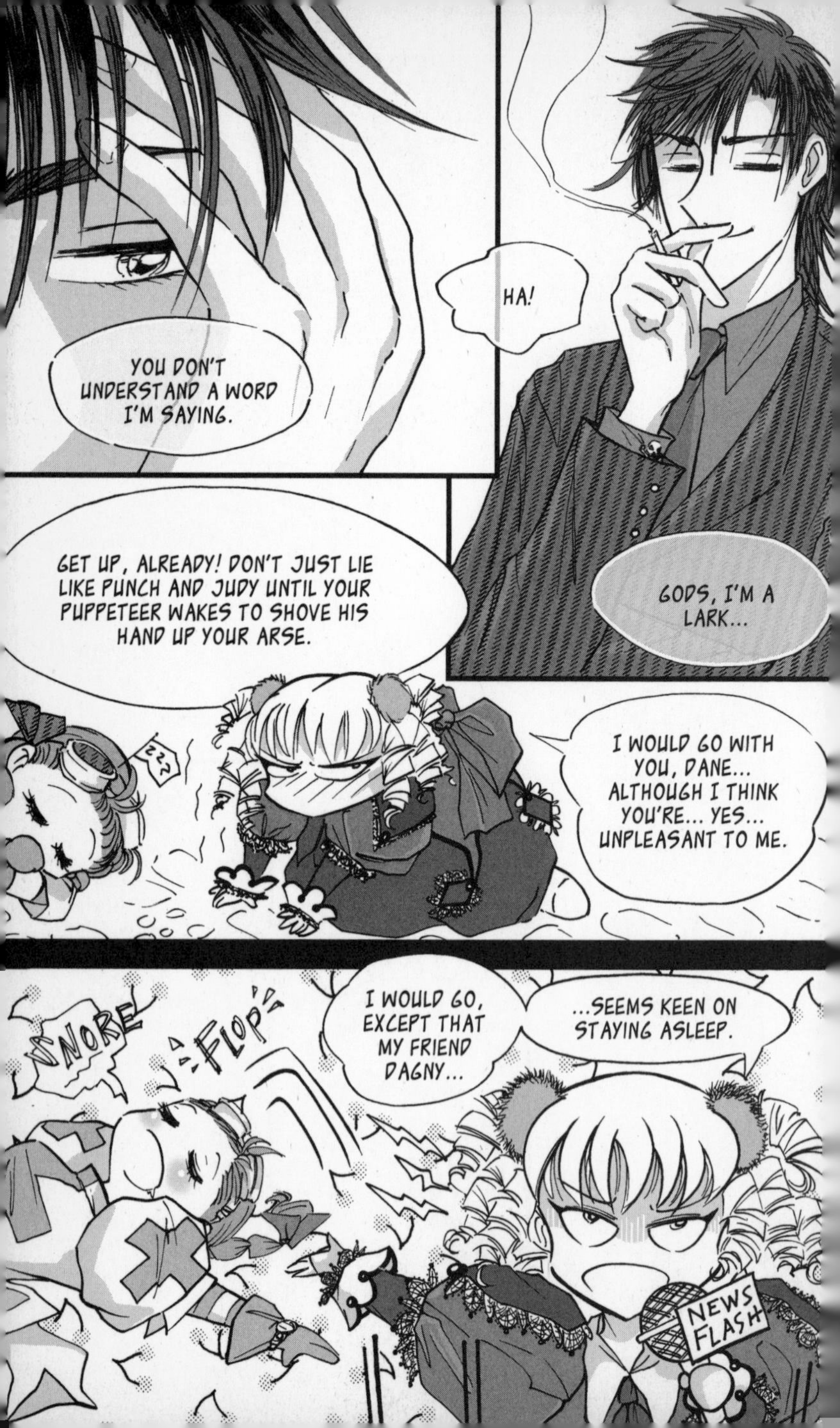
YOU DON'T UNDERSTAND A WORD I'M SAYING.
HA!
GODS, I'M A LARK...
GET UP, ALREADY! DON'T JUST LIE LIKE PUNCH AND JUDY UNTIL YOUR PUPPETEER WAKES TO SHOVE HIS HAND UP YOUR ARSE.
I WOULD GO WITH YOU, DANE... ALTHOUGH I THINK YOU'RE... YES... UNPLEASANT TO ME.
SNORE
FLOP
I WOULD GO, EXCEPT THAT MY FRIEND DAGNY...
...SEEMS KEEN ON STAYING ASLEEP.
NEWS FLASH

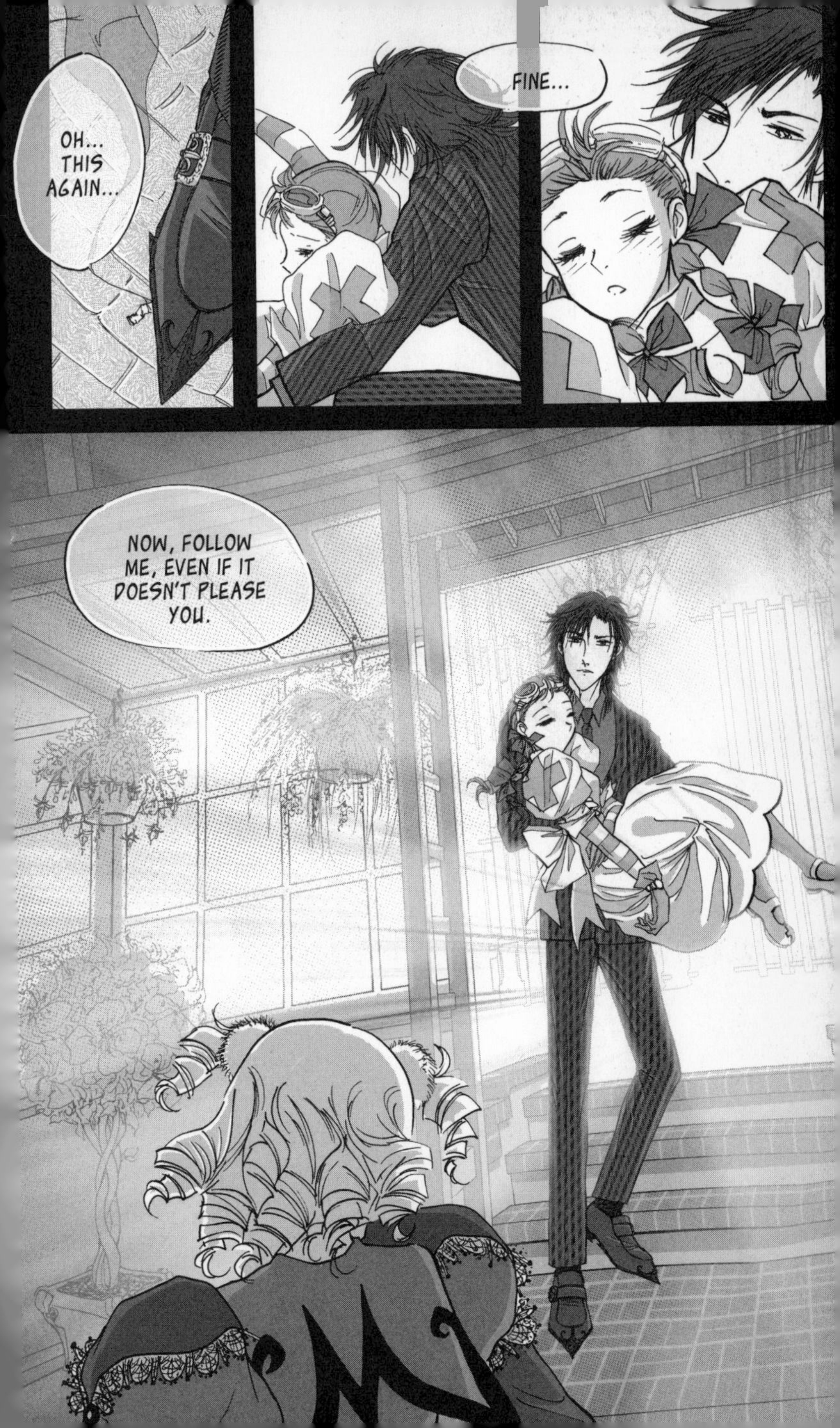
OH... THIS AGAIN...
FINE...
NOW, FOLLOW ME, EVEN IF IT DOESN'T PLEASE YOU.

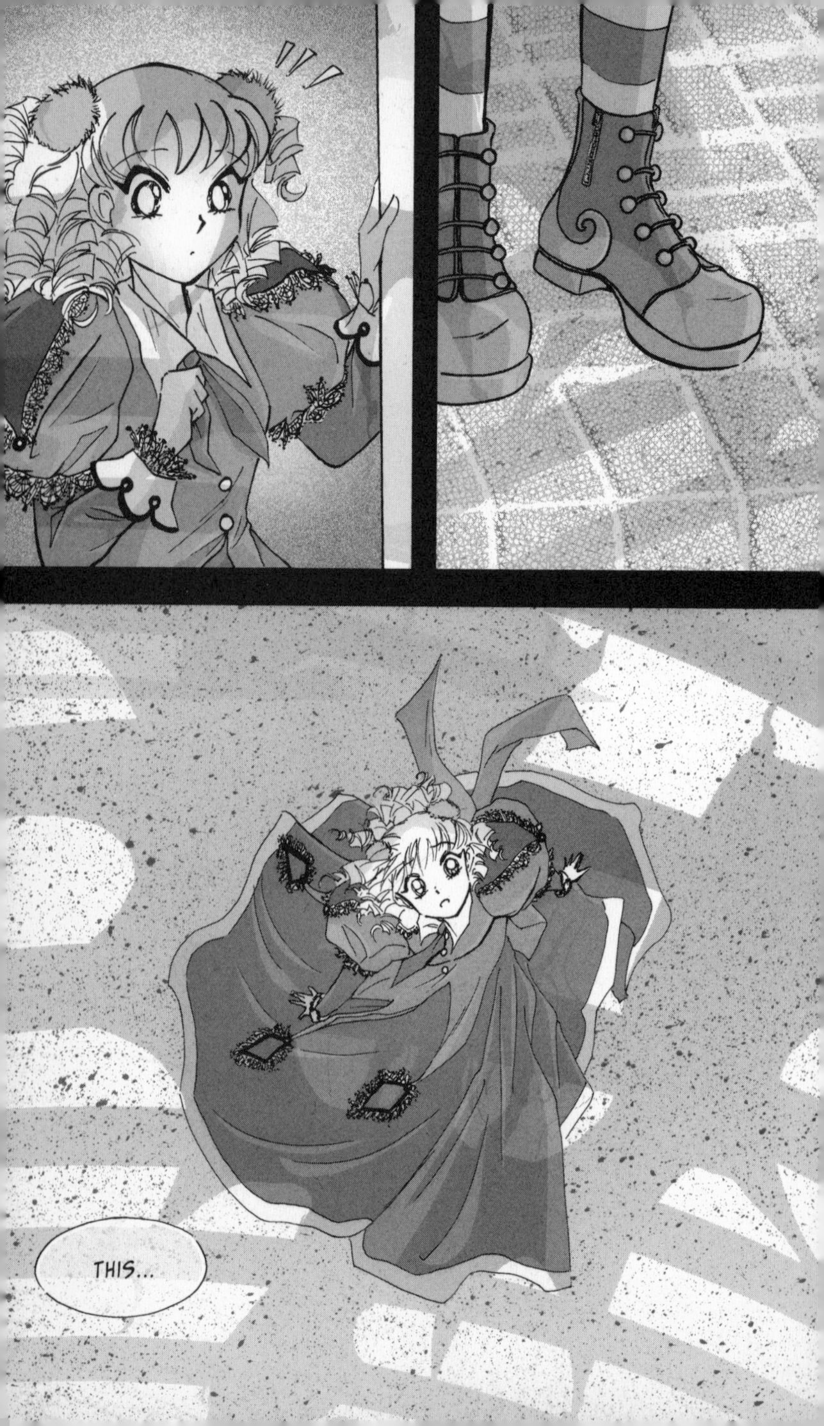
THIS...

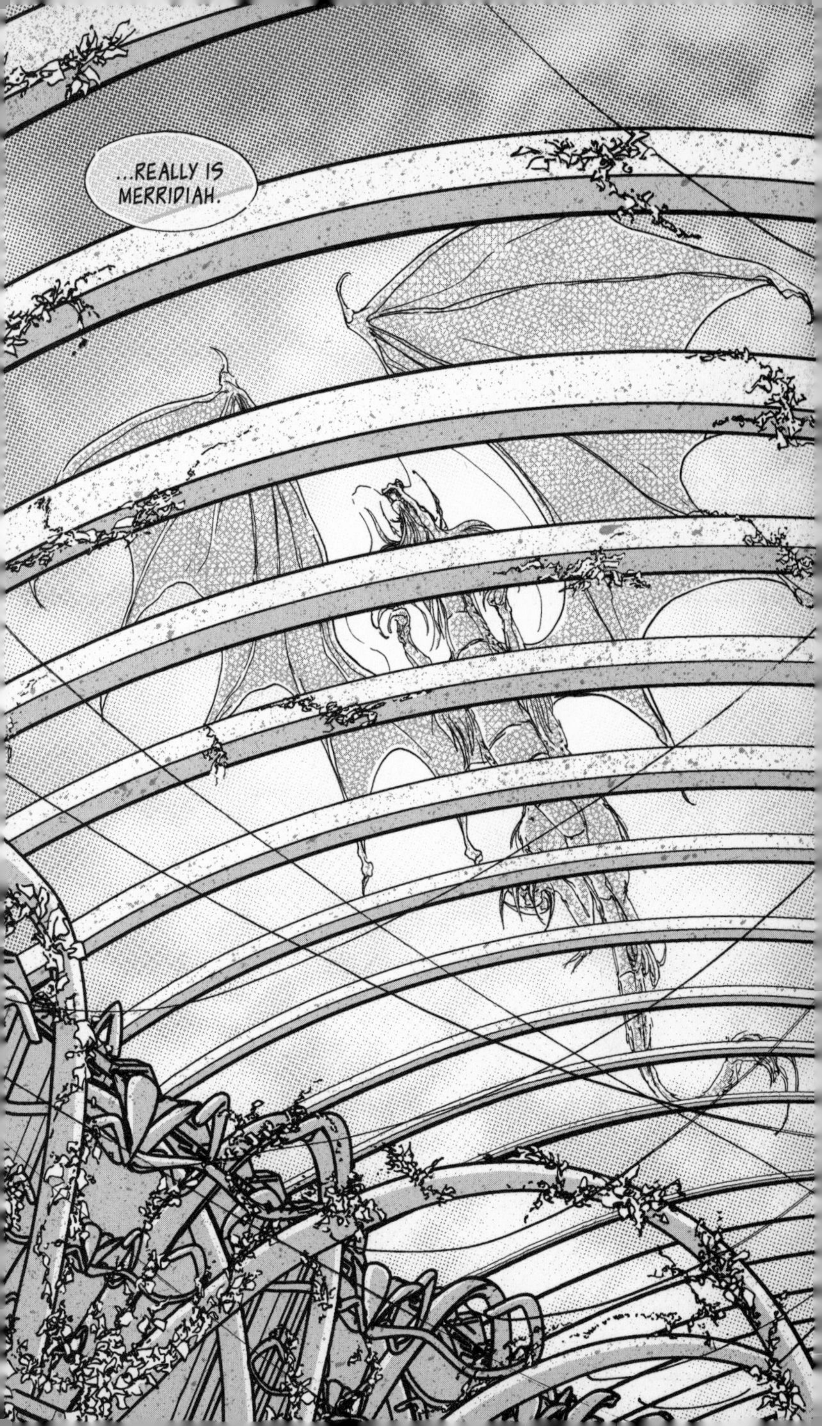
...REALLY IS MERRIDIAH.

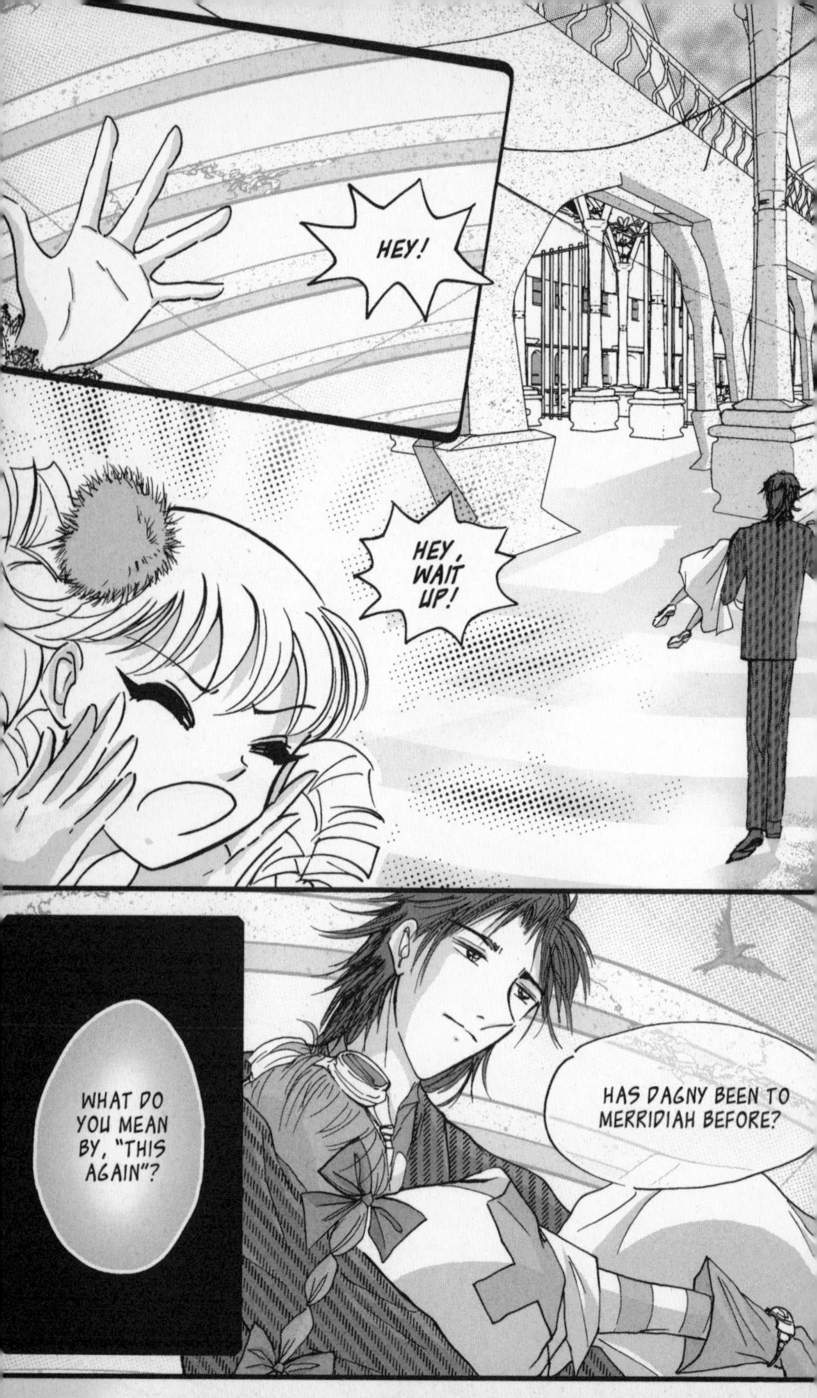
HEY!
HEY, WAIT UP!
HAS DAGNY BEEN TO MERRIDIAH BEFORE?
WHAT DO YOU MEAN BY, "THIS AGAIN"?

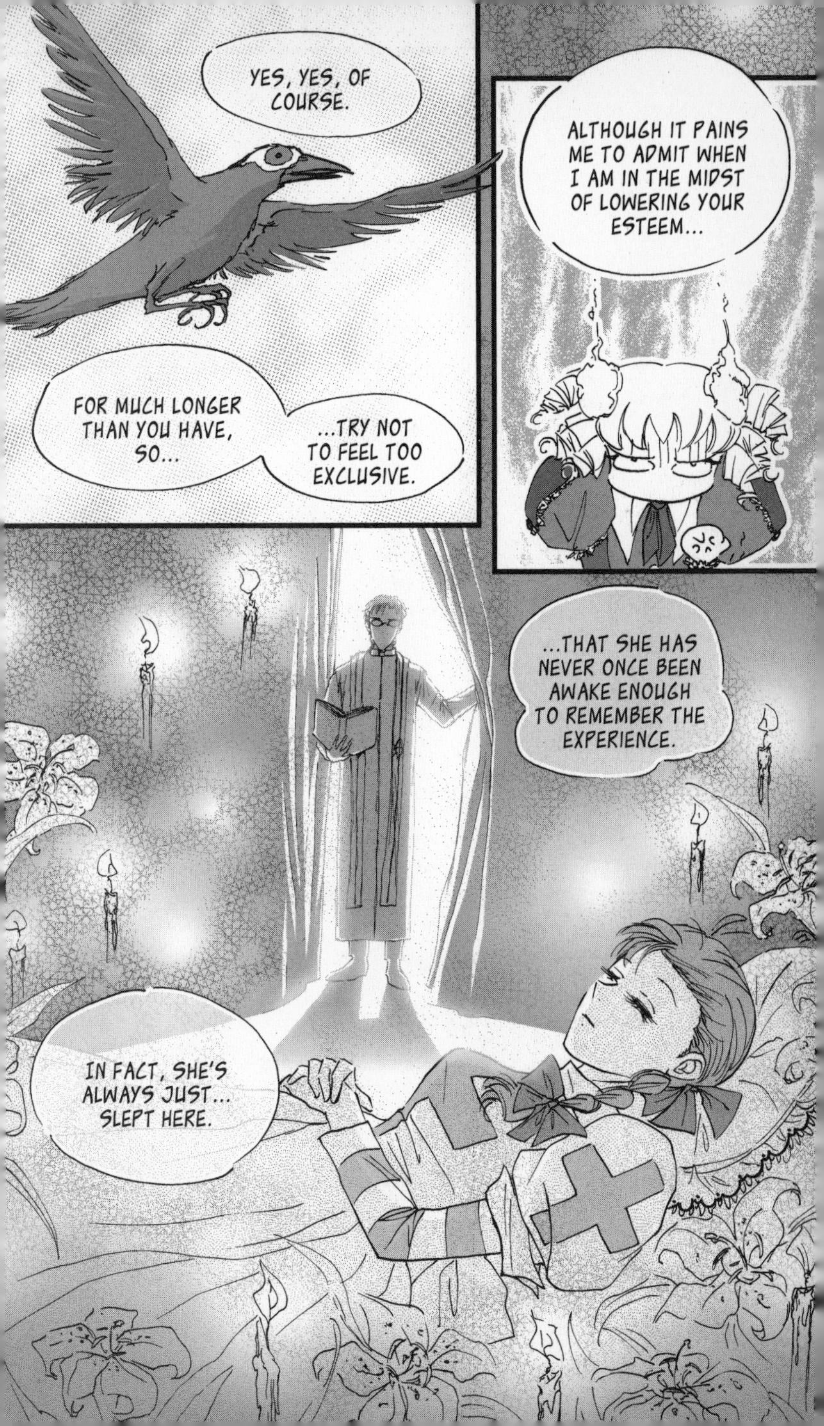
YES, YES, OF COURSE.
FOR MUCH LONGER THAN YOU HAVE, SO...
...TRY NOT TO FEEL TOO EXCLUSIVE.
ALTHOUGH IT PAINS ME TO ADMIT WHEN I AM IN THE MIDST OF LOWERING YOUR ESTEEM...
...THAT SHE HAS NEVER ONCE BEEN AWAKE ENOUGH TO REMEMBER THE EXPERIENCE.
IN FACT, SHE'S ALWAYS JUST... SLEPT HERE.

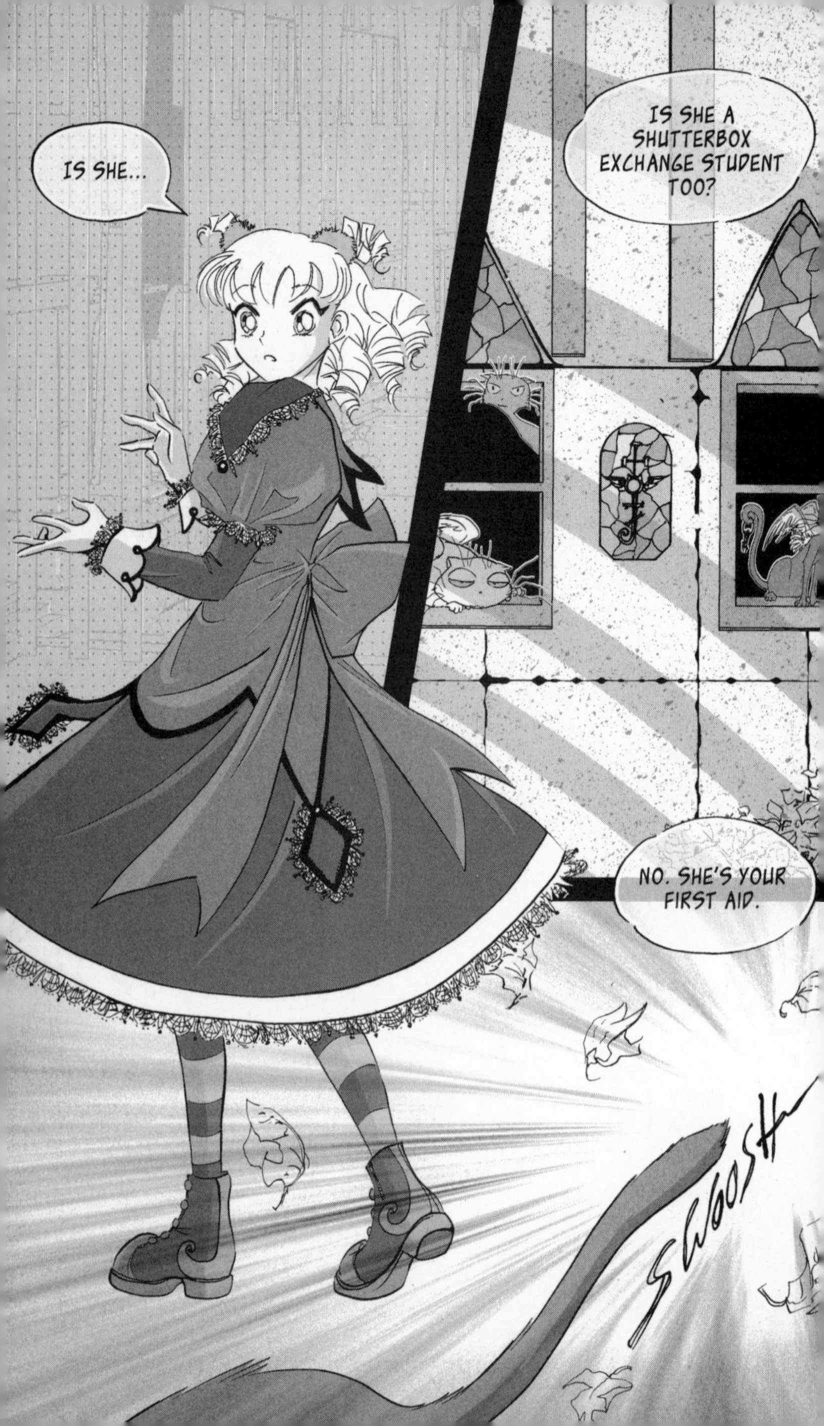
IS SHE...
IS SHE A SHUTTERBOX EXCHANGE STUDENT TOO?
NO. SHE'S YOUR FIRST AID.
SWOOSH

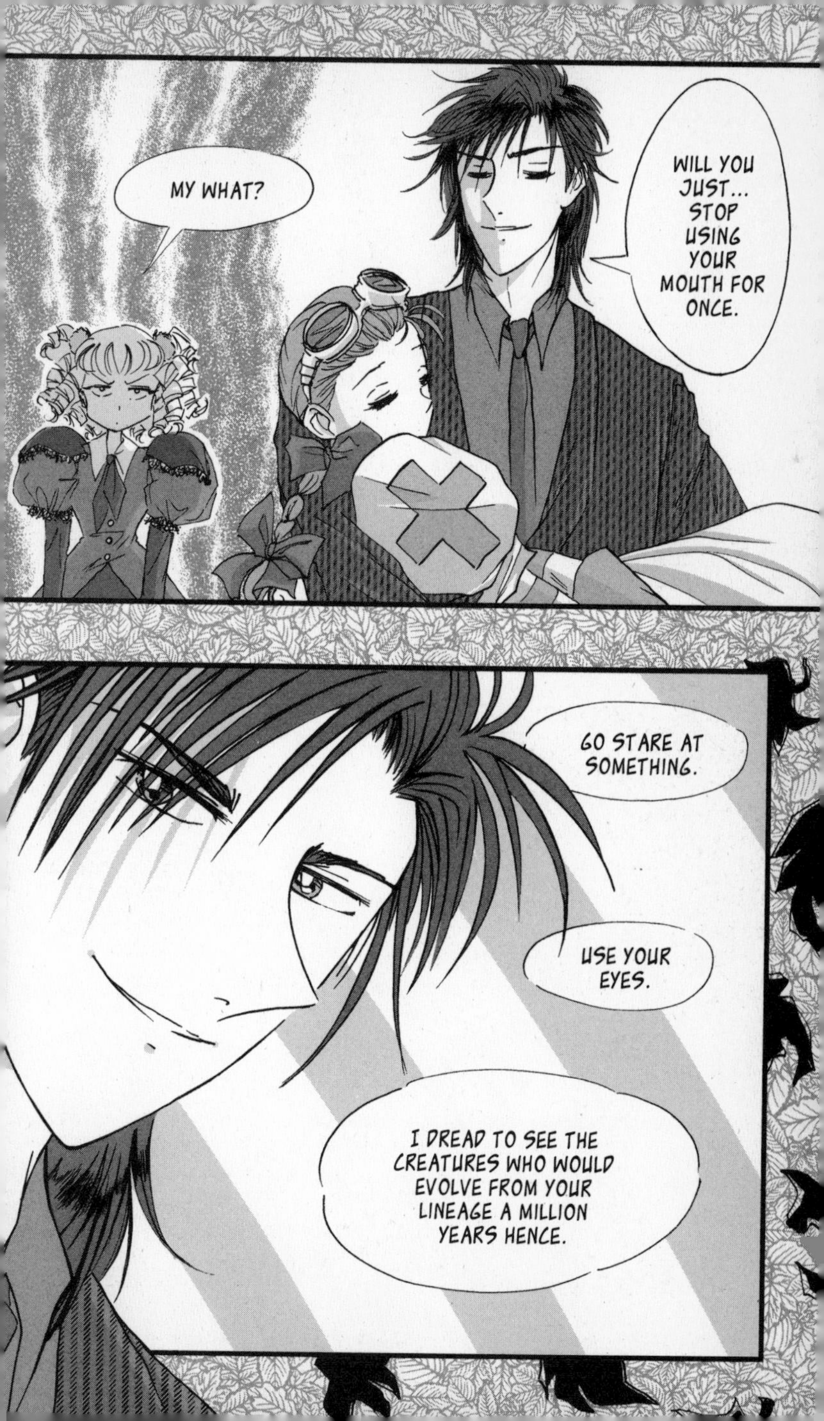
WILL YOU JUST... STOP USING YOUR MOUTH FOR ONCE.
MY WHAT?
GO STARE AT SOMETHING.
USE YOUR EYES.
I DREAD TO SEE THE CREATURES WHO WOULD EVOLVE FROM YOUR LINEAGE A MILLION YEARS HENCE.

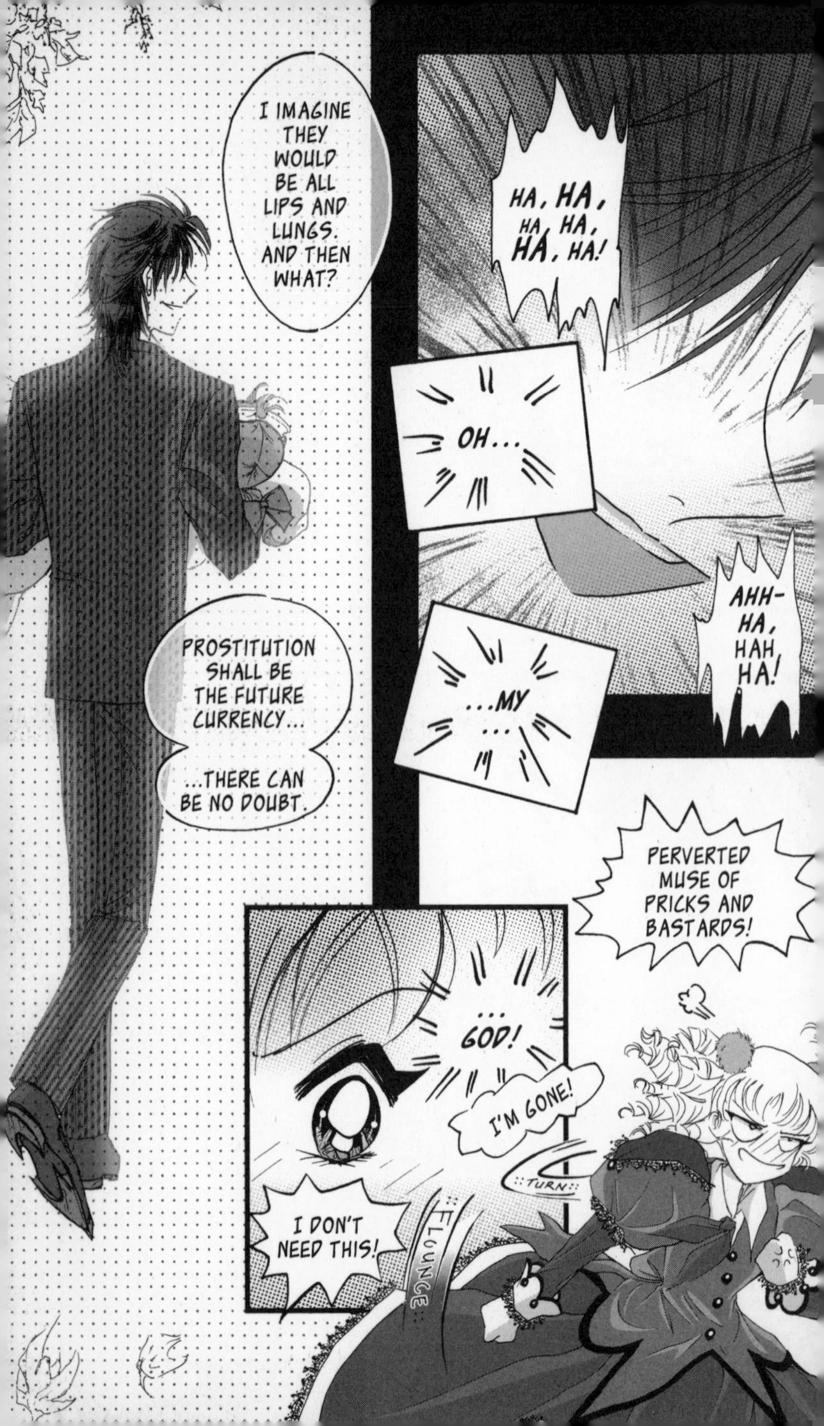
I IMAGINE THEY WOULD BE ALL LIPS AND LUNGS. AND THEN WHAT?
PROSTITUTION SHALL BE THE FUTURE CURRENCY...
...THERE CAN BE NO DOUBT.
HA, HA, HA, HA, HA, HA!
OH...
AHH-HA, HAH, HA!
...MY...
...GOD!
I'M GONE!
I DON'T NEED THIS!
FLOUNCE
TURN
PERVERTED MUSE OF PRICKS AND BASTARDS!

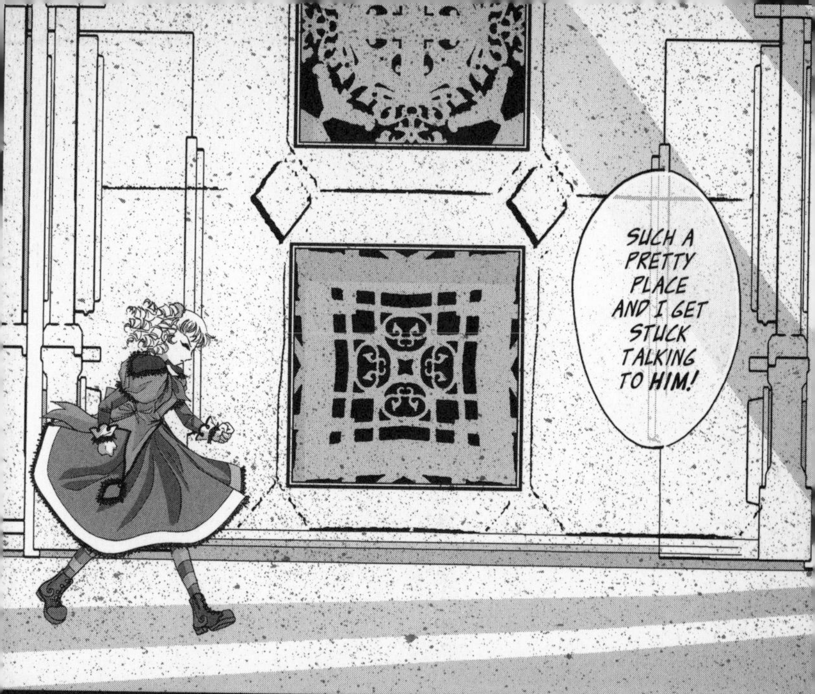
SUCH A PRETTY PLACE AND I GET STUCK TALKING TO HIM!
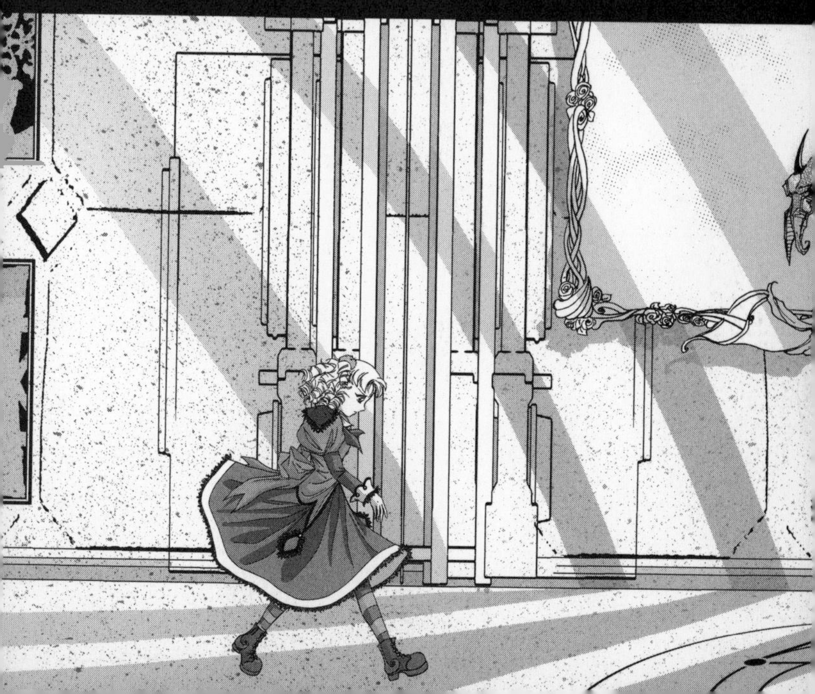

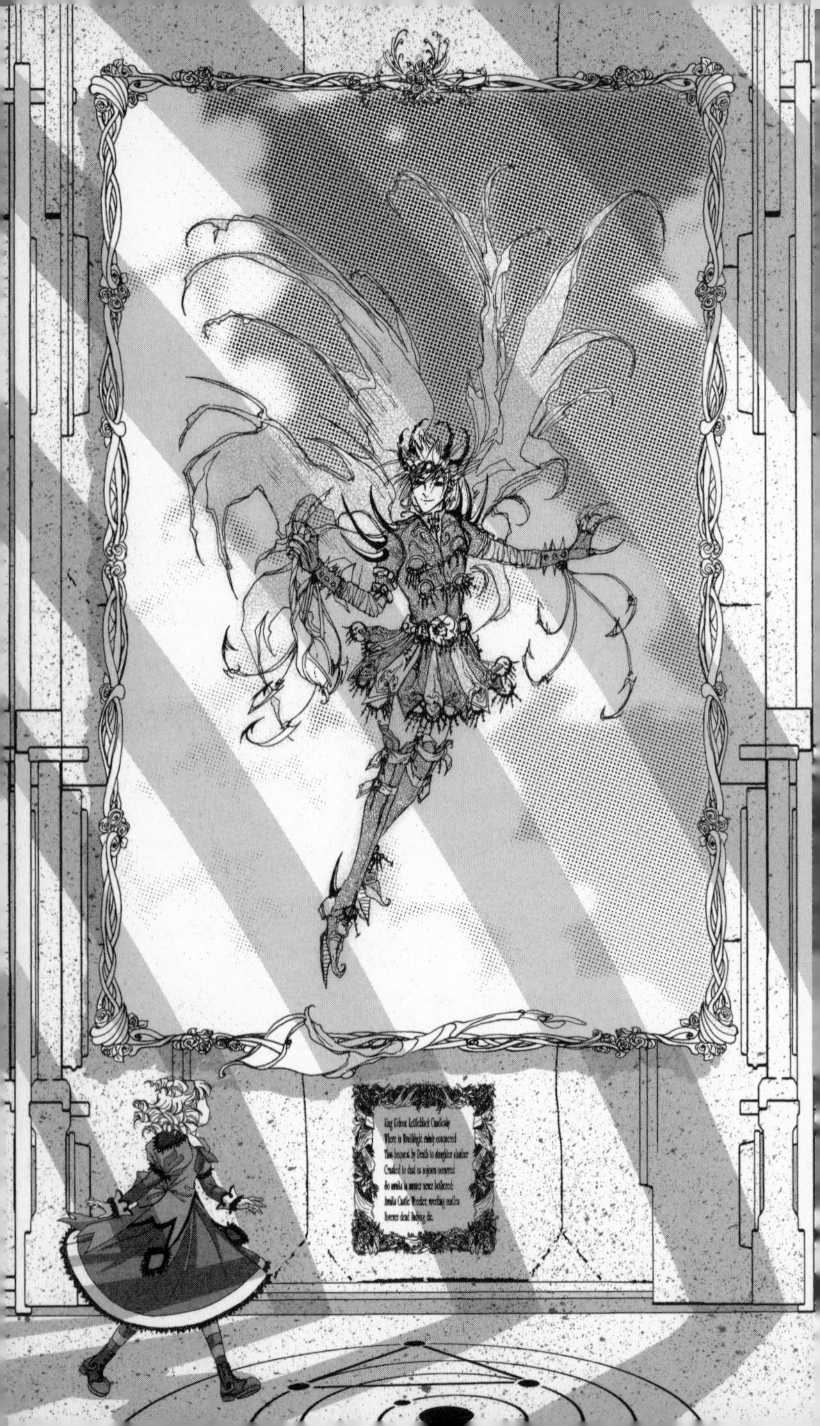

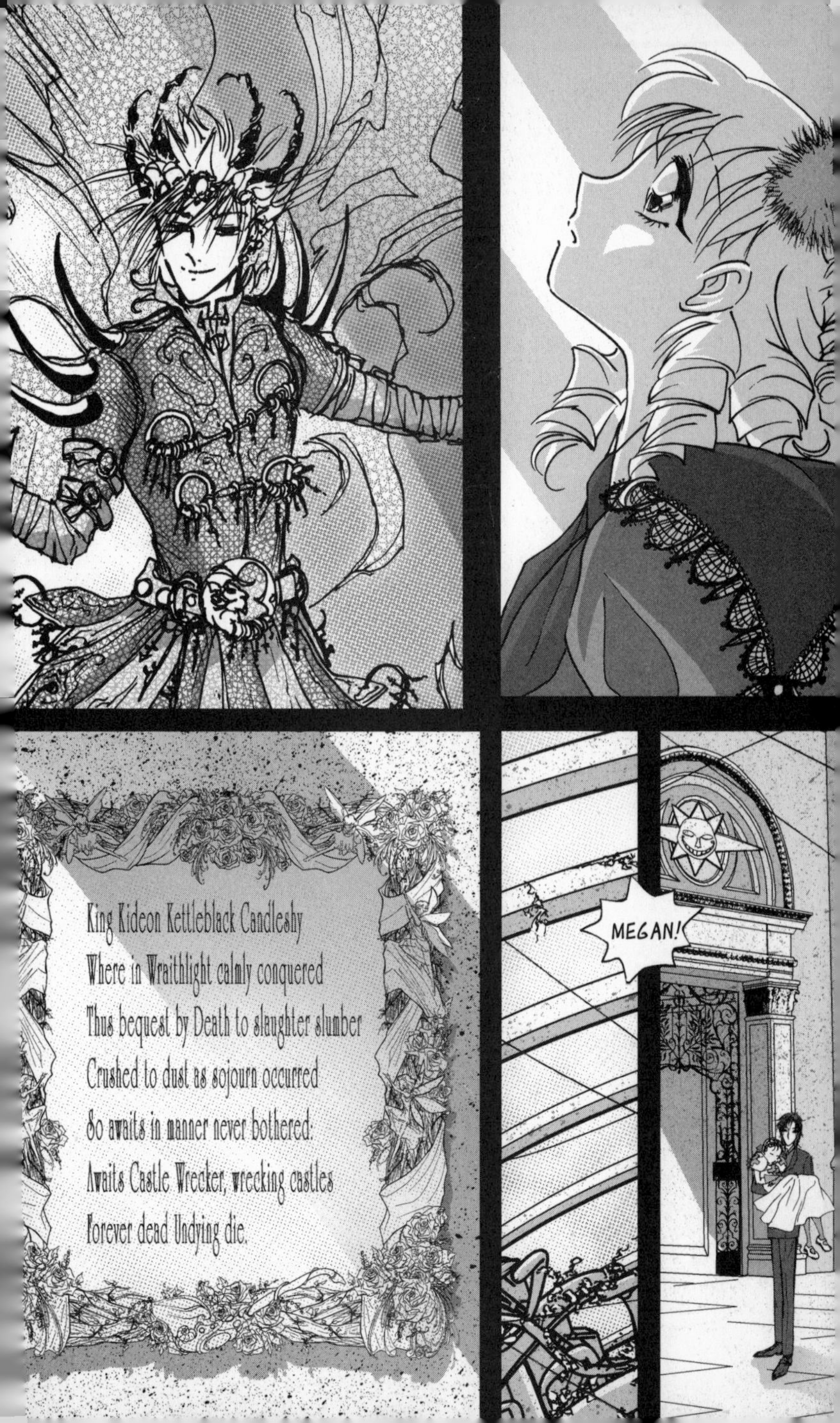
MEGAN!
King Kideon Kettleblack Candlesby
Where in Wraithlight calmly conquered
Thus bequest by Death to slaughter slumber
Crushed to dust as sojourn occurred
So awaits in manner never bothered:
Awaits Castle Wrecker, wrecking castles
Forever dead Undying die.

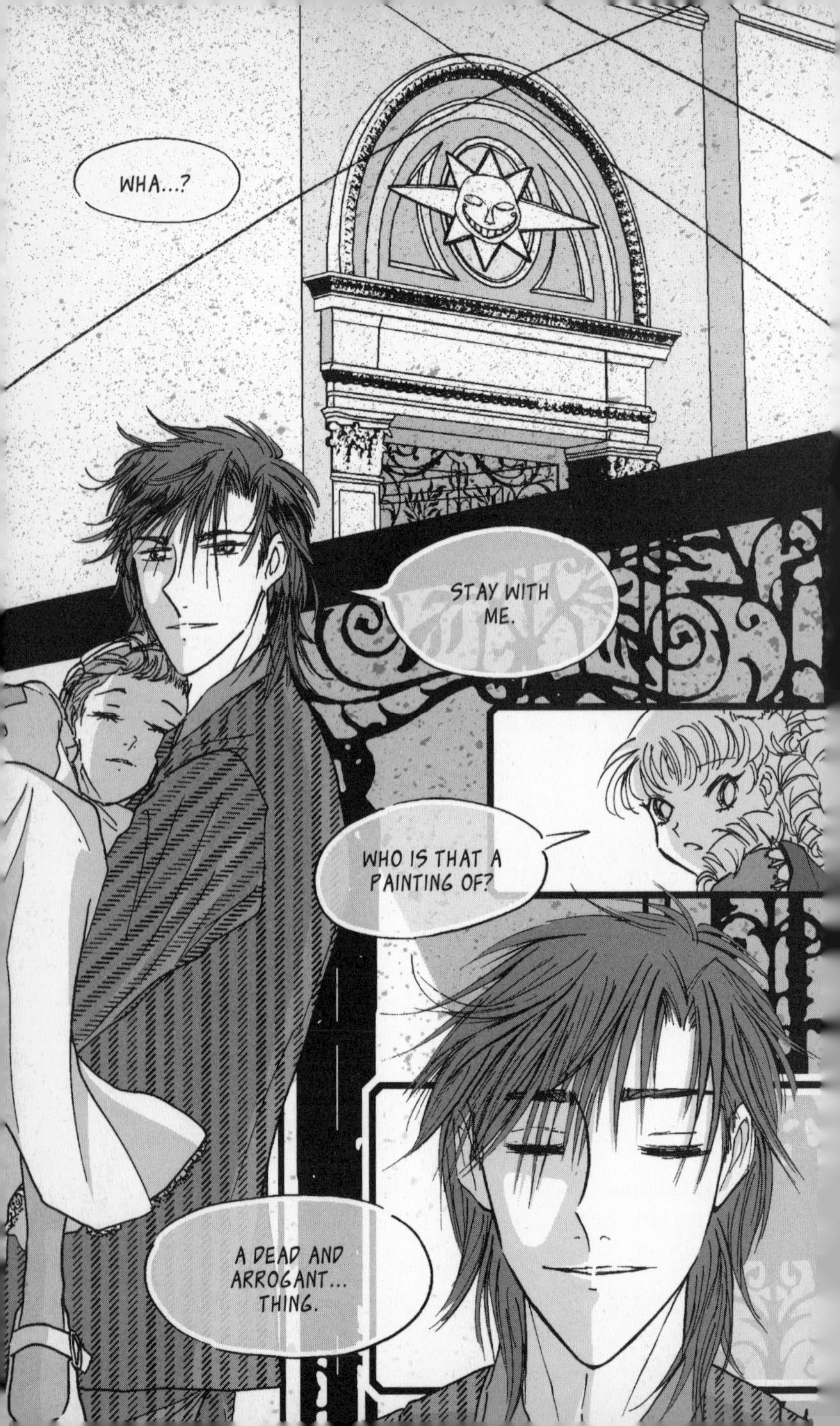
WHA...?
STAY WITH ME.
WHO IS THAT A PAINTING OF?
A DEAD AND ARROGANT... THING.

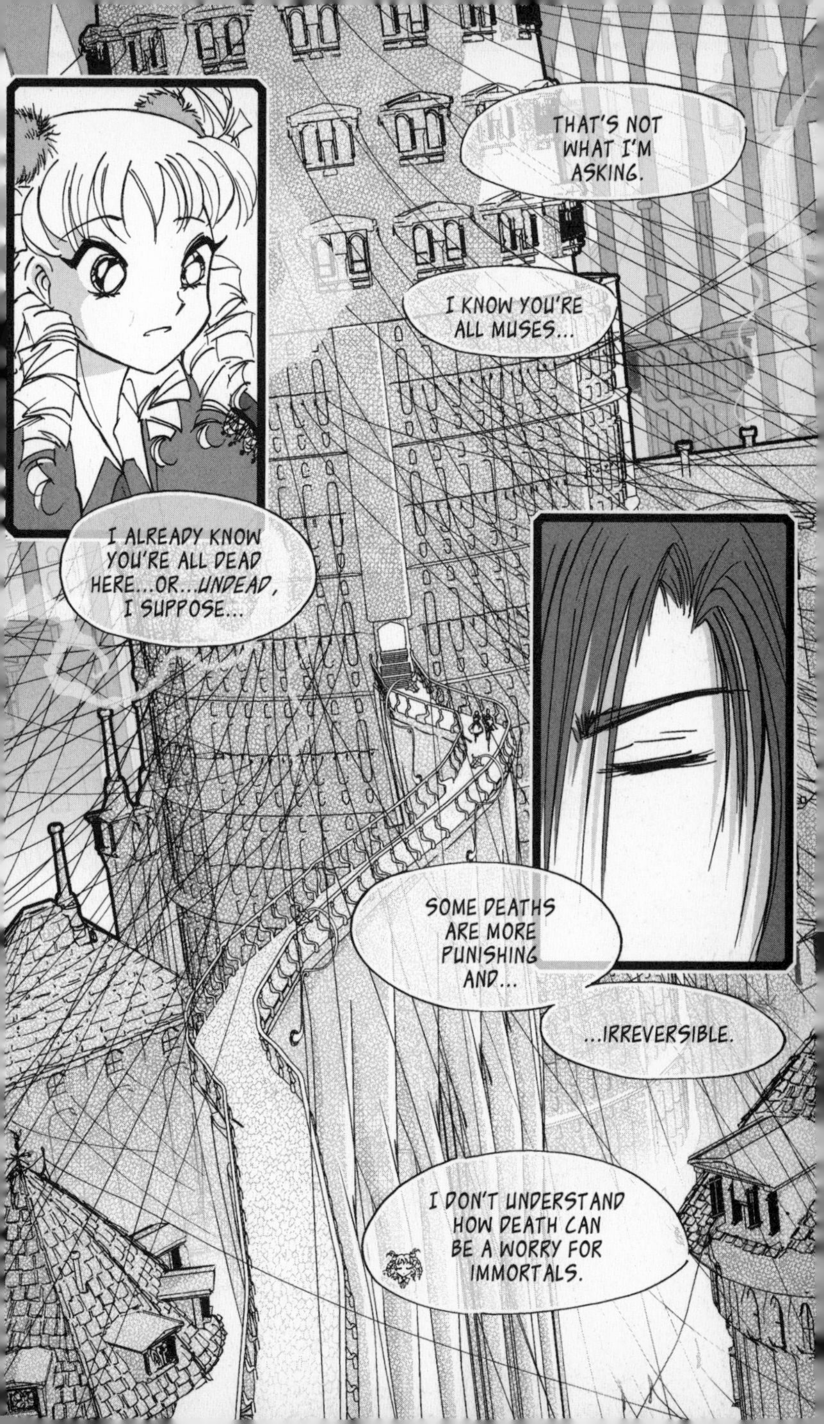
THAT'S NOT WHAT I'M ASKING.
I KNOW YOU'RE ALL MUSES...
I ALREADY KNOW YOU'RE ALL DEAD HERE...OR...UNDEAD, I SUPPOSE...
SOME DEATHS ARE MORE PUNISHING AND...
...IRREVERSIBLE.
I DON'T UNDERSTAND HOW DEATH CAN BE A WORRY FOR IMMORTALS.

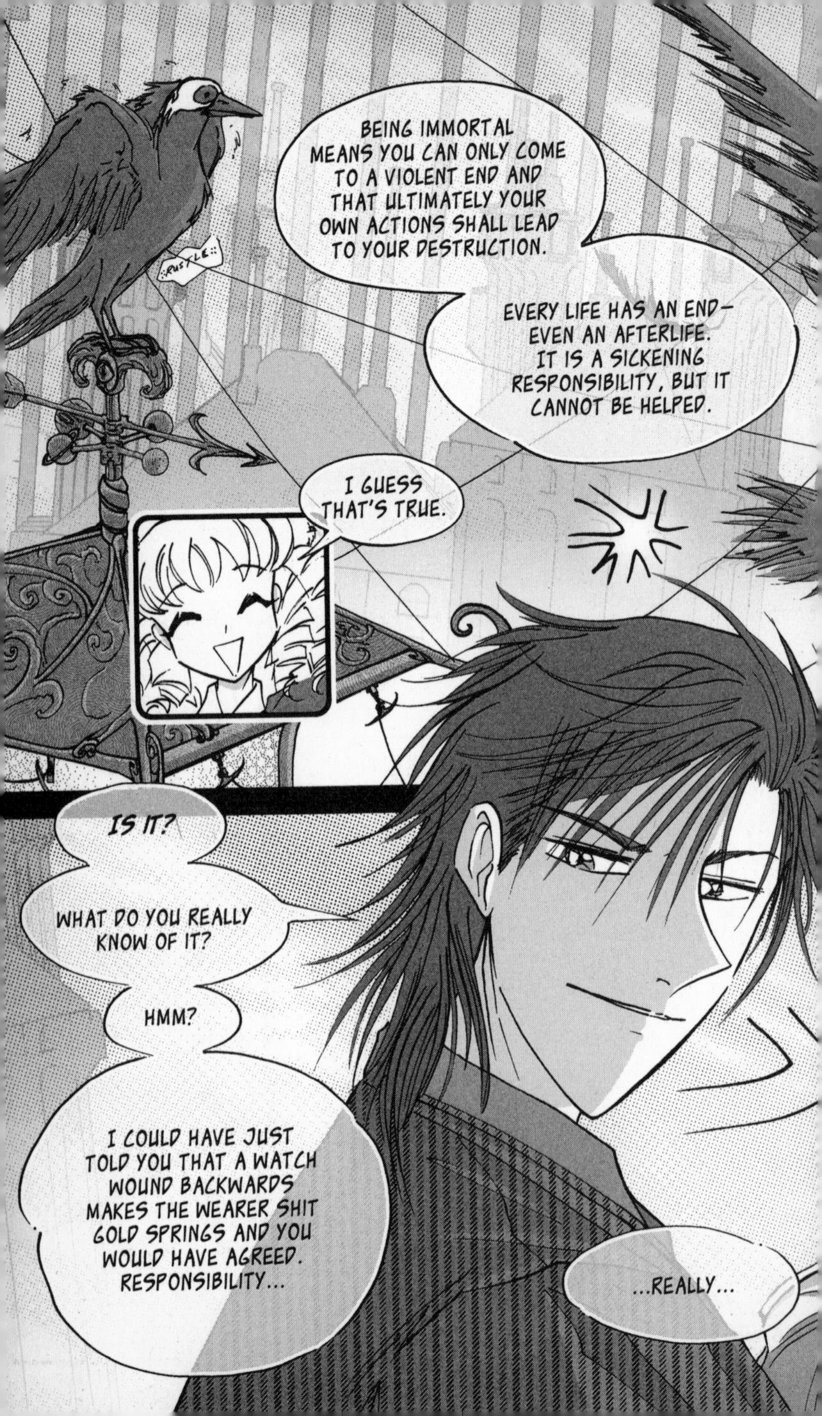
BEING IMMORTAL MEANS YOU CAN ONLY COME TO A VIOLENT END AND THAT ULTIMATELY YOUR OWN ACTIONS SHALL LEAD TO YOUR DESTRUCTION.
RUSTLE
EVERY LIFE HAS AN END— EVEN AN AFTERLIFE. IT IS A SICKENING RESPONSIBILITY, BUT IT CANNOT BE HELPED.
I GUESS THAT'S TRUE.
IS IT?
WHAT DO YOU REALLY KNOW OF IT?
HMM?
I COULD HAVE JUST TOLD YOU THAT A WATCH WOUND BACKWARDS MAKES THE WEARER SHIT GOLD SPRINGS AND YOU WOULD HAVE AGREED. RESPONSIBILITY...
...REALLY...

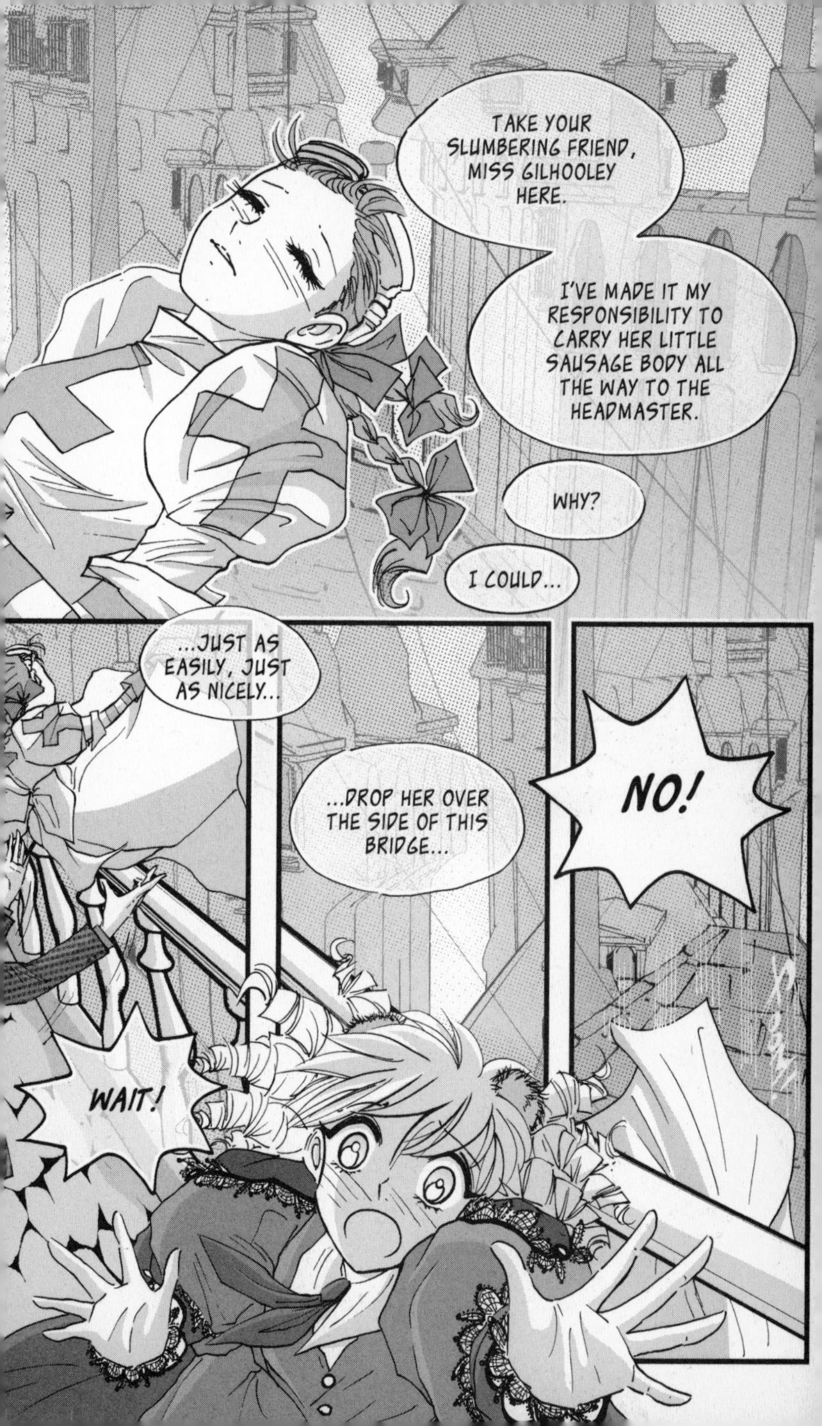
TAKE YOUR SLUMBERING FRIEND, MISS GILHOOLEY HERE.
I'VE MADE IT MY RESPONSIBILITY TO CARRY HER LITTLE SAUSAGE BODY ALL THE WAY TO THE HEADMASTER.
WHY?
I COULD...
...JUST AS EASILY, JUST AS NICELY...
...DROP HER OVER THE SIDE OF THIS BRIDGE...
NO!
WAIT!

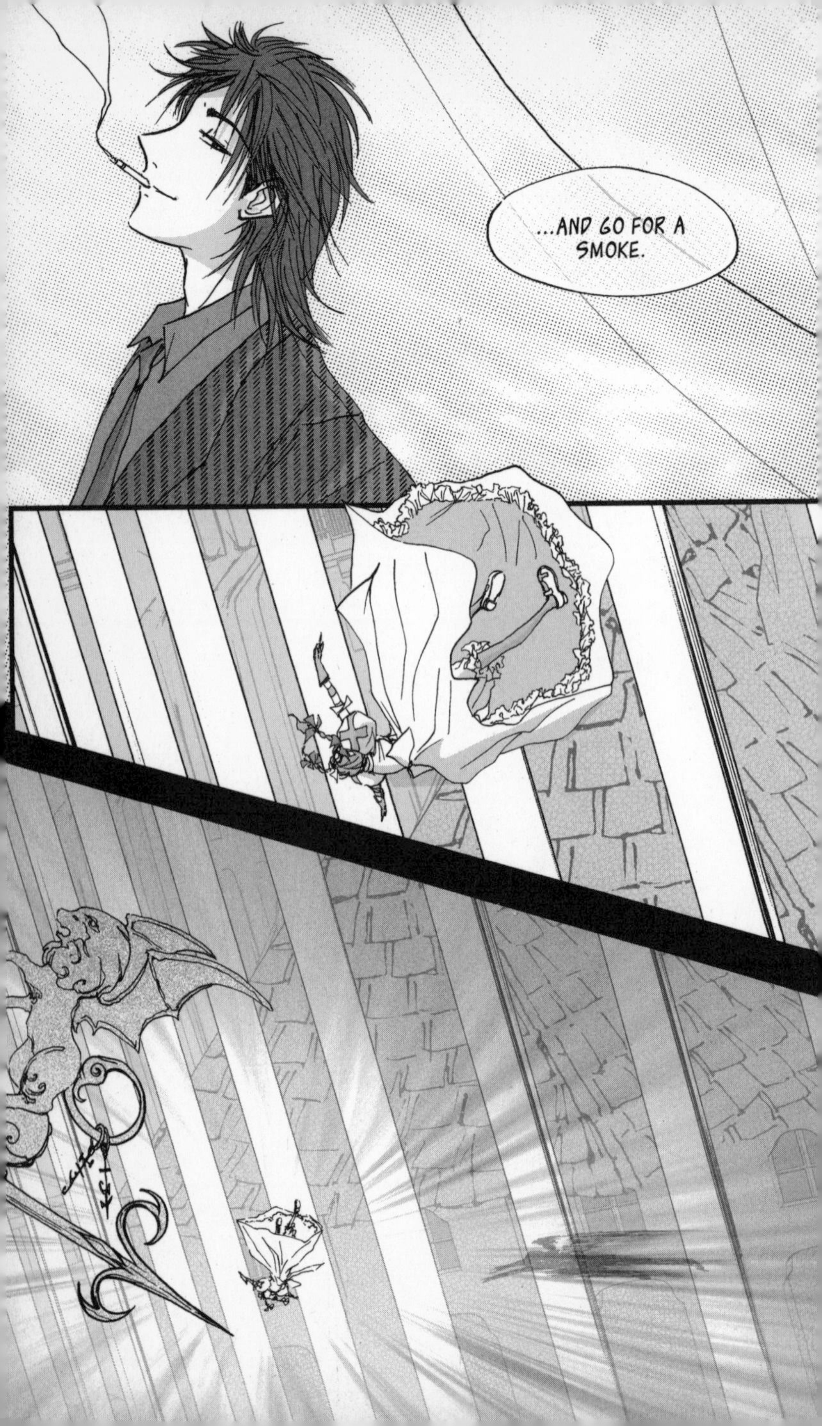
...AND GO FOR A SMOKE.

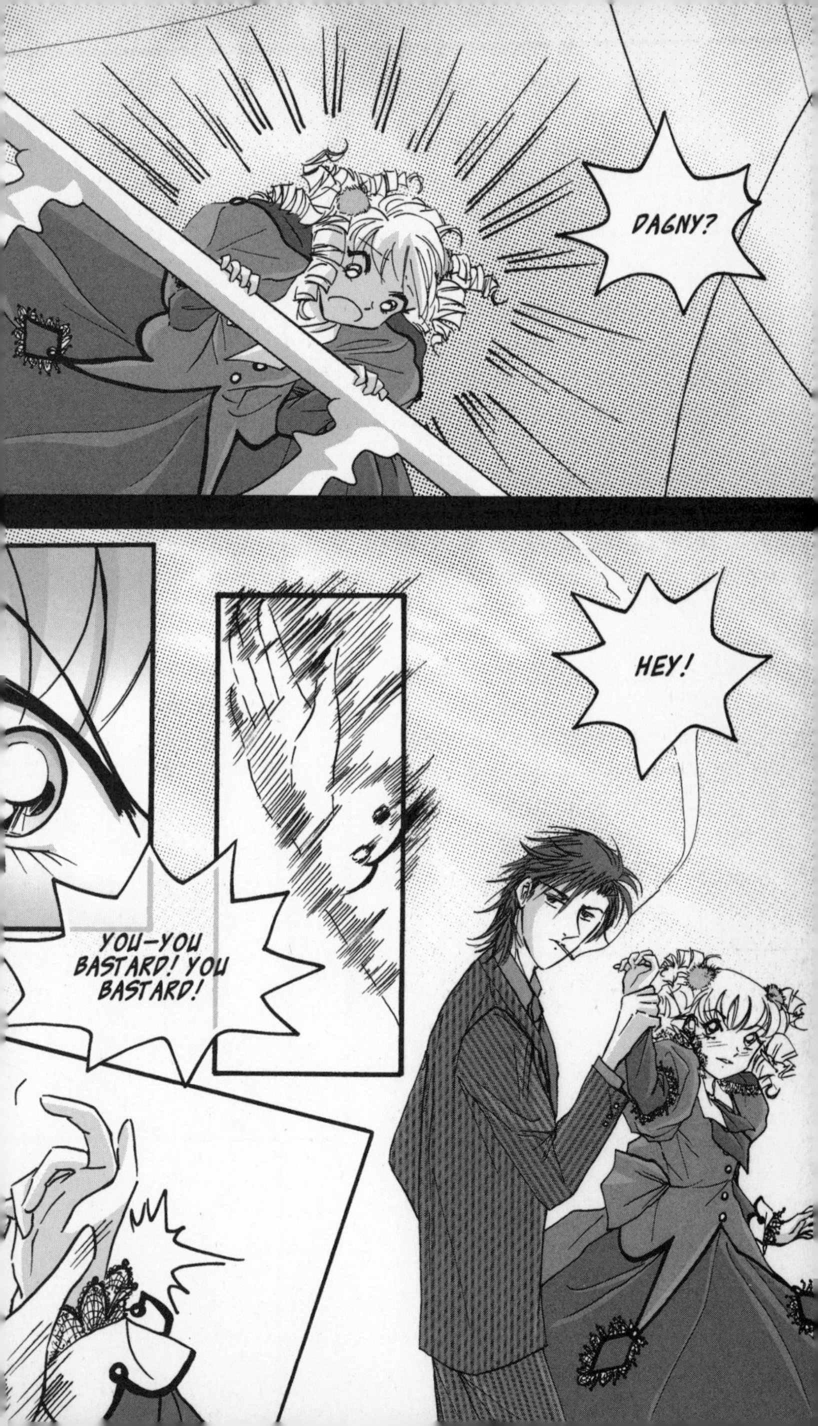
DAGNY?
HEY!
YOU—YOU BASTARD! YOU BASTARD!

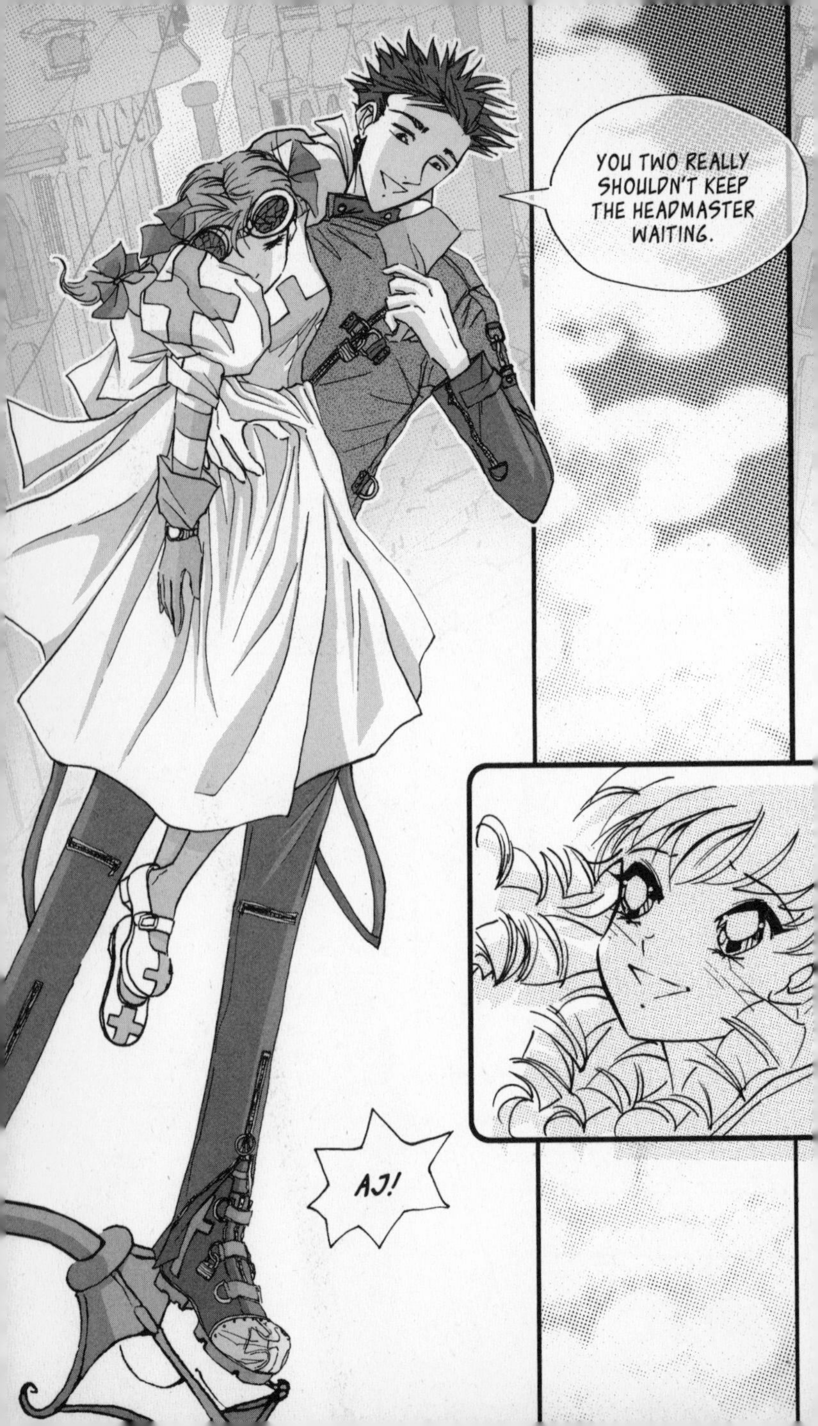
YOU TWO REALLY SHOULDN'T KEEP THE HEADMASTER WAITING.
AJ!

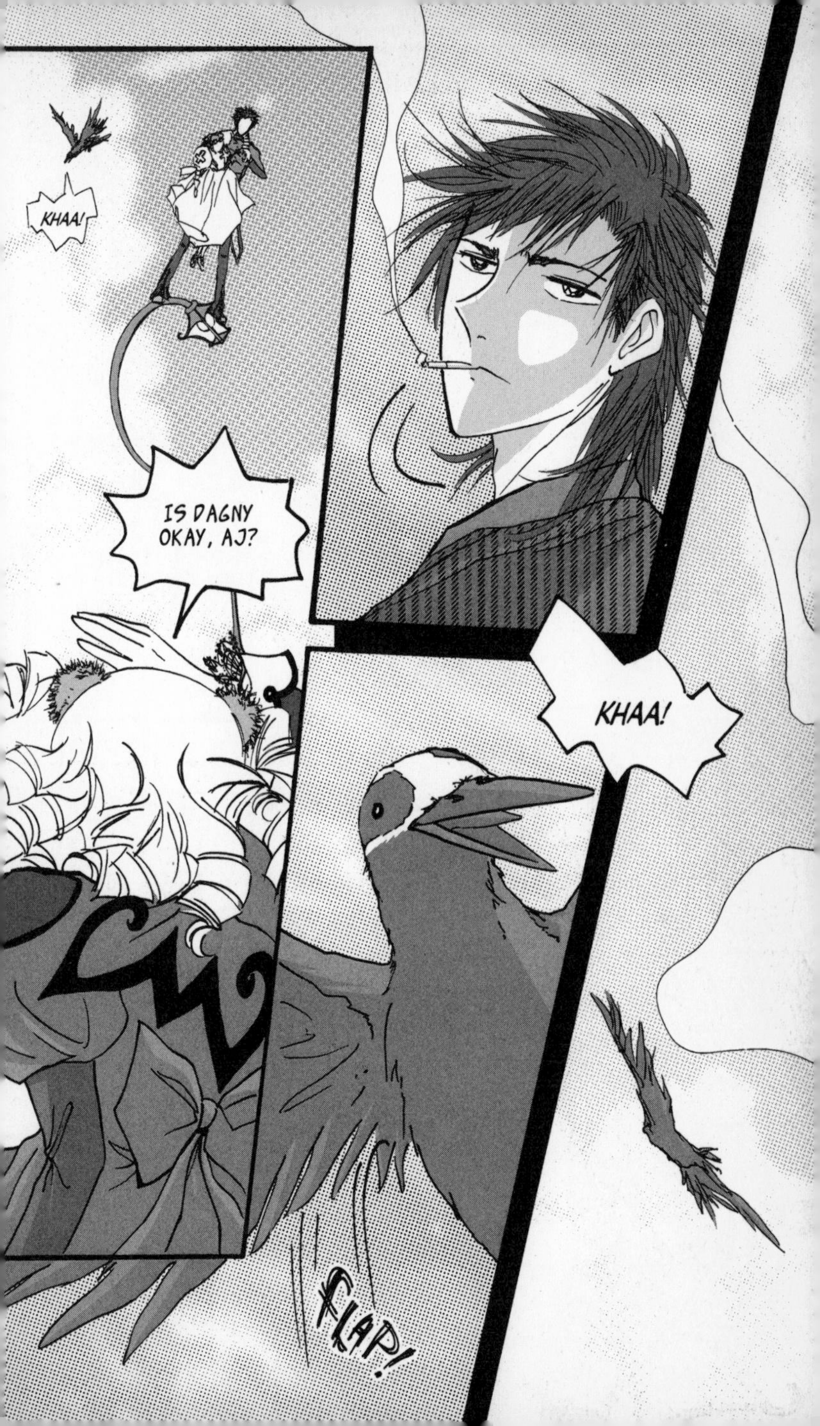
KHAA!
FLAP!
KHAA!
IS DAGNY OKAY, AJ?

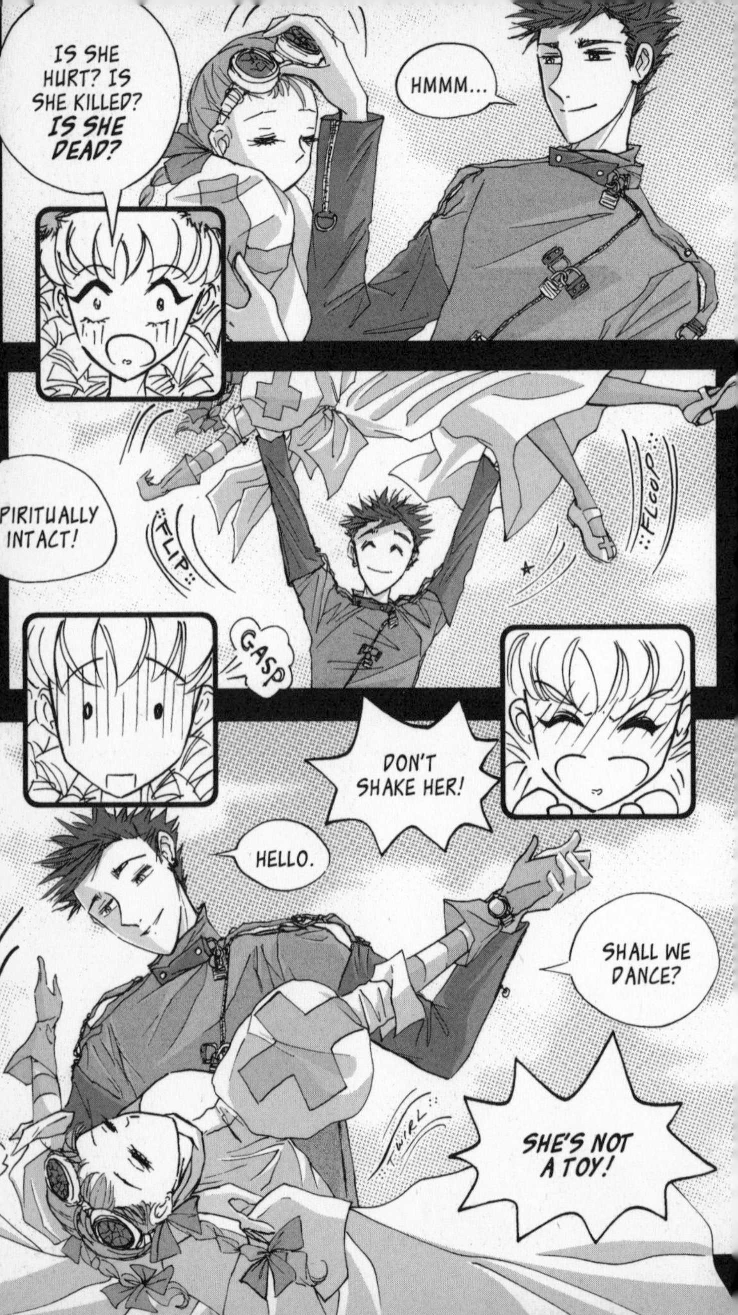
IS SHE HURT? IS SHE KILLED? IS SHE DEAD?
HMMM...
SPIRITUALLY INTACT!
FLIP
FLOOP
GASP
DON'T SHAKE HER!
HELLO.
SHALL WE DANCE?
SWING
FOP
TWIRL
SHE'S NOT A TOY!

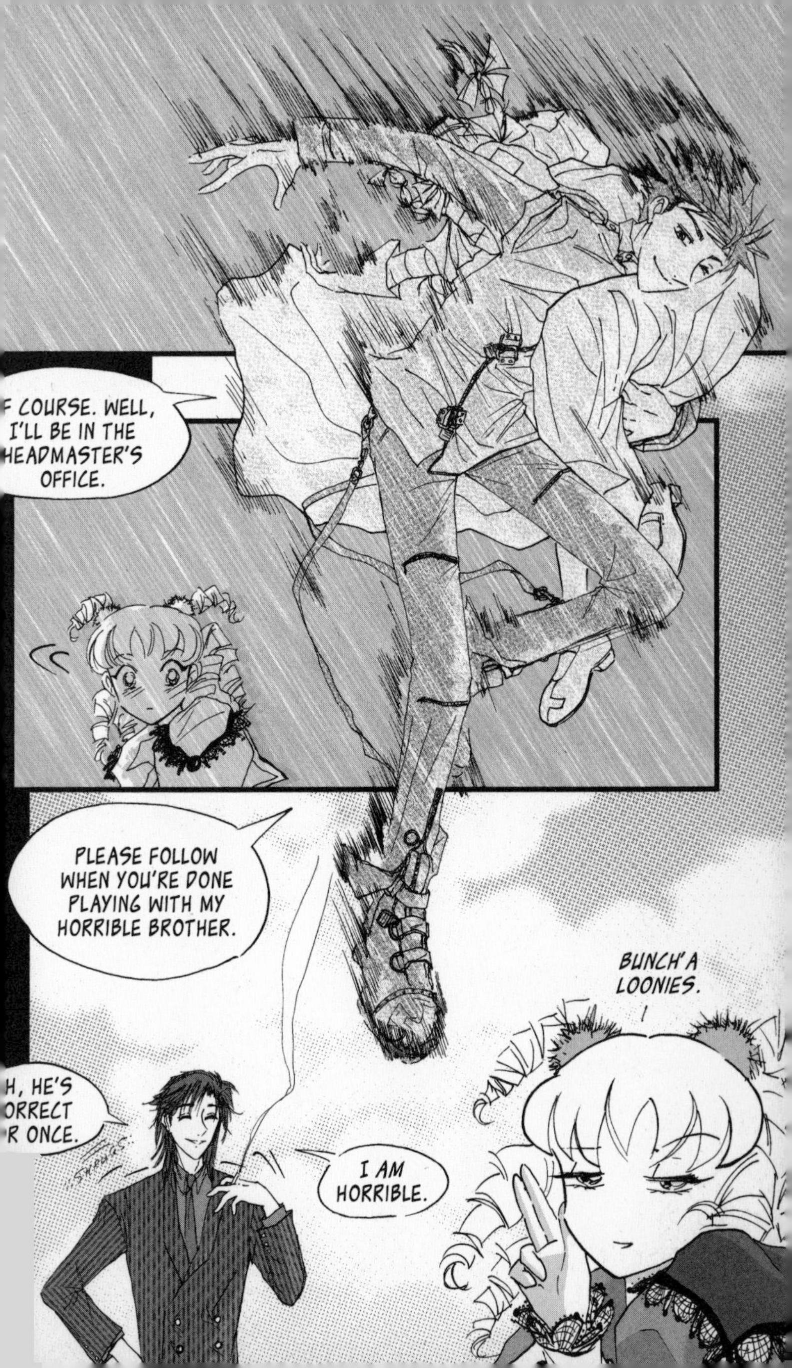
F COURSE. WELL, I'LL BE IN THE HEADMASTER'S OFFICE.
PLEASE FOLLOW WHEN YOU'RE DONE PLAYING WITH MY HORRIBLE BROTHER.
BUNCH'A LOONIES.
H, HE'S ORRECT R ONCE.
I AM HORRIBLE.

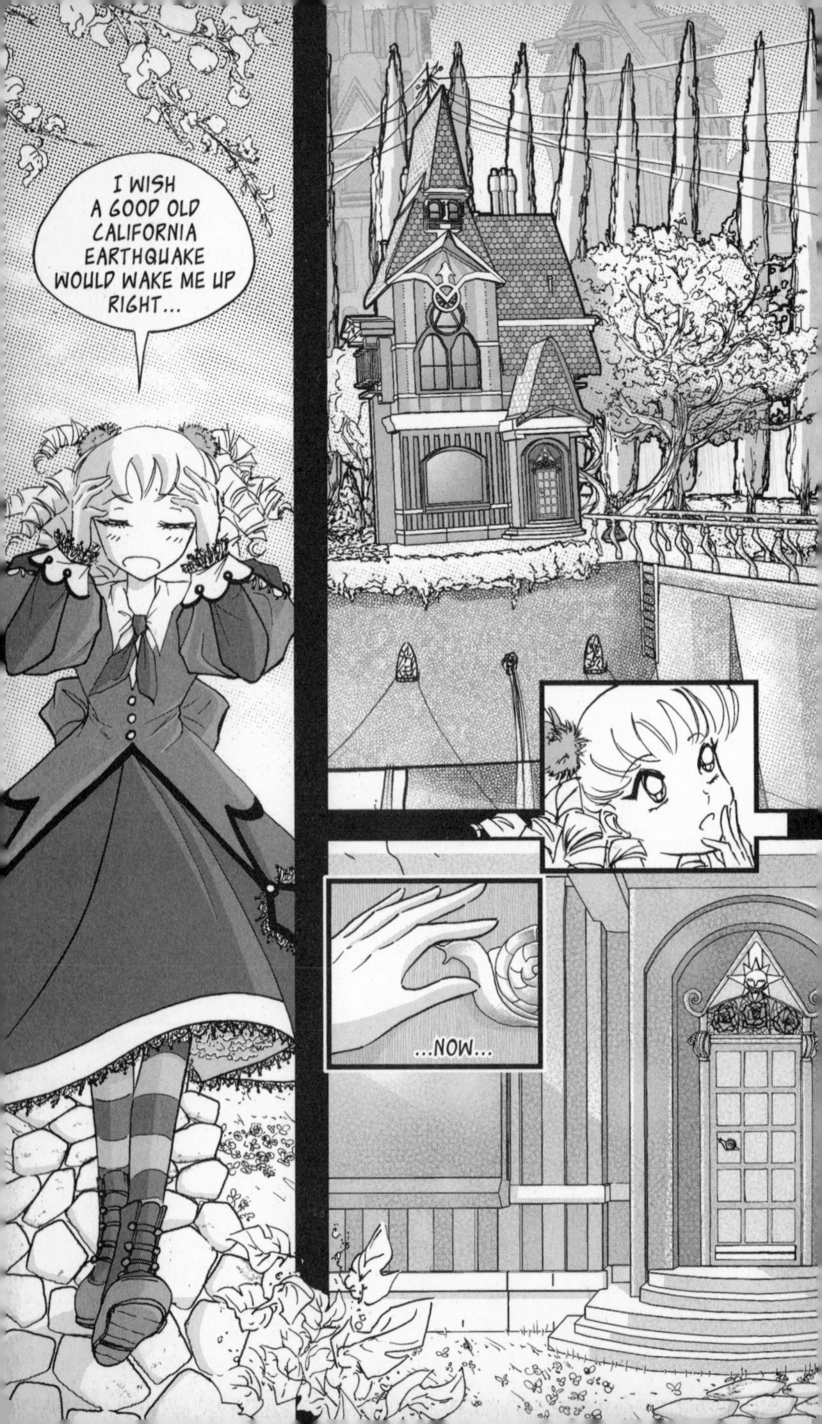
I WISH A GOOD OLD CALIFORNIA EARTHQUAKE WOULD WAKE ME UP RIGHT...
...NOW...

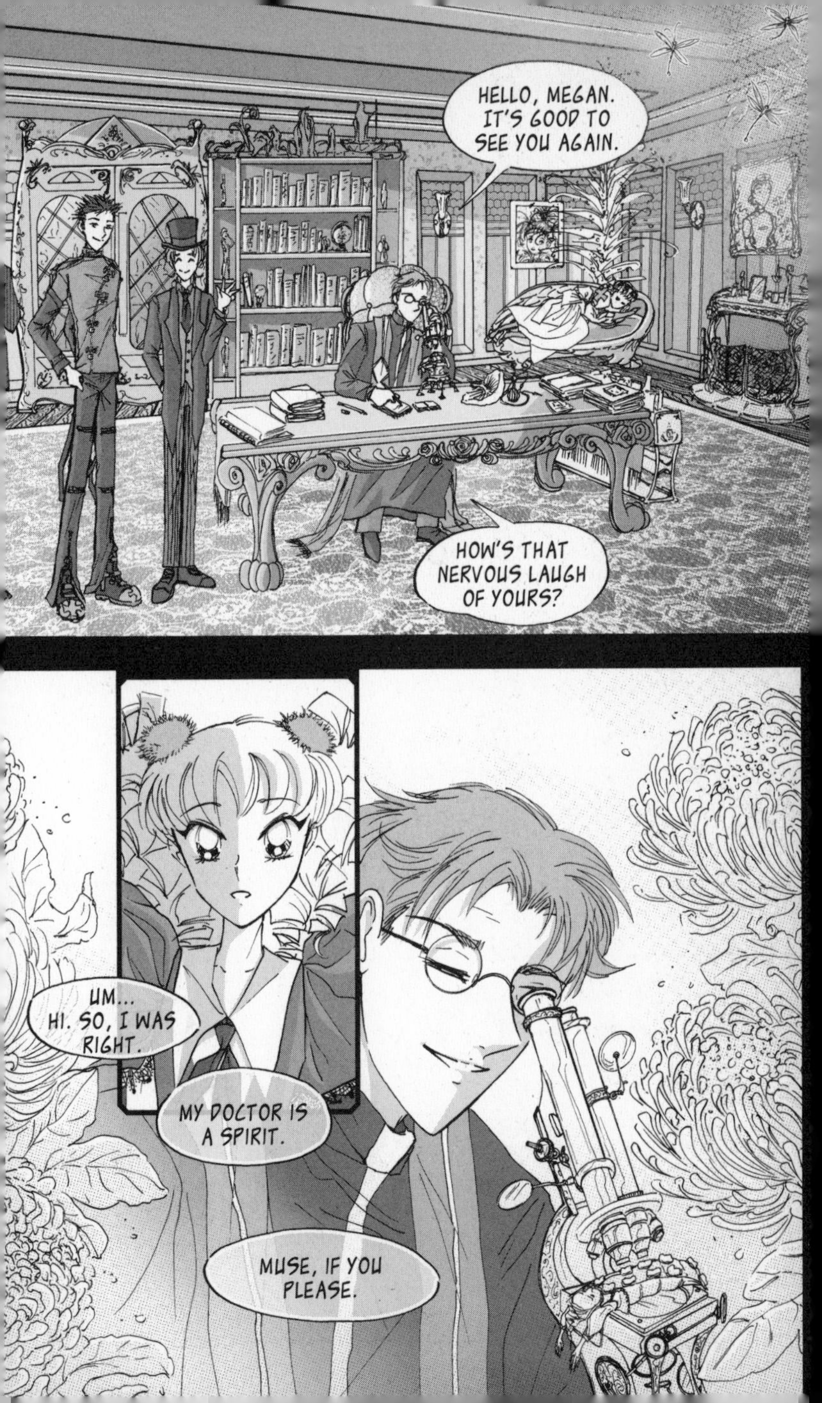
HELLO, MEGAN. IT'S GOOD TO SEE YOU AGAIN.
HOW'S THAT NERVOUS LAUGH OF YOURS?
UM... HI. SO, I WAS RIGHT.
MY DOCTOR IS A SPIRIT.
MUSE, IF YOU PLEASE.

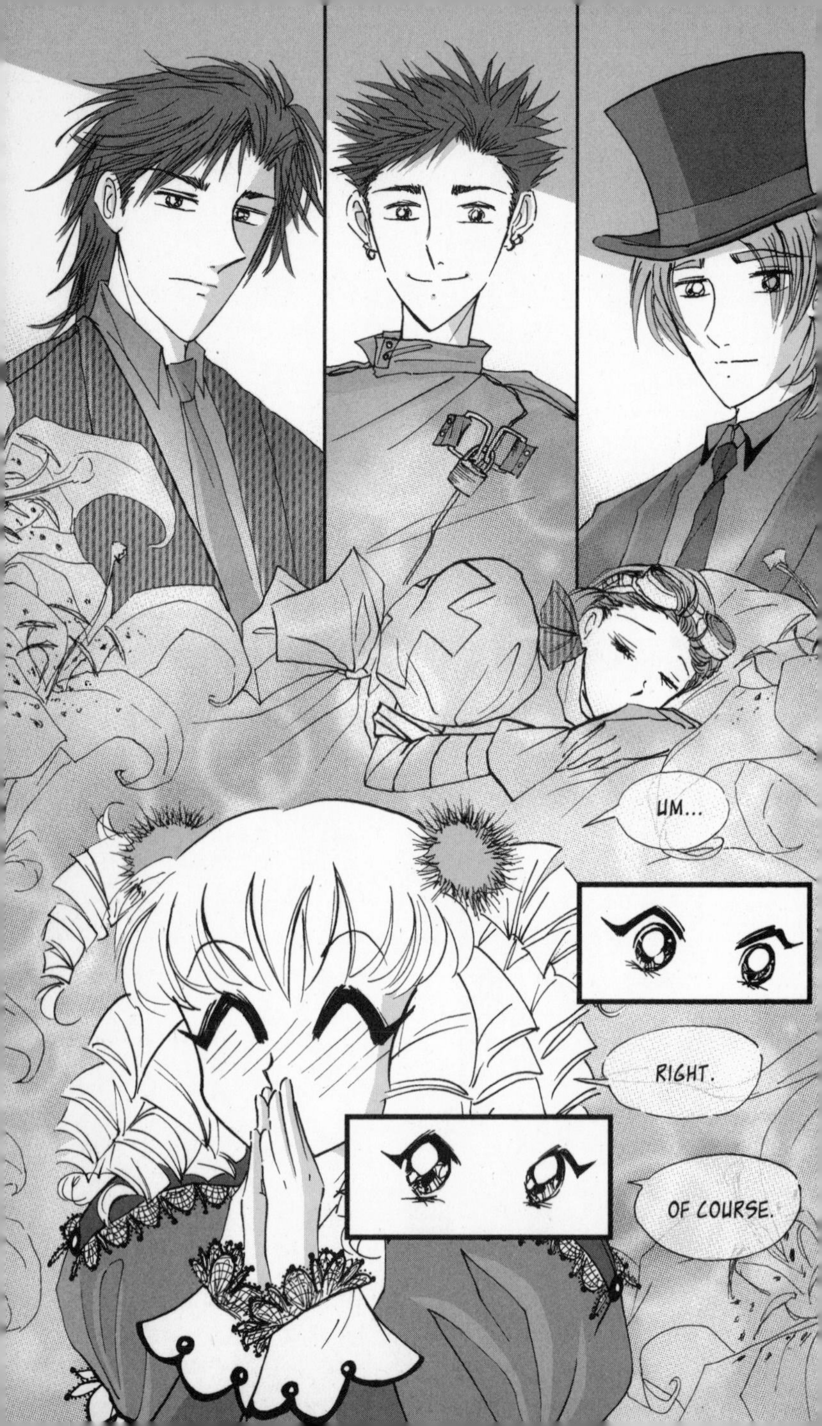
UM...
RIGHT.
OF COURSE.

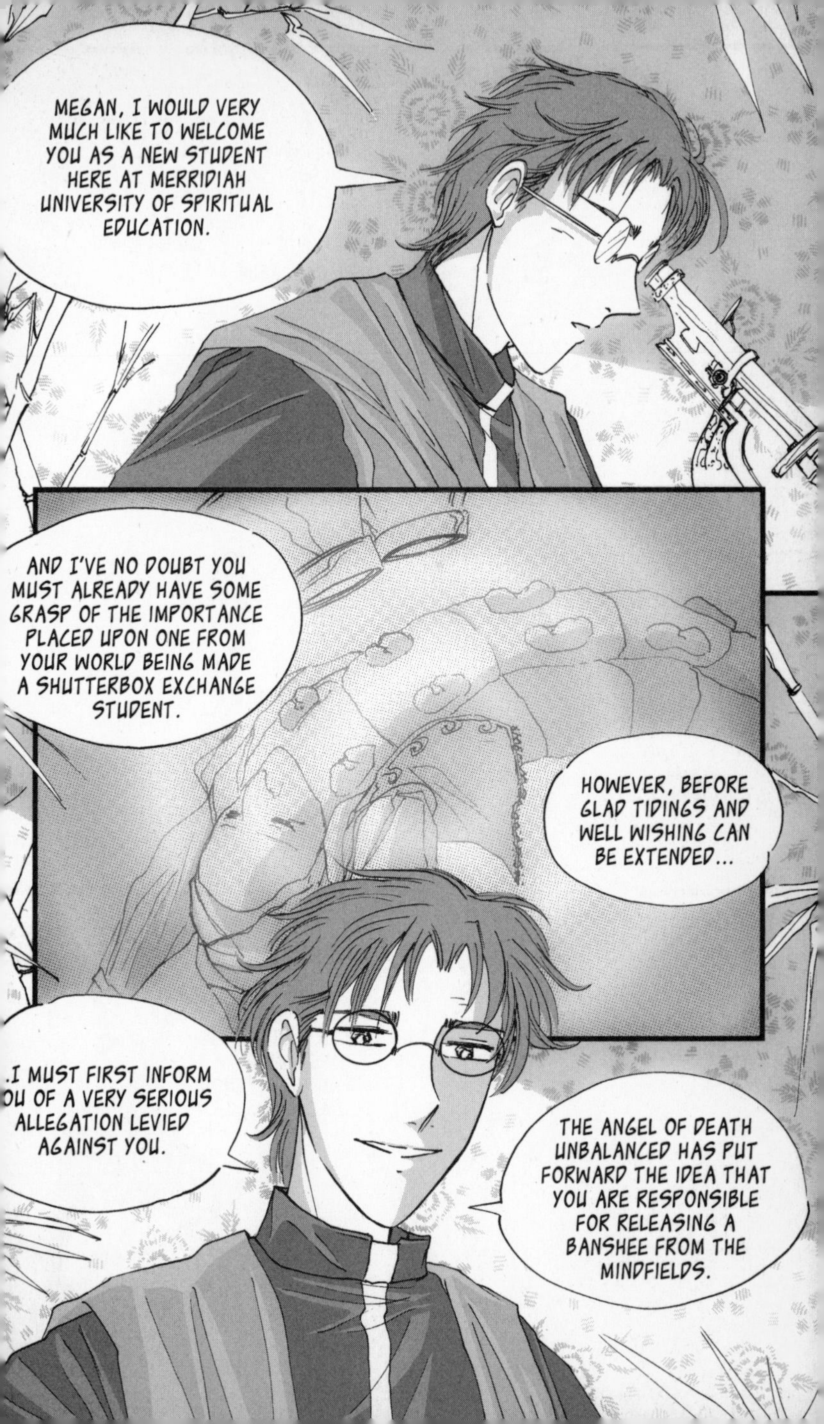
MEGAN, I WOULD VERY MUCH LIKE TO WELCOME YOU AS A NEW STUDENT HERE AT MERRIDIAH UNIVERSITY OF SPIRITUAL EDUCATION.
AND I'VE NO DOUBT YOU MUST ALREADY HAVE SOME GRASP OF THE IMPORTANCE PLACED UPON ONE FROM YOUR WORLD BEING MADE A SHUTTERBOX EXCHANGE STUDENT.
HOWEVER, BEFORE GLAD TIDINGS AND WELL WISHING CAN BE EXTENDED...
.I MUST FIRST INFORM OU OF A VERY SERIOUS ALLEGATION LEVIED AGAINST YOU.
THE ANGEL OF DEATH UNBALANCED HAS PUT FORWARD THE IDEA THAT YOU ARE RESPONSIBLE FOR RELEASING A BANSHEE FROM THE MINDFIELDS.

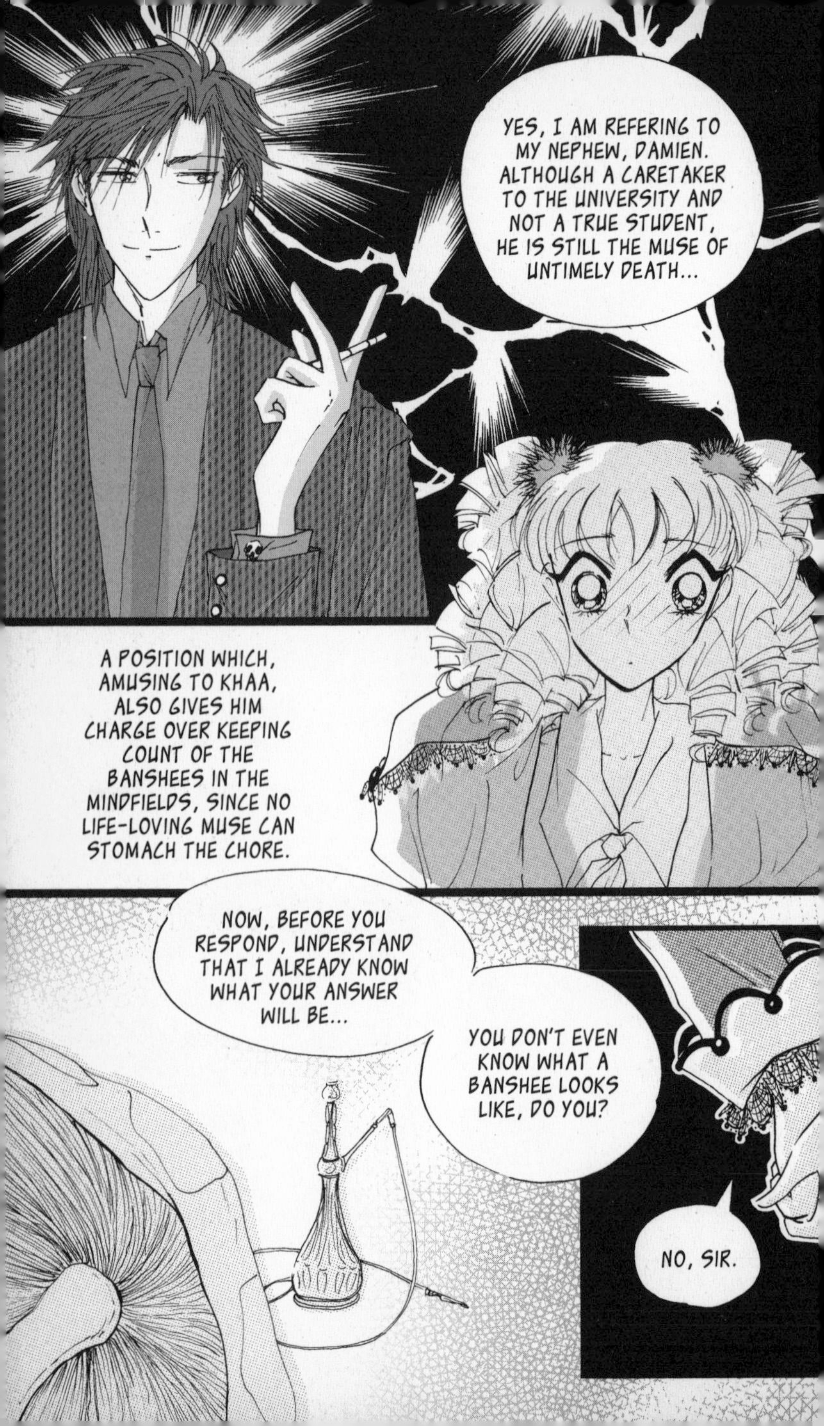
YES, I AM REFERING TO MY NEPHEW, DAMIEN. ALTHOUGH A CARETAKER TO THE UNIVERSITY AND NOT A TRUE STUDENT, HE IS STILL THE MUSE OF UNTIMELY DEATH...
A POSITION WHICH, AMUSING TO KHAA, ALSO GIVES HIM CHARGE OVER KEEPING COUNT OF THE BANSHEES IN THE MINDFIELDS, SINCE NO LIFE-LOVING MUSE CAN STOMACH THE CHORE.
NOW, BEFORE YOU RESPOND, UNDERSTAND THAT I ALREADY KNOW WHAT YOUR ANSWER WILL BE...
YOU DON'T EVEN KNOW WHAT A BANSHEE LOOKS LIKE, DO YOU?
NO, SIR.

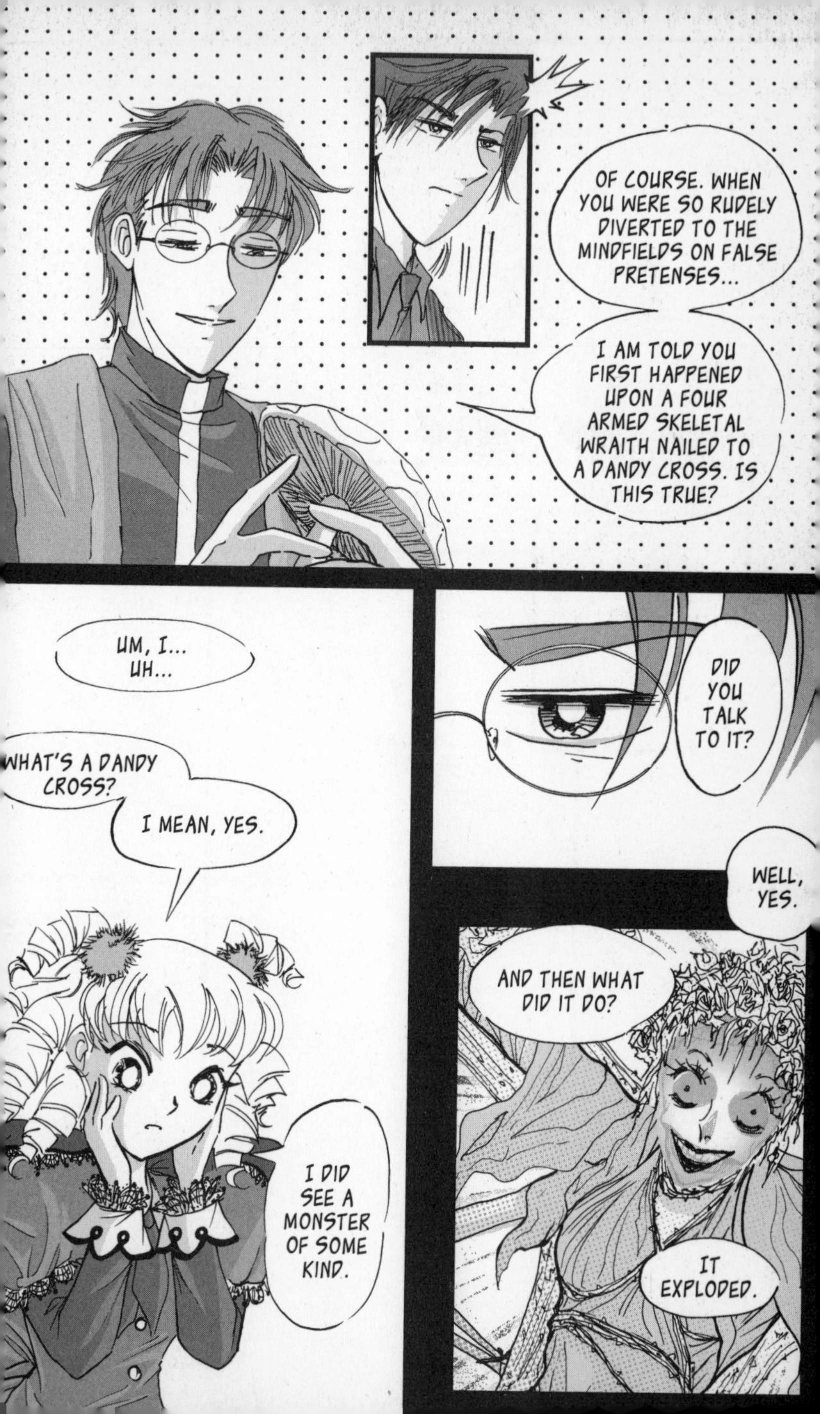
OF COURSE. WHEN YOU WERE SO RUDELY DIVERTED TO THE MINDFIELDS ON FALSE PRETENSES...
I AM TOLD YOU FIRST HAPPENED UPON A FOUR ARMED SKELETAL WRAITH NAILED TO A DANDY CROSS. IS THIS TRUE?
UM, I... UH...
WHAT'S A DANDY CROSS?
I MEAN, YES.
I DID SEE A MONSTER OF SOME KIND.
DID YOU TALK TO IT?
WELL, YES.
AND THEN WHAT DID IT DO?
IT EXPLODED.

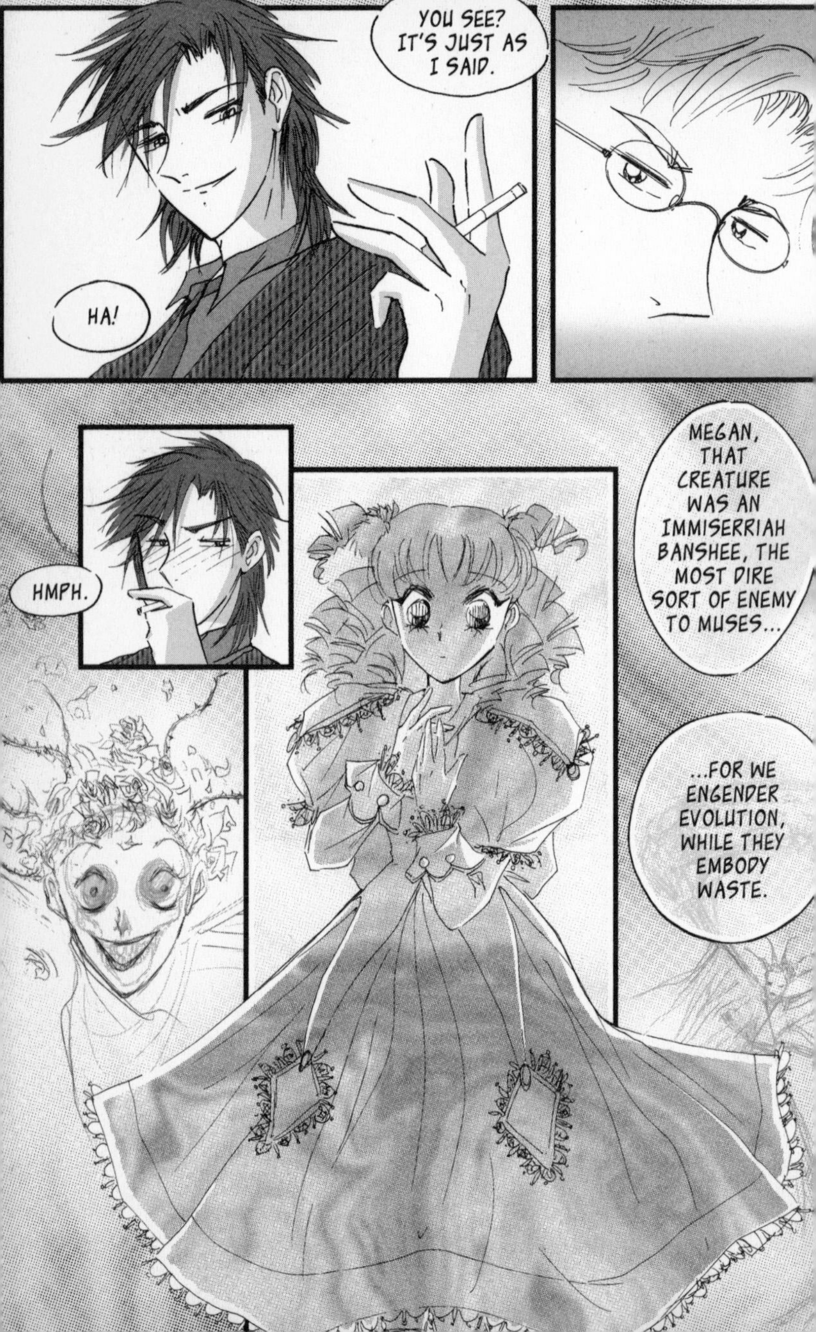
YOU SEE? IT'S JUST AS I SAID.
HA!
MEGAN, THAT CREATURE WAS AN IMMISERRIAH BANSHEE, THE MOST DIRE SORT OF ENEMY TO MUSES...
...FOR WE ENGENDER EVOLUTION, WHILE THEY EMBODY WASTE.
HMPH.

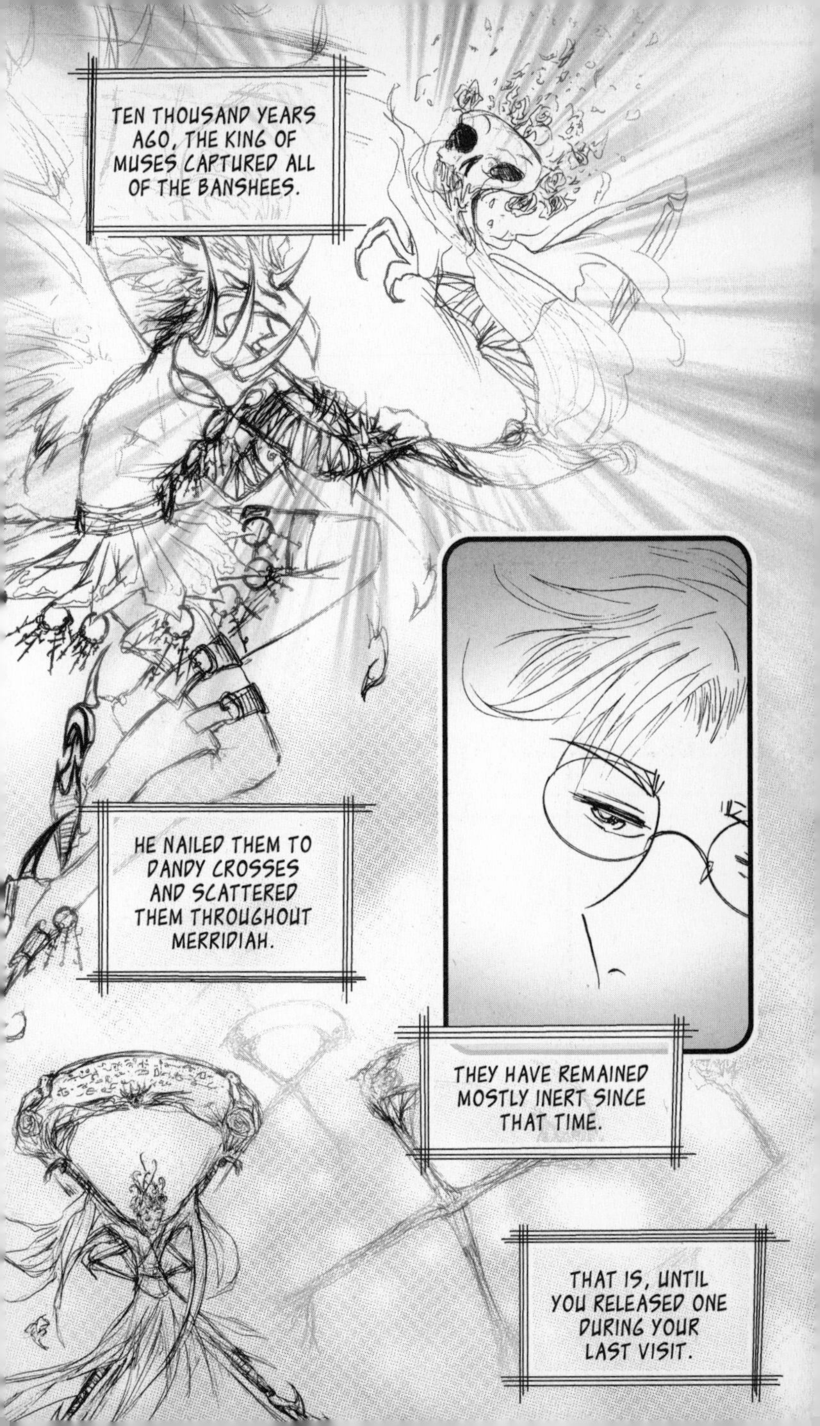
TEN THOUSAND YEARS AGO, THE KING OF MUSES CAPTURED ALL OF THE BANSHEES.
HE NAILED THEM TO DANDY CROSSES AND SCATTERED THEM THROUGHOUT MERRIDIAH.
THEY HAVE REMAINED MOSTLY INERT SINCE THAT TIME.
THAT IS, UNTIL YOU RELEASED ONE DURING YOUR LAST VISIT.

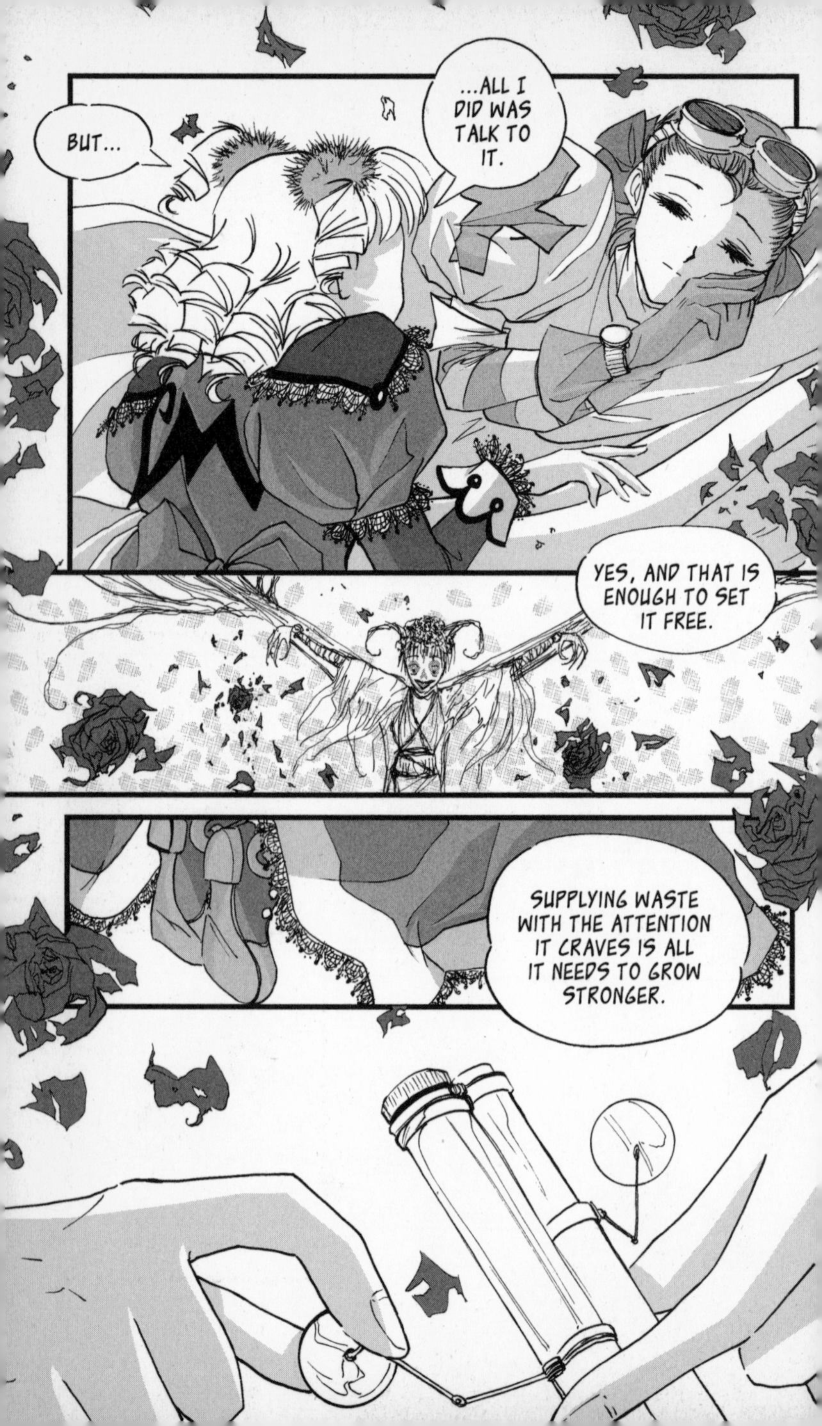
...ALL I DID WAS TALK TO IT.
BUT...
YES, AND THAT IS ENOUGH TO SET IT FREE.
SUPPLYING WASTE WITH THE ATTENTION IT CRAVES IS ALL IT NEEDS TO GROW STRONGER.

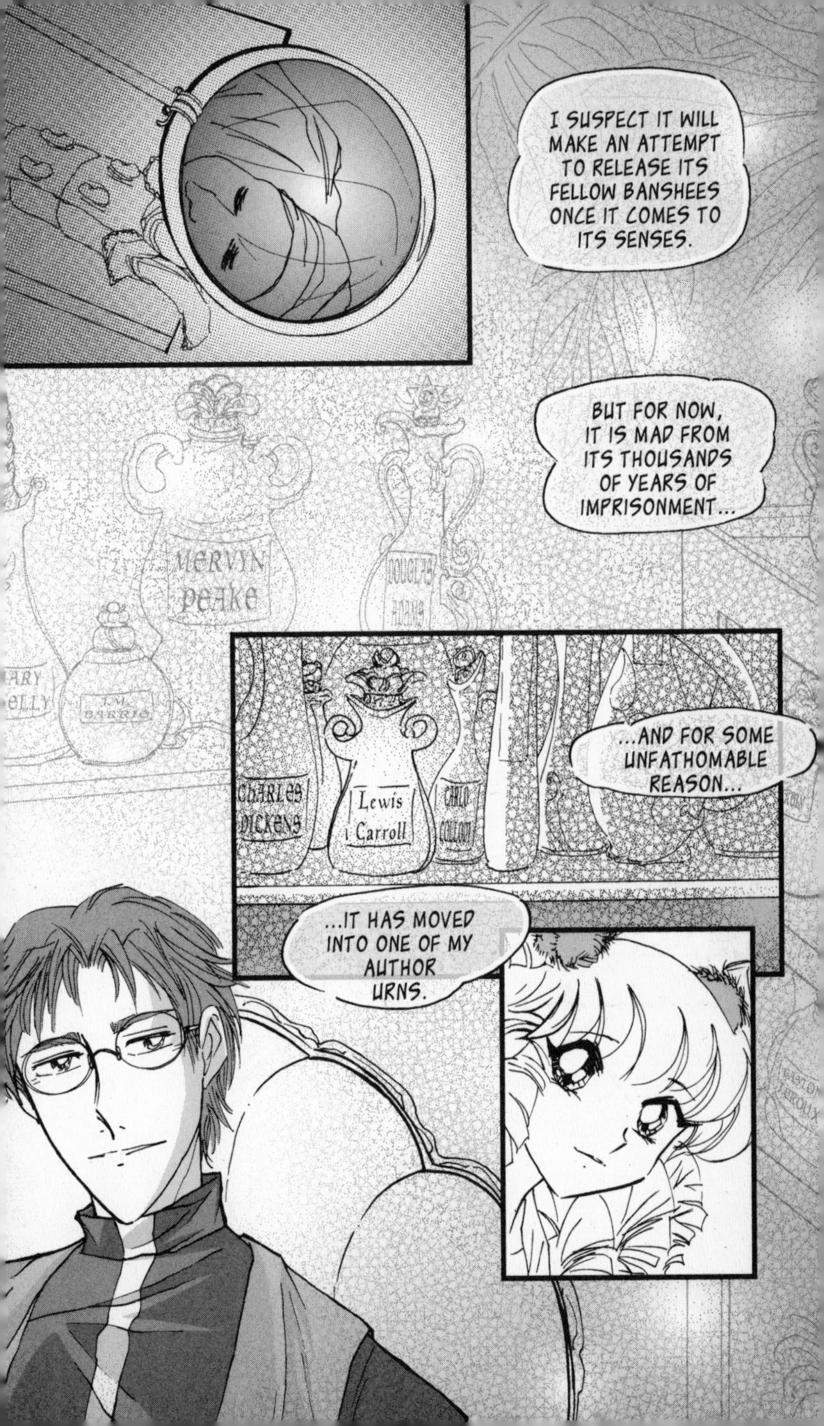
I SUSPECT IT WILL MAKE AN ATTEMPT TO RELEASE ITS FELLOW BANSHEES ONCE IT COMES TO ITS SENSES.
BUT FOR NOW, IT IS MAD FROM ITS THOUSANDS OF YEARS OF IMPRISONMENT...
MERVIN PEAKE
...AND FOR SOME UNFATHOMABLE REASON...
CHARLES DICKENS
Lewis Carroll
CARLO COLLODI
...IT HAS MOVED INTO ONE OF MY AUTHOR URNS.

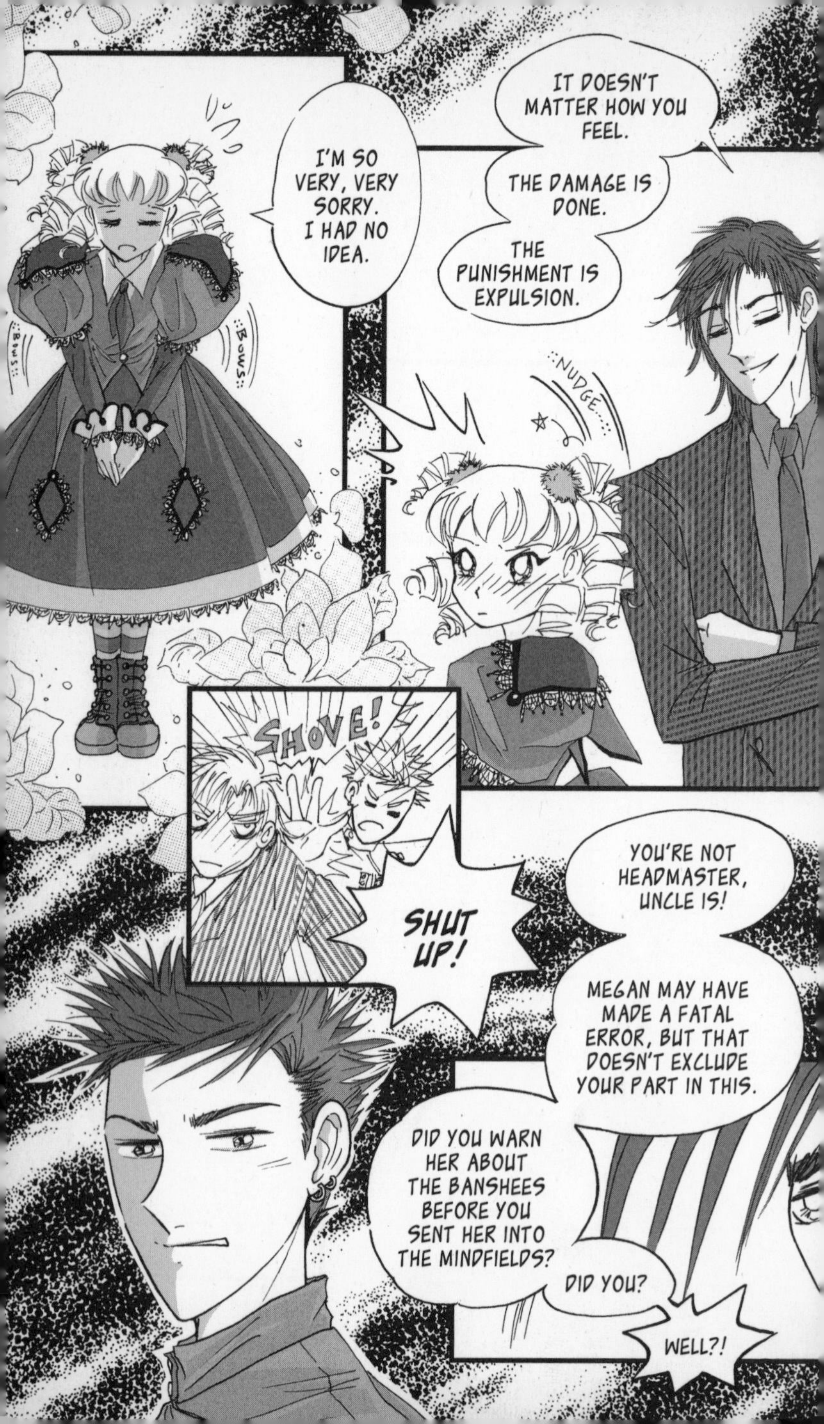
::BOWS::
::BOWS::
I'M SO VERY, VERY SORRY. I HAD NO IDEA.
IT DOESN'T MATTER HOW YOU FEEL.
THE DAMAGE IS DONE.
THE PUNISHMENT IS EXPULSION.
::NUDGE::
SHOVE!
SHUT UP!
YOU'RE NOT HEADMASTER, UNCLE IS!
MEGAN MAY HAVE MADE A FATAL ERROR, BUT THAT DOESN'T EXCLUDE YOUR PART IN THIS.
DID YOU WARN HER ABOUT THE BANSHEES BEFORE YOU SENT HER INTO THE MINDFIELDS?
DID YOU?
WELL?!

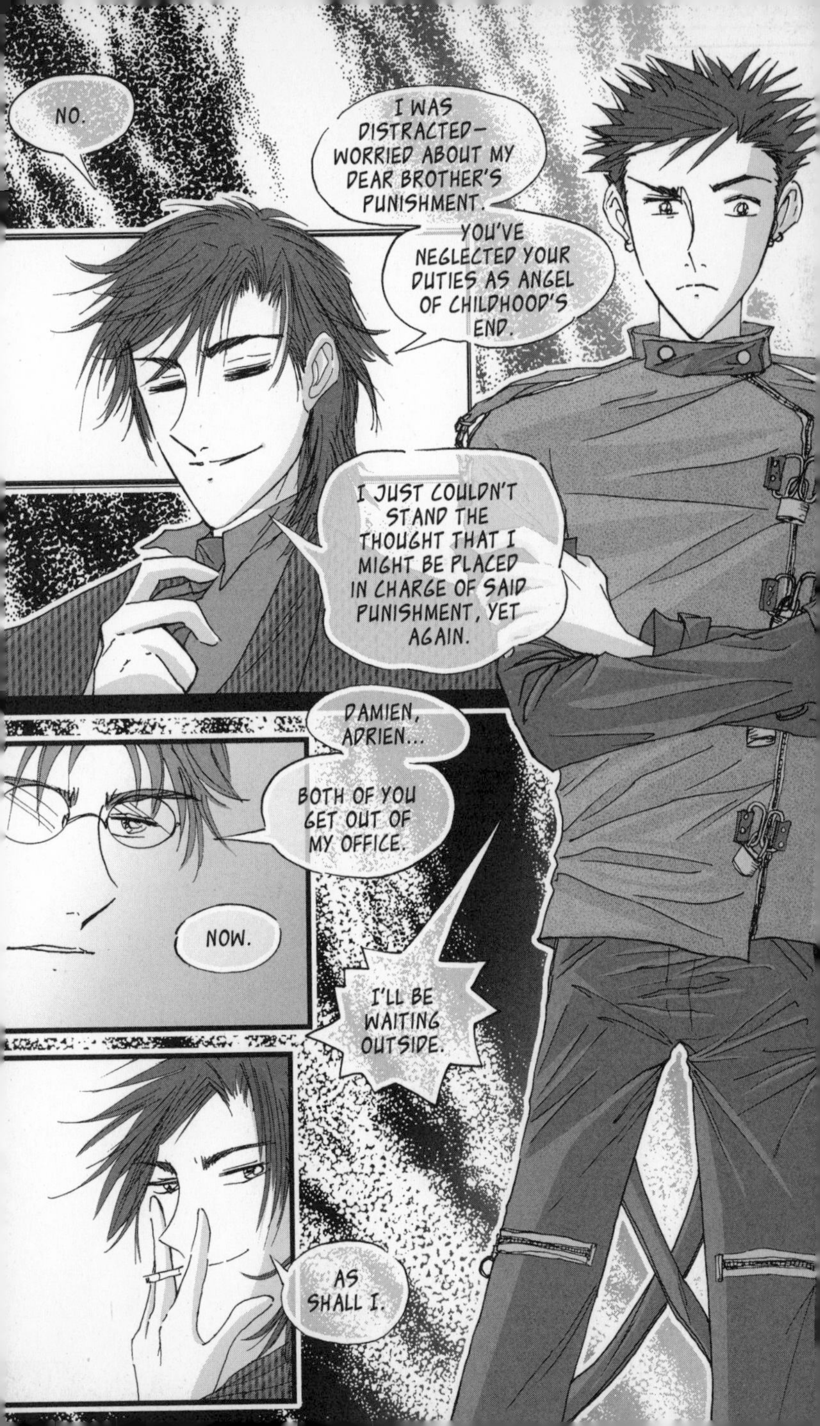
NO.
I WAS DISTRACTED— WORRIED ABOUT MY DEAR BROTHER'S PUNISHMENT.
YOU'VE NEGLECTED YOUR DUTIES AS ANGEL OF CHILDHOOD'S END.
I JUST COULDN'T STAND THE THOUGHT THAT I MIGHT BE PLACED IN CHARGE OF SAID PUNISHMENT, YET AGAIN.
DAMIEN, ADRIEN...
BOTH OF YOU GET OUT OF MY OFFICE.
NOW.
I'LL BE WAITING OUTSIDE.
AS SHALL I.

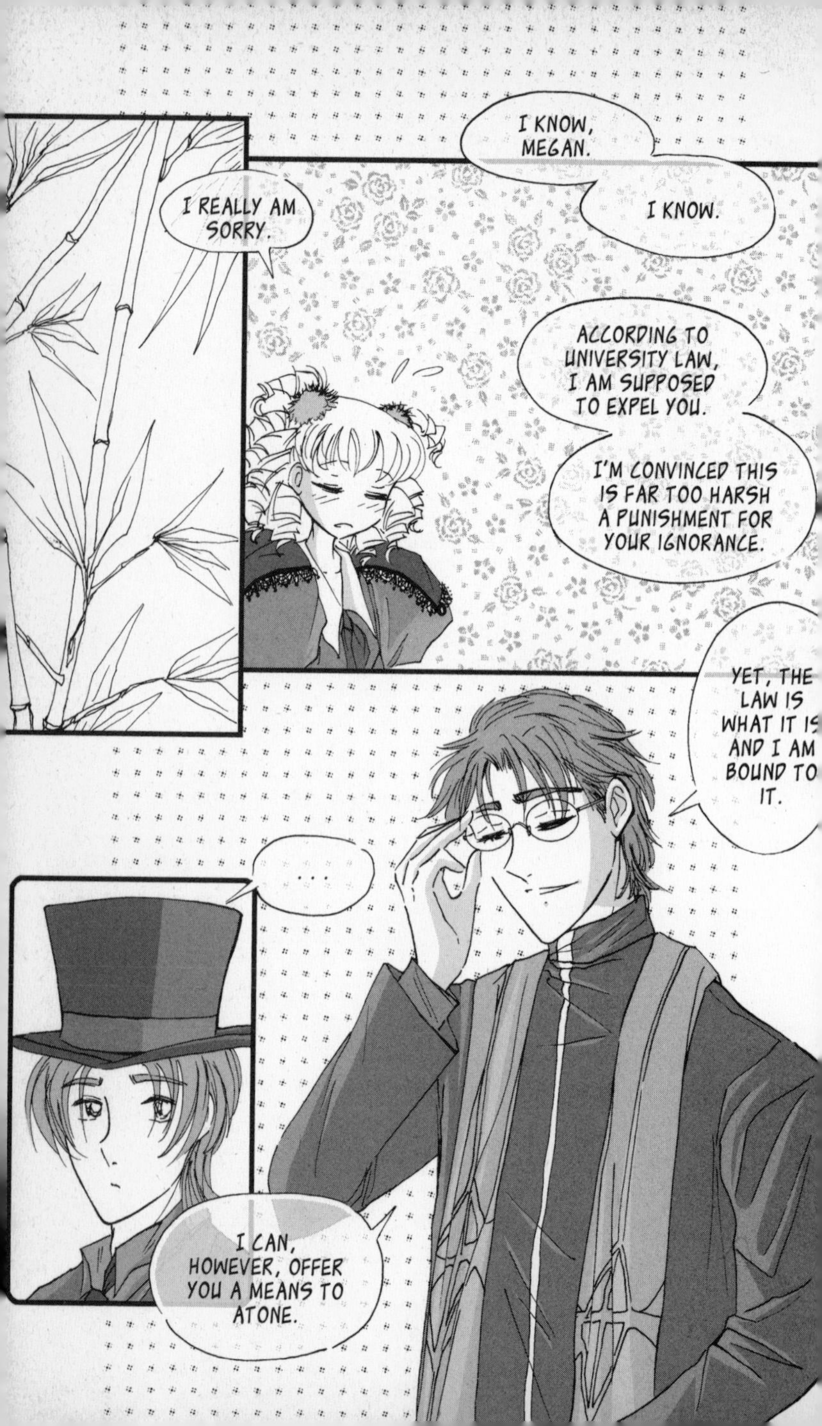
I REALLY AM SORRY.
I KNOW, MEGAN.
I KNOW.
ACCORDING TO UNIVERSITY LAW, I AM SUPPOSED TO EXPEL YOU.
I'M CONVINCED THIS IS FAR TOO HARSH A PUNISHMENT FOR YOUR IGNORANCE.
YET, THE LAW IS WHAT IT IS AND I AM BOUND TO IT.
. . .
I CAN, HOWEVER, OFFER YOU A MEANS TO ATONE.

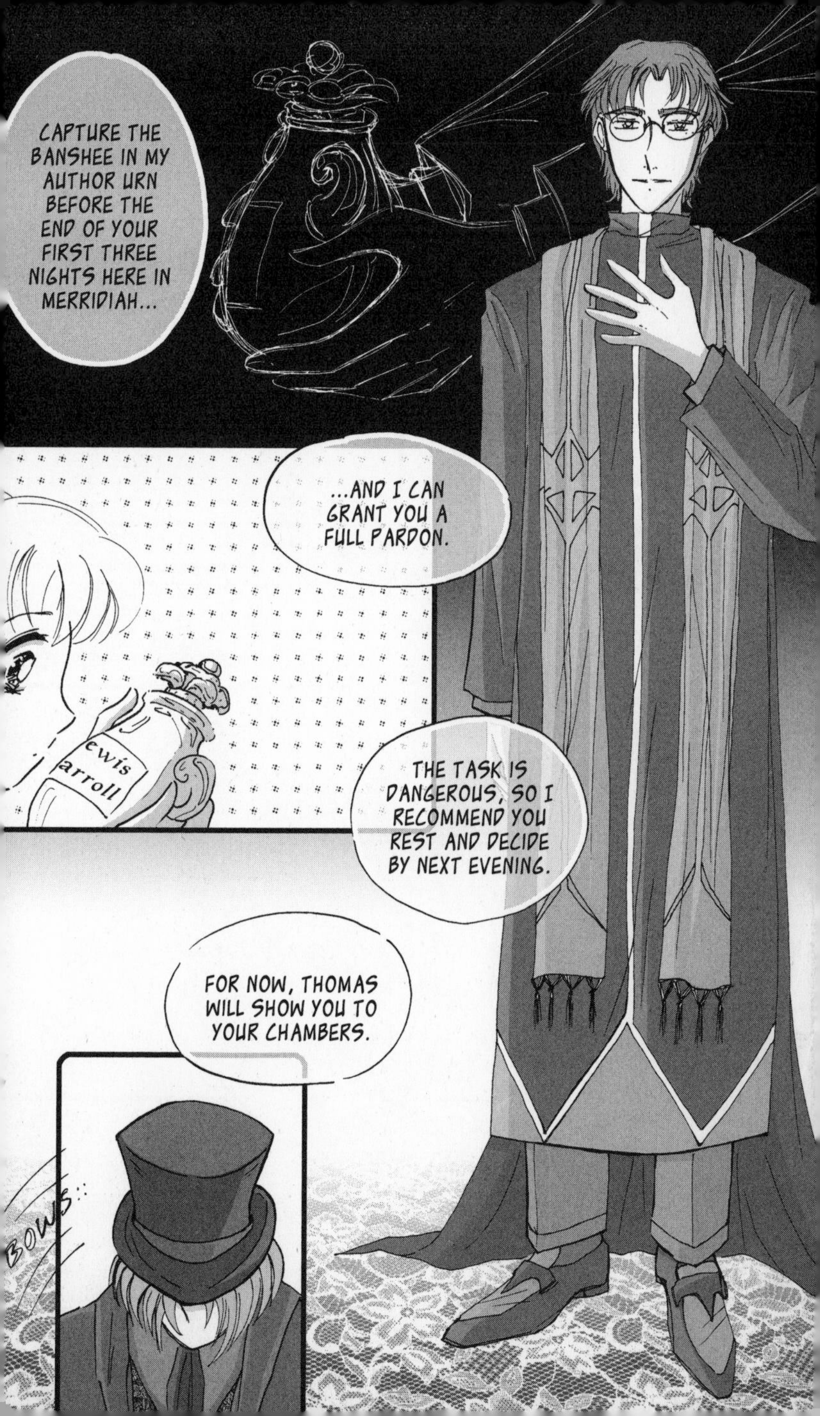
CAPTURE THE BANSHEE IN MY AUTHOR URN BEFORE THE END OF YOUR FIRST THREE NIGHTS HERE IN MERRIDIAH...
...AND I CAN GRANT YOU A FULL PARDON.
THE TASK IS DANGEROUS, SO I RECOMMEND YOU REST AND DECIDE BY NEXT EVENING.
FOR NOW, THOMAS WILL SHOW YOU TO YOUR CHAMBERS.
BOWS::

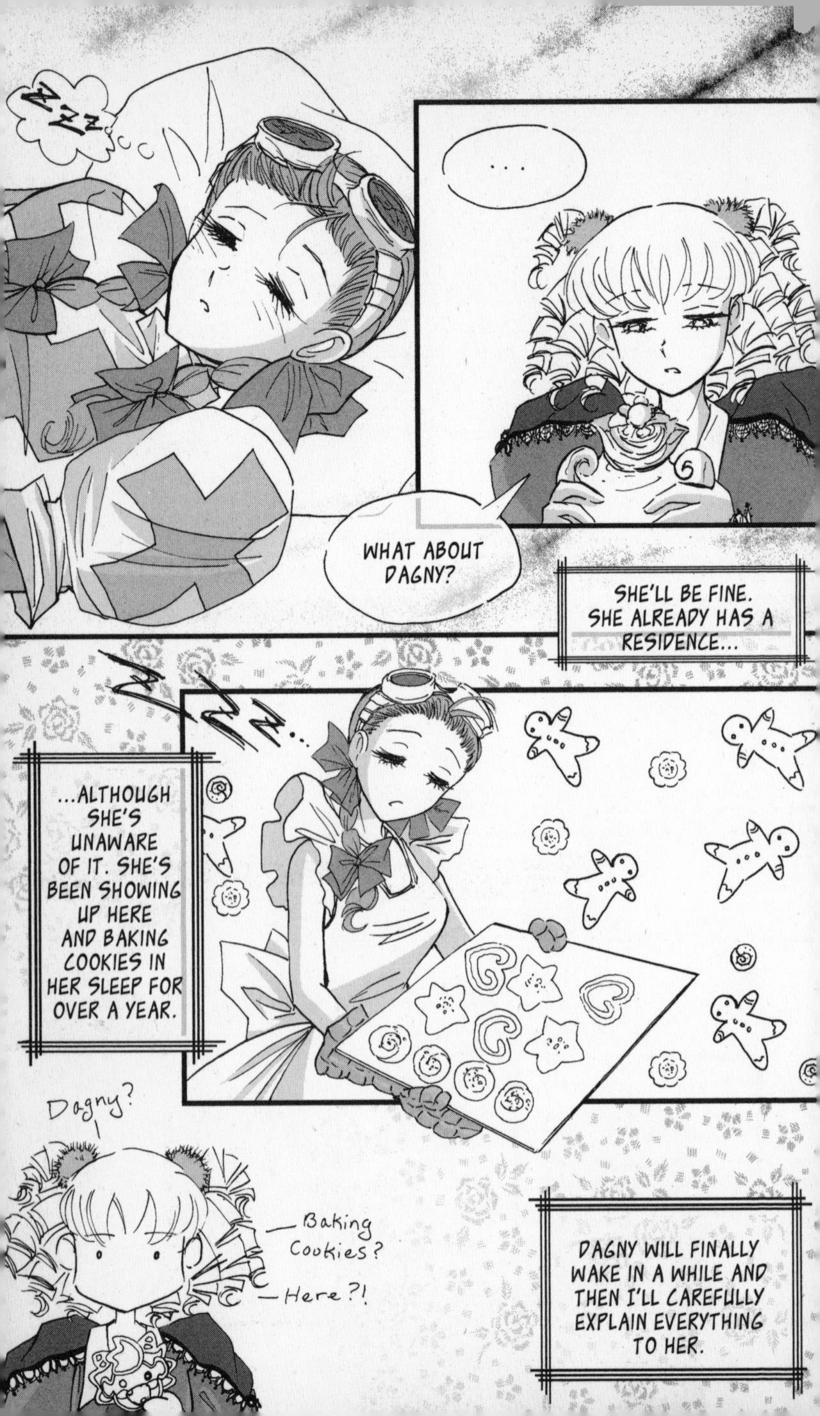
...
ZZZ...
WHAT ABOUT DAGNY?
SHE'LL BE FINE. SHE ALREADY HAS A RESIDENCE...
ZZZ...
...ALTHOUGH SHE'S UNAWARE OF IT. SHE'S BEEN SHOWING UP HERE AND BAKING COOKIES IN HER SLEEP FOR OVER A YEAR.
Dagny?
Baking Cookies?
Here?!
DAGNY WILL FINALLY WAKE IN A WHILE AND THEN I'LL CAREFULLY EXPLAIN EVERYTHING TO HER.

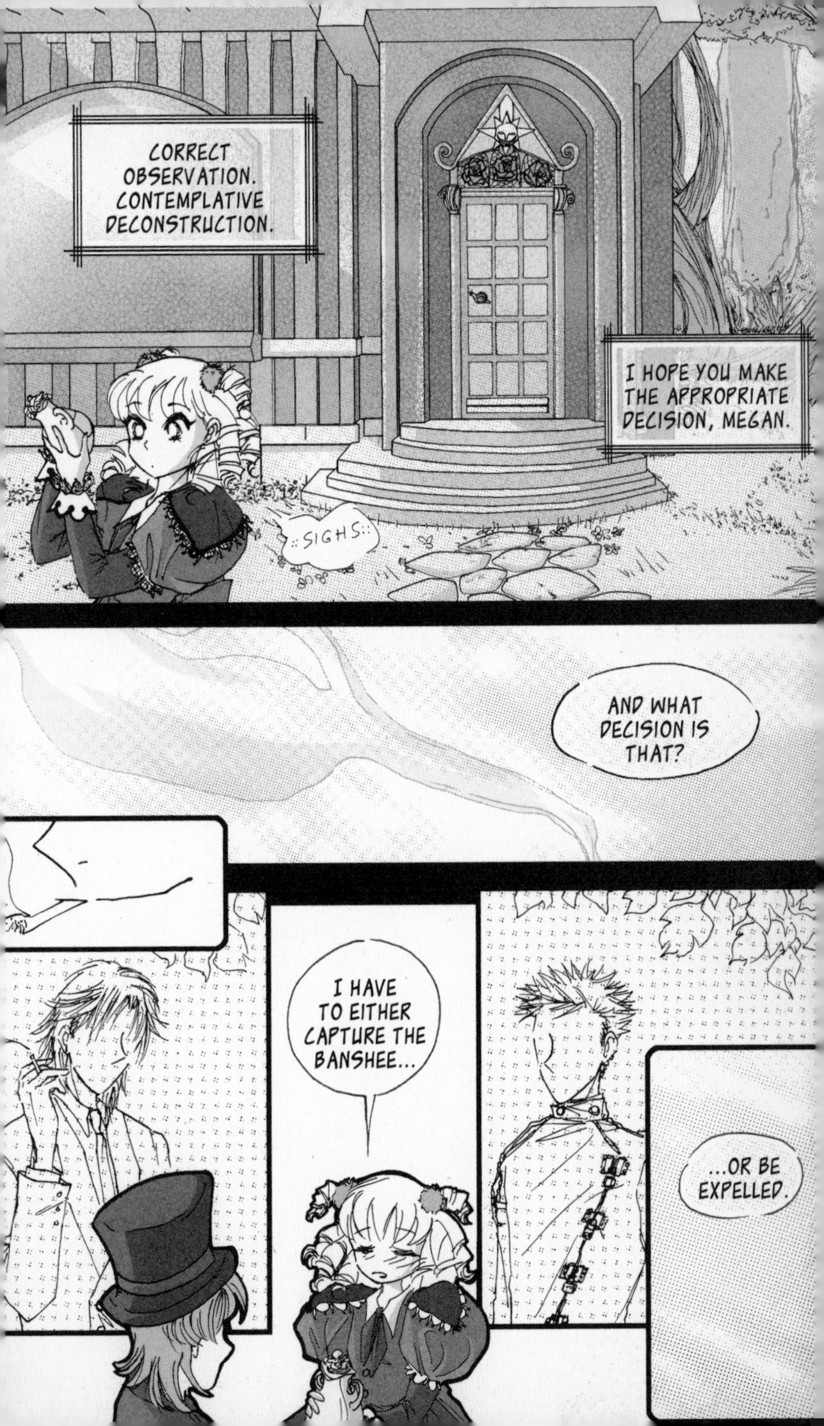
CORRECT OBSERVATION. CONTEMPLATIVE DECONSTRUCTION.
I HOPE YOU MAKE THE APPROPRIATE DECISION, MEGAN.
::SIGHS::
AND WHAT DECISION IS THAT?
I HAVE TO EITHER CAPTURE THE BANSHEE...
...OR BE EXPELLED.

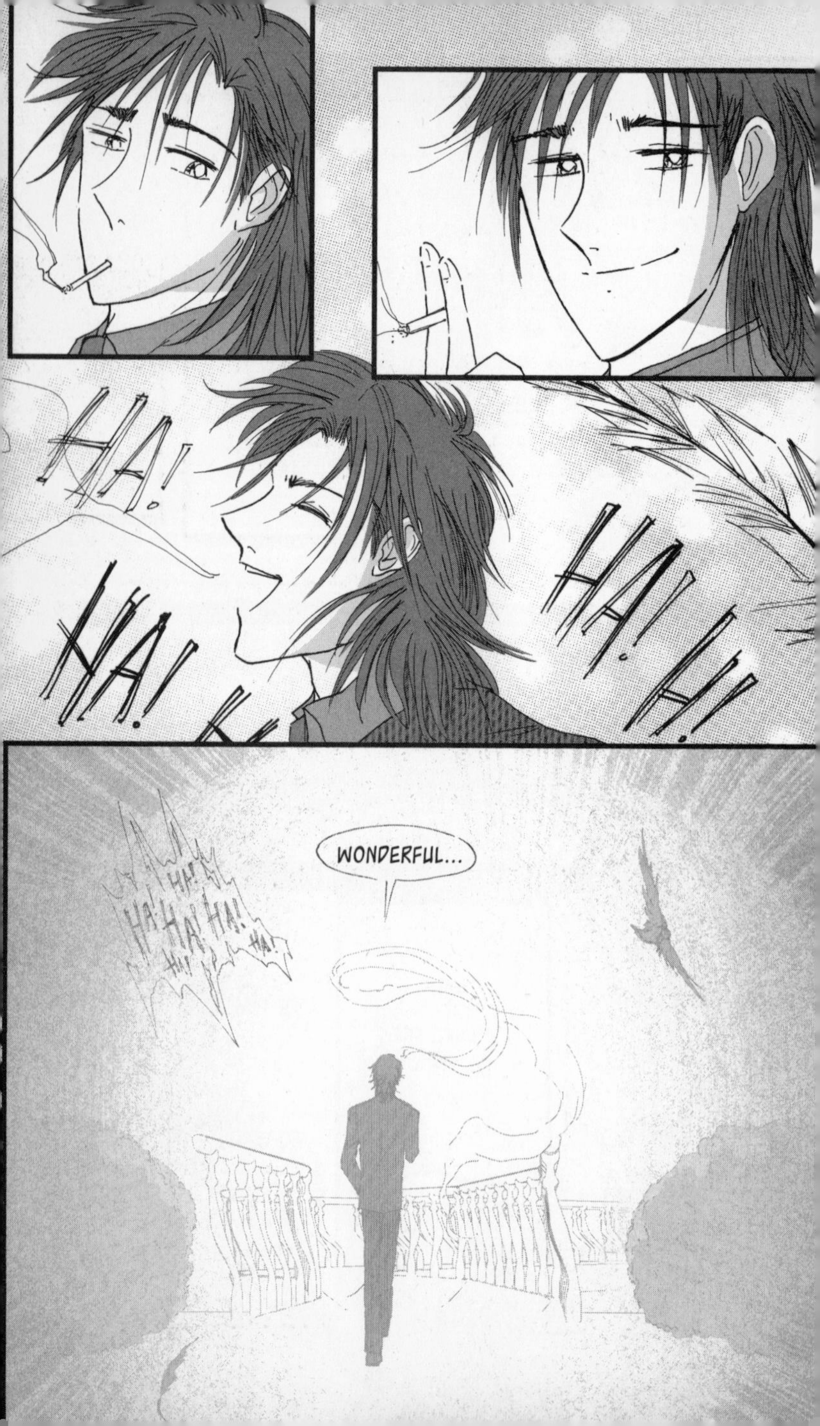
HA! HA!
HA! HA!
HA!
HA! HA! HA! HA! HA! HA! HA!
WONDERFUL...

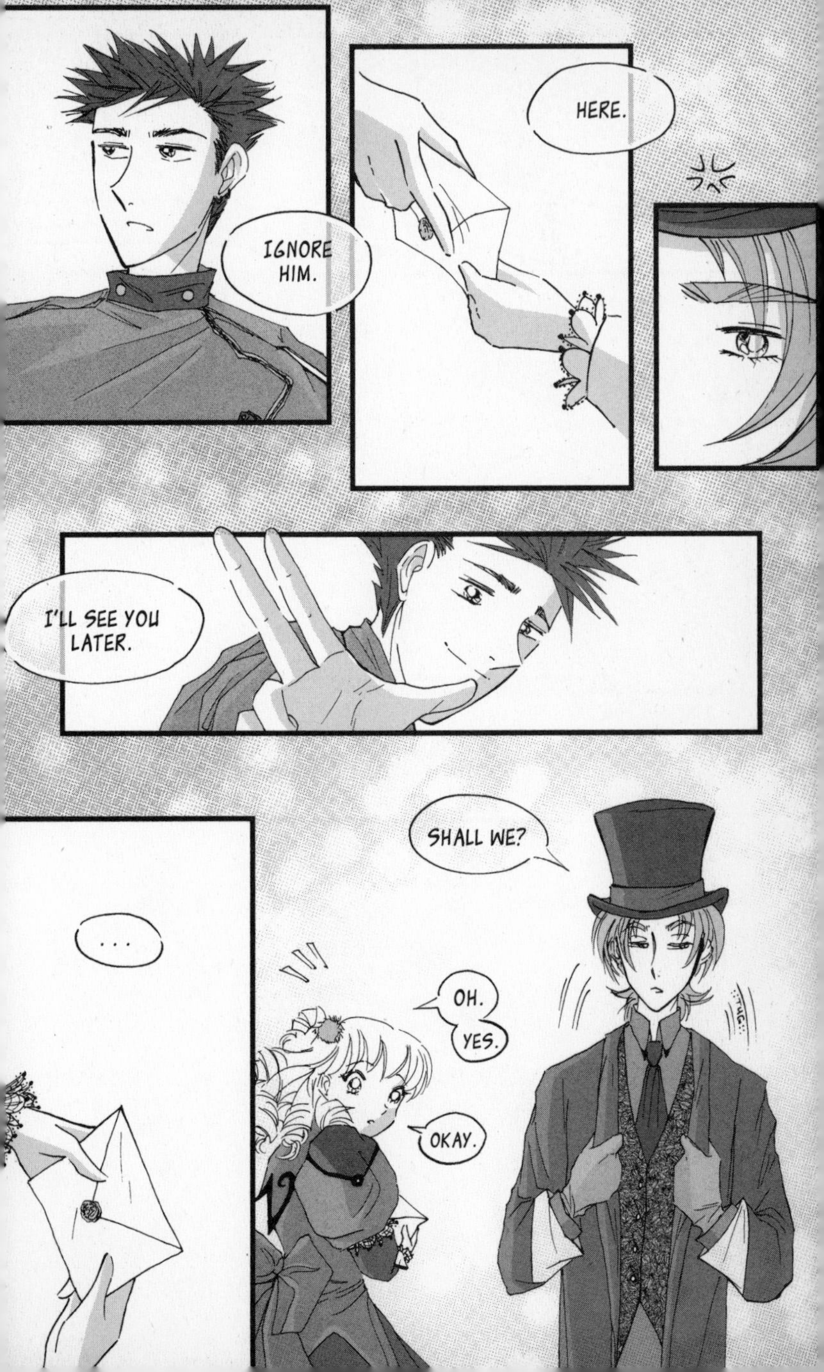
HERE.
IGNORE HIM.
I'LL SEE YOU LATER.
SHALL WE?
TUG
OH.
YES.
OKAY.
...

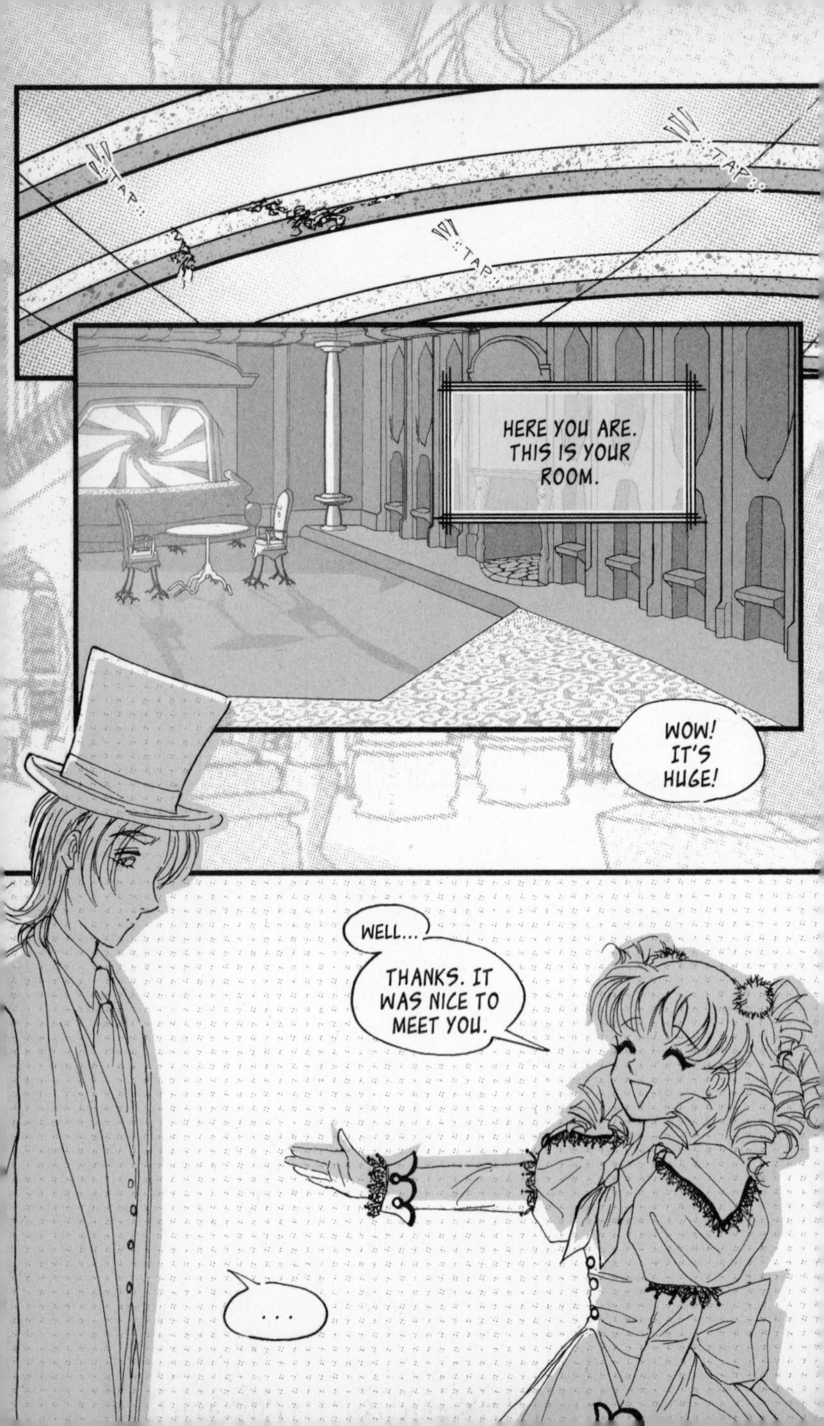
TAP...
TAP...
TAP!
HERE YOU ARE. THIS IS YOUR ROOM.
WOW! IT'S HUGE!
WELL...
THANKS. IT WAS NICE TO MEET YOU.
...

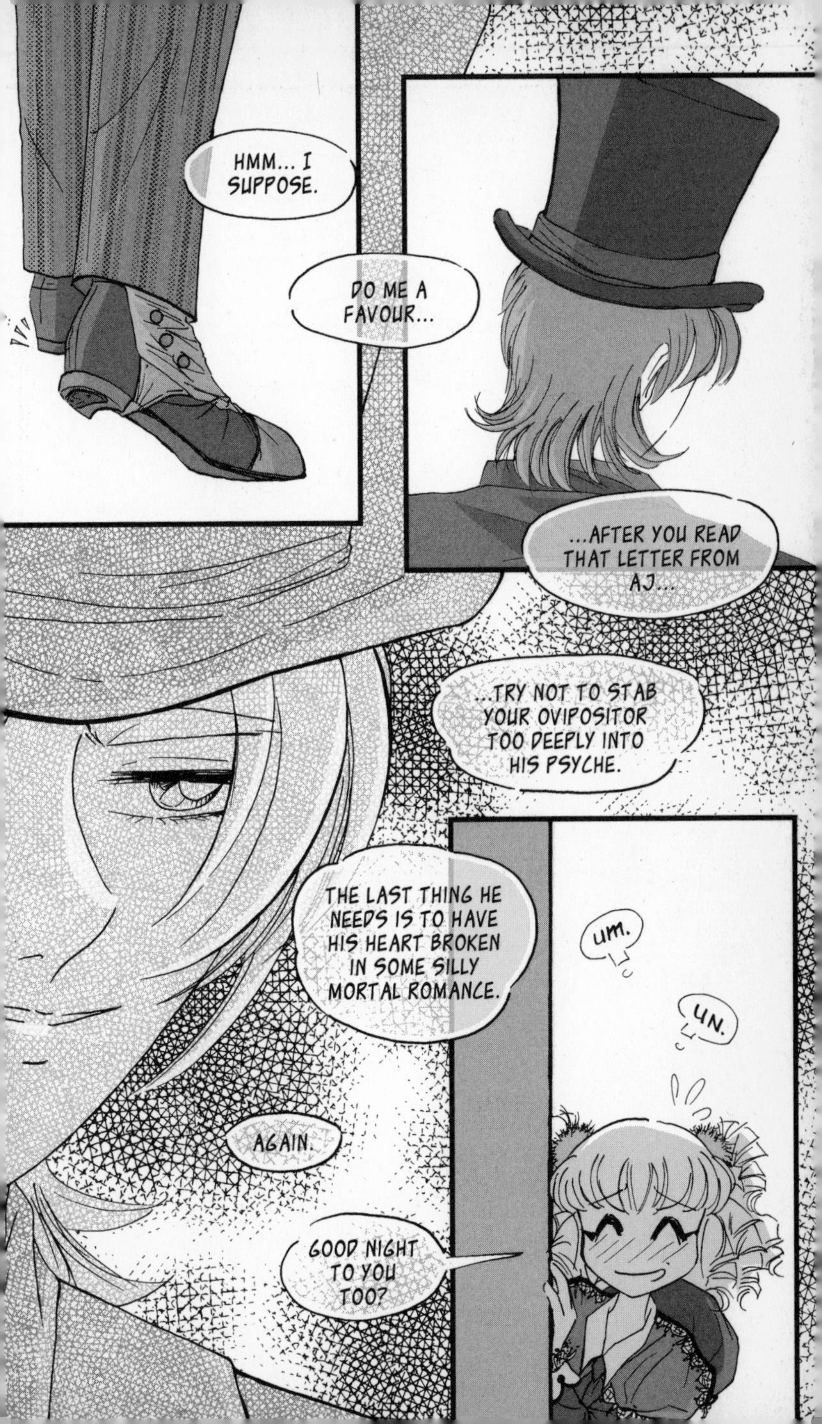
HMM... I SUPPOSE.
DO ME A FAVOUR...
...AFTER YOU READ THAT LETTER FROM AJ...
...TRY NOT TO STAB YOUR OVIPOSITOR TOO DEEPLY INTO HIS PSYCHE.
THE LAST THING HE NEEDS IS TO HAVE HIS HEART BROKEN IN SOME SILLY MORTAL ROMANCE.
AGAIN.
um.
un.
GOOD NIGHT TO YOU TOO?

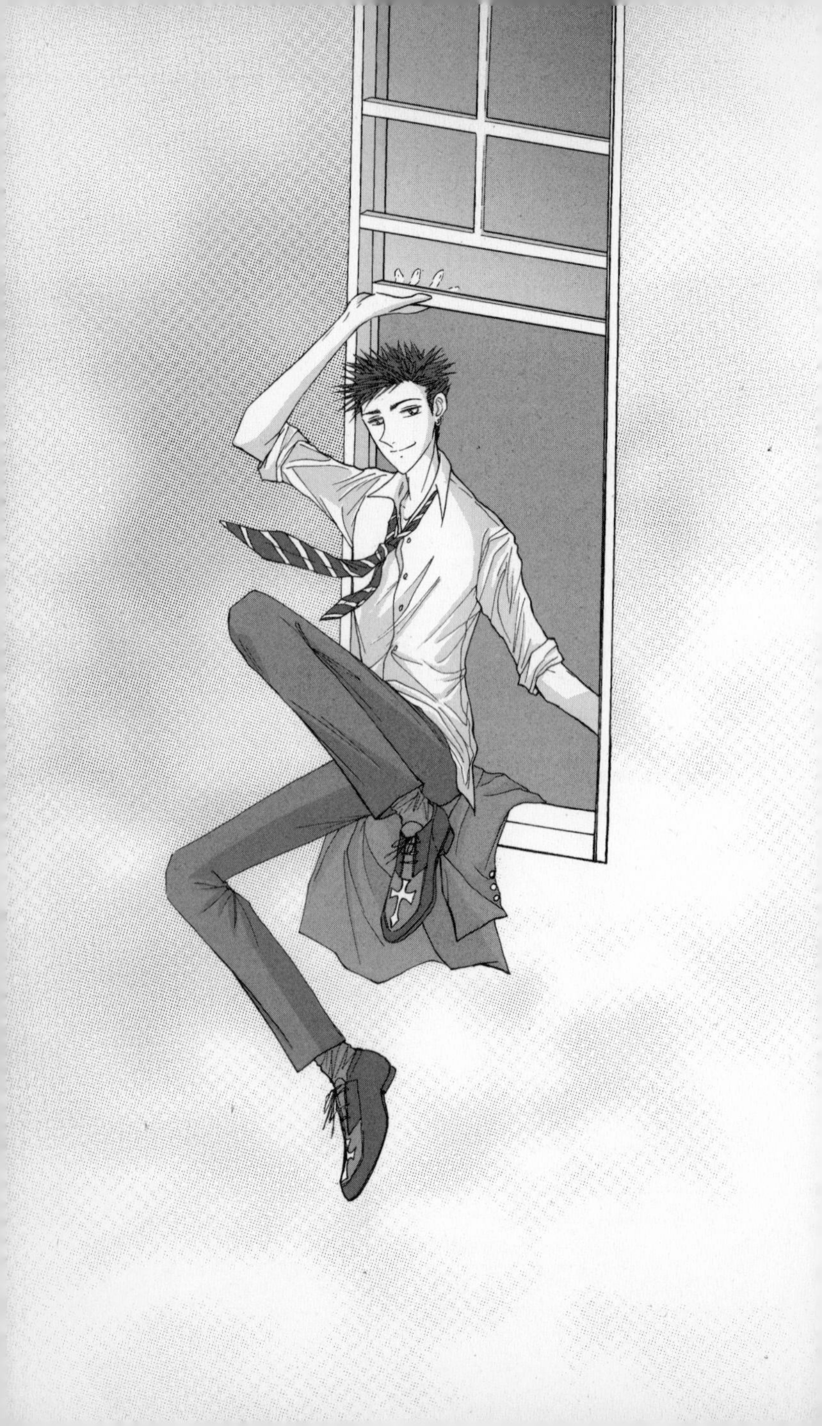

# Chapter Five:

## this is Elusion

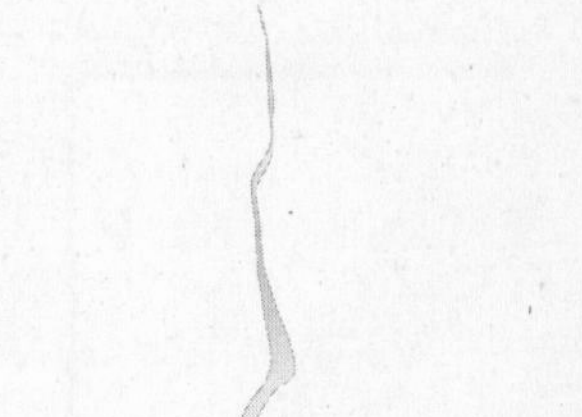
-AJ

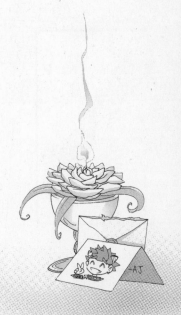

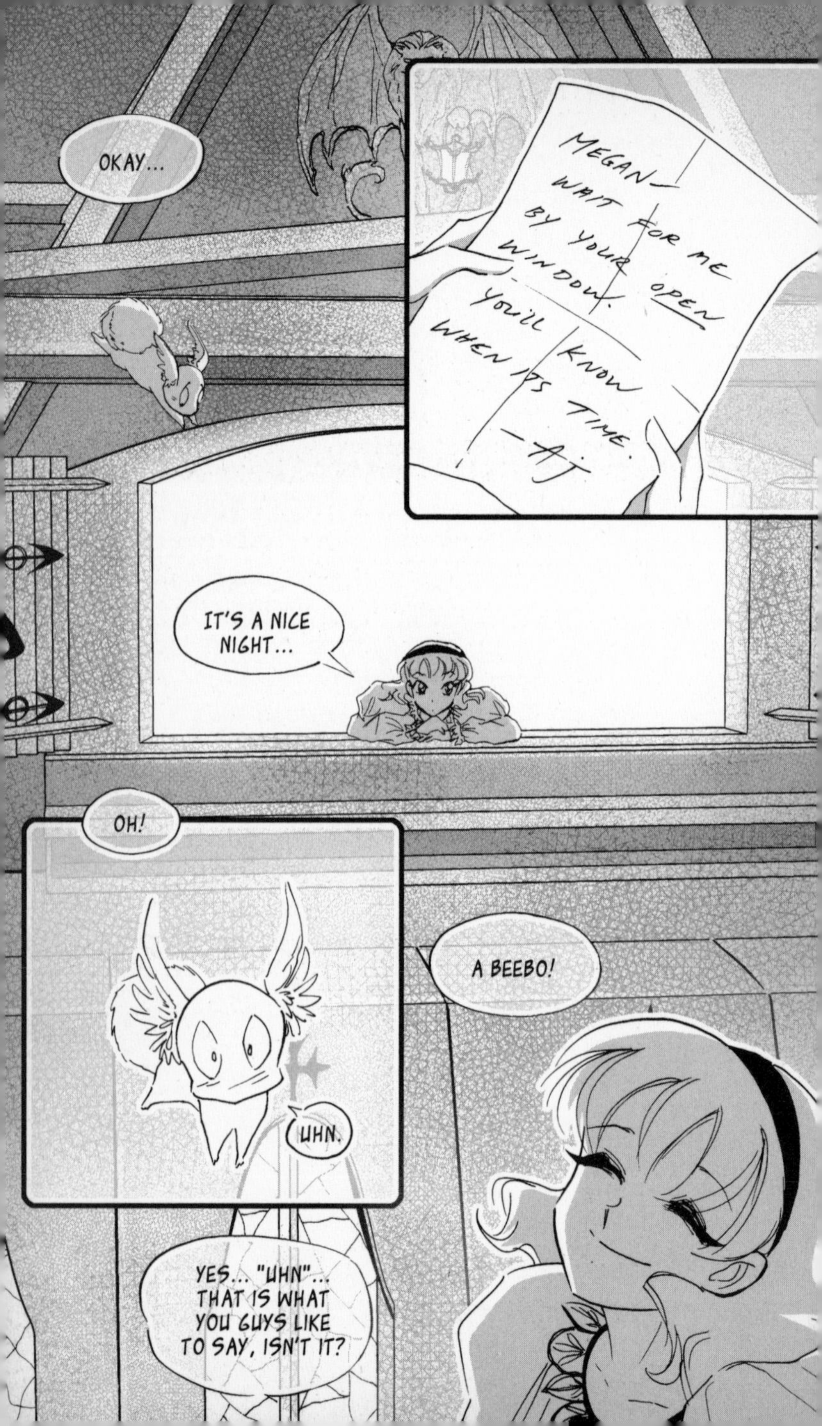
OKAY...
MEGAN—
WAIT FOR ME
BY YOUR OPEN
WINDOW.
YOU'LL KNOW
WHEN IT'S TIME.
—AJ
IT'S A NICE NIGHT...
OH!
A BEEBO!
UHN.
YES... "UHN"... THAT IS WHAT YOU GUYS LIKE TO SAY, ISN'T IT?

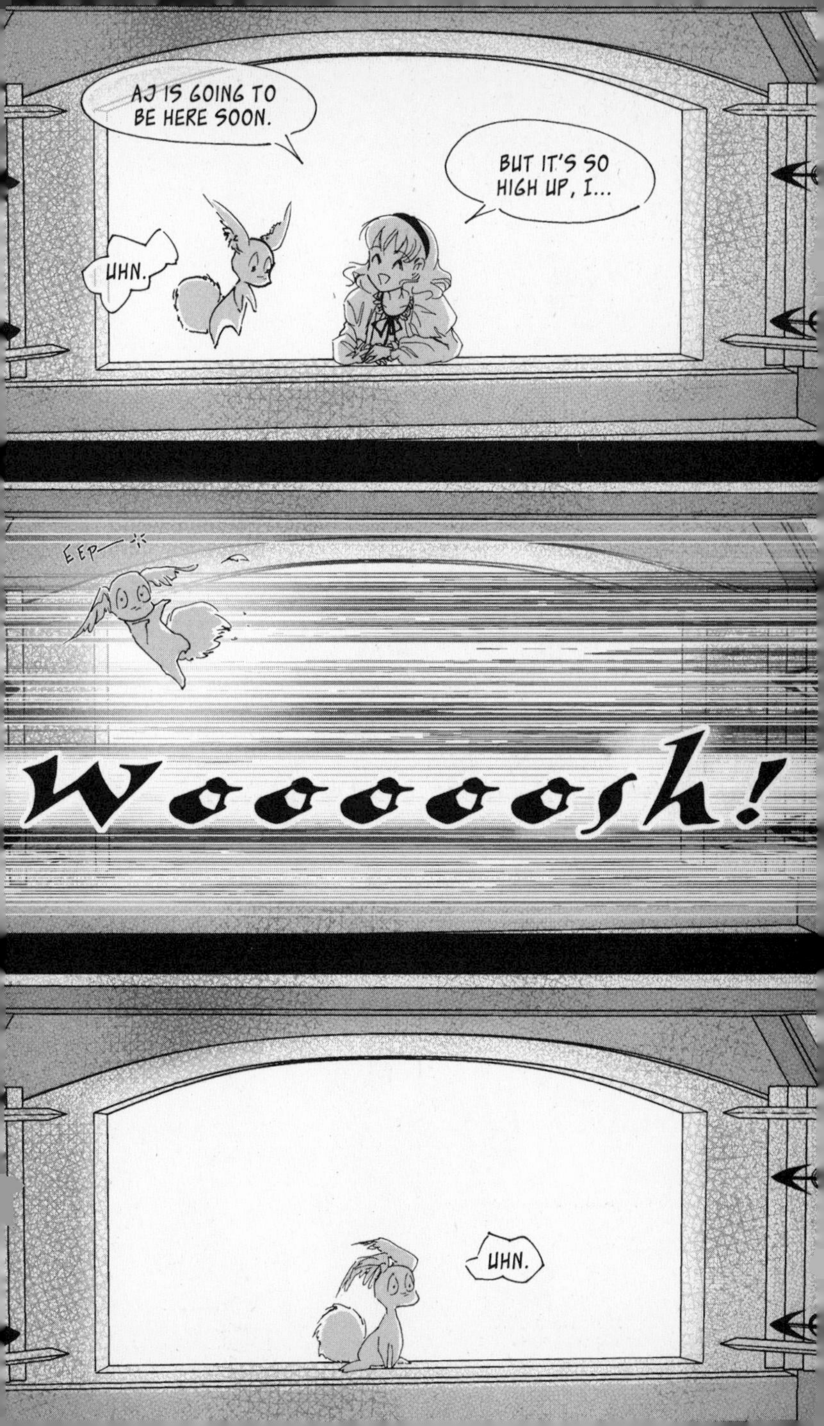
AJ IS GOING TO BE HERE SOON.
BUT IT'S SO HIGH UP, I...
UHN.
EEp—
Woooosh!
UHN.

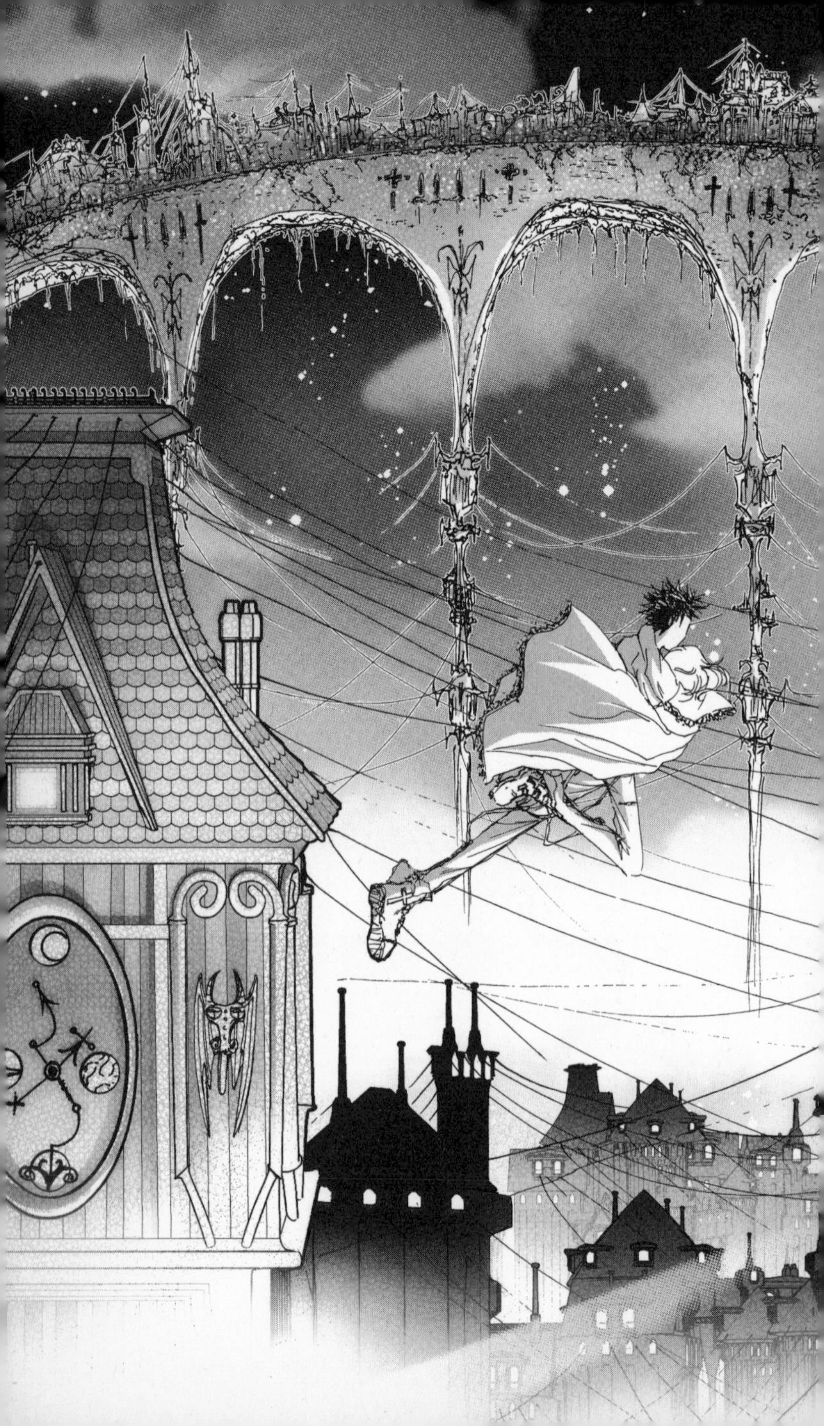

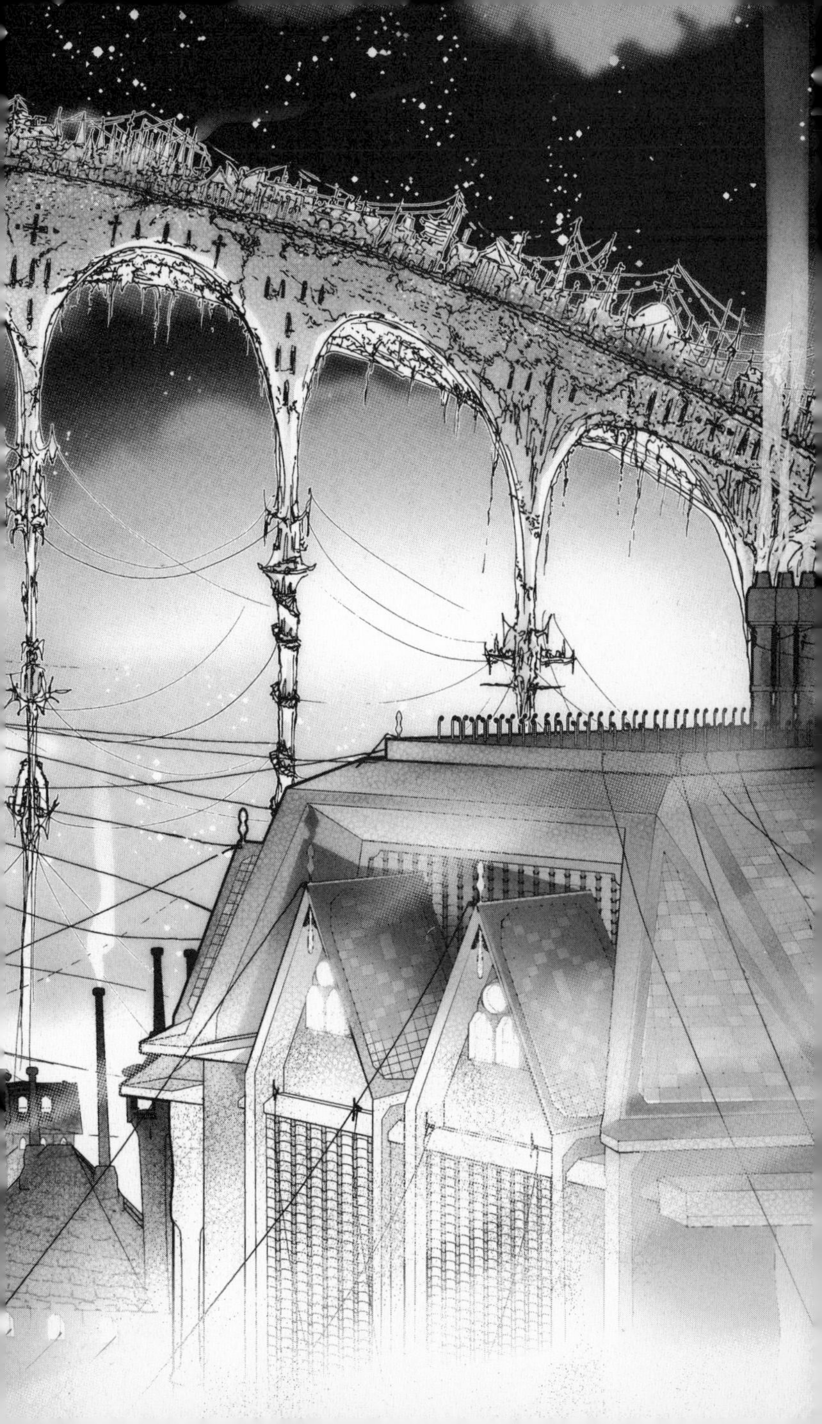

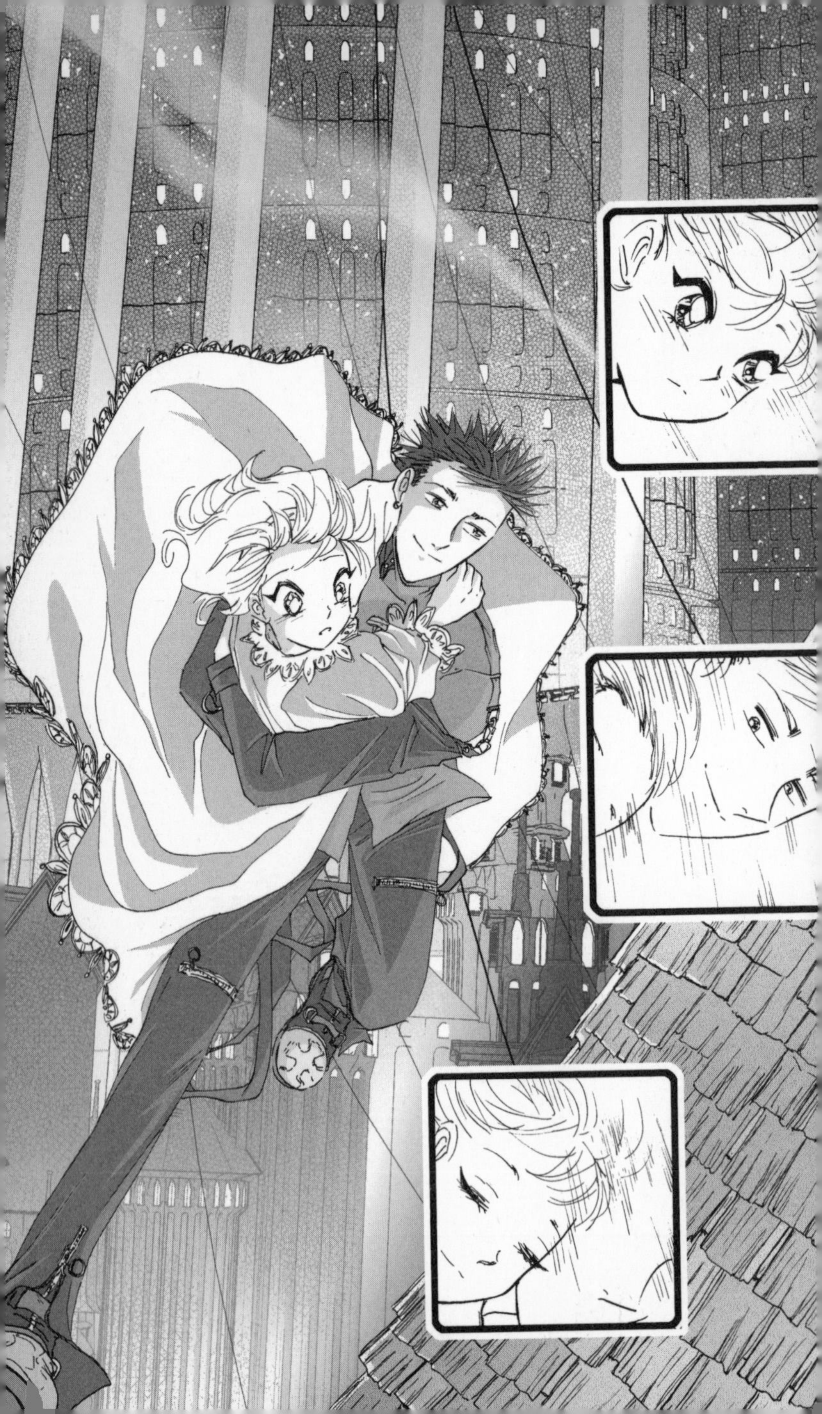

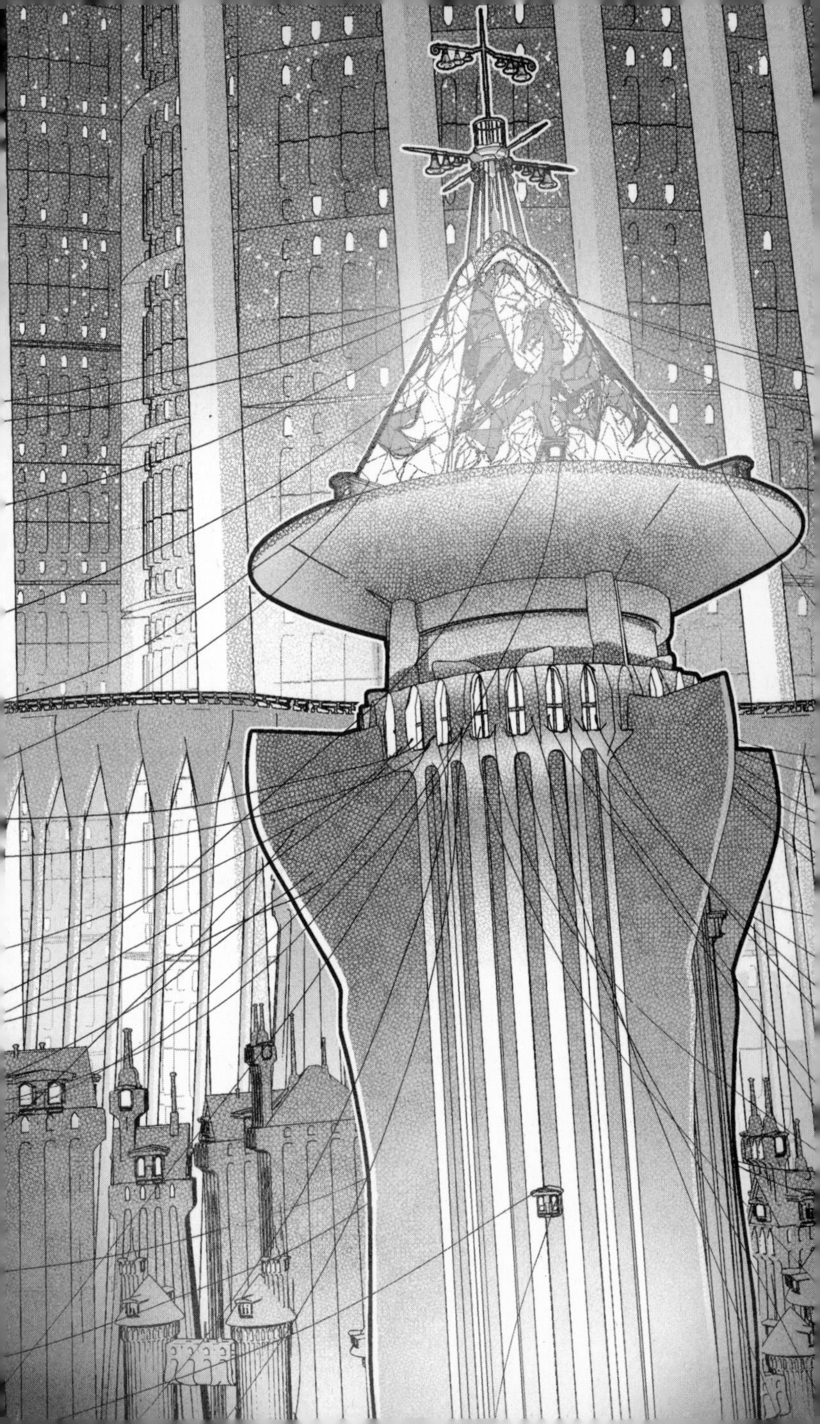

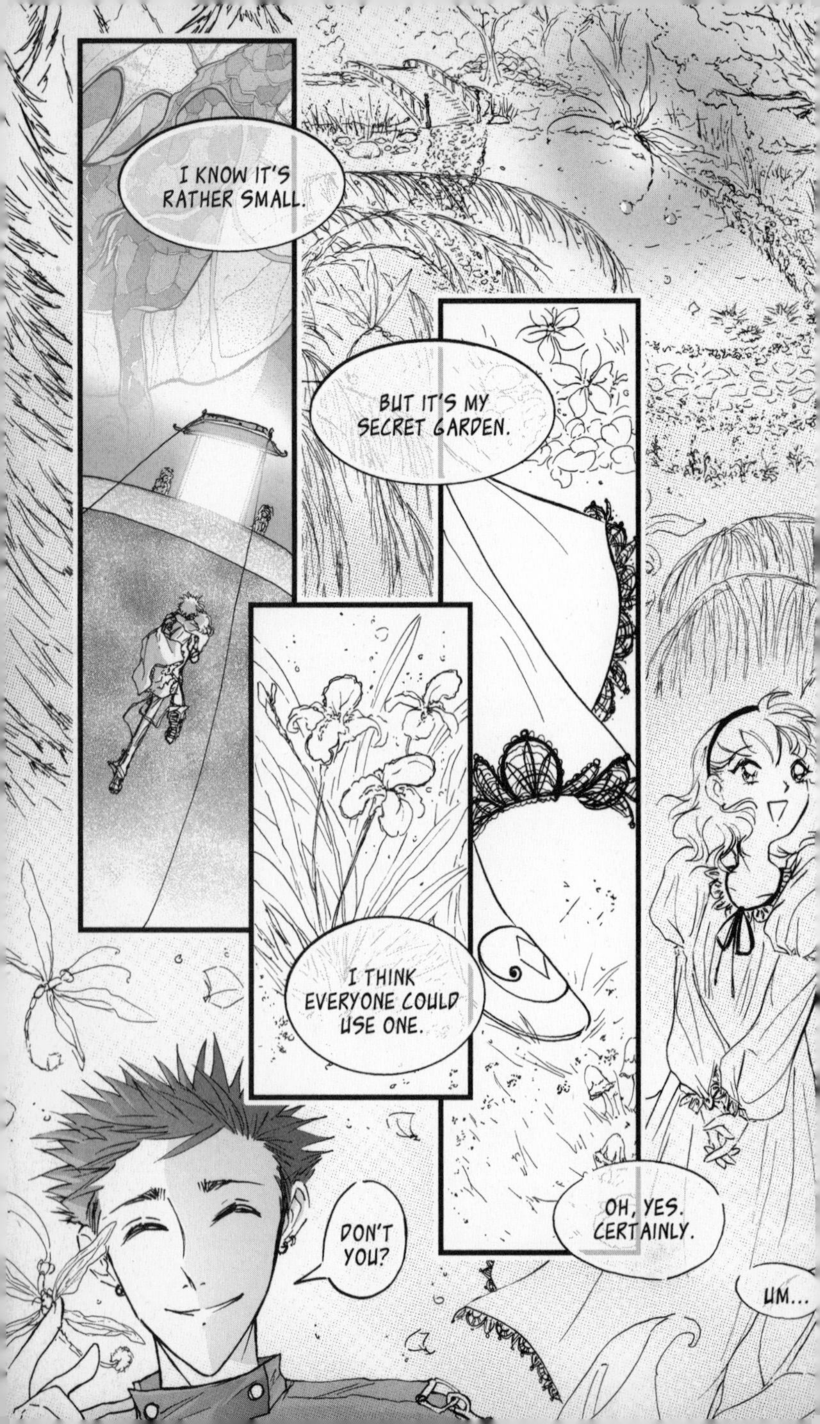
I KNOW IT'S RATHER SMALL.
BUT IT'S MY SECRET GARDEN.
I THINK EVERYONE COULD USE ONE.
DON'T YOU?
OH, YES. CERTAINLY.
UM...

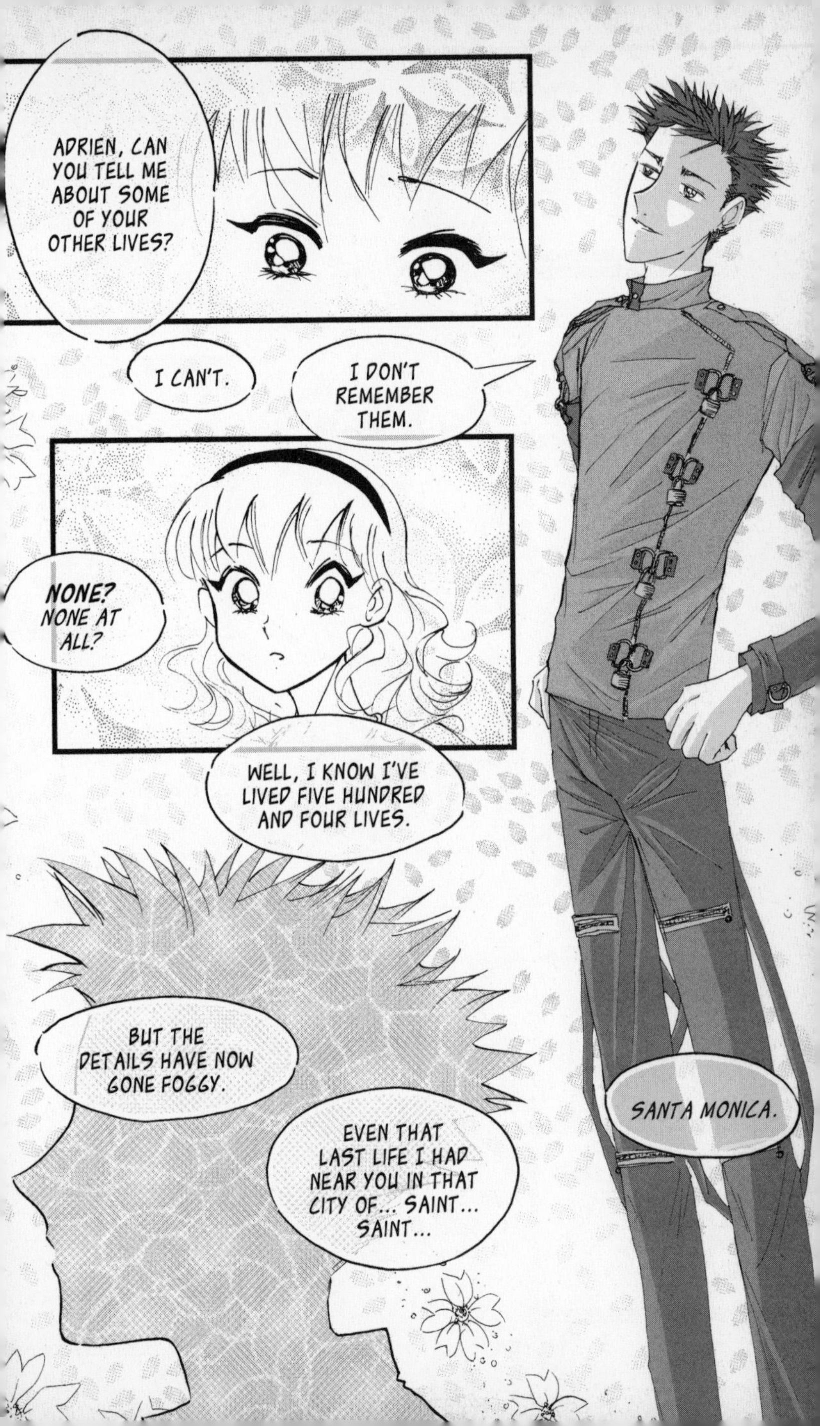
ADRIEN, CAN YOU TELL ME ABOUT SOME OF YOUR OTHER LIVES?
I CAN'T.
I DON'T REMEMBER THEM.
NONE? NONE AT ALL?
WELL, I KNOW I'VE LIVED FIVE HUNDRED AND FOUR LIVES.
BUT THE DETAILS HAVE NOW GONE FOGGY.
EVEN THAT LAST LIFE I HAD NEAR YOU IN THAT CITY OF... SAINT... SAINT...
SANTA MONICA.

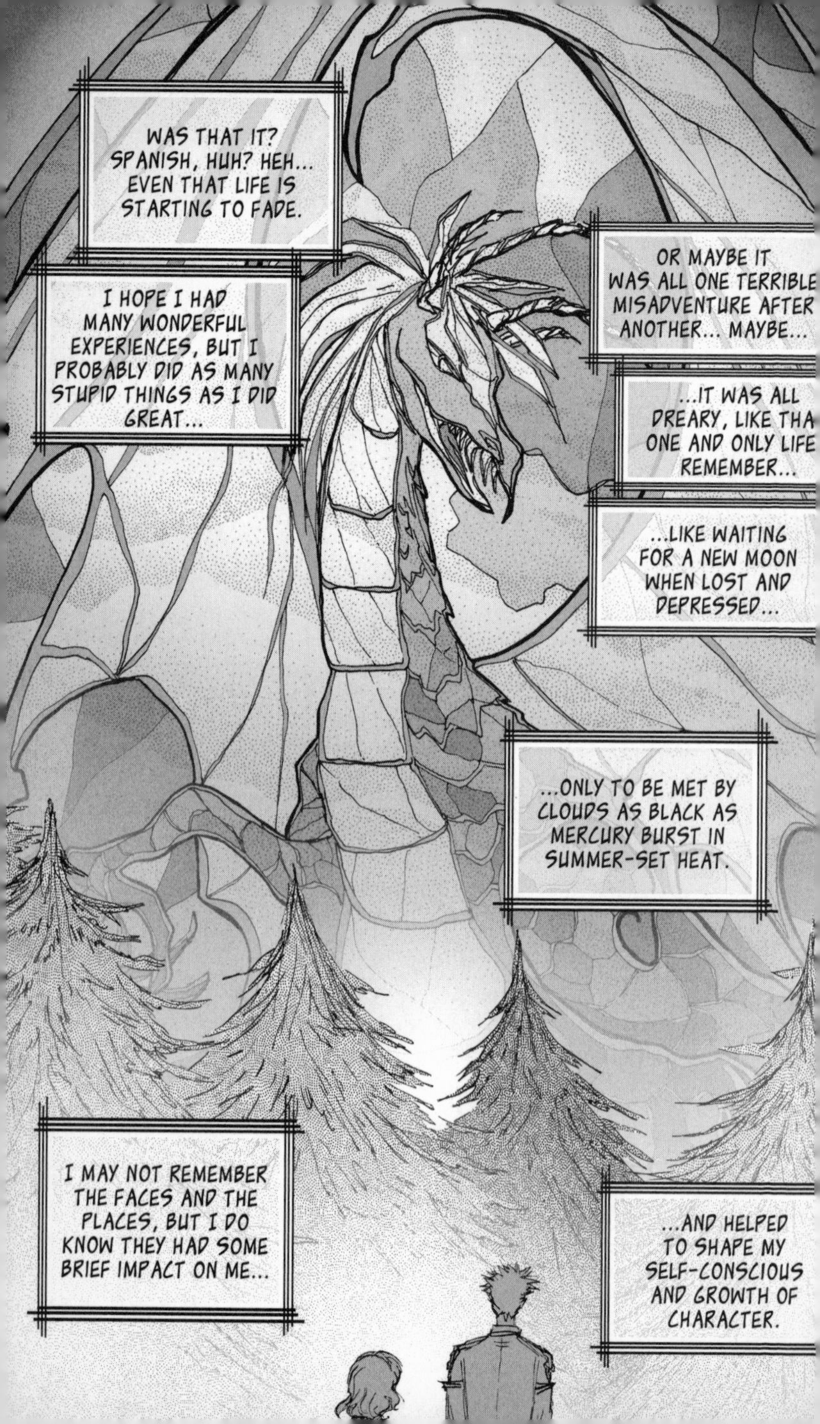
WAS THAT IT? SPANISH, HUH? HEH... EVEN THAT LIFE IS STARTING TO FADE.
I HOPE I HAD MANY WONDERFUL EXPERIENCES, BUT I PROBABLY DID AS MANY STUPID THINGS AS I DID GREAT...
OR MAYBE IT WAS ALL ONE TERRIBLE MISADVENTURE AFTER ANOTHER... MAYBE...
...IT WAS ALL DREARY, LIKE THA ONE AND ONLY LIFE REMEMBER...
...LIKE WAITING FOR A NEW MOON WHEN LOST AND DEPRESSED...
...ONLY TO BE MET BY CLOUDS AS BLACK AS MERCURY BURST IN SUMMER-SET HEAT.
I MAY NOT REMEMBER THE FACES AND THE PLACES, BUT I DO KNOW THEY HAD SOME BRIEF IMPACT ON ME...
...AND HELPED TO SHAPE MY SELF-CONSCIOUS AND GROWTH OF CHARACTER.

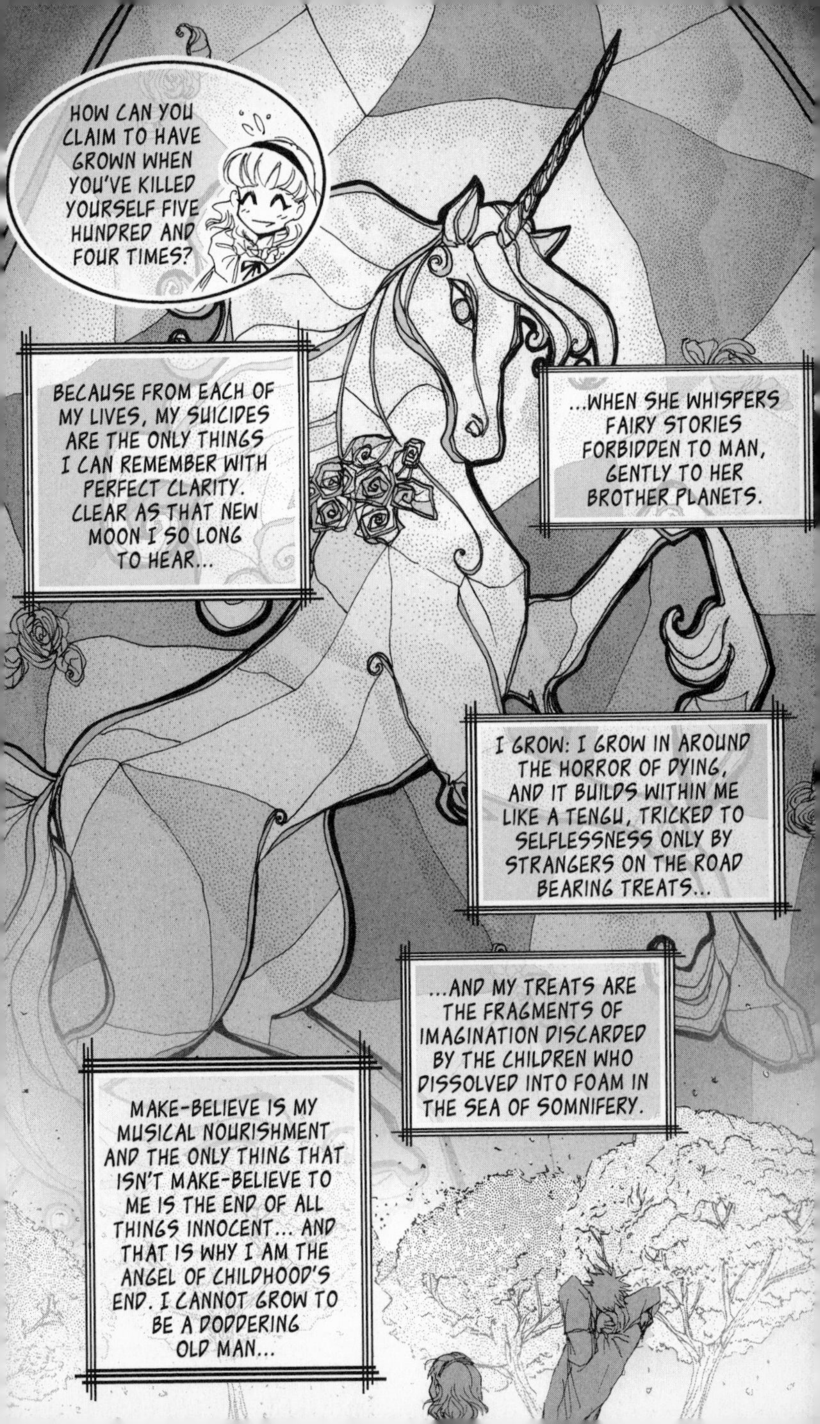
HOW CAN YOU CLAIM TO HAVE GROWN WHEN YOU'VE KILLED YOURSELF FIVE HUNDRED AND FOUR TIMES?
BECAUSE FROM EACH OF MY LIVES, MY SUICIDES ARE THE ONLY THINGS I CAN REMEMBER WITH PERFECT CLARITY. CLEAR AS THAT NEW MOON I SO LONG TO HEAR...
...WHEN SHE WHISPERS FAIRY STORIES FORBIDDEN TO MAN, GENTLY TO HER BROTHER PLANETS.
I GROW: I GROW IN AROUND THE HORROR OF DYING, AND IT BUILDS WITHIN ME LIKE A TENGU, TRICKED TO SELFLESSNESS ONLY BY STRANGERS ON THE ROAD BEARING TREATS...
...AND MY TREATS ARE THE FRAGMENTS OF IMAGINATION DISCARDED BY THE CHILDREN WHO DISSOLVED INTO FOAM IN THE SEA OF SOMNIFERY.
MAKE-BELIEVE IS MY MUSICAL NOURISHMENT AND THE ONLY THING THAT ISN'T MAKE-BELIEVE TO ME IS THE END OF ALL THINGS INNOCENT... AND THAT IS WHY I AM THE ANGEL OF CHILDHOOD'S END. I CANNOT GROW TO BE A DODDERING OLD MAN...

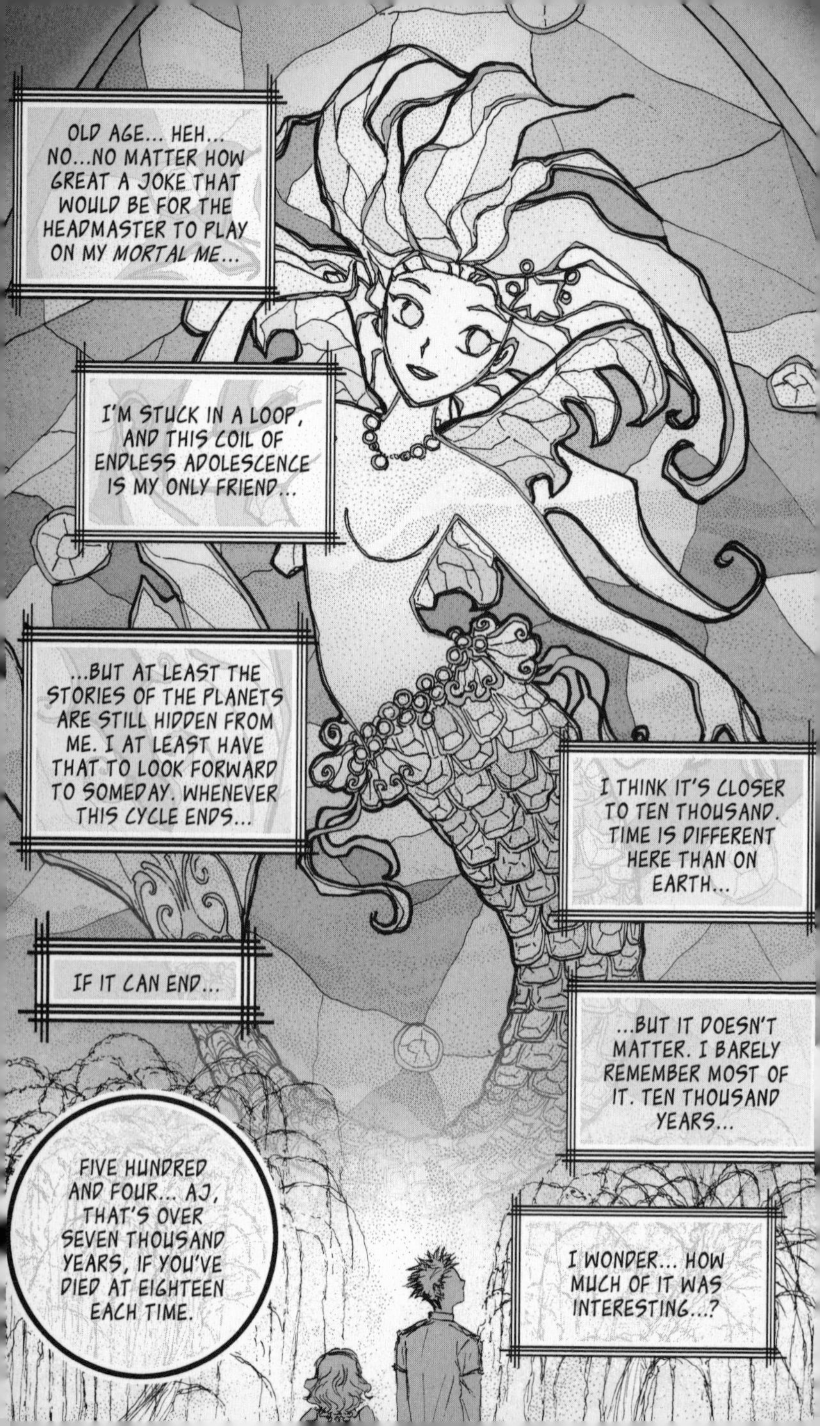
OLD AGE... HEH... NO...NO MATTER HOW GREAT A JOKE THAT WOULD BE FOR THE HEADMASTER TO PLAY ON MY *MORTAL ME*...
I'M STUCK IN A LOOP, AND THIS COIL OF ENDLESS ADOLESCENCE IS MY ONLY FRIEND...
...BUT AT LEAST THE STORIES OF THE PLANETS ARE STILL HIDDEN FROM ME. I AT LEAST HAVE THAT TO LOOK FORWARD TO SOMEDAY. WHENEVER THIS CYCLE ENDS...
IF IT CAN END...
FIVE HUNDRED AND FOUR... AJ, THAT'S OVER SEVEN THOUSAND YEARS, IF YOU'VE DIED AT EIGHTEEN EACH TIME.
I THINK IT'S CLOSER TO TEN THOUSAND. TIME IS DIFFERENT HERE THAN ON EARTH...
...BUT IT DOESN'T MATTER. I BARELY REMEMBER MOST OF IT. TEN THOUSAND YEARS...
I WONDER... HOW MUCH OF IT WAS INTERESTING...?

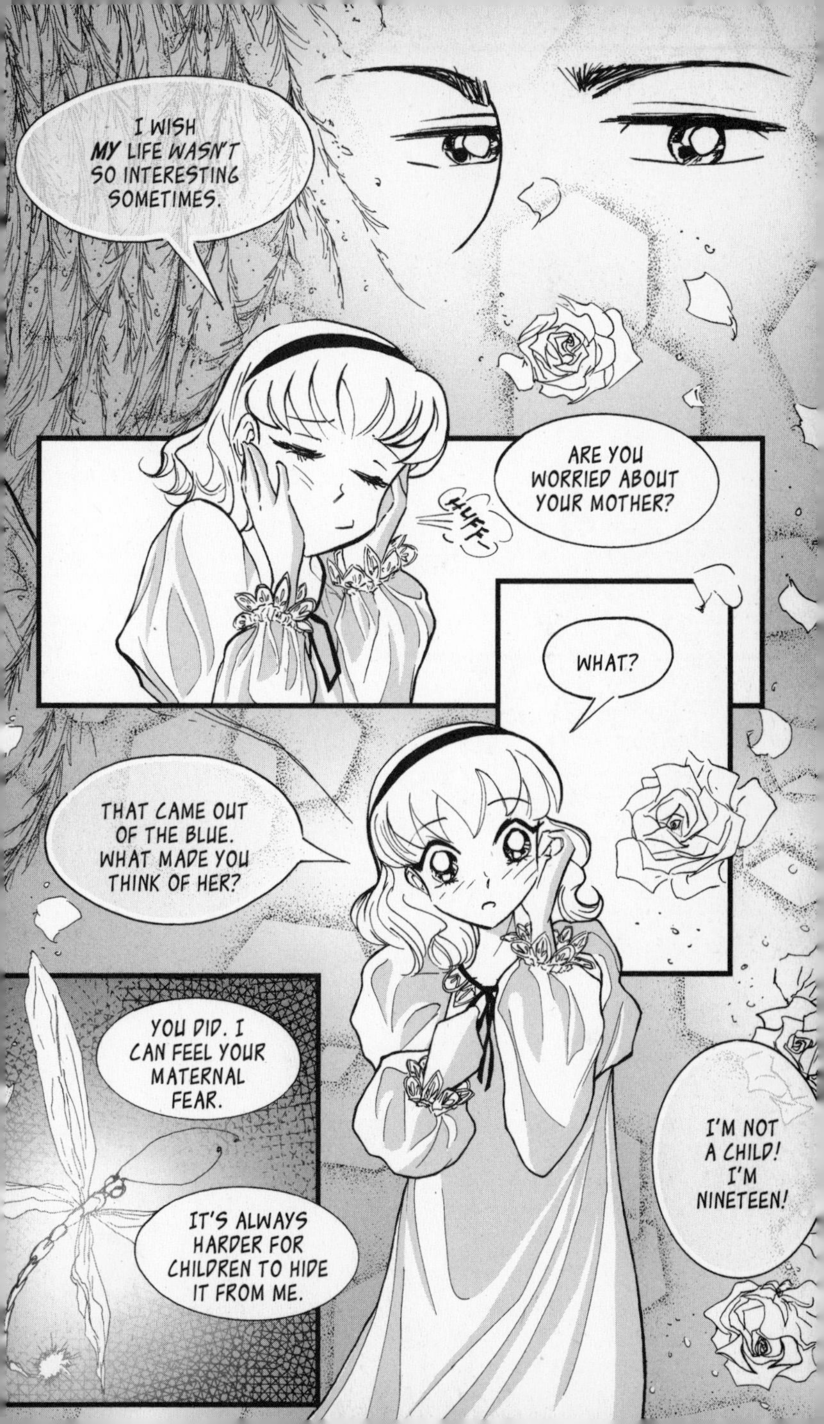
I WISH MY LIFE WASN'T SO INTERESTING SOMETIMES.
HUFF
ARE YOU WORRIED ABOUT YOUR MOTHER?
WHAT?
THAT CAME OUT OF THE BLUE. WHAT MADE YOU THINK OF HER?
YOU DID. I CAN FEEL YOUR MATERNAL FEAR.
IT'S ALWAYS HARDER FOR CHILDREN TO HIDE IT FROM ME.
I'M NOT A CHILD! I'M NINETEEN!

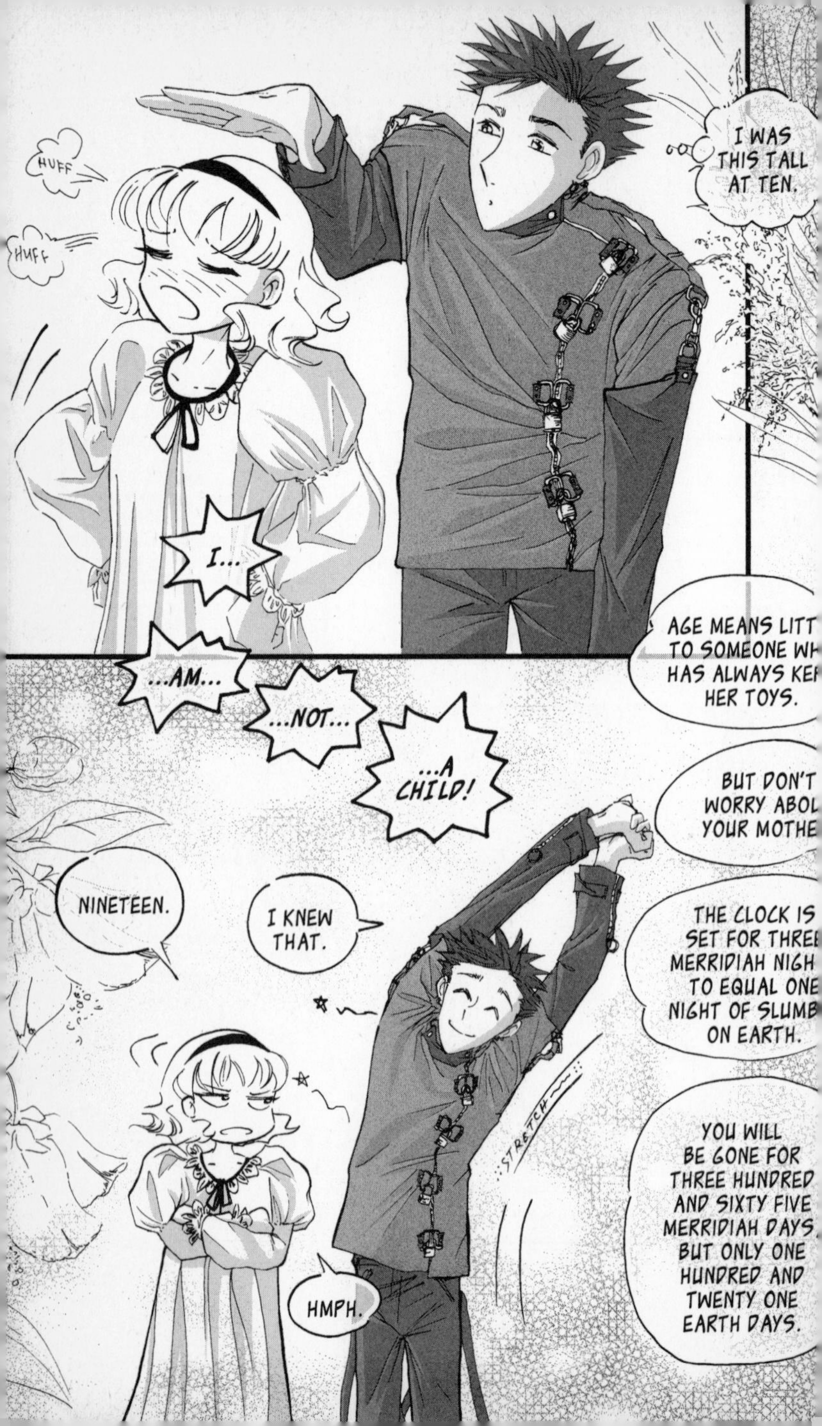
I WAS THIS TALL AT TEN.
HUFF
HUFF
I...
...AM...
...NOT...
...A CHILD!
AGE MEANS LITT TO SOMEONE WH HAS ALWAYS KE HER TOYS.
BUT DON'T WORRY ABOU YOUR MOTHE
THE CLOCK IS SET FOR THREE MERRIDIAH NIGH TO EQUAL ONE NIGHT OF SLUMB ON EARTH.
YOU WILL BE GONE FOR THREE HUNDRED AND SIXTY FIVE MERRIDIAH DAYS, BUT ONLY ONE HUNDRED AND TWENTY ONE EARTH DAYS.
NINETEEN.
I KNEW THAT.
STRETCH
HMPH.

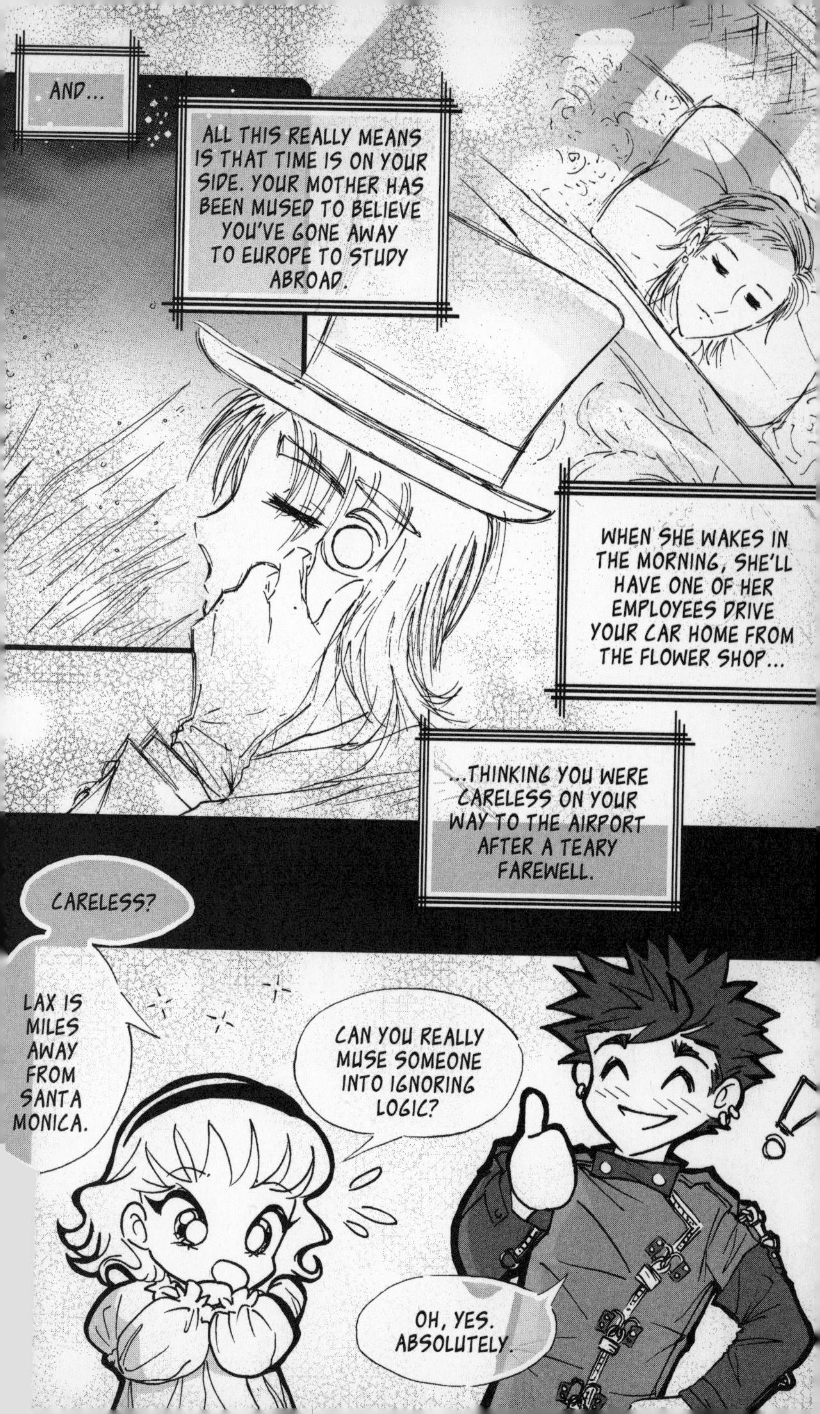
AND...
ALL THIS REALLY MEANS IS THAT TIME IS ON YOUR SIDE. YOUR MOTHER HAS BEEN MUSED TO BELIEVE YOU'VE GONE AWAY TO EUROPE TO STUDY ABROAD.
WHEN SHE WAKES IN THE MORNING, SHE'LL HAVE ONE OF HER EMPLOYEES DRIVE YOUR CAR HOME FROM THE FLOWER SHOP...
...THINKING YOU WERE CARELESS ON YOUR WAY TO THE AIRPORT AFTER A TEARY FAREWELL.
CARELESS?
LAX IS MILES AWAY FROM SANTA MONICA.
CAN YOU REALLY MUSE SOMEONE INTO IGNORING LOGIC?
OH, YES. ABSOLUTELY.

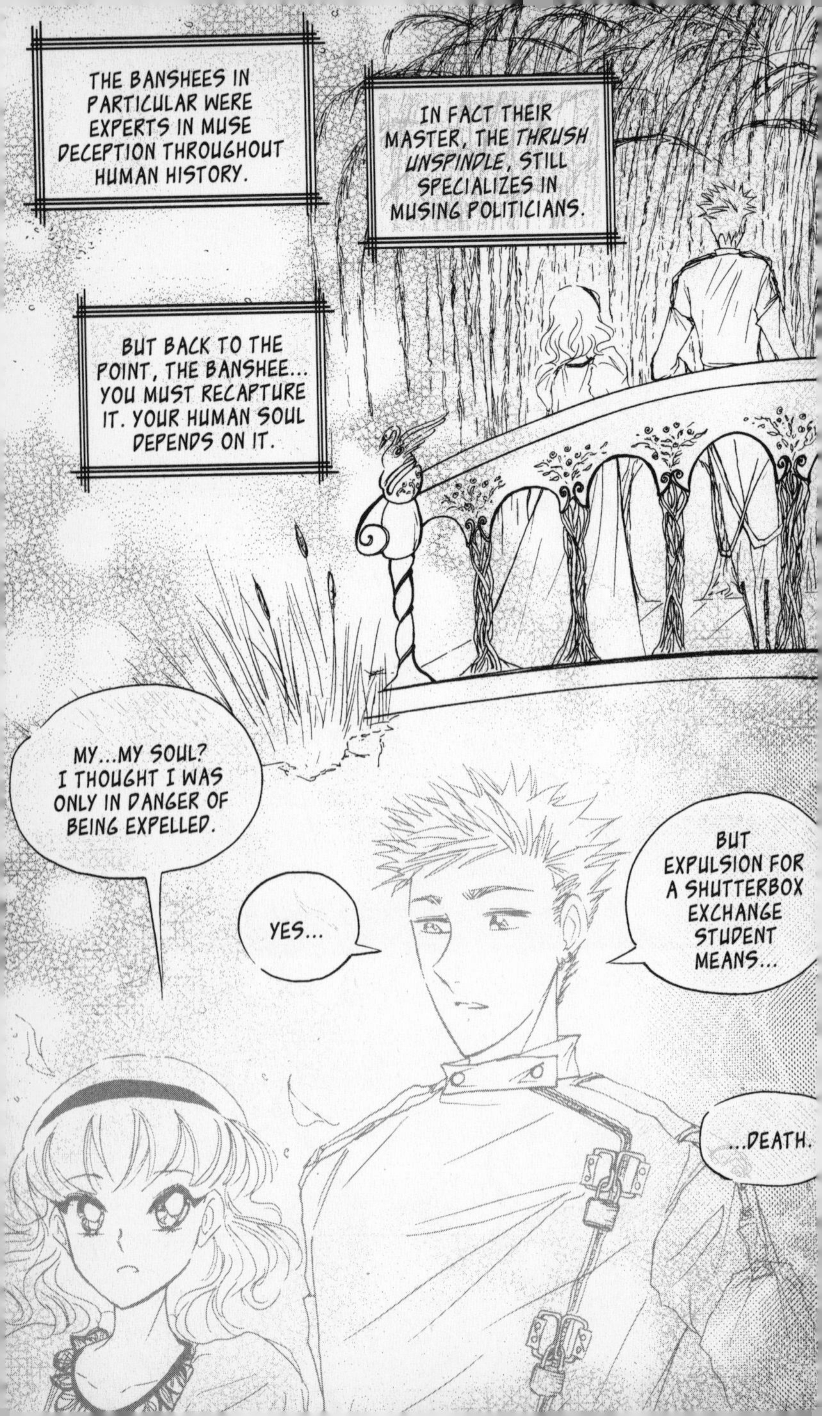
THE BANSHEES IN PARTICULAR WERE EXPERTS IN MUSE DECEPTION THROUGHOUT HUMAN HISTORY.
IN FACT THEIR MASTER, THE *THRUSH UNSPINDLE*, STILL SPECIALIZES IN MUSING POLITICIANS.
BUT BACK TO THE POINT, THE BANSHEE... YOU MUST RECAPTURE IT. YOUR HUMAN SOUL DEPENDS ON IT.
MY...MY SOUL? I THOUGHT I WAS ONLY IN DANGER OF BEING EXPELLED.
YES...
BUT EXPULSION FOR A SHUTTERBOX EXCHANGE STUDENT MEANS...
...DEATH.

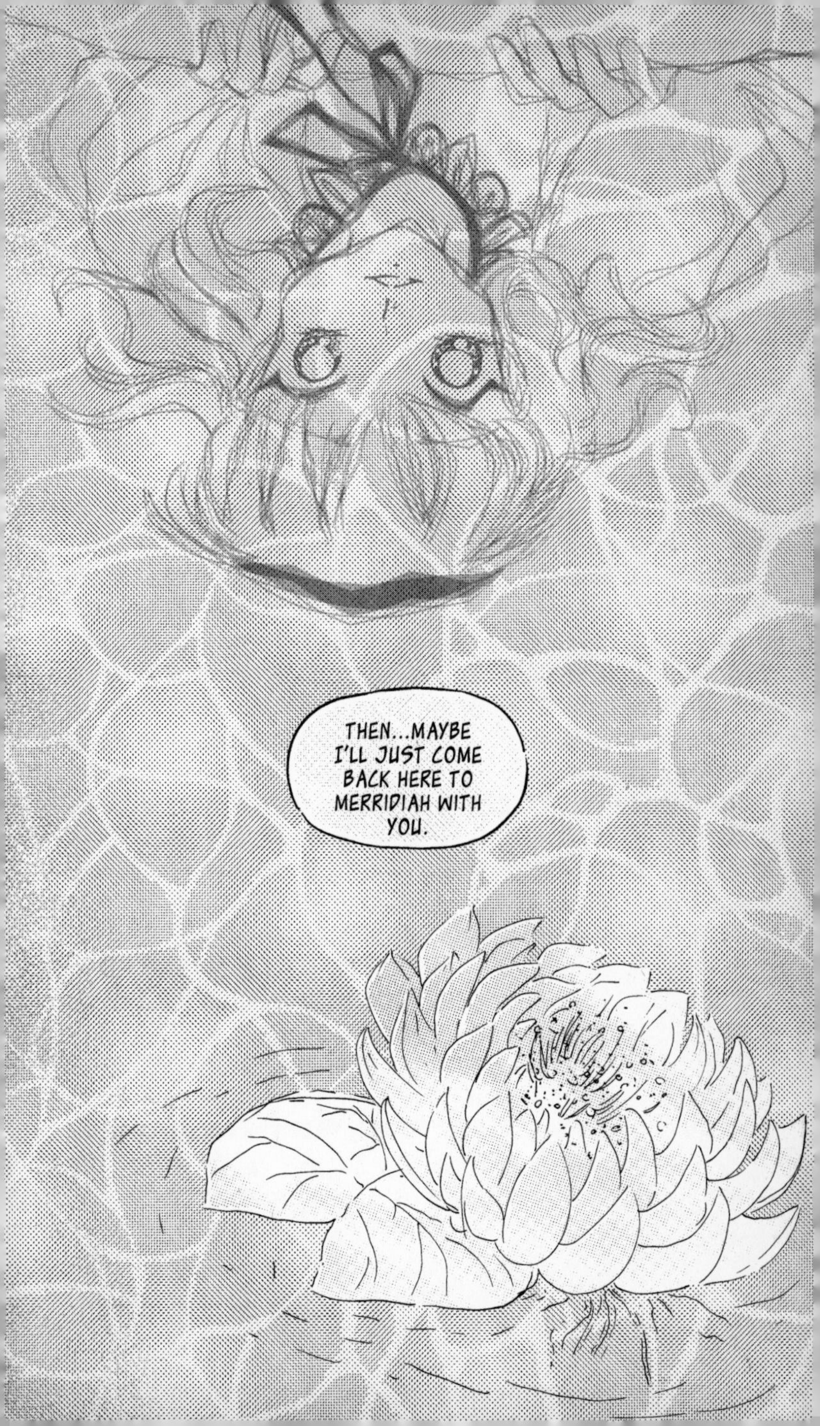
THEN...MAYBE I'LL JUST COME BACK HERE TO MERRIDIAH WITH YOU.

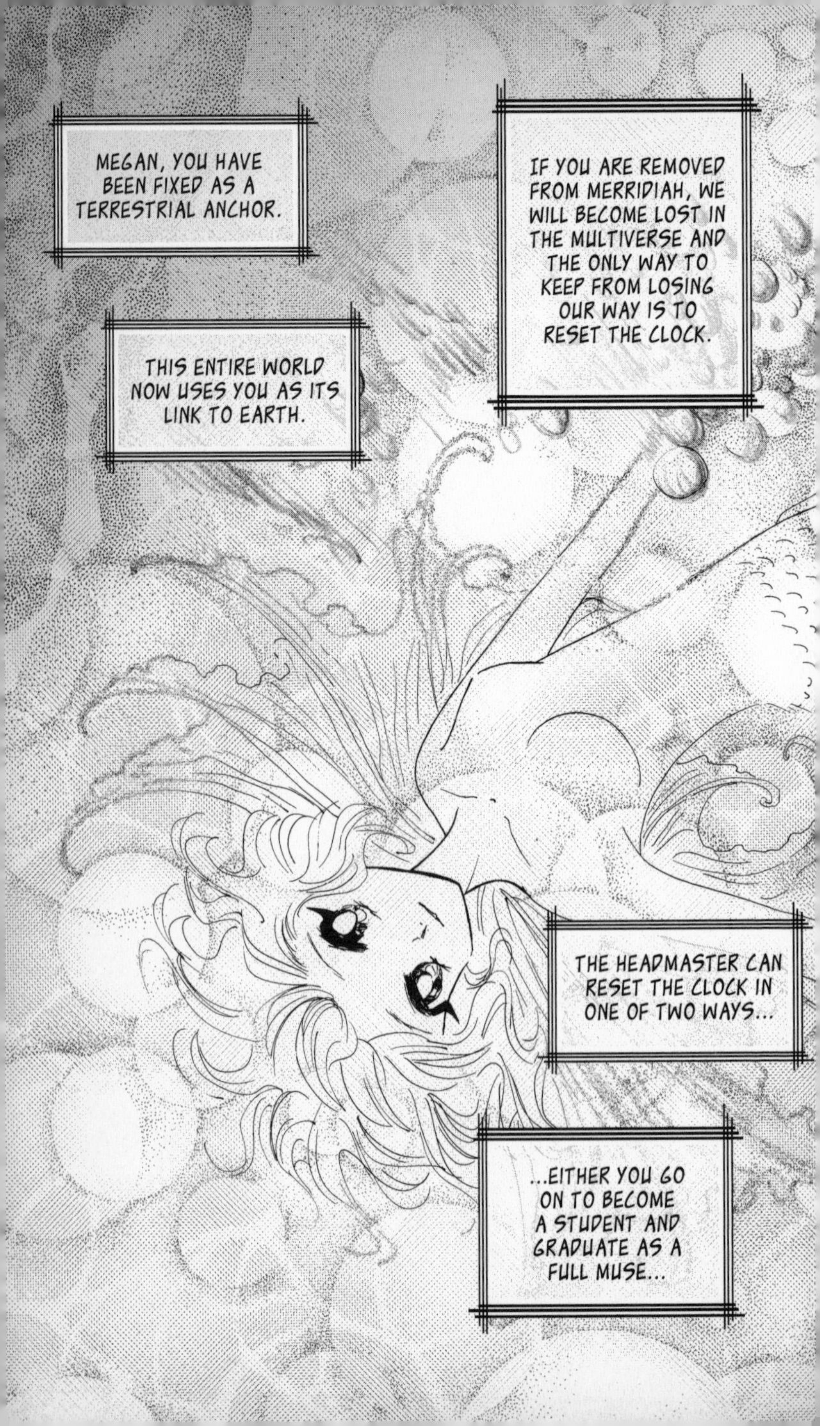
MEGAN, YOU HAVE BEEN FIXED AS A TERRESTRIAL ANCHOR.
THIS ENTIRE WORLD NOW USES YOU AS ITS LINK TO EARTH.
IF YOU ARE REMOVED FROM MERRIDIAH, WE WILL BECOME LOST IN THE MULTIVERSE AND THE ONLY WAY TO KEEP FROM LOSING OUR WAY IS TO RESET THE CLOCK.
THE HEADMASTER CAN RESET THE CLOCK IN ONE OF TWO WAYS...
...EITHER YOU GO ON TO BECOME A STUDENT AND GRADUATE AS A FULL MUSE...

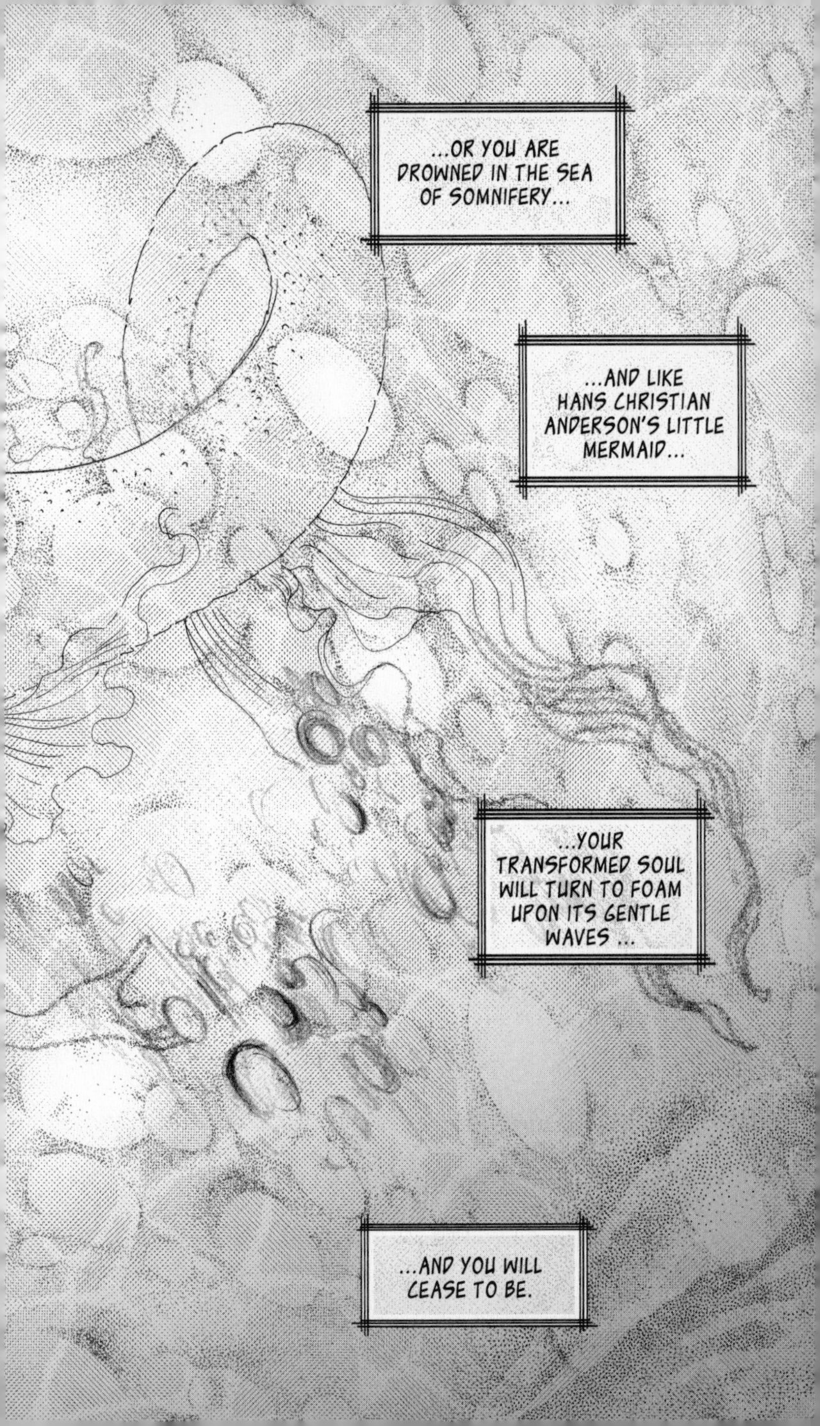
...OR YOU ARE DROWNED IN THE SEA OF SOMNIFERY...
...AND LIKE HANS CHRISTIAN ANDERSON'S LITTLE MERMAID...
...YOUR TRANSFORMED SOUL WILL TURN TO FOAM UPON ITS GENTLE WAVES ...
...AND YOU WILL CEASE TO BE.

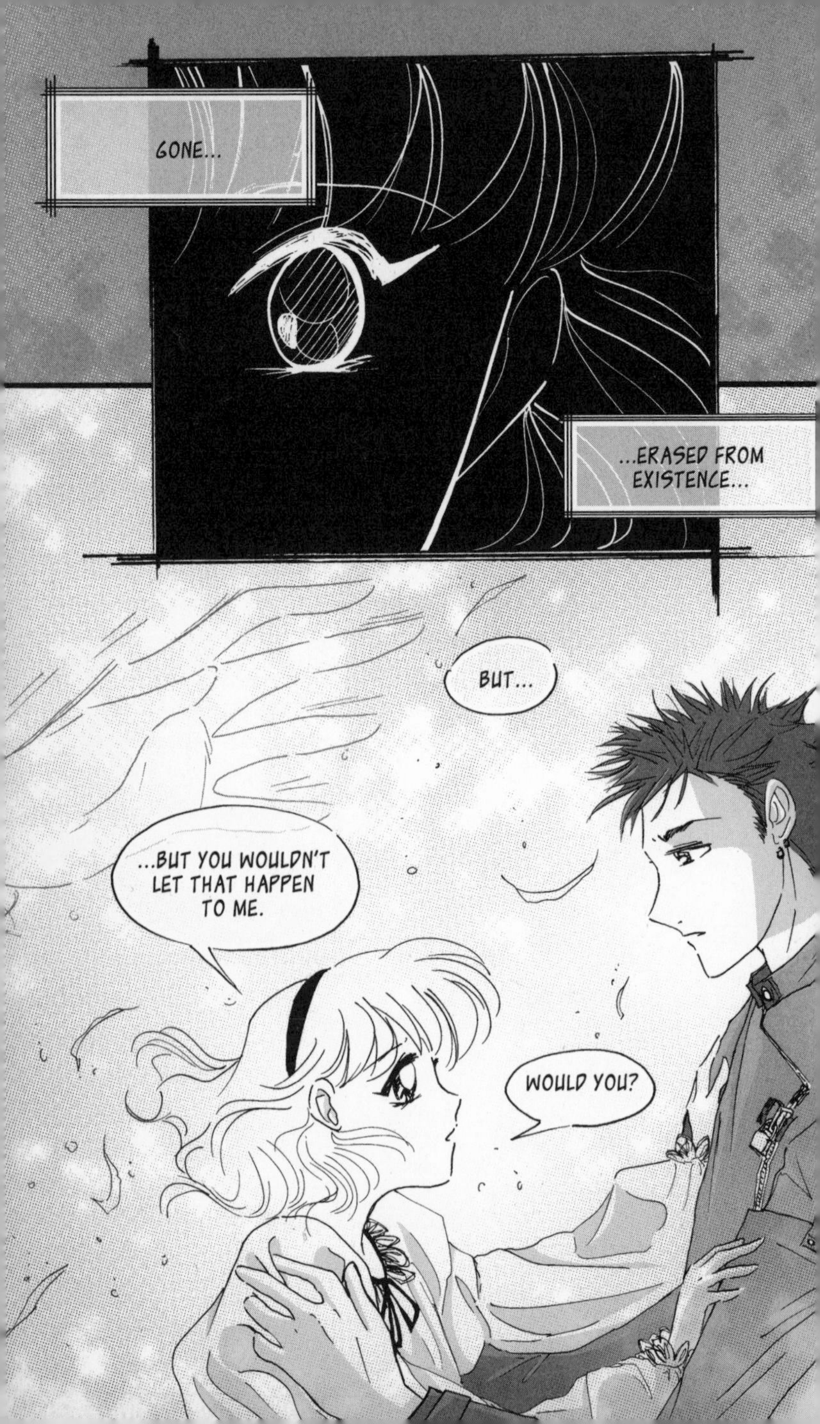
GONE...
...ERASED FROM EXISTENCE...
BUT...
...BUT YOU WOULDN'T LET THAT HAPPEN TO ME.
WOULD YOU?

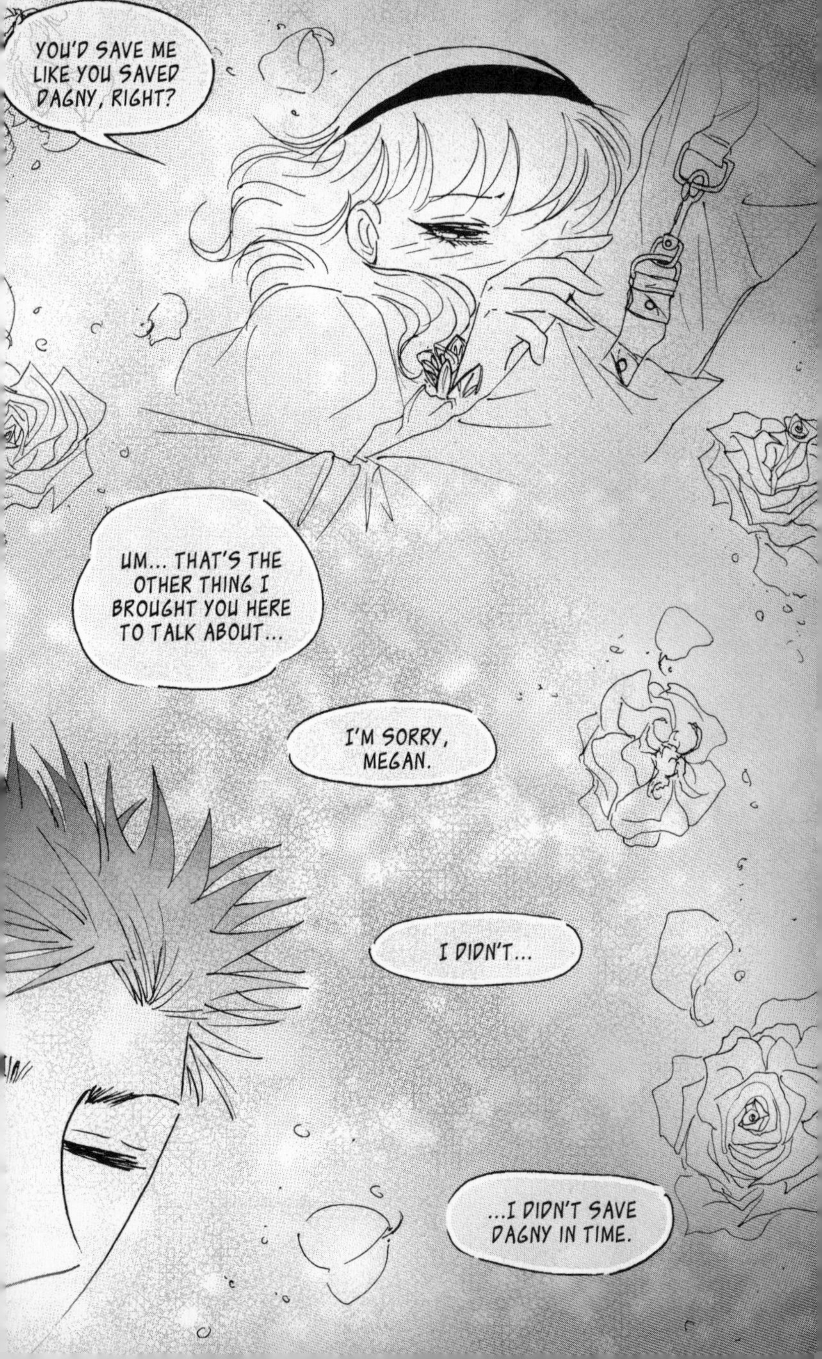
YOU'D SAVE ME LIKE YOU SAVED DAGNY, RIGHT?
UM... THAT'S THE OTHER THING I BROUGHT YOU HERE TO TALK ABOUT...
I'M SORRY, MEGAN.
I DIDN'T...
...I DIDN'T SAVE DAGNY IN TIME.

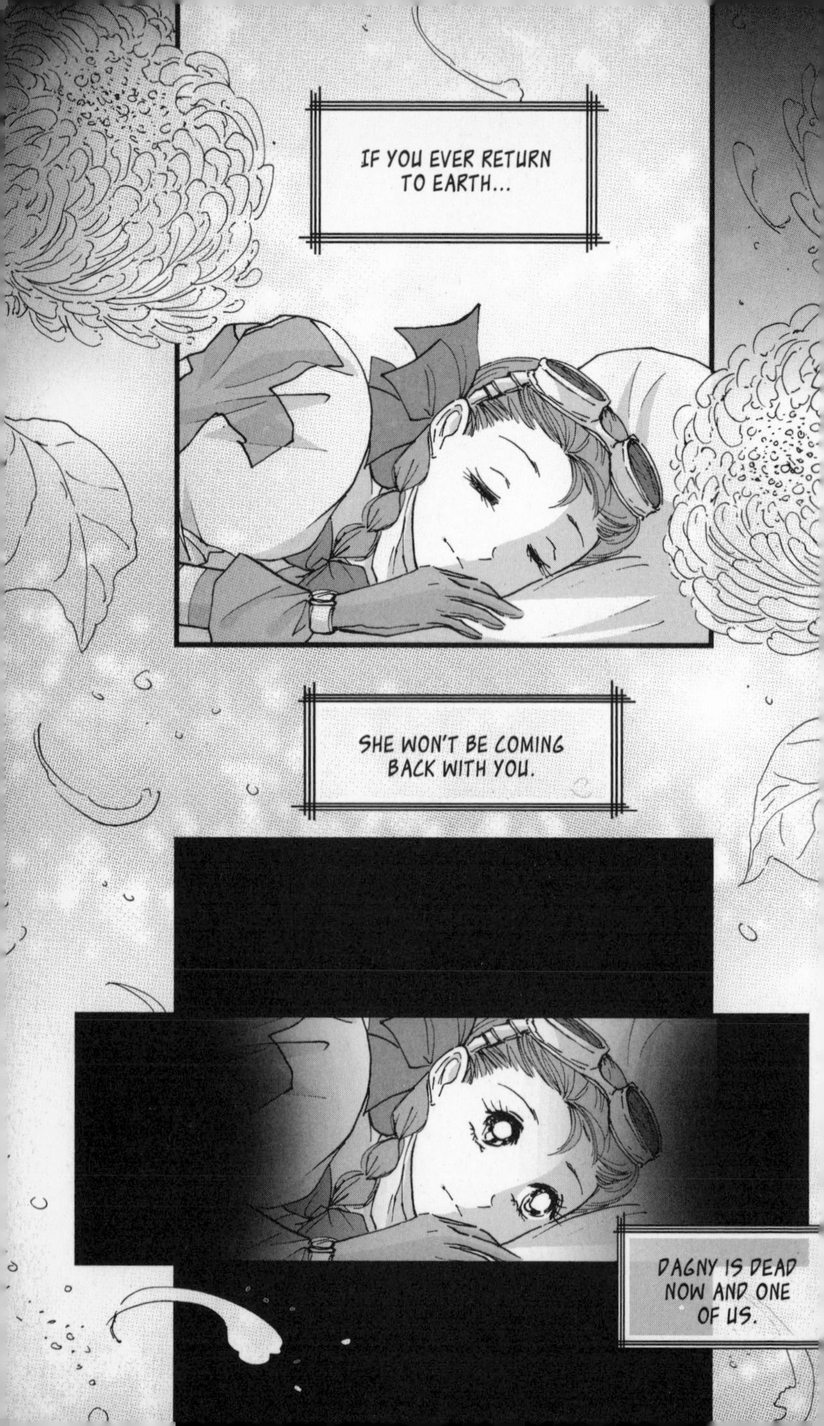
IF YOU EVER RETURN TO EARTH...
SHE WON'T BE COMING BACK WITH YOU.
DAGNY IS DEAD NOW AND ONE OF US.

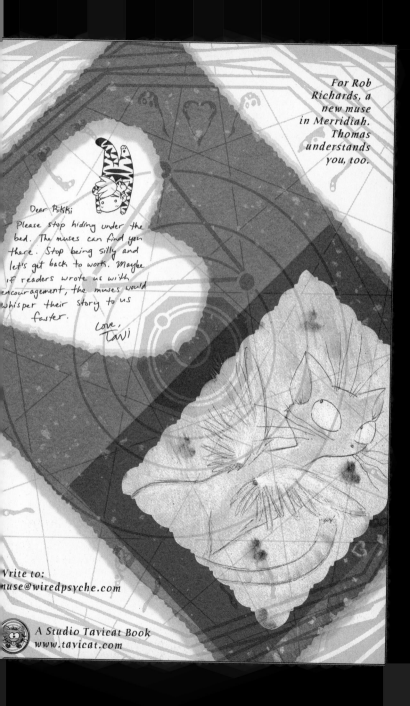

For Rob Richards, a new muse in Merridiah. Thomas understands you, too.

Dear Bikki

Please stop hiding under the bed. The muses can find you there. Stop being silly and let's get back to work. Maybe if readers wrote us with encouragement, the muses would whisper their story to us faster.

Love,
Tavi

Write to:
muse@wiredpsyche.com

A Studio Tavicat Book
www.tavicat.com

Hello Diary,
My Camera Ghost reappeared last night, but I must say...this photo I found tacked to my door this morning concerns me more.

Mayu:
It's pointless, isn't it?
All the unreasonable behaviour.
Let's be friends. Come see me at my boutique. —D

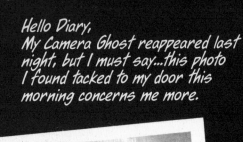

My Camera Ghost is advising me not to go to Dane's boutique... I sense a terrible struggle coming next...

# A Brief Tour of Merridiah University

BY

ADRIEN J. CRANDALL

AND

THOMAS K. JENKINS

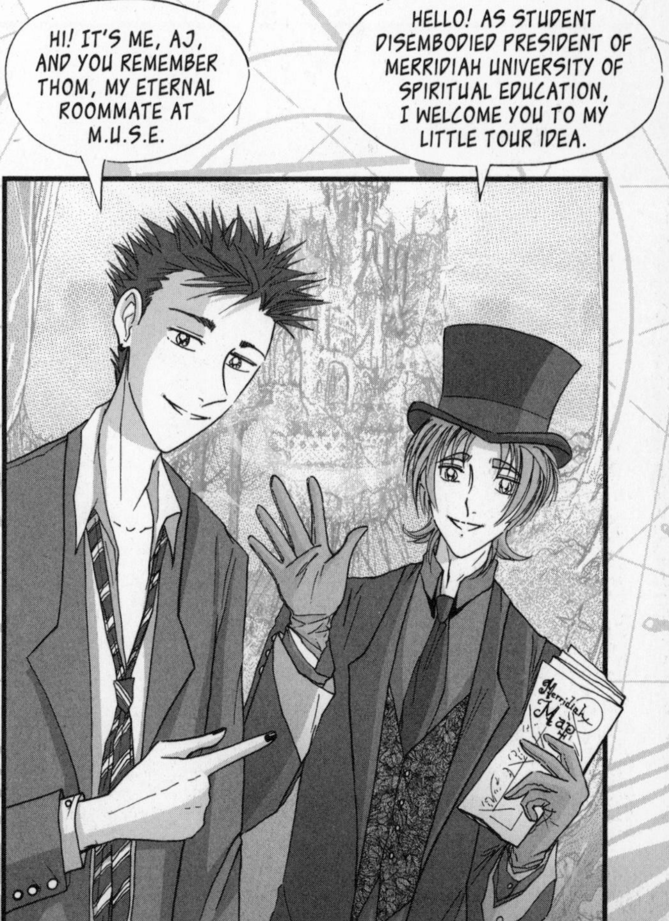
HI! IT'S ME, AJ, AND YOU REMEMBER THOM, MY ETERNAL ROOMMATE AT M.U.S.E.
HELLO! AS STUDENT DISEMBODIED PRESIDENT OF MERRIDIAH UNIVERSITY OF SPIRITUAL EDUCATION, I WELCOME YOU TO MY LITTLE TOUR IDEA.

## The World of Merridiah

Hello. AJ here. First off, let me explain the absurd nature of the World of Merridiah itself. As I'm sure you already know, the universe that houses both Merridiah and Earth is just a dynamic collection of human senses colliding with dimensions, three perceived and six imperceptible. I assume you must already know this because some flippant fairy probably whispered it to you in your sleep, or disguised itself as a howling cat, berserk in the night. You thought it was some mad feline, but really it was the way of the world being explained to you bit by bit. True clarity always sounds like this to the living, just an insane wash of howls.

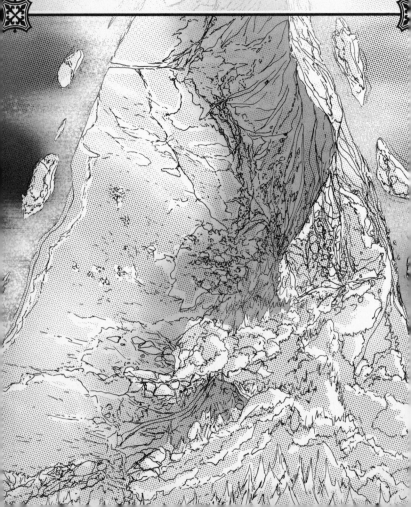

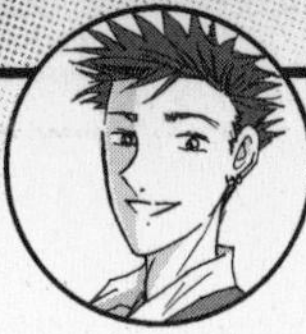

So! The multiverse is an endlessly vast expanse of profound sections of probability that are divided up into an infinite number of alternate realities. Divided by whom, no one in Merridiah knows—well except maybe my uncle, the headmaster, but in ten thousand years he's never fessed up. You terrestrial-bound humans of Earth interact with the physical elements of your world using your five physical senses, senses that in turn invisibly make contact with the nine dimensions, of which Earth proper is the first three dimensions and Merridiah is the seventh, eighth, and ninth. The fourth, fifth, and sixth dimensions are occupied by Immiserriah, the world that is home to our natural enemies, the banshees.

Merridiah is similar to Earth but there is only one continent, and it stretches like a halo around the circumference of the Meridian, from North to South (Merridiah University occupies the North-West). This continent is twenty-five thousand miles long, but only nine miles wide. I speak in miles because my last life on Earth was in America. It should be noted that due to the ethereal nature of our world, if the metric system is your preference, Merridiah is also twenty-five thousand kilometers long and nine kilometers wide. Twenty-five and nine. Those are always the numbers, no matter what system you're used to. So, if you want to move like a bullet in Merridiah, it pays to think of distances in terms of inches, but yourself in terms of yards. That's one of my little secrets.

Merridiah is not what some might call Heaven, nor is it a Purgatory or a Hell. Merridiah is simply the highest three dimensions attached to your Earth's reality, and being the highest imperceptibly means that our physics are closer to the kind of ethereal matter that the human soul is composed of. Therefore, some humans, if they ever find their way to Merridiah at all, usually only do so after they have shed that mortal flesh which binds their five senses to the first three dimensions, that skin which keeps the skeleton in, and hides the soul under pounds of protein and water. Having been born into Merridiah first, we muses have never had any need to walk as mortals among you. We are content to call you via our WiredPsyche, and talk to you in your dreams. It sure works better than the caterwauls of the mad fairy hiding behind your fence.

I say we have no need to live as humans on Earth, although, need is not desire. If we are dreaming near the Sea of Somnifery, the chances are we may wake to find ourselves born to human parents on Earth, and it seems my desires keep leading me back to the Sea, life after life, after life...

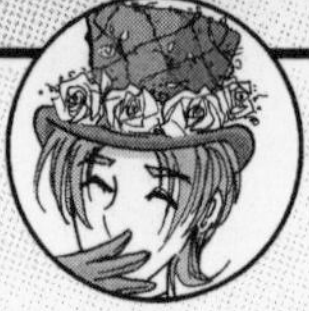

Merridiah University

Hi, this is Tina–er, I mean, Thom. Heh. So, anyway, I thought you might like to see a directional map of the University. This view is the back of the University and it faces North. The castle houses perhaps a million muses, but it's thought to be able to hold at least a hundred million. The legend of how the castle was built is hidden in a book called The Threadbare Heart, written long before I came into existence. I've never found a copy, but I'm told that it explains how the chains at the bottom of the University are actually anchors, and if they were ever broken, the whole place would sail off into the sky. What a dreadful inconvenience that would be.

A. Tower of Enneadiah's Antennae.
B. Olde Kettledrum and South Dorm Catacombs somewhere here.
C. East Bridge to City of Undanoth.
D. West Bridge to City of Seth.
E. City of Seth.
F. The Mindfields, usually this direction.
G. Well of Armour, realm of Groshuvein Chatter.
H. The Crater of the Banshees' Necropolis (headstones not visible from this height).
I. The Sea of Somnifery.
J. Long Morning Cafe somewhere here.
K. Adrien's Tower Garden right around here.
L. Black Spire, Shade Terra, and the entrance to the Hourglass Hollow beyond here.

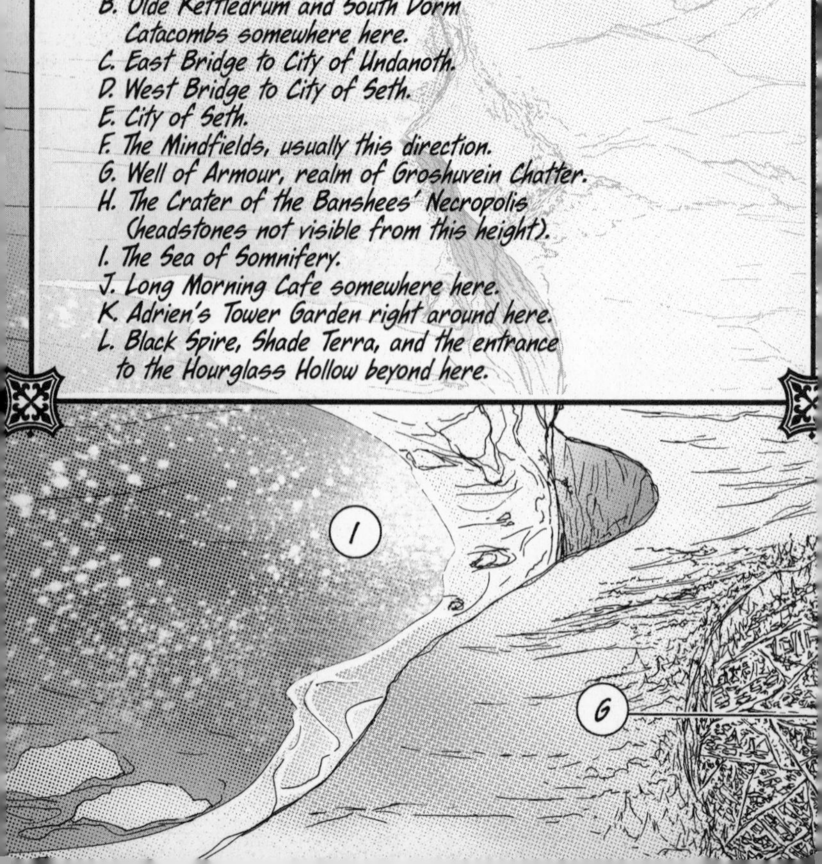
I
G

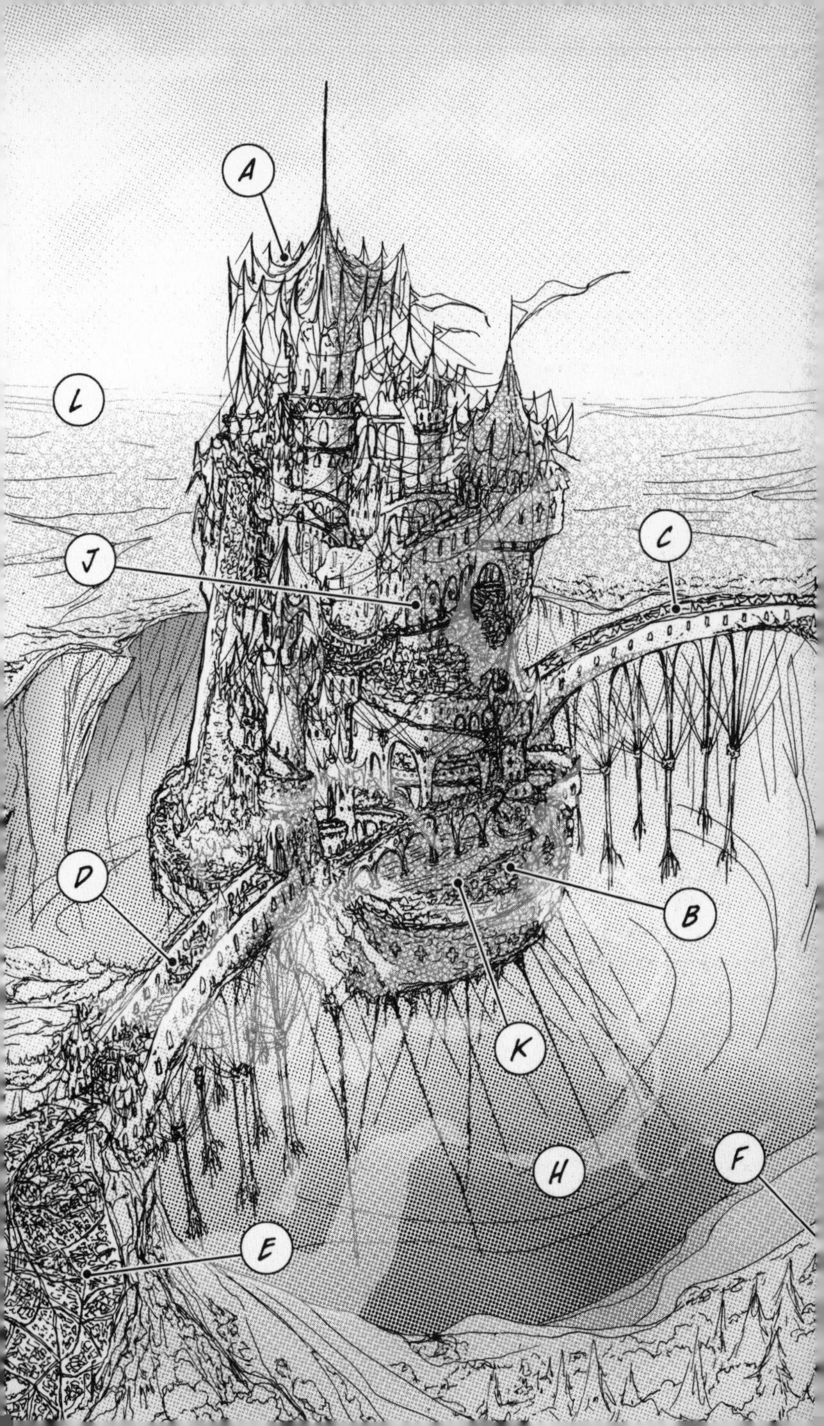
A
L
C
J
D
B
K
H
F
E

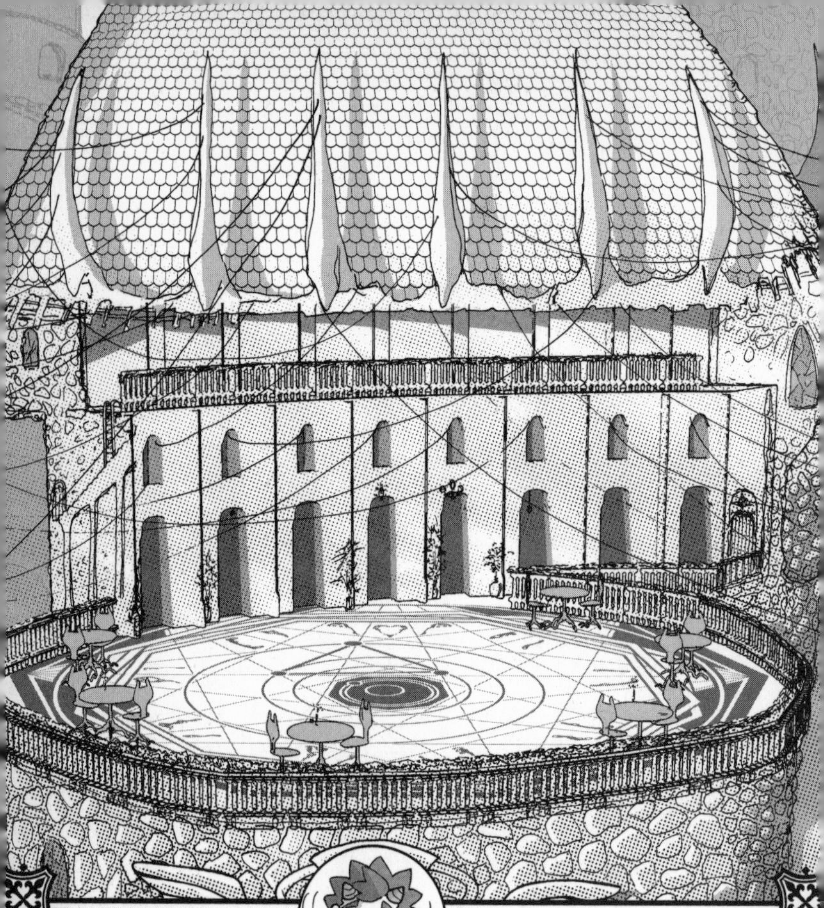

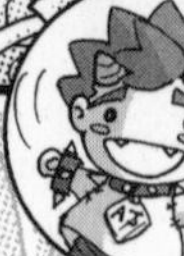

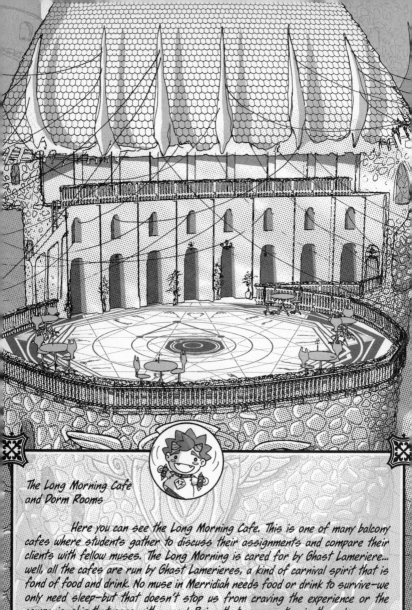

*The Long Morning Cafe and Dorm Rooms*

*Here you can see the Long Morning Cafe. This is one of many balcony cafes where students gather to discuss their assignments and compare their clients with fellow muses. The Long Morning is cared for by Ghast Lameriere... well, all the cafes are run by Ghast Lamerieres, a kind of carnival spirit that is fond of food and drink. No muse in Merridiah needs food or drink to survive—we only need sleep—but that doesn't stop us from craving the experience or the companionship that goes with a meal. Being that conversation is the only purpose of a meal, a single breakfast can last all the way into night—but then I never get up that early.*

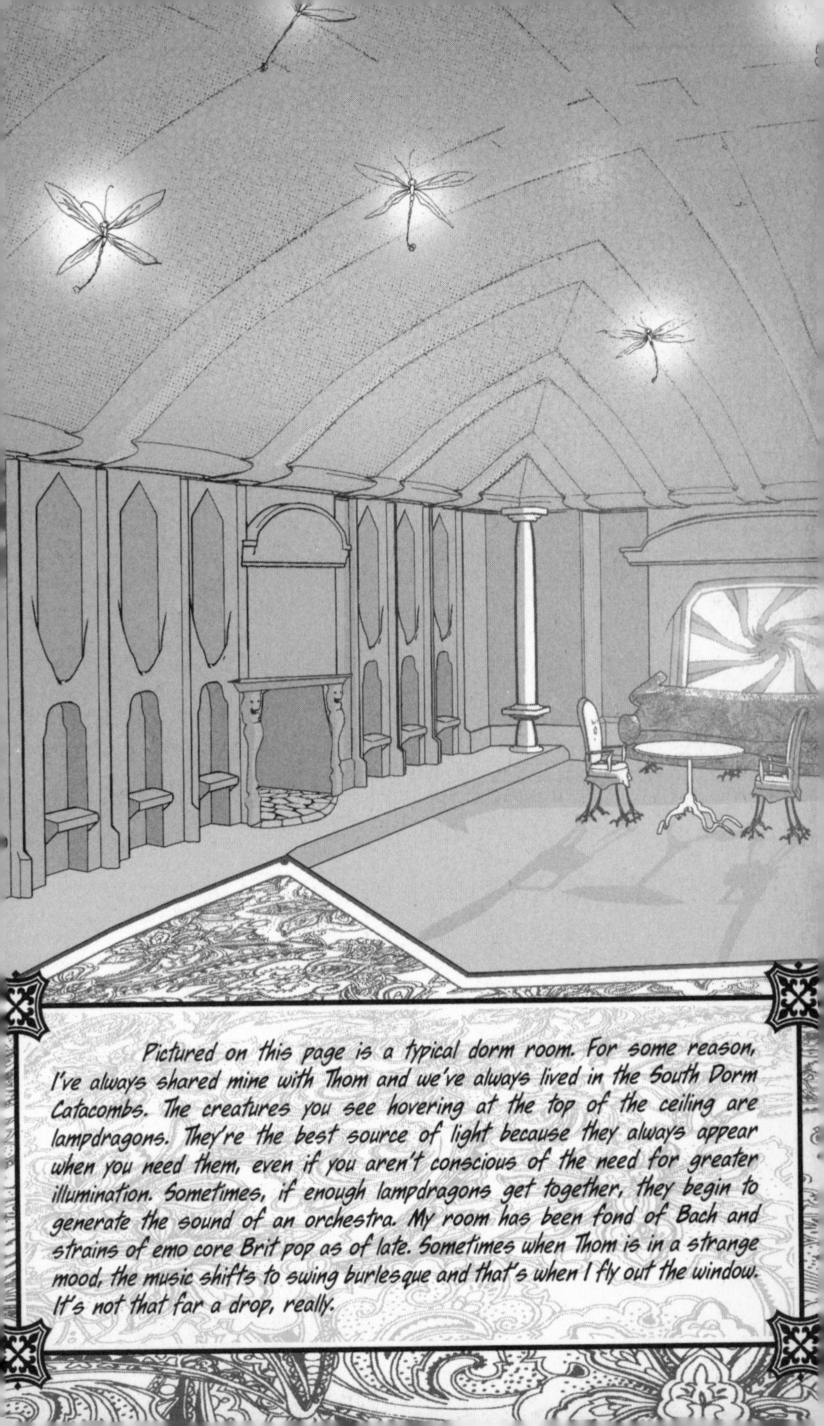

Pictured on this page is a typical dorm room. For some reason, I've always shared mine with Thom and we've always lived in the South Dorm Catacombs. The creatures you see hovering at the top of the ceiling are lampdragons. They're the best source of light because they always appear when you need them, even if you aren't conscious of the need for greater illumination. Sometimes, if enough lampdragons get together, they begin to generate the sound of an orchestra. My room has been fond of Bach and strains of emo core Brit pop as of late. Sometimes when Thom is in a strange mood, the music shifts to swing burlesque and that's when I fly out the window. It's not that far a drop, really.

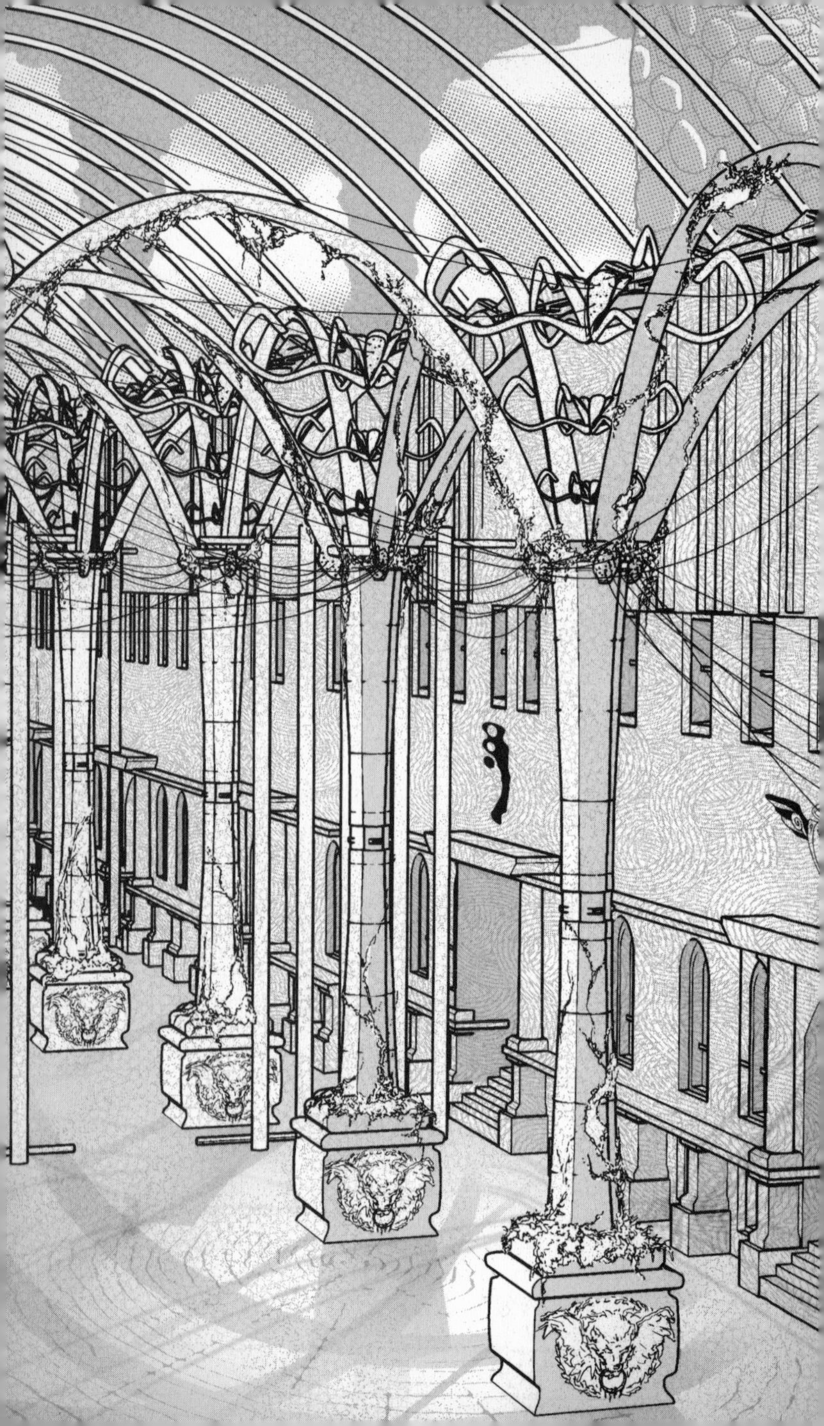

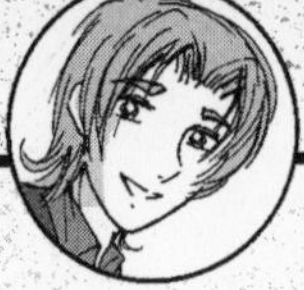

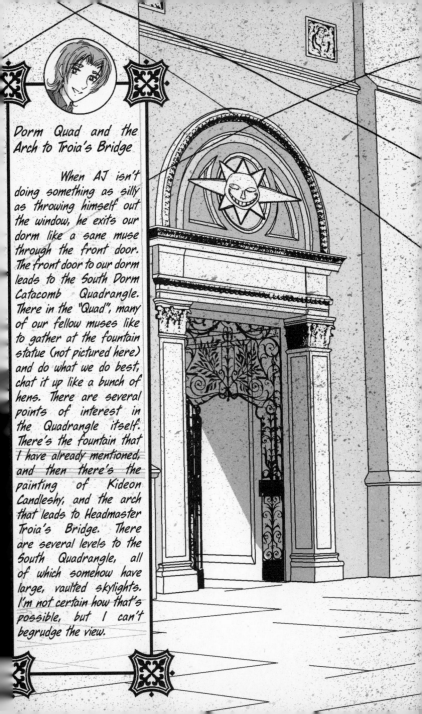

## Dorm Quad and the Arch to Troia's Bridge

When AJ isn't doing something as silly as throwing himself out the window, he exits our dorm like a sane muse through the front door. The front door to our dorm leads to the South Dorm Catacomb Quadrangle. There in the "Quad", many of our fellow muses like to gather at the fountain statue (not pictured here) and do what we do best, chat it up like a bunch of hens. There are several points of interest in the Quadrangle itself. There's the fountain that I have already mentioned, and then there's the painting of Kideon Candleshy, and the arch that leads to Headmaster Troia's Bridge. There are several levels to the South Quadrangle, all of which somehow have large, vaulted skylights. I'm not certain how that's possible, but I can't begrudge the view.

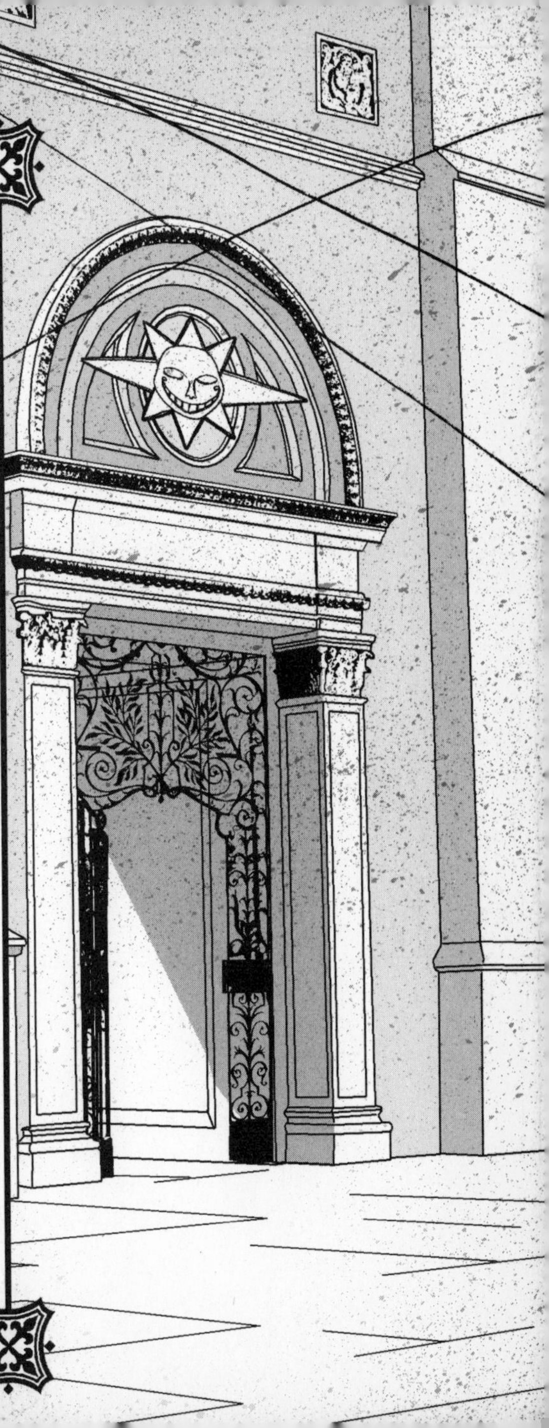

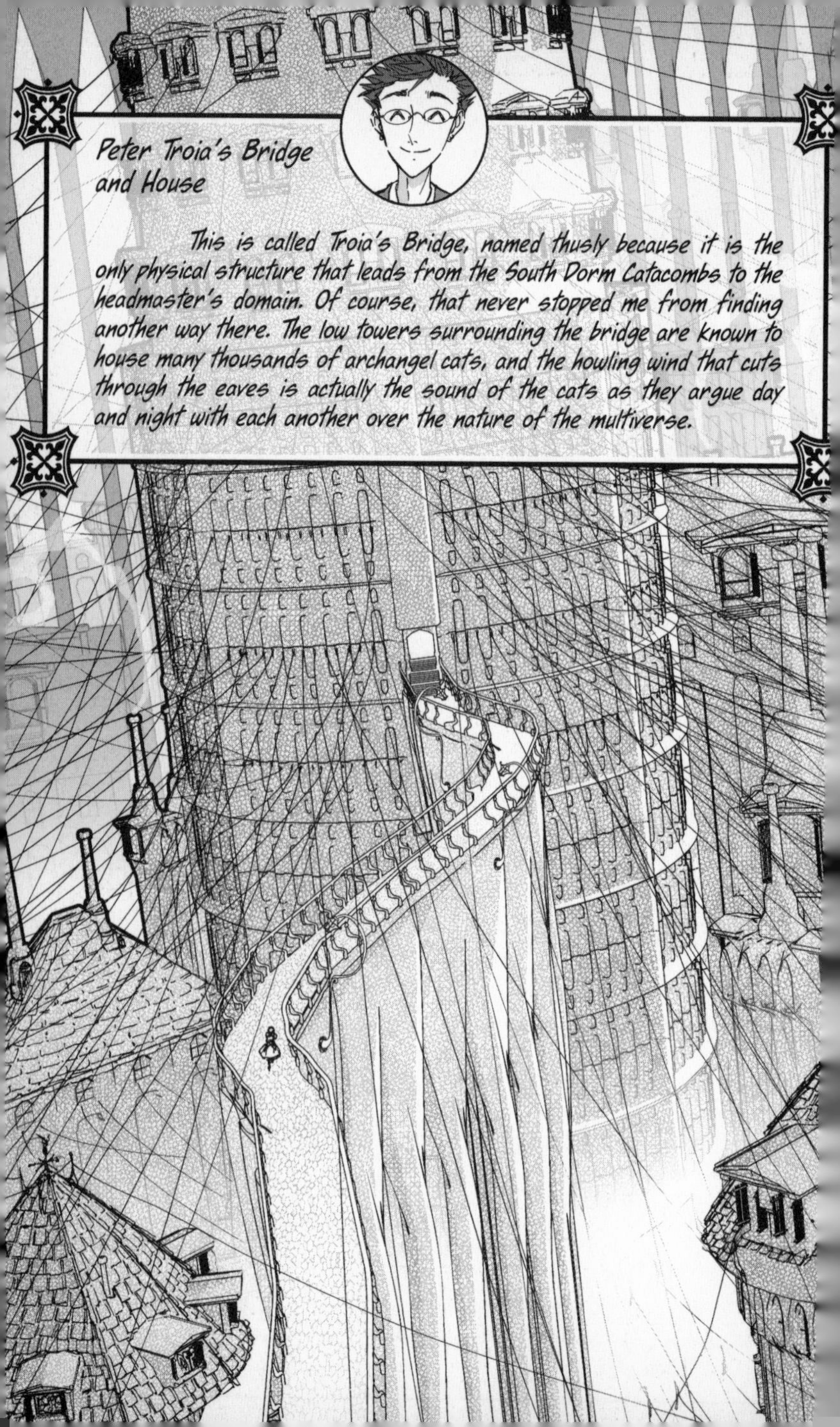
Peter Troia's Bridge and House
This is called Troia's Bridge, named thusly because it is the only physical structure that leads from the South Dorm Catacombs to the headmaster's domain. Of course, that never stopped me from finding another way there. The low towers surrounding the bridge are known to house many thousands of archangel cats, and the howling wind that cuts through the eaves is actually the sound of the cats as they argue day and night with each other over the nature of the multiverse.

*Below is Troia's house and office in its current incarnation, which he calls Olde Kettledrum. It is set as a brick and terra-cotta Victorian—and I say current because my dear uncle likes to change his surroundings every five hundred years. Olde Kettledrum is said to be the most terrestrial-centric and rational place in all of Merridiah, and that's because it's the only structure that changes at the whim of its builder, with an interior that accurately represents the dimensions of its exterior. I like it. It's a whole lot cozier than the old Greco-Roman temple he used to hide himself away in.*

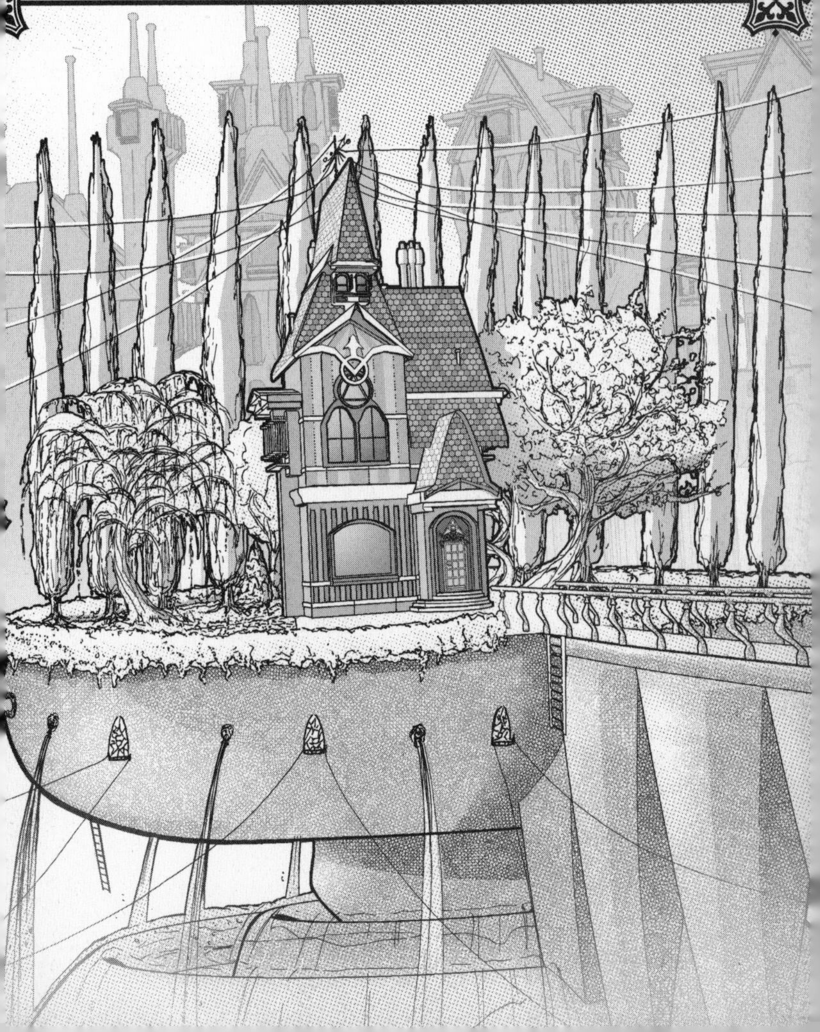

# ALSO AVAILABLE FROM 🌀 TOKYOPOP®

## MANGA

.HACK//LEGEND OF THE TWILIGHT
@LARGE
ABENOBASHI: MAGICAL SHOPPING ARCADE
A.I. LOVE YOU
AI YORI AOSHI
ANGELIC LAYER
ARM OF KANNON
BABY BIRTH
BATTLE ROYALE
BATTLE VIXENS
BRAIN POWERED
BRIGADOON
B'TX
CANDIDATE FOR GODDESS, THE
CARDCAPTOR SAKURA
CARDCAPTOR SAKURA - MASTER OF THE CLOW
CHOBITS
CHRONICLES OF THE CURSED SWORD
CLAMP SCHOOL DETECTIVES
CLOVER
COMIC PARTY
CONFIDENTIAL CONFESSIONS
CORRECTOR YUI
COWBOY BEBOP
COWBOY BEBOP: SHOOTING STAR
CRAZY LOVE STORY
CRESCENT MOON
CROSS
CULDCEPT
CYBORG 009
D•N•ANGEL
DEMON DIARY
DEMON ORORON, THE
DEUS VITAE
DIABOLO
DIGIMON
DIGIMON TAMERS
DIGIMON ZERO TWO
DOLL
DRAGON HUNTER
DRAGON KNIGHTS
DRAGON VOICE
DREAM SAGA
DUKLYON: CLAMP SCHOOL DEFENDERS
EERIE QUEERIE!
ERICA SAKURAZAWA: COLLECTED WORKS
ET CETERA
ETERNITY
EVIL'S RETURN
FAERIES' LANDING
FAKE
FLCL
FLOWER OF THE DEEP SLEEP
FORBIDDEN DANCE
FRUITS BASKET
G GUNDAM

GATEKEEPERS
GETBACKERS
GIRL GOT GAME
GIRLS' EDUCATIONAL CHARTER
GRAVITATION
GTO
GUNDAM BLUE DESTINY
GUNDAM SEED ASTRAY
GUNDAM WING
GUNDAM WING: BATTLEFIELD OF PACIFISTS
GUNDAM WING: ENDLESS WALTZ
GUNDAM WING: THE LAST OUTPOST (G-UNIT)
GUYS' GUIDE TO GIRLS
HANDS OFF!
HAPPY MANIA
HARLEM BEAT
HONEY MUSTARD
I.N.V.U.
IMMORTAL RAIN
INITIAL D
INSTANT TEEN: JUST ADD NUTS
ISLAND
JING: KING OF BANDITS
JING: KING OF BANDITS - TWILIGHT TALES
JULINE
KARE KANO
KILL ME, KISS ME
KINDAICHI CASE FILES, THE
KING OF HELL
KODOCHA: SANA'S STAGE
LAMENT OF THE LAMB
LEGAL DRUG
LEGEND OF CHUN HYANG, THE
LES BIJOUX
LOVE HINA
LUPIN III
LUPIN III: WORLD'S MOST WANTED
MAGIC KNIGHT RAYEARTH I
MAGIC KNIGHT RAYEARTH II
MAHOROMATIC: AUTOMATIC MAIDEN
MAN OF MANY FACES
MARMALADE BOY
MARS
MARS: HORSE WITH NO NAME
MINK
MIRACLE GIRLS
MIYUKI-CHAN IN WONDERLAND
MODEL
MY LOVE
NECK AND NECK
ONE
ONE I LOVE, THE
PARADISE KISS
PARASYTE
PASSION FRUIT
PEACH GIRL
PEACH GIRL: CHANGE OF HEART
PET SHOP OF HORRORS

03.30.04T

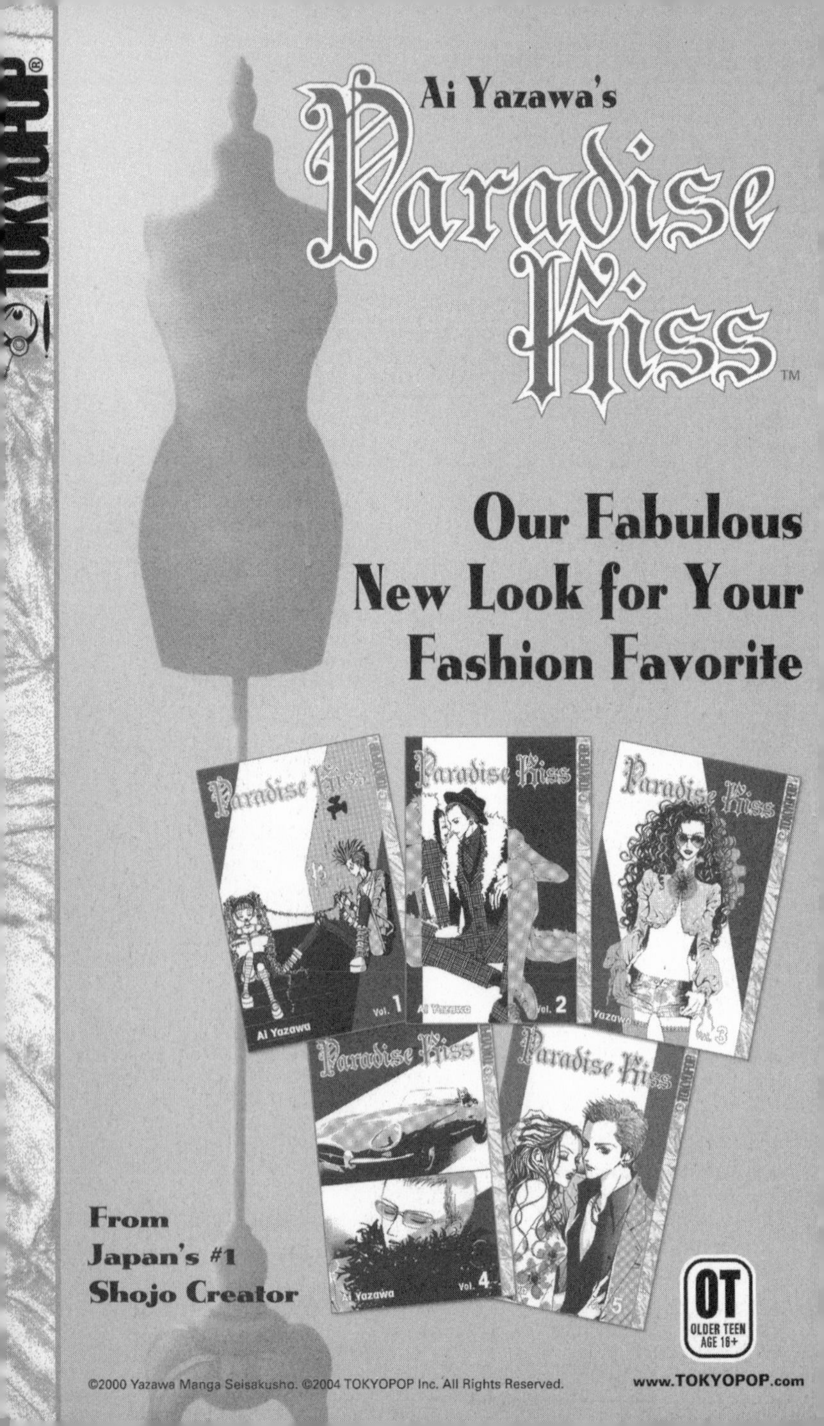
TOKYOPOP®
Ai Yazawa's
Paradise Kiss™
Our Fabulous
New Look for Your
Fashion Favorite
Paradise Kiss
Ai Yazawa
Vol. 1
Vol. 2
Vol. 3
Vol. 4
5
From
Japan's #1
Shojo Creator
OT
OLDER TEEN
AGE 16+
©2000 Yazawa Manga Seisakusho. ©2004 TOKYOPOP Inc. All Rights Reserved.
www.TOKYOPOP.com

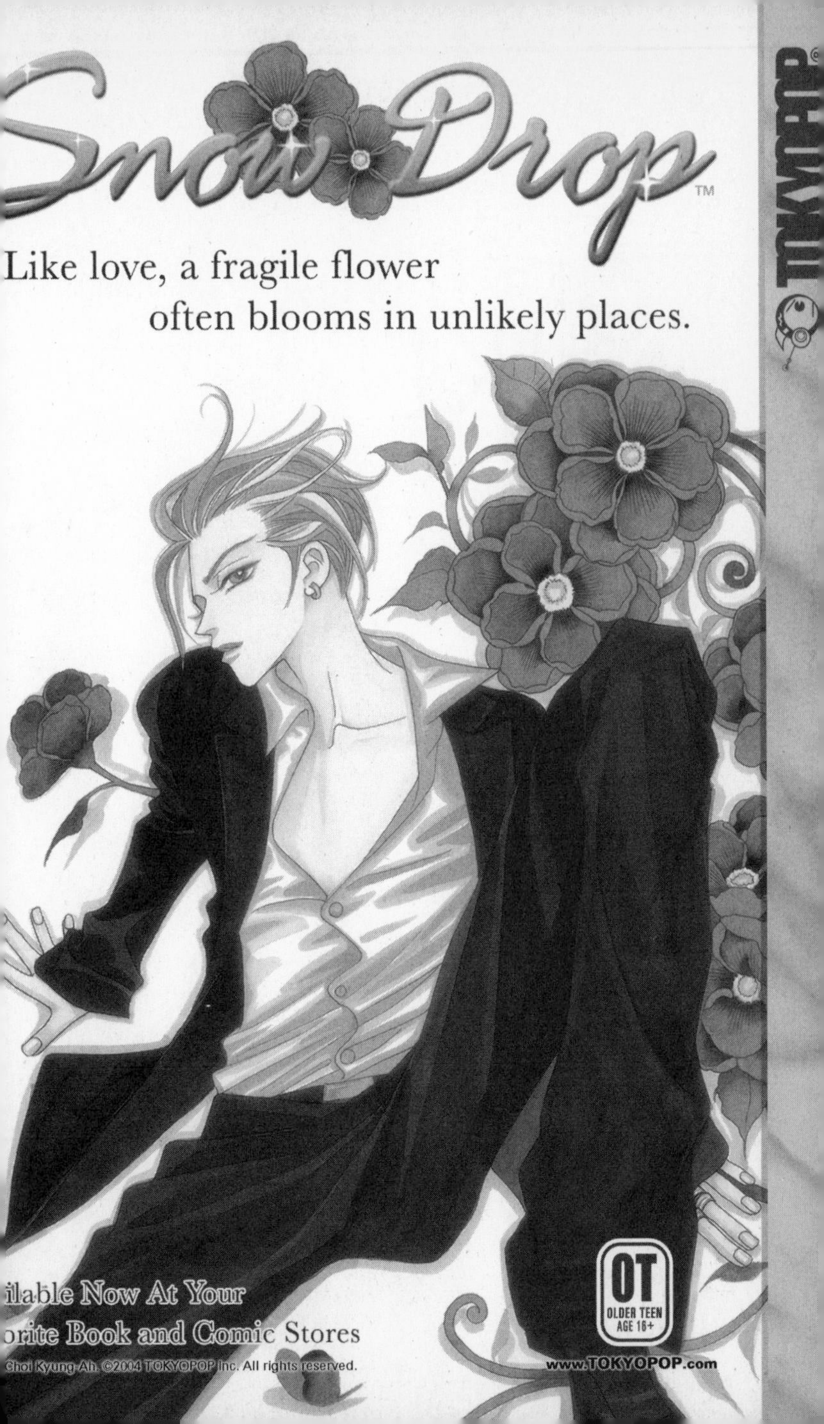
Snow Drop™
Like love, a fragile flower
often blooms in unlikely places.
TOKYOPOP
ilable Now At Your
orite Book and Comic Stores
Choi Kyung-Ah. ©2004 TOKYOPOP Inc. All rights reserved.
OT
OLDER TEEN
AGE 16+
www.TOKYOPOP.com

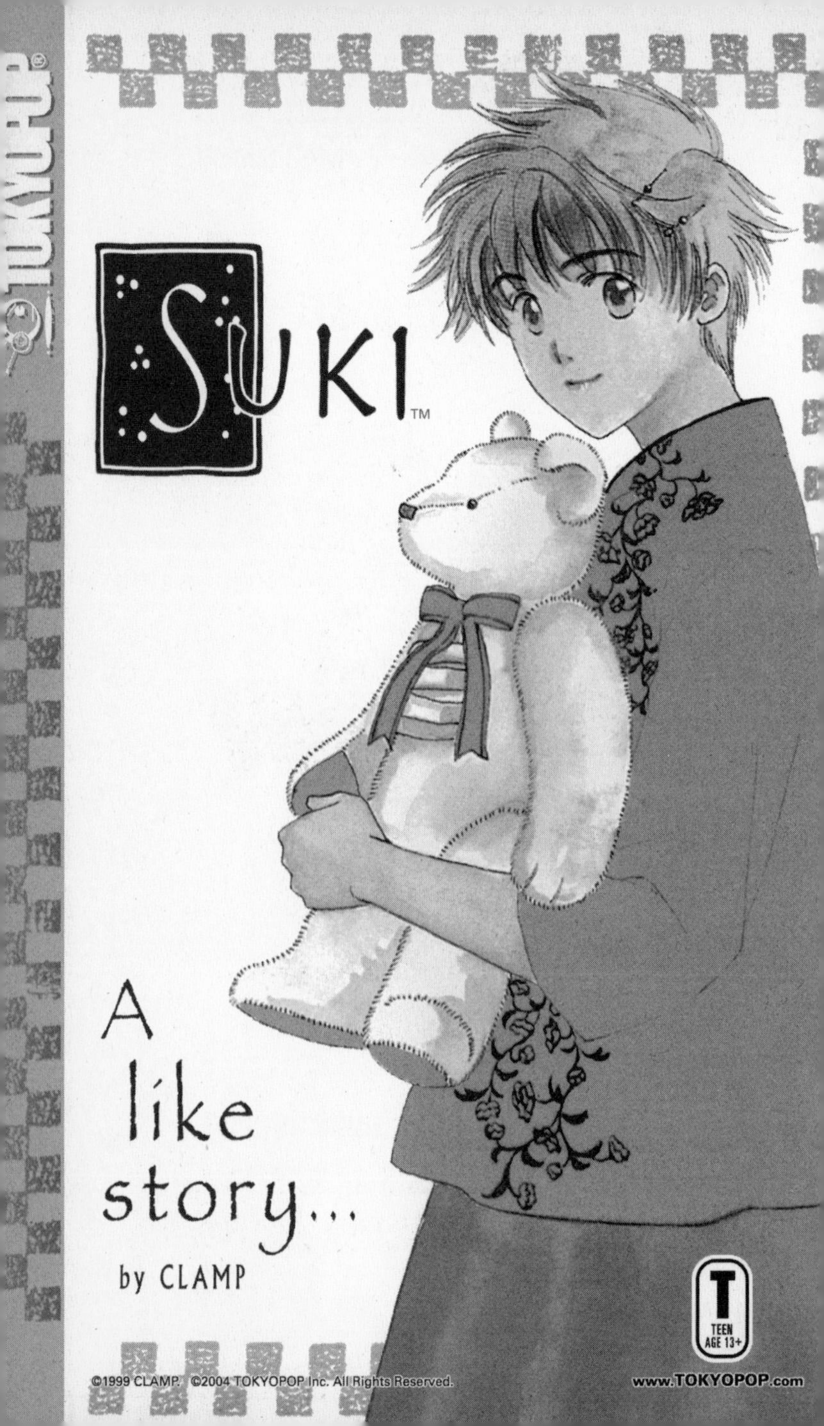
TOKYOPOP®
SUKI™
A like story...
by CLAMP
T
TEEN
AGE 13+
©1999 CLAMP. ©2004 TOKYOPOP Inc. All Rights Reserved.
www.TOKYOPOP.com

# PITA-TEN™

**By Koge-Donbo · Creator of Digicharat**

The girl next door is
bringing a touch of heaven
to the neighborhood.

# TOKYO
# BABYLON™

Welcome to Tokyo.
The city never sleeps.
May its spirits rest in peace.

TEEN
AGE 13+

www.TOKYOPOP.com

# Fruits Basket

*Life in the Sohma household can be a real zoo!*

TOKYOPOP®

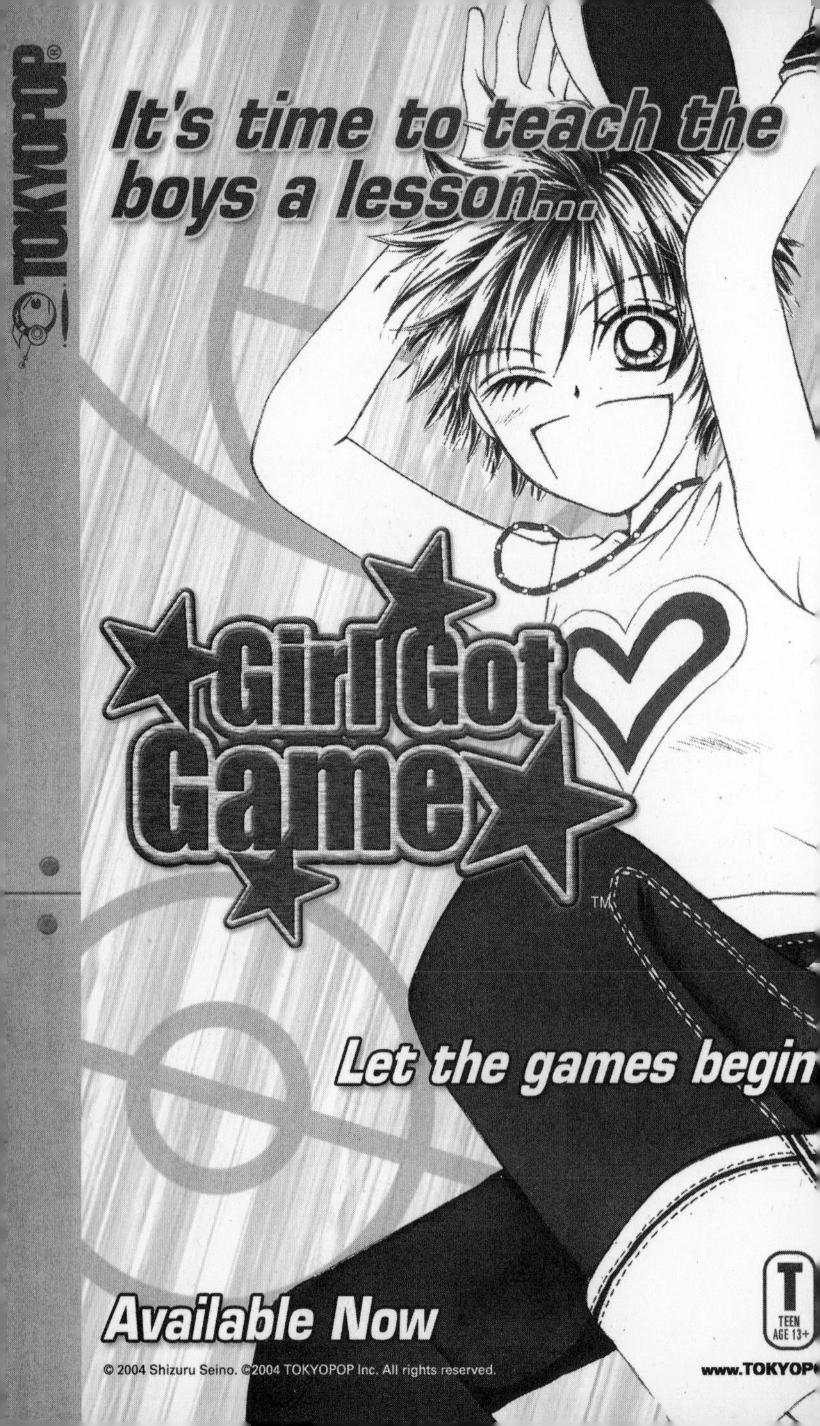
TOKYOPOP
It's time to teach the boys a lesson...
Girl Got Game
TM
Let the games begin
Available Now
T
TEEN
AGE 13+
© 2004 Shizuru Seino. ©2004 TOKYOPOP Inc. All rights reserved.
www.TOKYOP

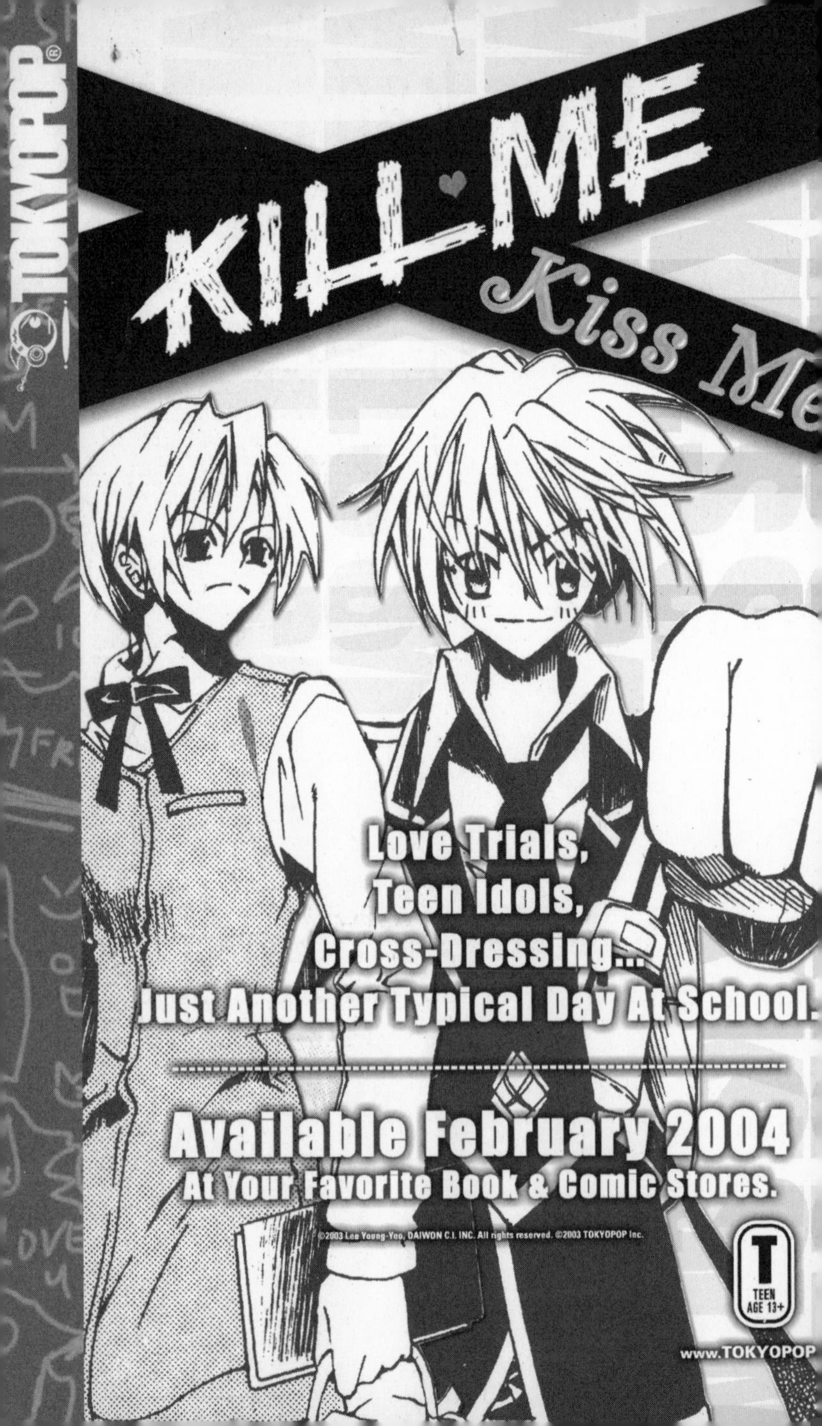
TOKYOPOP
KILL ME
Kiss Me
Love Trials,
Teen Idols,
Cross-Dressing...
Just Another Typical Day At School.
Available February 2004
At Your Favorite Book & Comic Stores.
©2003 Lee Young-Yoo, DAIWON C.I. INC. All rights reserved. ©2003 TOKYOPOP Inc.
T
TEEN
AGE 13+
www.TOKYOPOP